The Logic
of the Heart

The Logic

of the Heart

AUGUSTINE, PASCAL,
and the RATIONALITY OF FAITH

James R. Peters

B
Baker Academic
a division of Baker Publishing Group
Grand Rapids, Michigan

© 2009 by James R. Peters

Published by Baker Academic
a division of Baker Publishing Group
P.O. Box 6287, Grand Rapids, MI 49516-6287
www.bakeracademic.com

Printed in the United States of America

Library of Congress Cataloging-in-Publication Data

Peters, James R., 1957–
    The logic of the heart : Augustine, Pascal, and the rationality of faith / James R. Peters.
       p.   cm.
    Includes bibliographical references and index.
    ISBN 978-0-8010-3599-9 (pbk.)
    1. Faith—History of doctines. 2. Augustine, Saint, Bishop of Hippo 3. Pascal, Blaise, 1623–1662. 4. Hume, David, 1711–1776. I. Title.
    BT771.3.P48 2009
    231'.042—dc22
                                                 2008049506

I certainly don't think that the death required that "ye be born again" is the death of reason. If what the church teaches is not true, then the security and emotional release and sense of purpose it gives you are of no value and you are right to reject it. One of the effects of modern liberal Protestantism has been gradually to turn religion into poetry and restoration of self, to make truth vaguer and vaguer and more and more relative, to banish intellectual distinctions, to depend on feeling instead of thought, and gradually to believe that God has no power, that he cannot communicate with us, cannot reveal himself to us, indeed has not done so, and that religion is our own sweet invention. . . .

Of course, I am a Catholic and I believe the opposite of all of this. I believe what the Church teaches—that God has given us reason to use and that it can lead us toward a knowledge of him, through analogy; that he has revealed himself in history and continues to do so through the Church. . . . To believe all this I don't take any leap into the absurd. I find it reasonable to believe, even though these beliefs are beyond reason. . . .

[S]atisfy your demand for reason always but remember that charity is beyond reason and that God can be known through charity.

—Flannery O'Connor, *The Habit of Being*

CONTENTS

ACKNOWLEDGMENTS

My work on this book began at a National Endowment for the Humanities seminar on the philosophy of David Hume, held at Dartmouth College in Hanover, New Hampshire, in the summer of 1990. I am grateful to both the faculty and participants of that seminar for six weeks of a most engaging and lively exchange of ideas and arguments. Two professors there, Donald Livingston and Terence Penelhum, deserve special mention. From Donald Livingston—under whom as both an undergraduate and graduate student at Northern Illinois University I had the privilege of studying Hume's philosophy—I continued to learn to read Hume as a subtle and complex historical thinker whose skeptical vision is inextricably bound up with a humanistic Ciceronian concern for civil politics, humane social order, and the concord of the life of the passions. In Terence Penelhum I found a living and exemplary model of how a Christian philosopher ought to engage a great adversary like the "dreaded Scot, David Hume"—with unfailing seriousness tempered by humble charity and deep respect. Professor Penelhum's *God and Skepticism* is a towering classic from which I have greatly benefited.

My aim in *The Logic of the Heart* is to provide a clear and nontechnical philosophical defense of the rationality of Christian faith. I hope that my book will meet the interests of a wide range of readers, from academic philosophers and theologians to ordinary laypeople confronted with the challenges of postmodern accounts of religious pluralism and metaphysical skepticism. *The Logic of the Heart* is deeply indebted to the critiques of Enlightenment rationality found in such works as Alasdair MacIntyre's *Whose Justice? Which Rationality?* (1988) and *Three Rival Versions of Moral Enquiry: Encyclopaedia, Genealogy, and Tradition* (1990); Stanley Hauerwas's *A Community of Character: Toward a Constructive Christian Social Ethic* (1981) and *A Better Hope: Resources for a Church Confronting Capitalism, Democracy, and*

Postmodernity (2000); Alvin Plantinga's *Warranted Christian Belief* (2000); and the critiques of postmodernism in these works, as well as in David Bentley Hart's *The Beauty of the Infinite: The Aesthetics of Christian Truth* (2003). The uniqueness of *The Logic of the Heart* lies in its focus on Pascal's and Augustine's non-Enlightenment vision of human rationality, and in the comparative analysis of Pascal and Hume that elucidates the fundamental differences in their perspectives on theism and defends Pascal's account of reason and faith. Calling on this Augustinian and Pascalian account of the embeddedness of human rationality, *The Logic of the Heart* contends that human reasoning on ultimate issues of human life is inextricably bound up with those affections and feelings that reveal to us our proper place in creation. Reason can function properly only when reason is informed by the intuitions of the heart, as nurtured by historically constituted traditions of belief and practice.

In defending the inseparability of reason and affection, *The Logic of the Heart* bears some resemblance to two fine works of twentieth-century philosophy, C. S. Lewis's *The Abolition of Man* (1944) and William Wainwright's *Reason and the Heart: A Prolegomenon to a Critique of Passional Reason* (1995). Neither of these classic works, however, specifically defends the reasonableness of Christian faith for the postmodern world in the contexts of reason, affection, and embeddedness, loci shared among Augustine, Pascal, and Hume, on the one hand, and the postmoderns, on the other, but the sharing of which leads to widely divergent conclusions. *The Logic of the Heart* defends Augustinian and Pascalian "embedded reason" as a viable middle ground between the Enlightenment's affirmation of universal rational autonomy and radical postmodernism's affirmation of the poetics of self-creation.

A recurring theme in *The Logic of the Heart* is the importance of the Socratic tradition in understanding all three of the major philosophers whose arguments about faith and reason differently make up the substance of my work. For my appreciation and understanding of the Socratic vision of the philosophical quest I am especially indebted to three of the finest teachers I have ever known—Michael Gelven at Northern Illinois University and Kenneth Seeskin and the late Reginald Allen at Northwestern University. My debt to these three men is incalculable; in both word and deed, they have shown me what it means to love wisdom. Despite their noble efforts, I acknowledge that my own rendition of the Socratic vision of life comes up short, both in its eloquence and substance. I hereby exonerate them from any responsibility for my inadequate and halting efforts to convey in words the passion of spirit and clarity of insight they so generously shared with me.

I also wish to give special thanks to my colleagues at the University of the South—William Garland, James Peterman, Christopher Conn, and Andrew Moser—with whom I have enjoyed hours and years of philosophical conversation and from whom I have learned so much about deep and important philosophical matters. I would like also to thank my students at the University of the

South, not only for their fruitful insights and questions that have deeply shaped my own thinking, but also for their patience in permitting me to continue to be a mere apprentice for twenty-three years in that honorable craft known as the teaching of philosophy. I owe an especially warm thanks to three of my most thoughtful Christian friends—Jon Bruss, Wilmer Mills, and Dale Richardson—who graciously read and commented on my manuscript at various stages of its completion. Luther Leibensberger, cherished elder brother in the faith, has long provided yet another source of thoughtful insight on the life of faith. I would like to express as well my sincerest gratitude to David Haskell for his generous and perceptive comments on my text. David has taught me by word and example what it means to think with the heart. To these patient friends and cherished fellow pilgrims I owe a debt I cannot repay.

I am also deeply grateful to Bill Davis and Reg McLelland and their students at Covenant College in Lookout Mountain, Georgia, all of whom offered invaluable comments on earlier drafts of my chapters on Hume's case against miracles and Augustine's conception of charitable reason. During the last fifteen years, I have further benefited from the helpful comments on earlier versions of my text graciously provided by many friends and colleagues. I would like especially to thank Stanley Hauerwas, Tad Lehe, Scott Sinclair, the late Monroe Spears, and the late Cecil Woods. Tom Kennedy, outstanding former editor of the *Cresset*, offered invaluable counsel on an earlier draft of my chapter on Augustine. I am deeply grateful to Tom for his gracious editorial assistance and years of friendship. At a crucial stage in my life when I was a zealously skeptical college student, Dick Thompson convinced me through his generous and thoughtful spirit to rethink my blind faith in the wisdom of Bertrand Russell. Though I did not know it at the time, Dick Thompson provided me with a living witness to the logic of the heart. For his enthusiastic support, I would also like to thank my friend Creston Davis, now assistant professor of religion at Rollins College, who read my manuscript and introduced me to Robert Hosack, an editor of the highest caliber, at Baker Academic. I cannot thank Bob Hosack warmly enough for his willingness to work with me to bring this book—so long in the growing—to fruition. I would also like to express my gratitude and appreciation to the reviewer for Baker Academic whose penetrating advice led me to make crucial changes in my text. I am grateful as well to Brian Bolger and his editorial team at Baker Academic, whose keen eye for details has saved me much shame. For technical and practical assistance in the wearisome production of scores of drafts, I thank Tammy Elliot, who threw in graciousness, patience, and a warm smile—no extra charge.

At the core of my argument is a vision of the life of reason rooted in and sustained by love. With this in mind, I would, first, like to thank with all my heart my parents, June and Robert Peters, for their unfailing support and love for me. Growing up as their son, how could I not become a believer in the beauty and reality of unconditional love? My second set of parents, Clifford and Prudence Bedell, loved me before they knew me, which, no doubt, was easier than after they knew me. From their enduring and patient love of a son-in-law, I have learned much of the power of God's spirit. To my children, Nathaniel, Sasha, and Nadia, I owe my deepest thanks for enduring my broken attempts at loving them and for enriching my life in ways I cannot begin to describe. Above all, I would like to thank my wife, Cheri, who with unfailing grace and good sense has given me invaluable counsel on all that I have written. Without her love, support, and encouragement, both my mind and my heart would have faltered. To her I owe a debt both endless and unfathomable. To her I dedicate this book.

INTRODUCTION

AUGUSTINE, PASCAL, AND HUME
ON THE "EMBEDDEDNESS" OF REASON

Novalis, the German romantic poet and philosopher, once remarked that all
proper philosophizing is driven intrinsically by the longing to be at home in
the world, by the desire to bring to peace the restlessness that pervades much
of human life. Wisdom, within this view, and therefore also happiness and
well-being, rest on the ability to transpose the alienation and fragmentation
that characterize life into a marriage of nature and spirit, or as William
Wordsworth described it, a wedding between the human mind and "this
goodly universe."

> Norman Wirzba, "The Challenge of Berry's Agrarian Vision"[1]

Modernity, as everyone living in the closing years of the twentieth century can
see, is a double-edged phenomenon. The development of modern social institutions and their worldwide spread have created vastly greater opportunities
for human beings to enjoy a secure and rewarding existence than any type of
pre-modern system. But modernity also has a somber side, which has become
very apparent in the present century. . . .

On the whole, the opportunity side of modernity was stressed most strongly
by the classical founders of sociology. Marx and Durkheim both saw the modern
era as a troubled one. But each believed that the beneficent possibilities opened
up by the modern era outweighed its negative characteristics. . . . Max Weber
was the most pessimistic among the founding fathers, seeing the modern world
as a paradoxical one in which material progress was obtained only at the cost

---

1. Norman Wirzba, "The Challenge of Berry's Agrarian Vision," in *The Art of the Commonplace: The Agrarian Essays of Wendell Berry*, by Wendell Berry (Washington, DC: Shoemaker
and Hoard, 2002), vii.

of an expanded bureaucracy that crushed individual creativity and autonomy. Yet even he did not fully anticipate how extensive the darker side of modernity would turn out to be.

Anthony Giddens, *The Consequences of Modernity*[2]

In *The Consequences of Modernity*, social theorist Anthony Giddens characterizes the technological, consumer-driven culture of modernity as a culture of "disembeddedness."[3] Giddens argues that the cumulative impact of the social, economic, technological, and intellectual transformations of modernization has been to extricate the individual self from the traditional bonds of kinship to community, land, and history. His description of the modern, disembedded self echoes Max Weber's thesis that secularization and disenchantment are necessary corollaries to the rise of modern scientific culture. As Weber remarks in "Science as a Vocation," "The fate of our times is characterized by rationalization and intellectualization and, above all, by the 'disenchantment of the world.'"[4]

The legacy of modernity's disembeddedness is now a familiar theme in the writings of many contemporary social thinkers.[5] Alasdair MacIntyre and Stanley Hauerwas, in particular, argue that modernity's preoccupation with individual liberation and autonomy has tragically torn asunder the intricate fabric of the individual's social and historical identity. Modernity's zeal to free the rational individual from all forms of historical and traditional embeddedness has infected all the major institutions of modernity: the marketplace, academy, political arena, and church.[6] In the name of the right to forge one's

---

2. Anthony Giddens, *The Consequences of Modernity* (Stanford, CA: Stanford University Press, 1990), 7.

3. Ibid., 17–54.

4. Max Weber, *From Max Weber: Essays in Sociology*, trans. and ed. H. H. Gerth and C. Wright Mills (New York: Oxford University Press, 1946).

5. See, for example, Peter Berger, Brigette Berger, and Hansfried Kellner, *The Homeless Mind: Modernization and Consciousness* (New York: Vintage, 1973); Berry, *Art of the Commonplace*; Giddens, *Consequences of Modernity*; idem, *Modernity and Self-Identity: Self and Society in the Late Modern Age* (Stanford, CA: Stanford University Press, 1991); Christopher Lasch, *The Culture of Narcissism* (New York: Norton, 1979); Alasdair MacIntyre, *After Virtue* (Notre Dame, IN: University of Notre Dame Press, 1984); Wilfred M. McClay, *The Masterless: Self and Society in Modern America* (Chapel Hill: University of North Carolina Press, 1994); Charles Taylor, *Sources of the Self: The Making of the Modern Identity* (Cambridge, MA: Harvard University Press, 1989); and Norman Wirzba, *The Paradise of God* (Oxford: Oxford University Press, 2003).

6. Of the many works of both Hauerwas and MacIntyre that develop this critique of modernity, see esp. Stanley Hauerwas, *A Better Hope: Resources for a Church Confronting Capitalism, Democracy, and Postmodernity* (Grand Rapids: Brazos, 2000); idem, *A Community of Character: Toward a Constructive Christian Social Ethic* (Notre Dame, IN: University of Notre Dame Press, 1981); idem, *After Christendom? How the Church Is to Behave if Freedom, Justice, and a Christian Nation Are Bad Ideas* (Nashville: Abingdon, 1991); idem, *The Peaceable Kingdom: A Primer in Christian Ethics* (Notre Dame, IN: University of Notre Dame Press, 1983); MacIntyre,

own meaning and to improve the material conditions of human existence, modernity has severed individual from community, community from nature, natural from supernatural, and facts (as mere commodities) from human values (as mere private preferences).

Following Hauerwas and MacIntyre, I shall argue that those of us living in the so-called postmodern world, in which fundamental beliefs and practices central to modernity appear to have lost their authority and legitimacy, will suffer the consequences of our disembeddedness until we recognize the extent to which both modernity and mainstream secular postmodernity foster a pervasive ethos of disembeddedness. *The Logic of the Heart* seeks to remedy the disembeddedness of our postmodern condition by returning to the thought of two Christian thinkers of the past, Augustine and Pascal, whose perspectives on Christian faith and human reason provide us with a viable way to overcome modernity's unfortunate legacy of a deep and ugly divide between reason and affection and postmodernism's excessive preoccupation with its own gospel of radical autonomy.

While bequeathing to us a valuable legacy of resistance to various forms of tyranny over the individual self, modernity has perpetrated a damaging illusion of the radically autonomous, rational self. Similarly, while postmodernism has rightly exposed modernity's misunderstanding of the nature of rational objectivity and its failure adequately to foresee the potentially oppressive and exploitative uses to which such modern notions as rational progress and metaphysical essentialism might be put, it has utterly failed to offer any substantial opposition to the intoxicating modern consumer appetite for human autonomy.[7] In different ways, both modernity and postmodernity have succumbed to the *lure of autonomy*. Modernity's vision of autonomy fosters the distorted conception of the self-governing, ahistorical, nonsectarian, rational self. Following the brilliant but tragically modernist diatribes of Friedrich Nietzsche against the idols of modern culture, the postmodernism of the late twentieth-century Western academy has succeeded in unmasking the incoherence of the modern notions of pure rational objectivity and liberal individualism only to foist on us an even more virulent addiction to autonomous self-creation. The poverty of mainstream, radical, secular postmodernism

---

After Virtue; and idem, *Three Rival Versions of Moral Enquiry: Encyclopaedia, Genealogy, and Tradition* (Notre Dame, IN: University of Notre Dame Press, 1990).

7. In my critical discussion of radical postmodernism, I do wish to acknowledge with appreciation some of the significant contributions postmodernism has made to contemporary debates on the nature of human thinking. My critique of postmodernism focuses on those mainstream, secular postmodernists who insist that postmodern liberation requires an aversion to all realist traditions of metaphysical and theological thought, traditions that make definite claims about the nature of objective reality, in order to uphold the radical autonomy of human interpretation. Despite the severity of my criticisms of postmodernism as "hypermodern" rather than truly postmodern, I acknowledge the meritorious contributions of radical postmodernism to the current debates about rationality, objectivity, and the situatedness of all forms of human thinking.

is paradoxically that its professed remedy for the disorders of modernity is itself a form of self-imprisonment within a community of self-liberating and self-creating ironists.

By defending the rationality of faith in a God of grace who alone can satisfy our longings and heal our brokenness, Augustine and Pascal advocate the art of living as embedded creatures. Following such Christian thinkers as Alasdair MacIntyre, Stanley Hauerwas, Alvin Plantinga, and David Bentley Hart, *The Logic of the Heart* seeks to elucidate and defend an Augustinian and Pascalian account of the embeddedness of human rationality. Properly understood, human reasoning on ultimate issues of human life is inextricably bound up with those affections and feelings that reveal to us our proper place in creation. Reason can function properly, in other words, only when reason is informed by the intuitions of the heart as it is nurtured by historically constituted traditions of belief and practice. By insisting on reason's autonomous authority independent of the sensibilities of the heart, the Enlightenment inadvertently severed reason from the very source on which it depends for its own proper functioning. Similarly, by advocating the poetics of self-creation and extolling the freedom to construct our own worlds, mainstream postmodernism strips the self of its embeddedness in a world beyond mere human artifice, a world that has the power to bestow meaning and dignity on human life precisely because it is not a mere social construct. Augustine's and Pascal's vision of "passionate reason" provides a compelling account of human embeddedness and offers a viable middle ground between Enlightenment rational autonomy and mainstream postmodern poetics of self-creation.

The modern separation of the sacred from the secular may well have its origins in the worldview of the late medieval nominalists, who by rejecting essences denuded the created order of common forms, thereby reducing the natural order to a realm of valueless, formless individuals; in so doing, these nominalists forged an unbridgeable divide between the truths of reason and the truths of faith. This pioneering, premodern demarcation of the secular from the sacred was in turn reinforced through the epistemological turn of early modern philosophers. Thomas Hobbes, Galileo Galilei, and René Descartes all insisted on redirecting the path of learning away from the antiquated Aristotelian conception of Nature as teleological and toward a dualistic framework in which an objective, mechanized, and valueless natural order was set over against a subjective world of human ideas and sentiments. By abandoning the vision of an *enformed* Nature whose members remain unintelligible apart from their directedness toward their own proper ends, modern philosophy severed the objective realm of Nature from the subjective world of human consciousness. As a result, both the natural order of mathematical mechanism and the subjective order of human ideas and judgments were abstracted from ordinary, everyday human experience in which our encounters with self and world are embedded in an intricate and complex context of natural forms and are inextricably bound up with a world of historical and cultural traditions. By turning away from the world of ordinary human experience embedded in this web of contingent beings and historical forms of life, the great pioneering minds of modernity, such as Descartes, Benedict de Spinoza, John Locke, and Immanuel Kant, aspired to liberate human rationality by establishing human reason in and of itself as a universal, dispassionate, objective, and autonomous authority. By severing the valueless natural order from the subjective evaluating human mind, the framers of modernity brought into being the disembedded, autonomous mind.

Despite the fact that we live today in what many social thinkers term the "postmodern" world, this modern archetype of dispassionate, unbiased, and disembedded reason has in one form or another become so pervasive in our dominant intellectual, cultural, and political practices that for most of us the very idea of "passionate reason" seems an oxymoron. Now, it is no doubt true that most, if not all, of us have experienced ethical conflicts between what "reason" tells us we should do and what we desire or "feel like" doing: there is no denying that reason and passion do at times conflict. But this opposition between reason and *certain* of our passions and desires does not ipso facto require reason to function most properly in our lives only when it is freed entirely from the influence of *all* passion and *all* sensibility.

The core project of *The Logic of the Heart* is to recover a robust conception of passionate reason. Despite the legacy of modernity that pervades our lives today, I believe that we can reasonably embrace the following radical claims: first, that the proper function of reason in human life is to enable us truthfully to locate ourselves in our world and to live wisely by recognizing who we are and what our proper place is in this world; and second, that reason cannot perform this proper function apart from the guidance of the human heart. Indeed, I will argue that it is only by cultivating habits of love, properly understood, that we can discover the truth about ourselves and make fully rational judgments about the most pressing questions for any age: Who are we? How should we treat one another? And just what is our proper place in a diverse world composed not only of diverse peoples and nonhuman forms of life, but also of human communities and natural landscapes? These are questions that cannot be answered by a dispassionate intellect, but only by "passionate reason."

This conception of "passionate reason" challenges three predominant modern or postmodern perspectives on the fundamental purposes of reason:

1. the modern technological, consumerist perspective, which assumes that reason's fundamental purpose is to master the cosmos by scientific manipulation of the forces and raw materials of nature;
2. the Enlightenment-based, dispassionate perspective, which assumes that reason's fundamental purpose is to gain objective knowledge of a material world of valueless, neutral facts;

3. the radical, secular postmodern perspective, which assumes that reason's fundamental purpose is to create reality, and thereby to exercise our interpretive freedom through the free play of our own artifices.

In contrast to these three mainstream conceptions of rationality, I shall defend an account of the rational self in which the final end of human reason is not to "see" reality dispassionately, or to master a reality of valueless entities, supplying us with endless commodities, or even to liberate us by unmasking metaphysical idols and constructing our own realities. Instead, the real purpose of reason is to allow us to be in communion with, to esteem and lovingly embrace, the truly Real; it is, as Wirzba puts it, to attain "a wedding between the human mind and 'this goodly universe.'"[8] In the same vein, following Augustine and Pascal, I contend that our proper *telos* as rational creatures is to cultivate rational love and passionate acknowledgment of God as our highest good and of our fellow humans as dependent icons of divine, infinite goodness.

At this point a sober reader might well inquire whether such a vision of passionate reason can have any validity in a post-Christian, secularized world. What, one might well ask, would it mean for us to conceive of the work of reason as leading us to wholeness, and the purpose of philosophy as enabling us to find our proper place in the world? Can it still make sense today to conceive of human life and indeed the philosophical quest as driven by a humble yearning, even an erotic desire, to partake in a magnificent banquet of nature and spirit in which the human self finds its true fulfillment?

A careful reading not only of the Christian philosophers Augustine and Pascal, but also of the robustly anti-Christian modern skeptic David Hume, can help us to recover a vision of passionate rationality that is more than mere romantic fantasy. This vision of "passionate reason" rejects the misguided, Enlightenment-based myth of the rational person as an autonomous, critical individual who exercises a universal, dispassionate, and objective rationality. Equally unsustainable is the radical postmodern mythos of the self-creating, world-constituting, autonomous community of self-creators. By contrast, the conception of passionate reason acknowledges the complex and intricate interdependence of our beliefs, affections, historical experience, cultural forms of life, and the objective goodness of God and God's creation. One cannot function rationally in isolation from the "heart," for it is only when the affections are properly oriented to the ends of human life that people can think rationally about themselves, find their proper place in the scheme of things, and acknowledge that the world is neither our creation nor our intellectual shopping mall. Central to this outlook is the conviction that our world is an aesthetic whole, an order of inherently good beings, an order we are meant to

8. Wirzba, "Challenge of Berry's Agrarian Vision," vii.

honor and respect, rather than to master or lay claim to as our own creation. Nothing in this world, not even our own individual selves, is ever simply our own. Ironically—so at least I shall argue—acknowledging our place in God's creation and reason's dependence on the heart is profoundly, and even eternally, liberating. Our embeddedness should not offend us but serve as cause for ecstatic celebration.

My argument develops as an examination of Augustine's philosophy of faith seeking understanding and the modest skepticism of two modern philosophers who were among the earliest, most original skeptics of the modern, intellectual faith in "progress through scientific objectivity" and "enlightenment through disinterested, autonomous reason." These two modern philosophers, Blaise Pascal and David Hume, should be understood as modern counterparts of Socrates, warning their rationalist contemporaries of the dangers of a distinctively modern philosophical hubris, the pride of an imperial and autonomous new rationality, offering instead a skeptical critique of the modern faith in purely rational foundations.

Yet Pascal and Hume do not extol the "higher" wisdom of irrational feelings over against the practice of coherent rational thinking, nor do they propound a kind of "safe" radicalism that in fact has little potency for calling into question the power structures of their worlds. On the contrary, Hume and Pascal risked significant censure as they sought to emphasize both the necessity of substantial rational inquiry and the severe limits of human reason in the face of serious social and religious controversy. In the following chapters, I hope, despite my own commitments and potential biases as a Christian philosopher, to demonstrate the originality and courage of both of these modern skeptics, one deeply Christian and the other vehemently anti-Christian, in their "Socratic," rather than comfortably "ironic," skepticism. In essence, I shall argue that what is needed today, at the end of modernity, is not the postmodern exaltation of autonomy and difference but a return to a healthy and balanced Christian skepticism about rational autonomy, which has the power to invigorate and transform lives.

In sum, I intend to defend the integrity and rationality of Christian faith in the context of the skepticism and uncertainty of the so-called postmodern world through Pascal and Hume, who in ultimately quite different ways stand in opposition to the mainstream of modern philosophy and yet offer substantial alternatives to radical postmodernism. For both Pascal and Hume, human nature compels us to believe in realities, the existence of which we cannot verify, a philosophical outlook that accords with the nonrational dimension of our human character. They insist on rendering philosophy human and on humbling our philosophical ambitions in accordance with the narrow limits of human reasoning. Yet despite their kinship in recognizing the limits of reason and in condemning dogmatic philosophers' proud lack of self-knowledge, Pascal and Hume come to radically different conclusions on the value of Christian faith. On this critical point of disagreement, Pascal's understanding of the role of reason and love in the life of Christian faith exposes the deficiencies of Hume's skeptical attack on Christian beliefs and practices.

Pascal's account of reason and faith is essentially Augustinian; two principles of Augustine's thought in particular illuminate what is ultimately at issue between Pascal and Hume. The first, "*credo ut intellegam*," sets forth a certain kind of priority of trust and love over understanding, and the second, "*fides quaerens intellectum*," proclaims a mutual dependence and harmony between reason and the heart. These two Augustinian principles play a fundamental role in Pascal's own philosophy. The scholarly characterization of Pascal as an irrationalist fails to perceive the complexity of his Augustinian conception of faith and rationality. Pascal's protests against reliance on reason alone are no more the utterances of an irrationalist than are Augustine's critical words against the dangers of Neoplatonism. Neither Pascal nor Augustine recommends divorcing the life of faith from the life of rational inquiry and reflection. Rather, both philosophers condemn as a distortion that philosophical conception of human reason in which reason has autonomous authority for judging *on its own* any and all claims regarding the human good. In contrast, Hume's attack on Christian faith reveals his failure to comprehend an Augustinian stance on the interrelationship of love, faith, and reason. Although rightly rejecting the autonomy of reason, Hume's understanding of the nature and rationality of the Christian faith fails seriously to consider how reason, faith, and love are interrelated.

Indeed, Hume's infamous attacks on the Christian faith reveal a woeful ignorance about the power of love both in the life of faith and in the process of transforming us into creatures able to make sense of the rationality of Christian faith. Ultimately, Hume's anti-theistic skepticism begs the question: his most forceful criticisms of the Christian life are compelling only if one already presupposes a naturalistic, nontheistic framework.

One of the instructive lessons that emerges from a comparative study of Augustine, Pascal, and Hume is that our conception of rationality cannot be separated from our metaphysics—that is, from our understanding of the nature of the world and the human self. In his neoclassical ethics of virtue, Hume develops a perceptive and intricate account of the role of the passions in moral judgment. Yet Hume never considers it plausible to believe that the moral judgments we form on the basis of our passions reveal to us objective features of a morally ordered universe. That Hume finds such a move implausible results primarily from how Hume interprets the meaning of human experience naturalistically. In other words, having presupposed a naturalistic framework in which it makes no sense to regard human judgments concerning good and evil or virtue and vice as having any real ethical correspondence to the objective order of nature, Hume naturally resists regarding our moral sentiments as reliable sources of information about the objective world order outside the psychological constitution of humans. Hume takes the objective world as a realm of valueless facts about which we can have no rational certainty as one of his starting points. In contrast to Hume, from an Augustinian perspective, the objective world order cannot be a realm merely of valueless facts, because there simply are no such things as mere, valueless facts. Whatever exists, on an Augustinian view, exists as something possessing a unifying form that distinguishes it as an embodiment of inherent goodness and as an icon of the divine reality. In an important sense, then, for the Augustinian "valueless facts" are simply not real. This fundamental difference in metaphysical outlook deeply affects how Augustine and Hume conceive of the virtues and come to judge the merits of Christian faith. When Hume concludes that a rational person cannot embrace the Christian faith, he presupposes a prior, nontheistic conception of the world in which this rational person must navigate. When Augustine concludes that assenting to Christ by faith is eminently rational, he presupposes an entirely un-Humean set of metaphysical beliefs about the self and world.

Of course, the claim that Augustine and Hume disagree in their metaphysics hardly makes for surprising news. Yet it is vitally important to grasp that one's conception of the nature of the world impacts one's view of the proper function of human reason. If we agree with Hume's naturalistic outlook, we may well have no other reasonable choice but to conclude that religious faith, at least the traditional Christian faith, is indeed irrational. That Hume would be right about the irrationality of faith if the world is, in fact, an arena of valueless facts becomes clear, ironically, when we take seriously the Augustinian understanding of the connection between rationality and human nature. For Augustine, as well as Pascal, the rationality of faith is inextricably bound up with a conception of human nature as unhealthy and incomplete apart from divine grace. Insofar as a major purpose of being *rational* for people is to help us find out and become properly aligned to the truth about ourselves, it is rational, according to Augustine and Pascal, to believe in Christ because only through faith in Christ can reason perform its proper function. But, of course, if Hume is right divine grace is a human fabrication, and the road to genuine human health lies not in humbly submitting to God's love but in reconciling ourselves to our naturalistic destiny. Hume, like Augustine and Pascal, finally upholds a basically functionalist conception of rationality: to be rational about one's beliefs is basically to form and moderate one's beliefs in accordance with the proper function of reason. On Hume's account, the purpose of our rationality is to find peace and tranquility as the complex passionate reasoners that we are, living in a world of facts indifferent to our human sentiments. Hume thinks he can show that faith in the supernatural, in fact, offers little real benefit in enabling the wise person to be reconciled to this human condition. And yet, what Hume seems never to have realized is the difficulty he gets himself into when he does not critically examine the interrelationship of his conception of rationality and his naturalistic worldview. His conception of rationality presupposes—and thus cannot be used as a prior premise to defend—his metaphysical naturalism. Perhaps under the influence of the Enlightenment thinkers from whom Hume strove to distance himself, he is finally unable to recognize that there is no single, neutral standard of rationality by which we can adjudicate substantial philosophical disagreements independently of metaphysical context. Unlike Pascal and Augustine, Hume seems unaware of the role faith plays, even if it is a faith in naturalism, in a person's very conception of what it means to be rational.

I have written this book out of the conviction that the basic Augustinian and Pascalian position on faith and understanding is well suited for a postmodern age disillusioned with the idols of hard facts, passionless reason, absolute foundations, and the amoral rhetoric of consumerism and materialism. Augustine's and Pascal's conception of a situated and dialectical reason, of a reason dependent on the heart, of a reason nurtured and transformed by God's love, provides a viable middle ground between the Enlightenment idolatry of reason and the radical postmodernist's idolatry of autonomy and its call for the end of traditional philosophy and theology as unwarranted and oppressive metanarratives. Both Hume and Pascal tried in their own ways to caution us against the pretensions of philosophers who insist that we live by reason alone. I shall attempt in what follows to place these two dialectical opponents against each other. In the end, whether we opt for Hume's or Pascal's position on the merits of Christian faith depends on a question at the core of our human nature: "What are people for?" As an Augustinian, my own response to this question cannot help but reflect my own conviction that we are characterized at the core of our being by a desire and a yearning for God's perfect and inexhaustible *agape* love, and that we are made for the purpose of abiding in this love for all eternity. While reasonable people may well dispute my conclusions, I deeply believe that individuals committed to, opposed to, or even curious about the meaning of human life have much to learn from a careful study of Augustine, Pascal, and Hume.

1

AUGUSTINE, PASCAL, AND HUME FOR THE POSTMODERN WORLD?

I would be quite happy to continue and to show here the whole chain of other truths that I had deduced from these first ones. . . . I have always remained firm in my resolve not to suppose any principle but the one I have just used to demonstrate the existence of God and the soul, and to take nothing to be true that does not seem to me clearer and more certain than have the demonstrations of the geometricians been previously. And still I dare say not only that I have found the means of satisfying myself in a short time regarding all the main difficulties commonly treated in philosophy, but also I have noted certain laws that God has so established in nature and has impressed in our souls such notions of these laws that, after having reflected sufficiently, we cannot deny that they are strictly adhered to in everything that exists or occurs in the world.

René Descartes, *Discourse on Method*, part 5[1]

Objectivity, in practice, means that one studies or teaches one's subject *as such*, without concern for its relation to other subjects or to the world—that is, without concern for its truth. If one is concerned, if one cares, about the truth or falsity of anything, one cannot be objective: one is glad if it is true and sorry if it is false; one believes it if it is judged to be true and disbelieves it if it is judged to be false. Moreover, the truth and falsity of some things cannot be objectively demonstrated, but must be determined by feeling and appearance, intuition and experience. And

---

1. René Descartes, *Discourse on Method and Meditations on First Philosophy*, trans. Donald A. Cress, 3rd ed. (Indianapolis: Hackett, 1993), 23.

this work of judgment cannot take place at all with respect to one thing or one subject alone. The issue of truth rises out of the comparison of one thing with another, out of the study of the relations and influences between one thing and another and between something and many others.

Wendell Berry, *Home Economics*[2]

In this chapter I will set forth my case that the three philosophers I have chosen for my inquiry are especially relevant for the postmodern era, for a time when a diverse array of thinkers in many different disciplines have called into question major presuppositions and fundamental convictions of modern philosophy. Given the great resurgence of interest among philosophers and theologians today concerning how we should now assess the rationality of religious faith in the wake of the demise of modernity's doctrine of autonomous reason, and, indeed, whether it even makes sense to talk of objective truth, it is especially worthwhile to examine closely the Humean, Pascalian, and Augustinian views on the complex relationship of rationality, theistic belief, and human nature. These philosophers not only acknowledge that people cannot live by "hard" evidence alone, and that certain of our fundamental beliefs are neither self-evident nor incorrigible, but they also develop in a somewhat similar fashion a justification for these fundamental beliefs in terms of the indispensable role they play in human life. Yet Hume, unlike Pascal and Augustine, is determined to expose the lack of evidential grounding for theistic beliefs as a major defect and, indeed, as an insuperable impediment to faith.

For Augustine, Pascal, and Hume, the fundamental question about faith is not simply whether such belief is based on reason—that is, a belief supported by empirical or logical premises—but whether it is wise, given our lack of unambiguous evidence, to assent to the existence of, and indeed commit our lives to, a transcendent God.[3] By directing our attention away from the simple matter of the presence or absence of objective evidence to the question of how

---

2. Wendell Berry, *Home Economics* (New York: North Point, 1987), 91–92.

3. I do not mean to suggest that for Hume the lack of rational evidence for theistic belief is unimportant. On the contrary, Hume expends much energy in showing his Enlightenment contemporaries that their commitment to rational belief conflicts with their Christian faith. But Hume's own attitude to rational belief is more subtle than that of his Lockean contemporaries, for Hume recognizes that as humans we cannot live by evidence alone. Once Hume undermines the evidentialist case for religious belief, he then must show why we should not embrace faith with the self-knowledge that such faith is not supported by rational evidence. Although Hume permits himself to utter such Enlightenment platitudes as, "The wise man proportions his beliefs to the evidence" (see his essay "Of Miracles," in *Enquiries Concerning Human Understanding and Concerning the Principles of Morals*, ed. L. A. Selby-Bigge and P. H. Nidditch, 3rd ed. [Oxford: Clarendon, 1975], 110), he knows full well that the wise man cannot and should not always attempt to limit his beliefs in this way. My contention is that Hume relies primarily on his psychological diagnosis of religious belief to back up his stance that such belief is unwise. We could say that for Hume, as well as for Pascal, the truly appropriate statement would be, "The wise person proportions his or her beliefs to human nature."

people can believe wisely, Augustine, Hume, and Pascal recognize that the justification of a person's religious commitment ultimately hinges on an account of human nature. For Augustine and Pascal, Christian faith is rationally justified insofar as it makes sense of the human condition and enables us to align ourselves with our true nature. In sharp contrast, for Hume, Christian faith and theism in general ultimately are rationally unjustified because they violate our human nature and impair our efforts to align ourselves with our true nature.

Skeptics of Modernity: Embedded Rationality versus Rational Autonomy

> The madman is not the man who has lost his reason. The madman is the man who has lost everything except his reason.
>
> G. K. Chesterton, *Orthodoxy*[4]

One particularly significant insight shared by Hume, Pascal, and Augustine centers on the importance of the passions in guiding the dictates of reason. These three philosophers insist that reason must not be permitted complete autonomy from the life of the passions. While their specific accounts of the proper role of the passions in human ethical and religious judgments differ markedly, they agree that reason alone, operating in isolation from our passions, is insufficient for the tasks of determining how we ought to live and of guiding us to live properly in accordance with our human limitations. To appreciate something of their basic stance on the necessity of the passions, it may be instructive to compare the characteristically modern form of philosophical rhetoric, the propositional assertion [P], with a different form of persuasion, the metaphoric mode of expression [M], characteristic of the craft of the literary or dramatic poet. Consider, for example, the following two statements:

[M] "How sharper than a serpent's tooth it is
   To have a thankless child" (*King Lear* 1.4.295–96).

[P] The daughter's cold ingratitude evoked in her father a piercing sense of betrayal and regret.

Unless we already had been discipled in the wisdom of twentieth-century Anglo-American positivistic philosophy of language, or some other modern account of meaning that divorces fact from value, we would not presume that the statements [M] and [P] are identical in their cognitive meaning; most of

---

4. G. K. Chesterton, *Orthodoxy* (Garden City, NY: Image Books, 1959), 19.

us, at least in our preenlightened condition of everyday life, would intuitively recognize a crucial difference between the poetical [M] and the "merely descriptive" [P] forms of utterance, a difference that would not be reducible to some noncognitive, "aesthetic" embellishment inherent only in the poetical. For while both assertions more or less describe the same painful human experience, their forms of expression differ so poignantly that few but the most artless of readers would dare presume that the meaning of [M] may be reduced without loss of significance or cognitive content to that of [P].

And yet what is it about the poetic utterance of King Lear that moves us deeply and strikes us as so vivid and instructive? Is it not that the uniqueness of the poetic is a function of its brilliant use of metaphor? But then, we might well ask, "What makes the metaphor in this case so powerful?" Is not the special power of metaphor here that Lear's utterance moves us not only *to think* but also *to feel* something of the sharpness and bitterness of a child's ingratitude? We recoil from the idea of the thankless child through our grasp of Shakespeare's metaphor: our impression of the serpent's tooth evokes in us a sense of revulsion; we feel a loathing of the bite of serpentine fangs that, in its juxtaposition with the weight of human ingratitude, clarifies for us what it means to dishonor our parents. And, clearly, we fail to "grasp" the metaphor adequately if we do not feel its power, as it is meant to evoke in us a bitter, stinging sense of disapproval. In moving us both to think and to feel this distaste, Shakespeare shows us what it means for a parent to be treated with ingratitude and what it means for all of us who are children to neglect our parents: in pursuit of our own selfish ambitions, all of us, like Lear's daughters, have failed to love and honor those who have sacrificed years for our benefit. Through metaphor, the poetic utterance has the power to evoke in us a *feeling recognition* of the wrongfulness of betraying one's parents. Such a feeling recognition fuses heart and intellect in such a way that to divorce the component of cognitive judgment from our affections would be to distort the essential character of that very recognition.

By use of metaphor, in other words, Shakespeare transforms us from being indifferent, neutral spectators in the audience to being sympathetic participants in Lear's distress. On the one hand, a neutral spectator *could* view Lear's suffering merely as a fact. On the other hand, a feeling participant who understands Lear's pain knows that betrayal is more than a neutral fact; betrayal is *essentially* an ethical phenomenon—it is cruel, ugly, and repugnant. As witnesses of Lear's fall into madness, if we fail to feel revulsion at the cruelty of Lear's two older daughters, we simply fail to function properly as embedded cognitive persons. To grasp the essence of filial ingratitude we must go beyond a mere spectator's knowledge of the necessary and sufficient conditions of filial ingratitude as a "moral phenomenon"; in other words, an adequate understanding of filial ingratitude requires more from the viewer than simply a neutral type of *knowing that*. More importantly, *knowing* the nature of filial ingratitude requires *acknowledging* and even sympathetically feeling its repugnant and dehumanizing character. And yet such acknowledgment is unattainable to one lacking in a proper response of the will and the affections, for acknowledging the reality of ingratitude requires that one not be indifferent or neutral toward either its perpetrator or its victim. Put more precisely, acknowledging the ethical status of ingratitude necessitates in the beholder a form of personal participation: the sympathetic knower must enter into the suffering of Lear and must empathize with his pain in order to acknowledge its real character as a moral offense. In this act of personal knowing—"I acknowledge the dignity of the sufferer and recoil from the offense of ingratitude"—the viewer cannot reason properly and thus believe truly without engaging in a complex activity of ethical acknowledgment in which thinking, willing, and feeling are inextricably intertwined. Knowledge as participation thus binds together thinking and being: only by becoming a sympathetic participant in suffering can the viewer acknowledge Lear's plight and thus think truthfully about its meaning. This remarkable form of passionate knowledge, rooted in a unique kind of participation and enacted through acknowledgment, unites "being in the truth" with "thinking about the truth," fusing being and thinking in a complex form of *knowing as acknowledging*. In this act of acknowledging moral reality, rational cognition cannot be merely abstract or indifferent, for it is embedded within a way of being that esteems and evaluates, rather than a way that merely observes.

Now the power of the poet's art to evoke in us this form of feeling knowledge, a knowledge available to us only by participation in an emotional response and unavailable to the detached or "purely objective" intellectual, has particular relevance for our study of Hume, Pascal, and Augustine, all of whom agree that ethical first principles cannot be discovered through disinterested "pure reason." Moreover, they all contend that our ethical judgments ultimately arise from uncertain, fallible intuitions that are essentially bound up with our passions of approval and disapproval—put more precisely, in the case of Augustine, with the order and nature of our loves. They all seek in their own distinctive ways to persuade us of the role of "passion" or the "heart" in forming the fabric of our moral world. As philosophers, Hume, Pascal, and Augustine may well succeed in defending the place of the passions in our ethical lives and in clarifying for us the nature of our ethical concerns. But the poet or novelist has the special power to move us to a feeling recognition and proper estimation of ethical reality. The art of the poet thus shows rather than tells, presents rather than merely describes or defends, our ethical landscape. What the philosopher describes, and then attempts to defend by argument, the poet can show with the immediacy of concrete experience. The relative advantage of poetical language is that it more forcefully and directly engages our passions and thereby brings us to feel such complex sentiments as ingratitude; by awakening our ethical sentiments, the poet enables us to understand the ethical dimensions of our lives. One of the poet's advantages over the reflective philosopher turns on the fact that fundamental insights about the human condition are available to us only as we are moved either to approve or to disapprove of actions and events that cause joy or sorrow to people. The philosopher, in turn, has the relative advantage of serving as the reflective critic who creates an interpretive space within which we are able to check the potential prejudices and shortcomings of our sentiments. The philosopher enjoys the special power and freedom of self-conscious reflection; from this vantage point the philosopher may articulate, clarify, and subject to critical analysis the complex matrix of individual beliefs and sentiments, as well as the social forms and practices that constitute our embedded moral lives. In their own distinctive ways, Hume, Pascal, and Augustine, as inheritors of the Socratic tradition of the philosophical quest for self-understanding, acknowledge the dependence of rational reflection on the affections and yet defend in no uncertain terms the supreme importance of rational reflection and criticism.

Clearly then, for Hume, Pascal, and Augustine ethical insights require more than a mere intellectual and disinterested apprehension of facts. Indeed, for these philosophers the very ability to perceive ethical or religious "facts" depends on the proper ordering of our passions. Hume, for example, insists that our ethical judgments about human character and action can arise only through the proper engagement of our sentiments. In a similar way, for Pascal ethical knowledge is fundamentally a matter of knowledge of the heart. And for Augustine the interconnected knowledge of self and God depends on the purifying effect of the virtue of charity. Each offers an analysis of reason and sentiment that makes sense of the special power of poetic metaphor and literary narrative *to reveal* what is true. While the literary artist, through image and metaphor, can move our hearts and thus bring us to a feeling of recognition of the forms and contours of our ethical world, the particular province of the philosopher is to reflect on and assess our ethical beliefs and practices; indeed, such philosophical reflection without the enrichment of lived, existential intuitions will not only be empty but may also misdirect and blind us as to who we really are.

Personal Knowing in Dickens's Hard Times

Modernity certainly has its literary artists who oppose, as do Pascal and Hume, modern philosophy's excessive reliance on reason apart from feeling and passion. Charles Dickens's *Hard Times* is a good example of a work of literature that shows narratively rather than tells philosophically of the folly of living by "reason" alone. As a preface to our inquiry into the thought of Hume and Pascal, it may be instructive to consider Dickens's narrative argument in its relation to the modern philosophical quest for rational progress.

Riding in the wake of modern reformers such as Francis Bacon, René Descartes, and Jeremy Bentham, Dickens's character, Sir Thomas Gradgrind, opens *Hard Times* by proclaiming his revolutionary vision of a brave new world of rational "Facts": "Now, what I want is, Facts. Teach these boys and girls nothing but Facts. Facts alone are wanted in life. Plant nothing else, and root out everything else. You can only form the minds of reasoning animals upon Facts; nothing else will ever be of any service to them. This is the principle on which I bring up these children. Stick to the Facts, sir!"[5]

Gradgrind, a "man of facts and calculations," seeks to found a new social world liberated from the forces of fancy and ignorance and peopled by rational citizens, who, rooted in the soil of genuine Facts, could enjoy the fruits of real happiness. For modern progressives such as Gradgrind, rational social progress awaits the dawning of a new era enlightened by a renewed reason. And he is confident that in this age of progress the march of knowledge will not falter, for its feet will be planted firmly on a pathway of hard Facts. Yet as we discover through Dickens's narrative of self-deception and false enlightenment, Gradgrind comes, through the suffering of his beloved, eldest daughter, to see that people cannot live by Facts alone, for the so-called Facts that Gradgrind espouses allow no room for the needs of the human heart, for sentiments beyond primitive self-interest, and, in particular, for those most essentially human of sentiments, trust and love. Gradgrind begins to understand this defect in his vision when finally confronted by the suffering and desperation of his unhappy daughter Louisa:

"Father, you have trained me from my cradle?"

"Yes, Louisa."

"I curse the hour in which I was born to such a destiny."

He looked at her in doubt and dread, vacantly repeating: "Curse the hour? Curse the hour?"

"How could you give me life, and take from me all the inappreciable things that raise it from the state of conscious death? Where are the graces of my soul? Where are the sentiments of my heart? What have you done, O father, what have you done with the garden that should have bloomed once, in this great wilderness here?"

She struck herself with both her hands upon her bosom.

"If it had ever been here, its ashes alone would save me from the void in which my whole life sinks. I did not mean to say this; but, father, you remember the last time we conversed in this room?"

He had been so wholly unprepared for what he heard now, that it was with difficulty he answered, "Yes, Louisa."

"What has risen to my lips now, would have risen to my lips then, if you had given me a moment's help. I don't reproach you, father. What you have never

5. Charles Dickens, *Hard Times*, ed. George Ford and Sylvere Monod, 2nd ed. (New York: Norton, 1996), 7.

nurtured in me, you have never nurtured in yourself; but O! If you had only done so long ago, or if you had only neglected me, what a much better and much happier creature I should have been this day!"

On hearing this, after all his care, he bowed his head upon his hand and groaned aloud.

"Father, if you had known, when we were last together here, what even I feared while I strove against it—as it has been my task from infancy to strive against every natural prompting that has arisen in my heart; if you had known that there lingered in my breast sensibilities, affections, weaknesses capable of being cherished into strength, defying all the calculations ever made by man, and no more known to his arithmetic than his Creator is—would you have given me to the husband whom I am now sure that I hate?"

He said, "No. No, my poor child."

"Would you have doomed me, at any time, to the frost and blight that have hardened and spoiled me? Would you have robbed me—for no one's enrichment—only for the greater desolation of this world—of the immaterial part of my life, the spring and summer of my belief, my refuge from what is sordid and bad in the real things around me, my school in which I should have learned to be more humble and more trusting with them, and to hope in my little sphere to make them better?"[6]

As he painfully comes to realize, the Facts of Gradgrind's world constitute a barren landscape, for they include no more than the material features of a self-seeking, industrial world, the statistics of material efficiency, and the principles of "material progress." Thus the story of *Hard Times* is for Gradgrind a painful journey from a proud, if also self-deceived, philosophy of "progress" that stifles the human heart and damages human lives, to a truer and more humble enlightenment. The turning point in his own self-understanding comes in a moment of painful uncertainty: "'Some persons hold,' he pursued, still hesitating, 'that there is a wisdom of the Head, and that there is a wisdom of the Heart. I have not supposed so; but, as I have said, I mistrust myself now. I have supposed the head to be all-sufficient. It may not be all-sufficient; how can I venture this morning to say it is! If that other kind of wisdom should be what I have neglected, and should be the instinct that is wanted, Louisa.'"[7]

Gradgrind comes to appreciate that there is more to the Truth than just the Facts. But, ironically, for Gradgrind such an insight about the wisdom of the heart can be attained only through a prior act of relying on the heart in which he trusts that his daughter truthfully reports the nature and cause of her own suffering. Only because he first acknowledges that he deeply cares for Louisa, and thus will trust her own account of her predicament, does it become possible for Gradgrind to see his daughter's plight as evidence of the inadequacy of his own rational system. Let us not overlook how a more

---

6. Dickens, *Hard Times*, 161.
7. Dickens, *Hard Times*, 166.

stubborn disciple of Gradgrind's rational philosophy could persist indefinitely in accepting Louisa's crisis as real in a sense, and yet interpret her testimony in a way compatible with the basic commitments of his philosophy of facts. In other words, contrary to Kant's Enlightenment optimism that mere rational consistency precludes disregard for human dignity, a hardened Gradgrindian utilitarian has the rational option of reinterpreting all supposed counterevidence to his outlook as a manifestation of self-delusion or some other form of self-alienation.

Gradgrind falters and doubts his own philosophical system only because of his fundamental choice to place his trust and love for his daughter above his faith in his own rational system. Without this act of commitment, which is rooted in the affection of his heart, he would not feel compelled to take seriously the principles of the wisdom of the heart espoused by his daughter. Most significantly, then, Gradgrind's awakening to the wisdom of the heart occurs only because he first *believes in* the veracity of his daughter—"*credo ut intellegam.*" His intellectual reflection, in which he humbles himself and strives to reassure his daughter that he trusts her sense of the wisdom of the heart, depends on his prior act of trusting his own daughter.[8]

Bacon and Descartes: Seeds for the Enlightenment

Gradgrind's vision, though unique in its details, and specifically intended by Dickens as a satire of Bentham's utilitarianism, actually bears the unmistakable form and blueprint of an ingenious early modern philosophical vision of a new *scientia*. It is a revolutionary vision heralded in Bacon's *Novum Organum* and Descartes's *Meditations*, *Discourse on Method*, and the unfinished *Rules for the Direction of the Mind*. To appreciate the prophetic nature of Dickens's story, it may be useful to review some of the basic features of this modern intellectual revolution that sowed the seeds for the Enlightenment.

In his *Novum Organum* of 1620, Bacon embarked on the discovery of true knowledge with a word of warning: "They who have presumed to dogmatize on nature, as on some well investigated subject, either from self-conceit or arrogance, and in the professorial style, have inflicted the greatest injury on

---

8. From the point of view of our contemporary, postmodern skepticism of Enlightenment objectivity and the modern conception of rational autonomy, Dickens's critique of the Gradgrind philosophy has a prophetic tone. Since the 1850s, when Dickens wrote *Hard Times*, we have intellectually and culturally lived through the decline of the age of rational progress. Much debate remains on just what lies ahead. Today many intellectual critics, philosophers, and theologians are debating the implications of the demise of the Enlightenment for the most fundamental questions concerning the rationality of religious belief and the life and authority of the church. What these debates often lack is an understanding of the integrity and rationality of the Christian faith, as defended specifically by Augustine and Pascal, in the face of the challenges and perplexities of our postmodern world.

philosophy and learning."[9] Such a warning is necessary, Bacon presumes, for he believes that the modern mind of the early seventeenth century is still dominated by the imprecise and sterile method of Aristotelian logic, a "logic [that] rather assists in confirming and rendering inveterate the errors founded on vulgar notions than in searching after truth."[10] If there is to be genuine progress in the sciences, he argues, those seeking the truth must reject the speculative metaphysics of the past and pursue a new method of empirical reasoning. In contrast to the unproductive methodology of past thinkers, and of the Scholastics in particular, this new method of empiricism would both humble the pretensions of the human mind and render intelligible for the first time the book of nature. And insofar as he thinks that "knowledge and human power are synonymous,"[11] and that the new science will afford much knowledge, Bacon, as does Gradgrind, confidently looks ahead to our technological mastery of the forces of nature:

> We must next, however, proceed to the supports and corrections of induction, and thence to concretes, the latent process, and latent conformations, and the other matters, which we have enumerated in the twenty-first aphorism, in order that, like good and faithful guardians, we may yield up their fortune to mankind upon the emancipation and majority of their understanding; from which must necessarily follow an improvement of their estate, and an increase of their power over nature. For man, by the fall, lost at once his state of innocence, and his empire over creation, both of which can be partially recovered even in this life, the first by religion and faith, the second by the arts and sciences. For creation did not become entirely and utterly rebellious by the curse, but in consequence of the Divine decree, "in the sweat of thy brow shalt thou eat bread," she is compelled by our labors (not assuredly by our disputes or magical ceremonies), at length, to afford mankind in some degree his bread, that is to say, to supply man's daily wants.[12]

So in 1620 Bacon foresees a bright future. Seizing in particular on the promise of scientific renewal on the horizon, Bacon implores his reader to part company with the old ways of Aristotelian Scholasticism, with its emphasis on formal causes and teleological explanations, and to embrace a new intellectual covenant. He assures us that we can now look forward to unlocking Nature's secrets and regaining rightful mastery over Nature's subjects if only we take care to follow assiduously the steps of the new inductive method.

Just a few years later in 1628, Descartes laid the groundwork for one of the most distinctive and influential features of Cartesian philosophy—a

9. Francis Bacon, *Novum Organum*, ed. Joseph Devey (New York: P. F. Collier and Son, 1902).
10. Ibid., 13.
11. Ibid., 11.
12. Ibid., 290.

purportedly new methodology for attaining a purely objective system of knowledge built on an indubitable foundation of unassailable "intuitions." Heralding this new system of rational discovery, Descartes writes in the *Rules for the Direction of the Mind*: "The whole method consists entirely in the ordering and arranging of the objects on which we must concentrate our mind's eye if we are to discover some truth. We shall be following this method exactly if we first reduce complicated and obscure propositions step by step to simpler ones, then starting with the intuition of the simplest ones of all, try to ascend through the same steps to a knowledge of all the rest."[13]

Like Bacon, Descartes formulates his system of clear and distinct ideas as an alternative to the well-meaning but inconclusive inquiries of past philosophers. For Descartes, true *scientia* must necessarily be completely beyond doubt. Given the rather heroic grandeur of such a level of human understanding, it is not surprising that Descartes insists that achieving such knowledge demands the most rigorous of strategies. Both in the *Discourse on Method*, published in 1637, and in the *Meditations*, published in 1644, he is relentless in his ambition to achieve certain knowledge through a strict method of establishing clear and distinct foundations. Even in his earliest philosophical work, the *Rules*, Descartes is confident that his ambitious desire for such firm knowledge is not in vain. So Descartes reassures his reader that:

> All knowledge [*scientia*] is certain and evident cognition. Someone who has doubts about many things is no wiser than one who has never given them a thought; indeed, he appears less wise if he has formed a false opinion about any of them. Hence it is better never to study at all than to occupy ourselves with objects which are so difficult that we are unable to distinguish what is true from what is false, and are forced to take the doubtful as certain; for in such matters the risk of diminishing our knowledge is greater than our hope of increasing it. So, in accordance with this Rule, we reject all such merely probable cognition and resolve to believe only what is perfectly known and incapable of being doubted. Men of learning are perhaps convinced that there is very little indubitable knowledge, since, owing to a common human failing, they have disdained to reflect upon such indubitable truths, taking them to be too easy and obvious to everyone. But there are, I insist, a lot more of these truths than such people think—truths which suffice for the sure demonstration of countless propositions which so far they have managed to treat as no more than probable. Because they have thought it unbecoming for a man of learning to admit to being ignorant on any matter, they have got so used to elaborating their contrived doctrines that they have gradually come to believe them and pass them off as true.[14]

13. John Cottingham, Robert Stoothoff, and Dugald Murdoch, eds. and trans., *The Philosophical Writings of Descartes* (Cambridge: Cambridge University Press, 1984), 20.
    14. Ibid., 10–11.

To a significant extent, the scientist Bacon, the philosopher Descartes, and the social reformer Gradgrind all share an intellectual vision and possess the same remarkable confidence in its realization. It is this basic vision of rational autonomy that will become the chief cornerstone of the dominant traditions of modern Western philosophy.

Fundamental to this modern vision are three significant convictions, the first concerning what went wrong with the philosophies of the past and the second and third concerning how best to remedy philosophy's dismal past. With respect to the diagnosis of the past, the adherents of this outlook take a dim view of premodern philosophical systems. Indeed, they are firmly convinced that even the best minds of the past were led astray by their uncritical reliance on untested theories, mere custom, untutored common sense, and the fancies of the human heart. Here one encounters that distinctively modern philosophical diagnosis of the philosophical projects of the past as plagued by a common disorder: such efforts have been retarded by their lack of objectivity. Rather than discipline themselves according to the canons of objectivity, even the greatest minds of the past have relied on unreflective opinion and uncertain sentiment. Modern advocates of objective reason, like Bacon and Descartes, propose an essentially twofold remedy for philosophy's benighted past. This remedy embodies two of the fundamental articles of modernity's faith in pure reason. What is needed to correct the inherent bias of past philosophies and pave the way for genuine rational progress, Descartes and his Enlightenment heirs contend, is a radically new mental posture in which one strictly governs one's beliefs and assents only to those conclusions certified by a rational, and thus unbiased, apprehension of foundational certitudes. Only with such a union of, first, an enlightened new rational methodology and, second, a purified and unbiased set of rational foundations will it be possible to remedy the errors of the past. For Bacon the recovery of a truly rational methodology depends on the proper collating of pure observations of true science; for Descartes the recovery requires a rigorous methodology of accessing incorrigible rational intuitions that are discoverable only through a subjective turning within one's private consciousness. In a similar fashion, for Gradgrind the road to progress is paved with the foundations of measurable, utilitarian Facts. Though differing to some degree with respect to the proper methodology and content of this progressive, new rationality, all three modern philosophical programs share a common vision of a nonsectarian, universal rationality whose essential character is its autonomy. For Bacon, Descartes, Gradgrind, and the advocates of modern objective rationality who followed in their wake, the power and promise of human rationality lies in its fundamental disembeddedness from the entire fabric of human social and historical contingency.

Descartes and Gradgrind presume that human reason will function properly only when it is divorced from the sentiments and passions of the human heart. Their motives are properly noble: that we might attain an enlightenment sufficient to nurture our children and procure our general happiness. The Augustinian, on the contrary, argues that one must first believe in order to understand, and that understanding comes not through the intellect alone, but from a mind directed and counseled by the heart. In fact, a careful investigation of the arguments of Pascal and Hume supports such an Augustinian alternative.

All the same, we would do well not to be as dismissive of this modern quest for rational autonomy as the prophets of modern enlightenment were of their own past. Living in times of political and religious turmoil, it is not surprising that many modern philosophers were deeply attracted to this new "scientific" vision of objective progress in theory and practice. That such gifted men as Locke, Bacon, and Descartes should have felt the lure of a "scientific" program of education, free of bias and devoted only to objective facts and pure foundations, is understandable and laudable; they presumed that this new conception of objective reason would provide a common ground on which rational beings could think and live, free from the destructive effects of sectarian intolerance and human presumption. In one form or another, those who shared this vision of rational enlightenment sought a rigorous method that, by setting aside the biases of historical situation, religious commitment, and subjective belief, could get straight to the Facts and thus rely on a purely objective set of criteria for the peaceful resolution of all disputes.

My quarrel with Descartes, Bacon, and the Enlightenment thinkers they anticipate is not directed against their honorable intentions. But despite such noble intentions, Descartes's profound belief in the viability of an ambitious foundationalism bequeathed an unfortunate legacy in the form of modernity's mistaken understanding of the authority of autonomous reason—reason that stands apart from tradition, culture, family, and individual affection. The modern philosophical perspective so brilliantly but misguidedly set forth by Descartes fails to recognize that as mere humans we have no choice but to live in the absence of any absolute, purely rational, clear, and distinct truths. As finite humans, we must acknowledge that the normative standards of human beliefs and practices are historically situated and that our fundamental moral intuitions are embedded within a context of shared affections, cultural forms, and religious inheritances.

Interestingly enough, for Augustine and Pascal finite humans can hope to attain a kind of certainty on ultimate matters, but this is a kind of spiritual or ethical certainty rooted in faith and nurtured by participation in a community of fellow believers. Put another way, both Augustine and Pascal contend that true wisdom and ultimate clarity about human life are attainable only through a historical community of faith. They further argue that true rational enlightenment is possible only through acknowledgment of our dependence on a source of healing goodness outside ourselves that can be accessed only through the guidance and transformation of the affections.

Embedded Reason in Augustine, Pascal, and Plantinga

Despite their serious disagreements, Augustine, Pascal, and Hume all agree that any philosophical system extolling rational autonomy inevitably fails to comprehend the essentially dependent character—the radical embeddedness—of human rationality. Whether Descartes ever intended entirely to oppose his own Augustinian tradition, the historical impact of his methodology was the founding of a tradition, exemplified in the Enlightenment philosophies of such great modern thinkers as Locke and Kant, that declares that we may believe only after autonomous reason apart from faith and affection has granted us permission. Such a doctrine conceives of rational authority as independent from any form of faith; faith in its various and sundry human expressions must submit to the authority of autonomous reason. Rather than embrace the humility about human understanding basic to Socratic, Augustinian, Pascalian, and Humean perspectives, modernity declares in effect "*intellego ut credam*," "I must first understand in order to believe."[15]

Now, although Hume and Pascal hold fundamentally opposing views regarding the wisdom of believing in an unseen God, both uphold a conception of embedded human reason. The dominant trend of modern philosophy, brilliantly initiated by such well-intentioned thinkers as Bacon, Descartes, and Locke, sought certain foundations for human thinking; moving to Pascal and Hume, we find an outlook that insists on a Socratic form of human philosophy—one that neither boasts of possessing final, infallible knowledge nor recommends that, bereft of such final certainty, people should therefore cease to pursue the examined life and abandon the philosophical quest to understand the true nature of the world.

Unfortunately, in the history of modern philosophy the Cartesian and ultimately un-Socratic quest for certainty, rooted as it was in a faith in autonomous reason, dominated and overshadowed the more humble approach of such modern "Socratic thinkers" as Pascal and Hume. It is clear today,

---

15. As we shall see, the true Augustinian declares "*credo ut intellegam, et intellego ut credam.*" In other words, while reason cannot properly function apart from faith, faith in turn must be nurtured and refined by rational insight. On a related note, my critique of Descartes is not meant to deny that, in some respects, his philosophy is deeply indebted to and is shaped by important Augustinian insights. My quarrel with Descartes takes issue with his conception of the essential nature of reason as autonomous and his confidence in the powers of human reason to diagnose and solve fundamental philosophical problems independently of the historically constituted influences of character and culture. For an especially fine analysis of this fundamental contrast between Cartesian and Augustinian outlooks, see Ann Hartle, *Death and the Disinterested Spectator* (Albany: State University of New York Press, 1986), esp. 191–213.

however, that few if any philosophers hold out much hope for the attainment of indubitable first principles; indeed, one of the definitive marks of our so-called postmodern age is the widespread abandonment of this modern quest for certain foundations. Whereas much of modern philosophy inherited and embraced the Cartesian and Lockean ideal of a system of knowledge built on indubitable truths, the mainstream currents of philosophical thought today, both in the analytic and continental traditions, have rejected this ideal of knowledge. This model of a structure of certain knowledge, erected firmly on a basis of indubitable, objective foundations, is a model known to contemporary philosophers as modern foundationalism;[16] it is familiar to most current students of philosophy not so much as a venerable and viable inheritance, but as an epistemological fossil worthy of study simply to comprehend its

16. It is worth clarifying at the outset that I do not mean to give the impression that I am joining ranks with those "antifoundationalist" postmodern thinkers who condemn traditional Western philosophies and religions for being "foundationalist." The epistemological stance I reject is not foundationalism per se, which is simply the theory that some of our beliefs are basic or known immediately and serve as the foundations for beliefs we know inferentially, but a very strong version of foundationalism that holds that our basic beliefs must be immediately knowable to any rational mind who attends carefully to them and must be indubitable. Both Pascal and Hume offer what are in my judgment convincing arguments that humans cannot and should not try to govern their beliefs according to the standards of the modern foundationalist. While I hold that few if any of our beliefs are so certain as to be indubitable to any attentive rational thinker, I see no good reason to deny that we hold some of our beliefs without having inferred them from other more basic beliefs. In some sense, then, I want to argue that some of our beliefs are known immediately.

One problem with the current debate surrounding foundationalist epistemologies is that historically there have been many variants of foundationalist theories of knowledge, a fact that seems at times to be overlooked in postmodern critiques of "foundationalism." When Pascal attacks Descartes's account of rationality, for instance, it would be a mistake to infer that he rejects either foundationalism per se or the importance of governing our beliefs rationally. On the contrary, Pascal clearly thinks that we know some things intuitively; what Pascal rejects is a Cartesian account of what we might call the "security of our intuitions." For Pascal, it is dangerous for philosophers to believe that any of our beliefs can afford us complete security from skeptical doubts, for such illusions of epistemic power can deceive us into overlooking our need for grace. To this extent, Pascal's critique of Cartesian foundationalism is of a piece with Aquinas's assessment of the limits of philosophy apart from divine grace. For an excellent analysis of Aquinas's "nonmodern" foundationalist theory of human knowledge, see Scott MacDonald, "Theory of Knowledge," in *The Cambridge Companion to Aquinas*, ed. Norman Kretzmann and Eleonore Stump (Cambridge: Cambridge University Press, 1993), 160–95; and Ralph McInerny, "Ethics," in Kretzmann and Stump, *The Cambridge Companion to Aquinas*, 196–231.

Finally, it is important to note that postmodernists who attack foundationalism generally are not really attacking epistemological foundationalism at all but are attacking any perspective on human life that seeks to ground one's ethical and political claims on some set of fundamental beliefs about the nature of the world as it is in and of itself. Here "antifoundationalist" really means "antimetaphysical" or "antirealist." To be an "antifoundationalist" in this sense is to deny, as does Richard Rorty, that we can even make intelligible sense out of the notions of an objective world order independent of human interpretive frameworks and of philosophical thinking as aiming at bringing us into contact with this objective world.

demise and avoid its fate. So Stephen Toulmin notes in his work *Cosmopolis* that the Cartesian program, which so dominated the mainstream of modern philosophical thinking, "is now seen to have led the enterprise of philosophy into a dead end."[17]

Clearly, during the last half century in the philosophical academy there has been a growing sense of dissatisfaction with the very notion of certain foundations or pure facts.[18] Today, informed scholars both in philosophy and in other domains of the academy have come to reject this Enlightenment project on the general grounds that human life affords us little if any pure evidence untainted by the history, culture, and personal experience of those particular individuals engaged in reasoning. Against the background of modernity's

17. Stephen Toulmin, *Cosmopolis* (New York: Humanities, 1990), 168.

18. As "antimodernists" such as Toulmin, Hauerwas, and MacIntyre have shown, for several centuries now, since the dawn of modern science and technology, a deep-seated ambition has prevailed among the most influential modern philosophers to establish human institutions and philosophical theories on objective facts alone. The dream of many great figures of the Enlightenment, in particular, was to overcome the recurring violence and incessant disagreements of the past by securing for human society a set of social and political facts free from the bias of culture, tradition, and subjective experience. The noble ambition of the Enlightenment from Locke to Kant was to discover the universal and necessary rational foundations for human experience not only in science, but also in morality and politics. It is just this basic Enlightenment vision of rational belief that the Victorian rationalist W. K. Clifford expressed when he wrote in 1877, "It is wrong always, everywhere, and for anyone, to believe anything upon insufficient evidence" ("The Ethics of Belief," in *God, Man and Religion*, ed. Keith Yandell [New York: McGraw-Hill, 1973], 509). According to Clifford, who by this utterance simply echoes the outlook of many of his Enlightenment forebearers, humans should acknowledge their firm and absolute obligation to conform their beliefs to solid evidence, to the facts. For Clifford, as for Locke and Kant, exercising one's individual, autonomous capacity for rational criticism is essentially what it means to be rational.

And yet the unsettling question raised by a wide variety of modern and contemporary skeptics of the Enlightenment project is basically this: just how liberating can such an Enlightenment vision of rational "awakening" actually turn out to be if humans are simply unable to live solely by conforming their beliefs to objectively verifiable facts? To raise this question is to call into question on both theoretical and practical or pragmatic levels the appropriateness of the Enlightenment vision for human life. As many skeptics of the Enlightenment have argued, all our acts of apprehending facts are shaped by presuppositions and attitudes not themselves capable of being justified by appeal to the criterion of neutral and objective facts. Not only in morals, but even in the laboratory, how we perceive the world is determined in part by those values and commitments we bring with us rather than empirically observe in front of us. Given the inevitable embeddedness of human reasoning, the Enlightenment project of freeing ourselves from all sources of knowledge that are not objectively verifiable cannot be very liberating. First of all, it is impossible to carry out. Second, it betrays itself, insofar as the Enlightenment project is a human philosophical endeavor and as such depends on a range of specific aspirations and commitments that are not themselves rationally certifiable. And, finally, if humans cannot live by Enlightenment reason alone, then we will be blind to the truth about ourselves and will inevitably suffer if we seek to found our intellectual and practical endeavors on such an Enlightenment vision. By insisting on governing our beliefs strictly on the basis of objective, certain foundations, we may well even be in danger of betraying and violating our own humanity.

confidence in autonomous reason, it is remarkable that one notable feature of the present postmodern world is its suspicion of claims to objectivity and its lack of consensus even about what being rational means.

The news of the collapse of modernity's vision of autonomous reason and faith in rational progress has had major reverberations in almost every field of philosophy, and its impact has been especially fruitful in the area of philosophy of religion. Particularly influential in the world of analytical philosophy of religion are the works of Alvin Plantinga, Nicholas Wolterstorff, and William Alston, who attack the modern doctrine of autonomous reason and the modern skeptical, evidentialist attack on theistic belief as rationally subpar.[19] Modern skeptical evidentialists, such as Bertrand Russell, J. L. Mackie, and Anthony Flew, challenged religious faith on the grounds that unless one possesses objectively discernible and publicly certifiable evidence for belief in God, one's conviction that God exists is irrational. In reply to the evidentialist skeptic, Plantinga argues that the typical evidentialist case against theistic belief rests on modern foundationalist epistemology, and since the modern foundationalist criterion of rationality is self-negating, there is little cause for the reasonable theist to feel epistemic guilt in holding theistic convictions without evidential justification. On Plantinga's account, theistic belief does not need evidential support but may function instead as a fundamental starting point, a properly basic belief, in one's religious worldview. Plantinga contends that one can rationally believe that God exists without having evidential proof for God's existence and without inferring this belief from other beliefs certifiable as objectively warranted. In other words, Plantinga argues, the theist can hold his or her belief in God rationally without having "objective," publicly accessible, rational evidence to support it.

In response to critics who have charged Plantinga with epistemological anarchy, Plantinga has subsequently developed a substantial and thoroughgoing account of the nature of human rationality, detailed in his two-volume study of the general nature of rational warrant and justification, *Warrant and Proper Function*, and in a work specifically defending the rationality of Christian belief, *Warranted Christian Belief*. In these works, Plantinga unfolds a strategy for analyzing the meaning of rational belief—not in the epistemological abstraction of ahistorical, conceptual analysis, but in the

---

19. For a classic statement of the evidentialist case against religious belief, see Anthony Flew, *The Presumption of Atheism* (London: Pemberton, 1976), 13–30. For a rigorous critique of the evidentialist position, see Alvin Plantinga, "Is Belief in God Rational?" in *Rationality and Religious Belief*, ed. C. F. Delaney (Notre Dame, IN: University of Notre Dame Press, 1979), 22–77; idem, "Reason and Belief in God," in *Faith and Rationality*, ed. Alvin Plantinga and Nicholas Wolterstorff (Notre Dame, IN: University of Notre Dame Press, 1983), 16–93; Nicholas Wolterstorff, *Reason within the Bounds of Religion* (Grand Rapids: Eerdmans, 1976); and idem, "The Migration of the Theistic Arguments: From Natural Theology to Evidentialist Apologetics," in *Rationality, Religious Belief and Moral Commitment*, ed. Robert Audi and William Wainwright (Ithaca, NY: Cornell University Press, 1986), 38–81.

historically embedded, concrete context of a Christian framework of beliefs about human nature and natural function. Plantinga argues that we cannot make good sense of the nature of rationality, epistemic justification, or "warrant" without providing an account of the natural function of our cognitive faculties.[20] In *Warranted Christian Belief*, Plantinga characterizes the nature of rationality—a concept that he notes has distinct, though related, meanings—and the nature of warrant, the feature distinguishing knowledge from mere true belief, in terms of the proper functioning of our cognitive faculties.[21] Not surprisingly, this account of proper functioning is itself subtle and multifaceted. "A belief has warrant," Plantinga states, "if it is produced by cognitive processes or faculties that are functioning properly, in a cognitive environment that is propitious for that exercise of cognitive powers, according to a design plan that is successfully aimed at the production of true belief."[22] As Plantinga readily admits, given the complexity of his conception of proper cognitive functioning, any fleshed-out understanding of such proper functioning will inevitably be influenced by one's metaphysical and theological commitments. Indeed, according to Plantinga, we should not try to answer the question of what constitutes rational belief or knowledge apart from an inquiry into who we are as people. As Plantinga explains:

> What you properly take to be rational, at least in the sense of warranted, depends on what sort of metaphysical and religious stance you adopt. It depends on what kind of beings you think human beings are, what sort of beliefs you think their noetic faculties will produce when they are functioning properly, and which of their faculties or cognitive mechanisms are aimed at the truth. Your view as to what sort of creature a human being is will determine or at any rate heavily influence your views as to whether theistic belief is warranted or not warranted, rational or irrational for human beings. And so the dispute as to whether theistic belief is rational (warranted) can't be settled just by attending to epistemological considerations; it is at bottom not merely an epistemological dispute, but an ontological or theological dispute.[23]

By insisting that the nature of rationality must be understood as embedded within the larger context of human nature and even religious tradition,

---

20. Alvin Plantinga, *Warrant and Proper Function* (Oxford: Oxford University Press, 1993); and idem, *Warranted Christian Belief* (Oxford: Oxford University Press, 2000).

21. Specifically, Plantinga argues that Christian belief is warranted because it is (1) produced by a cognitive process functioning properly, (2) in an appropriate epistemic environment, and (3) according to a design plan successfully aimed at truth (see esp. *Warranted Christian Belief*, chs. 8 and 9). Plantinga's analysis of warranted Christian belief is stunning in its analytical rigor, historical richness, and remarkable clarity. I hope that my own analysis of faith, reason, and affection in Augustine and Pascal shows the deep affinity between their views and that defended by Plantinga as being essentially the outlook of Calvin and St. Thomas.

22. Plantinga, *Warranted Christian Belief*, xi.

23. Ibid., 90.

Plantinga disowns the Enlightenment project of treating epistemological issues concerning the nature of rationality and justification independently of one's "sectarian" religious and metaphysical framework. Indeed, insofar as he links his account of rationality and knowledge to a distinctively theistic understanding of human function, Plantinga develops a theory of human cognition that bears a much closer resemblance to the epistemologies of Pascal or Augustine than to those of modern proponents of autonomous reason.

Plantinga shares with both Augustine and Pascal the conviction that the question of what it is rational to believe is bound up with our conception not only of the proper function of reason in human life, but of the purpose, design, or meaning of human life itself. Ultimately, in the Augustinian tradition, the proper function of reason is not merely to make true judgments concerning a world of neutral, nonmoral facts, but to enable the rational individual to make proper contact with reality, a state of being that requires not only "true belief," but the transformation of the will and affections needed to put us in touch with—to align us fully with—reality. Assisted by divine charity, the proper function of reason is thus both cognitive and unitive. The perfection of reason requires our being transformed into the kind of persons we are designed to be—persons who are able not only to describe but also to affirm and become united with the God of love. Not surprisingly, for the Augustinian the path of such personal transformation cannot be undertaken by the dispassionate skeptic who is committed above all else to the authority of an impartial, neutral reason. On the contrary, the way to the human good, and indeed the way to being rational as a human, again for the Augustinian, is attainable only by those willing first to put their trust in the God of love before they can see clearly enough to understand God.[24]

24. The basic Augustinian conception of reason rooted in love, of what we might term "charitable reason," is beautifully described in the following passage, quoted in Plantinga's *Warranted Christian Belief* (297), from Jonathan Edwards's *A Treatise Concerning Religious Affections*. Edwards writes,

> Spiritual understanding consists primarily in a sense of heart of that spiritual beauty. I say, a sense of heart; for it is not speculation merely that is concerned in this kind of understanding: nor can there be a clear distinction made between the two faculties of understanding and will, as acting distinctly and separately, in this matter. When the mind is sensible of the sweet beauty and amiableness of a thing, that implies a sensibleness of sweetness and delight in the presence of the idea of it; and this sensibleness of the amiableness or delightfulness of beauty, carries in the very nature of it, the sense of the heart; or an effect and impression the soul is the subject of, as a substance possessed of taste, inclination and will.

Here Edwards envisions a way of knowing that is as much a matter of feeling and will as intellect. To comprehend why Edwards thinks that knowing God in particular requires a fusing of affection, will, and intellect, we need to take into account several key features of Edwards's conception of spiritual understanding. First of all, as Plantinga observes, for Edwards, knowledge of God is a matter of faith, and faith is possible only through the

To be sure, it is on this crucial question of the wisdom of the heart that Augustine and Hume diverge. On the one hand, Augustine and Pascal envision religious understanding as available only to those whose will, feelings, and intellect have been transformed in such a way that one's reason draws on and is shaped by healthy love. Augustine and Pascal affirm the rationality and virtue of "charitable reason." In contrast, while Hume also affirms in his own way the virtue of reasonableness, whereby the individual self unites passion and reason in order to function rationally, he rejects as incoherent and dangerous any such conception of human reason that is guided and shaped by religious virtues such as faith, hope, or charity. For Hume, the merging of theistic religious sentiments and human reason can lead only to the disturbance and disruption of our proper human nature. My aim is to carry out a sustained reflection on these three philosophers who, recognizing the interdependence of reason and the affections, disagree deeply about the validity and rationality of a remarkable and mysterious form of theistic practice, the life of reasonable faith, whereby reason and the heart are ultimately united in a "spiritual understanding" of the beauty and grandeur of God.

---

agency of God's grace working in the human subject. In describing the gift of spiritual understanding, Edwards insists that this knowledge of God is not simply an intellectual state of mind, whereby someone might in a detached way have a true belief about some aspect of the nature of God. Edwards insists that when it comes to knowing God, what it means to know God goes beyond our ordinary conception of mere "knowing facts about some being" and essentially includes not simply "knowing about God" but also "acknowledging God as God." To see how spiritual knowledge of God is a kind of acknowledgment involving both certain feelings, such as delight and awe, as well as certain acts of will, such as appreciation and affirmation, let us note that, like Augustine, for Edwards God cannot be reduced to a mere fact, even a very grand one. Consider how Edwards characterizes the nature of God as the "object" of spiritual understanding. For Edwards, God is not merely some existent object that one could grasp simply by means of a dispassionate propositional act of intellect correctly describing some neutral state of affairs. Rather, to know God is to know a magnificent reality; it is to know The Reality that by its very nature is of the greatest Beauty and Goodness. Edwards sees that, given God's nature as Beautiful, knowing God requires more than just affirming speculatively that God exists. It requires affirming and acknowledging God as God. To affirm God as God essentially involves willing and feeling as well as believing, and it is this knowing of God in the fullest sense that is the proper response of a rational creature, whose highest purpose lies in acknowledging and delighting in the beauty of God. To appreciate why knowing God as supremely beautiful involves a passionate intellectual response of affirming God as God, we might consider as an analogy the aesthetic experience of knowing a beautiful work of art as beautiful. A dispassionate person could be said to know facts about a beautiful work of art, but does it not make sense to say that until one feels and affirms the beauty of the work for what it is one does not know that work *as* beautiful? In the case of ordinary aesthetic experience, we understand that to know a work of art or a part of nature as beautiful requires experiencing it as such and this experience is not possible through the operations of "mere abstract intellect" alone. For an illuminating account of Edwards's conception of spiritual understanding, see William J. Wainwright, *Reason and the Heart: A Prolegomenon to a Critique of Passional Reason* (Ithaca, NY: Cornell University Press, 1995), 7–54.

Augustine, Pascal, and Hume as Socratic Apologists: Human Wisdom as Passionate Self-Knowledge

In his magisterial work *God and Skepticism*, Terence Penelhum explores how Pascal and Hume elucidate a philosophical way of life that steers a middle course between the Scylla of modern rationalist philosophy and the Charybdis of Pyrrhonism.[25] Building on Penelhum's insights, I argue in what follows that Pascal and Hume steer this middle course by pursuing a path of thinking through these extremes that is dialectical in two key respects. Both Pascal and Hume agree that the Pyrrhonist shows us the inevitable uncertainty of supposedly certain and indubitable first principles of dogmatic rationalists, or those who presume to attain certain knowledge. Yet they object to the radical Pyrrhonist on the grounds that our natural propensity to form beliefs about what is real independently of how the world appears to us—a propensity more instinctive than rational—blocks any resolve we might muster in our moments of radical skepticism to withhold assent to any claims about what is real. For both Hume and Pascal, in other words, people are by nature metaphysical realists. And yet both Hume and Pascal insist that human reason, left to itself, can attain no final or certain knowledge of the nature of reality in itself. Their strategy for overcoming the incessant quarrel between skepticism and dogmatism turns out to be dialectical, first of all, insofar as they recognize that we cannot overcome the dispute between rationalism and extreme skepticism by adopting either stance, for each mutually destroys the other's credibility; thus they argue that we can resolve this perennial intellectual conflict only through a creative synthesis that avoids their mutual errors and yet affirms their mutual insights. Let us note further that, for Pascal and Hume, this perennial antagonism is more than merely intellectual, for each stance ultimately manifests an excess that if left untreated will lead us into a particular form of human despair: for the dogmatist seeking certain knowledge, despair descends on the recognition that our foundational beliefs and commitments will never

25. Terence Penelhum, *God and Skepticism* (Dordrecht: Reidel, 1983), esp. 62–145. I am greatly indebted to Penelhum's erudite treatment of Pascal and Hume in this classic work. The description of Pascal and Hume as dialectical thinkers, however, is my own. By "dialectical" in this context, I specifically have in mind a way of thinking that resolves a tension between two rival positions by adopting a standpoint that is superior to them and explains why each is incapable of responding adequately to the challenge of its rival. Generally, in my analysis I use the term "dialectical" in a broader sense to refer to the Socratic conversational method of defending and challenging particular philosophical positions. More importantly, Socratic dialectic acknowledges that philosophical thinking never arrives at, or begins with, absolutely indubitable first principles but nevertheless insists on giving a rational account of what one believes. Both Hume and Pascal are also dialectical thinkers in this Socratic sense, which is precisely why I think they have much to teach us during a time in which the Cartesian project of attaining certainty and the Enlightenment project of founding human institutions and knowledge on pure, objective foundations have reached an impasse.

attain the status of being indubitable; for the Pyrrhonist, despair arises on recognizing our natural incapacity to suspend judgment and withhold assent concerning objective reality. Resolving this perennial debate requires not only the recognition of the distinctive vices of each side, but also the establishment of a livable form of philosophical reflection that accepts rather than resists our inherent limits as finite humans. For both Pascal and Hume, this conception of what it means to engage in philosophical inquiry articulates a rigorous strategy that acknowledges the limits of both reason and skepticism. As I shall try to show, their shared conception of a properly human form of philosophy is deeply Socratic: they extol the virtue of self-examination for beings who are unavoidably finite and fallible. In sum, Pascal's and Hume's dialectic contends that avoiding the philosophical distress that plagues the perennial debate between philosophy and skepticism requires an account of human rationality that explains why both sides of the perennial debate are defective and then provides a middle ground appropriate to our human condition—a stance midway between overweening confidence and excessive doubt concerning human reason.

At this point we can see how Pascal and Hume are dialectical in a second, specifically Socratic sense. Both thinkers affirm the virtue of leading a life of self-examination within the essential limits of our cognitive finitude. For both Pascal and Hume, philosophical reflection fails to be rational and thus fails to function properly when it fails to be rooted in, and to be in harmony with, the virtue of knowing ourselves to be finite both with respect to what we can know and with respect to what we can honestly doubt. Like Socrates, Pascal and Hume exhort us to live the examined life while at the same time acknowledging the intractable limits of human reason.

As Penelhum observes, it is nevertheless precisely on this matter of the properly humble, human philosophical perspective that Pascal and Hume so deeply disagree with each other: "Pascal urges us to conquer the wretchedness we find in the human life we enter by opening ourselves to faith; . . . Hume, thinking that faith, too, is another, needless source of anxiety and distress, holds that only by confining ourselves to secular concerns can peace of mind be a real possibility for us."[26] Exactly how is it that these two radical modern figures—so alike in their analysis of human limitations, of our limits regarding what we know and what we can doubt—could differ so deeply about the wisdom of embracing a theistic solution to our human predicament? Penelhum's most valuable insight is that Hume and Pascal disagree about faith fundamentally because they ultimately disagree about its teleological value. In other words, Penelhum's interpretation orients us to the proper overall context for appreciating why Pascal and Hume disagree about the wisdom of the heart. Both thinkers envision philosophy as a way to resolve a particular human

26. Ibid., 120.

dilemma manifested in the debate between two philosophical extremes. One requirement for a philosophical solution to this dilemma is that it must accord with our human nature by defending our need to believe without presuming to possess final and absolute knowledge. In other words, both thinkers insist that our philosophical conclusions reconcile us to our finite human nature. But they deeply disagree about the proper place of passionate Christian faith in living out an honest life of philosophical self-examination. To appreciate the significance of their disagreement on the propriety of Christian faith, it is necessary to comprehend clearly how Hume and Pascal are inheritors in their own distinctive ways of the Socratic conception of philosophy. Before we try to appreciate just why such kindred spirits so strongly oppose each other on the question of faith, it will be helpful to look further into their shared Socratic outlook. Toward that end, let us ask this question: what does it mean to uphold a basically Socratic conception of philosophy?

The fundamental character of Socratic philosophy is conversational, fallibilistic, and dialectical. The dialectical nature of Socratic philosophy has three distinctive features:

1. It espouses a unique type of qualified skepticism, one that denies, on the one hand, that people can attain final, certain knowledge of the meaning of human life, but one that insists, on the other hand, that we must commit our lives to critical rational questioning of our fundamental beliefs.

2. Socratic philosophy holds that the primary reason for engaging in philosophy is thus deeply practical: philosophy's primary purpose is to cultivate the virtue of self-understanding through critical conversation—not to gain power over others in a competitive agon of conflicting selves, or to achieve intellectual or material advantage, but to promote human excellence in all persons.

3. Socratic philosophy contends that, given the limits of human understanding, the materials for philosophical reflection must be the beliefs, commitments, and practices of our social lives, so that its aim cannot be to establish final, irreversible proof based on incorrigible foundations, but must instead be to gain self-understanding through a process of *anamnesis*, a kind of "remembering" or recovery of the self by clarifying, refining, and defending what we most deeply believe.

To appreciate what it means for a philosophical practice to embody these basic features, let us look in more detail at how Socrates engages in his characteristic method of philosophical dialectic.

In a typical Socratic dialogue, Socrates engages in a process of rigorous questioning in which the respondent is challenged to state, clarify, and defend one or more fundamental ethical beliefs. At its core Socratic philosophy is a method of questioning, an *elenchus*, for the sake of mutual self-enlightenment—for the questioner who carries on with the lifelong and never-ending quest for the truth about human excellence and for the respondent who cannot make progress without first acknowledging his or her own ignorance.

For Socrates, whose avowed purpose in practicing dialectic publicly in Athens is primarily to serve his polis, dialectical philosophy is to the inner person as medicine is to the physical body. Just as the proper excellence of the body is a matter of attaining a healthy balance, and thus the avoidance of disease, so human psychic excellence turns out to be a state in which one's actions and beliefs accord with one's finite nature and with one's proper place in the cosmos. Socratic piety thus requires self-knowledge, which has both a negative and a positive aspect. The negative dimension is the intractable limit of human reasoning; the first step in the cultivation of Socratic self-knowledge is one's confession of one's ignorance, one's admission that one lacks final and certain knowledge. The positive dimension of Socratic self-knowledge is the possibility of gaining clarity through the pursuit of wisdom, through a process of testing one's ethical convictions in an effort to determine whether one's most fundamental values and commitments can be coherently and honestly defended. Paradoxically, it is fundamental to Socratic philosophy that human thinkers must continually yearn for what they will never fully attain: the wisdom of living well while being grounded in an inerrant understanding of who we are.

Thus unlike the modern foundationalists, such as Descartes and Locke, who believe we could attain absolute and final knowledge based on absolutely certain foundations, Socrates acknowledges that neither our particular moral intuitions nor our general ethical principles will ever be self-evident or infallible. Instead, Socratic inquiry moves toward an articulation and defense of fundamental principles that must finally accord with and make sense of our particular moral beliefs and experiences. For Socrates neither our particular moral responses nor our philosophical articulations of fundamental principles are so certain that they are immune to any possible future refutation. Yet despite this lack of certainty, Socrates defends the wisdom of sacrificing his life for his fundamental beliefs. As Henry Teloh observes, "When Socrates states that he is justified in claiming to know something, he admits that his claim is open to revision. Truth is the aim, but justified belief—belief which satisfies a dialectic test—is the means, and our grasp of truth is dependent upon our best dialectical effort at any time."[27]

One of the hallmarks of the dialectical tradition is the shared commitment of its practitioners to pursue the best argument, viewing one's own past with a sense of critical respect. Socratic dialectic seeks to foster just

---

27. Henry Teloh, *Socratic Education in the Early Dialogues* (Notre Dame, IN: University of Notre Dame Press, 1989), 2.

this spirit of respect and criticism. Good dialectical thinkers seek to be fair and open-minded but are committed at the same time to honest criticism. Those committed to a Socratic form of "teaching," for example, will wish their students to understand why it is an unfortunate contemporary academic confusion to think that respecting others precludes honestly disagreeing with them. For those of us living in an age of postmodern suspicion about any and all sources of authority and power, we would be well served by cultivating the habits of Socratic dialectical inquiry. On the one hand, this way of thinking fits well with an age that has called into question the conception of autonomous reason and absolute knowledge that rose to prominence during the Enlightenment and has greatly influenced modern practices and institutions. And yet, on the other hand, with its commitment to the importance of attaining self-coherence in one's beliefs, actions, and emotions, the Socratic tradition would oppose those versions of radical postmodernism that regard rational discourse as mere expressions of the assertion of power and see the quest for self-understanding as futile on the grounds that the self, like all so-called objective realities, is nothing more than a human construct. Dialectical thinking seeks a middle ground that rejects the Enlightenment doctrine of absolute knowledge as unattainable but avoids inferring that the failure of the Enlightenment entails that human rationality is so relative to context, so driven by motives of self-assertion, and so tangled with ambiguous and self-negating discourse that the Socratic vision of a community of lovers of wisdom, of a community committed to the pursuit of self-unity, to the objective meaning of human life, and to the communal good of self-examination, is a mere illusion. Such a Socratic conception of what it means to engage in dialect is summarized by R. E. Allen:

> To construe philosophy as dialectic is to view it primarily as an activity, not a product, as a discovering of truth rather than a set of truths discovered. The dialectician is unlikely to be a man with an official doctrine, oral or otherwise. The whole spirit of Plato's teaching, insofar as his writing reflects the man who wrote, lies not in the promulgation of doctrine, not in expounding, as Aristotle and others have sought to expound, a necessary system demonstratively deduced from self-evident truths, but in leading men to see things for themselves. The aim, if you will, is education not instruction.[28]

In the spirit of such a humbled, critical inquiry, Socratic and Platonic dialectic invites us to take rational thinking seriously. In the Socratic tradition, the quality of our lives, both individually and communally, depends crucially on our commitment to honest self-understanding. Certainly Socrates does not

---

28. *The Dialogues of Plato*, trans. and with analysis by R. E. Allen, 4 vols. (New Haven: Yale University Press, 1984), 1:23.

believe that genuine wisdom can ever be attained by blindly following another. While the road to wisdom is better walked in the company of others than in solitude, we should not passively follow the way others have set before us.

Now, it is an important part of my defense of passionate reason that we understand how such texts as Augustine's *Confessions*, Hume's *Enquiry Concerning Human Understanding*, and Pascal's *Pensées* are works with significant and deep parallels to Socrates' *Apology*. In significant respects, Pascal and Hume are more Socratic than "modern" in their thinking. For one thing, as we have noted already, Pascal and Hume set out to refute the sort of philosophical programs that are unsuitable, in their view, for human life. Their opposition to modern foundationalism—to the position that we can establish a system of knowledge sufficient for resolving our primary philosophical disagreements on a set of self-justifying, indubitable first principles—resembles Socrates' denial that people possess divine knowledge. For Socrates, to presume to have final knowledge is to fail in self-knowledge. The method of *elenchus* accepts that all human theories and accounts are in principle revisable, where the need to revise and rethink one's beliefs is determined by one's success or failure in responding to challenges and objections set forth against one's position. Ironically, it is only through a humble recognition of one's ignorance that one has the initial human wisdom needed to endure the difficult self-examination provided through the *elenchus*. The fundamental point of similarity between Hume and Pascal, on the one hand, and Socrates, on the other, is not with the details of their methodologies, which are different, but with the demand for a rigorous philosophical method that acknowledges the fallible nature of human philosophizing.[29] If we look at the basis of their opposition to certain versions of modern foundationalism, we find both Hume and Pascal objecting on the grounds not only that such programs cannot work, but also that such programs are symptomatic of a lack of moderation and humility. To explore further the deeply Socratic character of Pascal's and Hume's philosophy, it will be useful to view them in their historical context, something I propose to do—however, only to a limited extent—by exploring their opposition to modern foundationalism and their importantly dissimilar relationships to the philosophical tradition of Augustine.

29. In arguing that both Hume and Pascal develop a Socratic form of philosophy, I do not mean to suggest that there are not fundamental methodological—let alone doctrinal—differences among the three. Neither Hume nor Pascal, for example, practices exactly the same conversational method as Socrates in the early dialogues. Yet among modern philosophers, Hume and Pascal are perhaps the most successful in expressing philosophical ideas in dialogue form. As Pamphilus remarks in the introduction to the *Dialogues*, those subjects on which humans cannot achieve full clarity and certainty are especially suited to dialogue form. In a similar fashion, Pascal often resorts to imaginary dialogue between the unbelieving skeptic and the believer in his defense of faith in the *Pensées*. These two modern thinkers follow Socrates in recognizing both the uncertainty of the human predicament and the appropriateness of conversational inquiry in seeking to make rational sense of it. It is in both of those senses that they are Socratic thinkers.

David Hume: Gadfly of Edinburgh

Hume in effect declares his opposition to immoderate philosophy in the opening section of the first *Enquiry* when he states: "Be a philosopher; but, amidst all your philosophy be still a man."[30] Here he enjoins us to accept the limits of human reasoning, to acknowledge philosophy's proper place in our social lives. With characteristic brevity, Hume thus sets the stage for his overall purpose in the first *Enquiry* of defending a moderate skepticism that conforms to the limits of reason and acknowledges our human nature as passionate and imaginative beings. The crux of Hume's argument regarding the limits of reason commences in section 4, where Hume divides human reasoning into two classes, and contends that our judgments may be considered rational, in the sense of being derived from reason, if and only if they are founded on the relations of ideas or on empirical matters of fact. But, as Hume proceeds to show, many of our most essential beliefs—such as the belief in causal connections, in the uniformity of nature, and in the existence of external objects outside of our perceptions—cannot be justified as rational in either of these respects. So, for instance, although people naturally infer that regularities in the past will continue in the future, this inference cannot be rationally justified on the basis of evidential reason. Our belief in the regularity of nature is neither logically necessary nor justified based on past experience, for we can easily conceive of the future being unlike the past, and we cannot justify drawing an inference concerning the future on the evidence of past experience alone unless we presuppose the principle of nature's uniformity in the first place.

Hume's next step is to argue that our inference that past associations will continue into the future results from a nonrational belief-forming mechanism. Such is also the case with our natural beliefs in causal powers inherent in physical objects and in the very existence of objects outside our perceptions: the generating mechanisms for these fundamental beliefs are nonrational (so Hume argues in sections 7, 8, and 12). In each of these instances of our believing nature, we form a belief not strictly speaking on the basis of rational evidence but at the prompting of nonrational propensities within human nature that operate despite our inability to give a satisfactory "rational justification" for the beliefs they produce. Now, for Hume the discovery of these nonrational natural beliefs requires a rethinking of the characteristic modern and specifically Lockean philosophical stance that people should above all else be guided by reason. We can best appreciate the Socratic character of Hume's analysis of these natural beliefs if we set it over against the Lockean conception of belief that itself becomes a kind of orthodoxy for many thinkers, including many modern religious apologists, of the Enlightenment. When we compare

---

30. David Hume, *An Enquiry Concerning Human Understanding*, in *Enquiries Concerning Human Understanding and Concerning the Principles of Morals*, ed. L. A. Selby-Bigge and P. H. Nidditch, 3rd ed. (Oxford: Clarendon, 1975), sec. 1, p. 9.

Hume to Locke, we can see the subtlety of Hume's conception of human believing. Hume holds in effect that it is irrational—in the sense that it does not make proper use of our cognitive faculties—to believe only in accordance with evidential reason.

Following Locke, at the outset of the first *Enquiry* Hume endorses an empiricist theory of the origin of ideas: all ideas, Hume maintains, must be derived from some past impression. Yet as Donald Livingston has argued, for Hume this empiricist doctrine undergoes subtle modification in the first *Enquiry* insofar as Hume also admits that the concepts basic to some of our natural beliefs—such as the concept of a necessary, causal connection—cannot be accounted for simply and straightforwardly on the basis of actual past impressions. Rather, it is only through the natural and involuntary operations of the imagination and sentiments that the human mind can conceive of and posit the reality of such things as causal powers and external objects.[31]

But how much of a real difference for the question of the validity of Christian theism does Hume's relaxing of the Lockean ethics of belief make in Hume's philosophy of religion? In one respect, it might not appear that Hume departs very significantly at all from Lockean epistemology, since Hume still demands that Christian theism have an evidential basis, and he speaks in a very Lockean manner throughout the first *Enquiry* when he insists on banishing those superstitious and metaphysical doctrines that he contends have no discernible foundation in our experience. Indeed, both Hume and Locke are similarly vexed by Christian enthusiasts and superstitious Schoolmen whose conceptual foundations, they contend, cannot be supported by rational evidence.[32] Clearly Hume and Locke regard it as a most serious problem that, as they see it, many members of the church are so passionately willing to renounce their reason, exercising belief even in the absence of sound evidence.

---

31. See Donald Livingston, *Hume's Philosophy of Common Life* (Chicago: University of Chicago Press, 1985), 60–90. It is a notable merit of Livingston's work to correct the tendency of Anglo-American philosophers who view Hume exclusively from the perspectives of classical empiricism and twentieth-century positivism. Livingston reveals the narrative and historical dimensions of Hume's philosophy of human life; for a specific discussion of the therapeutic aspect of Hume's thought, see esp. 3–4 and 9–33.

32. Both the opening and closing sections of the first *Enquiry* express Hume's concern to rid philosophy of the corrupting influence of abstruse, superstitious thinking. In his *Natural History of Religion*, Hume condemns both superstitious religion and religious enthusiasm. This antagonism to these two forms of religious thought and feeling also surfaces as a major Humean sentiment in the *Essays: Moral, Political and Literary*. See esp. Hume's essays "Of Parties in General" and "Of Superstition and Enthusiasm." While Hume deeply distrusts Christian sentiments, his own conception of the virtues is, as Don Livingston once noted to me in conversation, in one sense more Christian than Stoical. In his essay "Of Moral Prejudices," Hume denounces the Stoical ideal of passionless self-control as foolish and contemptible: for Hume, social existence necessitates genuine sympathy and thus vulnerability with regard to the lives of other humans. The Humean conception of friendship, in particular, borrows more from the Christian notion of charity than from the Stoical one of rational self-mastery.

But despite their shared suspicion arising from a profound tension between the canons of Enlightenment reason and popular expressions of faith, Hume in the *Enquiry* decisively refutes the Lockean model of rational man; in so doing he develops a critique of Christian theism more subtle than that of the Lockean evidentialist.

When Locke turns to investigating the proper relation of evidential reasoning and religious faith in *An Essay Concerning Human Understanding*, he unequivocally says that people have a fundamental obligation to govern their assent through reason and not to believe beyond what reason affirms. For Locke, we ought always to believe rationally, and believing rationally is believing in accordance with the evidence—not the sort of subjective experiences cited by zealous enthusiasts, but the immediate and certain evidence of our sensory ideas, introspective self-awareness, or logical intuitions. As does Hume, Locke holds that our beliefs are rational in the sense of deriving from reason if and only if they are grounded in logical or empirical evidence. Yet for Locke our obligation to proportion our beliefs to the evidence, to obey reason as "our last judge and guide in everything" is absolute.[33] "He that believes without having any reason for his believing," Locke remarks,

> may be in love with his own fancies; but neither seeks truth as he ought, nor pays the obedience due to his Maker, who would have him use those discerning faculties he has given him, to keep him out of mistake and error. . . . For he governs his assent right, and places it as he should, who, in any case or matter whatsoever, believes or disbelieves according as reason directs him. He that doth otherwise, transgresses against his own light, and misuses those faculties which were given him to no other end, but to search and follow the clearer evidence and greater probability.[34]

Note that Locke promotes an ethics of belief rooted in his own understanding of God's providence in endowing people with rational faculties. Presupposing that creatures have a moral obligation to use their God-given gifts in accordance with the intentions of their divine giver, Locke makes it clear that believing beyond what our evidence warrants violates our basic duty to God.

Interestingly enough, it is essentially this theory of our duty to reason that is espoused by Hume's character Cleanthes, who states in the *Dialogues* that rational believers must "proportion their assent to the precise degree of evidence which occurs."[35] Before we proceed further with our investigation of

Locke vehemently condemns religious enthusiasm as the malady of a "warmed or overweened brain" in *An Essay Concerning Human Understanding*, ed. Alexander Campbell Fraser (New York: Dover, 1959), 4.19.17.

33. Locke, *Essay*, 4.19.14.

34. Locke, *Essay*, 4.17.24.

35. David Hume, *Dialogues Concerning Natural Religion*, ed. Richard H. Popkin (Indianapolis: Hackett, 1980), 137. My brief analysis of the *Dialogues* cannot begin to do justice to

Hume's critique of Lockean epistemology, let me examine briefly how in the *Dialogues* themselves Hume also subjects a feature of Lockean philosophy to a brilliantly ironic, Socratic deconstruction. In part 1 of the *Dialogues*, Cleanthes praises Locke as the true prophet of a new, scientific approach to religious thinking: "Locke seems to have been the first Christian, who ventured openly to assert, that faith was nothing but a species of reason, that religion was only a branch of philosophy, and that a chain of arguments, similar to that which establishes any truth in morals, politics, or physics, was always employed in discovering all the principles of theology, natural and revealed."[36]

By the close of the *Dialogues*, after encountering Philo's devastating objections to Cleanthes's argument from design, we begin to understand Hume's artful irony: Cleanthes's endorsement of this new philosophical religion of Locke leads to consequences he never intended and does not appear to comprehend. If we follow the reasoning of Hume's heroic skeptical advocate, Philo, we discover that the Lockean commitment to "scientific theology," endorsed by

---

the Socratic character of the work as a whole. Any reasonable interpretation of the *Dialogues* must account for the apparent reversal in part 12 of Philo's antagonism to the argument from design and for the relative congeniality of the final conversation between Philo and Cleanthes in the same section. Penelhum proposes that we read Philo's stance in the final part of the *Dialogues* as a sign of Hume's own willingness to live with a form of institutionalized religion that has been so secularized and diluted as to have no real influence on human actions and affairs (see *God and Skepticism*, 135–39). As Penelhum observes, it is not so much that Philo changes his position as that Cleanthes comes to confess that true religion has no other function than to reinforce the principles and teachings of civil, secular morality. On the contrary, Cleanthes notes, when "religion distinguishes itself, and acts as a separate principle over men, it has departed from its proper sphere, and has become a cover to faction and ambition" (quoted in ibid., 139). Commenting on the significance of Cleanthes's view for the overall project of the *Dialogues*, Penelhum writes: "Hume was perceptive enough to see that a religious belief that seeks to commend itself to men of letters by supposedly scientific arguments that he can discredit will in time become nothing more than the domesticated non-denominational uplift with which we are all familiar today. To this, the most exacting Skeptic can conform with impunity" (ibid., 139). Penelhum's account of the real significance of the apparent reconciliation of Philo and Cleanthes at the end of the *Dialogues* supports my characterization of the *Dialogues* as Socratic in method. Essentially, Hume seeks through Philo's very guarded confession of belief and Cleanthes's open admission of the need for a domesticated faith to show that there is really no significant difference between their respective positions. The truly rational believer, in other words, turns out to be none other than the mitigated skeptic; thus Philo's closing confession that the true skeptic affirms the need for revelation is qualified by the further stipulation that such a revelation not be attributed to any kind of personal god. Philo serves to lead the Enlightenment reader to self-knowledge in much the way that the Socratic dialogues lead their readers to a rethinking of the relationship between virtue and knowledge. Hume hoped to produce in his readers a refined sympathy not for that popular version of Christian faith practiced in Scottish churches, but for a true religion purified of its dangerous and uncivil tendencies. Read in this way, Hume's *Dialogues* look remarkably like a secular humanist's Enlightenment counterpart to Socrates' sustained and uncompromising critique in the *Apology* of the basically Homeric values and practices of his fellow Athenians.

36. Hume, *Dialogues*, 138.

Cleanthes, permits him only the most diluted and attenuated form of religious belief—one that, for Philo and Hume, is so vacuous that it can have absolutely no significant bearing on our everyday lives. At best, insists Philo, the evidence of the world's design affords us only a minimal kind of religious belief, one that upholds nothing more substantial than that there must be some sort of ultimate principle or cause of the marvelous order of the universe. Hence, if with Cleanthes we are to remain true to the Lockean ethics of belief, we must, following Philo, acknowledge that the only kind of religion reason can support is one wholly insignificant for human affairs. In this way, Philo serves as a Humean-style Socratic critic, urging his Lockean rationalist fellow citizens to greater self-knowledge about the propriety of religious faith. As Socrates before his jurors, Philo serves as a gadfly by challenging the prevailing Enlightenment, Lockean conception of rational religious belief. Hume's ironic challenge presented through the character of Philo is that in order to retain their Lockean commitment to the authority of reason, Enlightenment Christians sympathetic to Locke must reject their Christian faith. If, following Locke, we believe that true piety demands our full allegiance to evidential reason, then, Philo argues, we must conclude that espousing Christian belief is in fact an act of egregious impiety!

Hume's *Enquiry Concerning Human Understanding* also exhibits an overall Socratic agenda calling us to live and think authentically within the severe limits of human reason. Basically what Hume provides in the first *Enquiry* is a fundamental Socratic critique of the Lockean conception of the authority of reason in the affairs of human life and in the traditional Christian belief in the wisdom of faith in a personal, transcendent God. Consider, first of all, how Hume sets out, in good Lockean form in the opening section of the first *Enquiry*, to justify his exploration of the "mental geography" of human nature. Human well-being, Hume declares, has repeatedly been threatened by the vain and pretentious efforts of abstruse metaphysicians.[37] At their worst, these proud and haughty abusers of human reason court religious superstition when "chased from the open country, these robbers fly into the forest, and lie in wait to break in upon every unguarded avenue of the mind, and overwhelm it with religious fears and prejudices."[38] Like Socrates, Hume conceives of the craft of philosophy as intended not merely for the comfort of the private intellectual, but also for the well-being of the social order; thus he calls practitioners to a life of honest self-examination and away from an addiction to destructive religious and philosophical practices. Yet in order for philosophy to benefit the social order in this way, Hume and Socrates agree that the philosopher must particularly confront and challenge his or her fellow citizens not to presume to know what is beyond the limits of human understanding.

37. See esp. Hume, *Enquiry*, sec. 1, pp. 11–12.
38. Ibid., sec. 1, p. 11.

Indeed, Hume's study of the human mind serves a moral and political end, as is evident throughout the *Enquiry*. True philosophy, for Hume, as for Locke, must teach us not to exceed our limits or succumb to the teachings of those who lack proper humility and self-knowledge. If the human social order is to protect itself against the socially pernicious influence of abstruse metaphysicians who claim to know what is in fact beyond human comprehension, it must expose the groundlessness of their systems by establishing the true limits of human reasoning. Insofar as the true philosopher carries out this task of unmasking philosophical conceit, he or she acts in the best interests of the state and represents a sort of civic piety.

There is, of course, one crucial difference between Socratic and Humean piety. Unlike the Socratic gadfly, Hume's philosopher does not place service to the state in the larger context of service to divine authority. Indeed, as I will discuss below, Hume appears to reach the radical conclusion that true piety actually requires that one not presume to believe anything substantial about the divine at all. As we shall see, Hume attempts to defend a secularized version of the Socratic skeptic. Hume's mitigated skeptic holds that belief in personal divinity, in a divinity whose moral character bears some resemblance to our conceptions of virtue, violates the standards of humility and true philosophical wisdom. But despite these entirely un-Socratic qualities, Humean piety is, nevertheless, a matter of knowing one's limits and thus one's place in a greater order. In this respect, the Humean philosopher exhibits the socially necessary virtues of self-knowledge and humility. Now, it is crucial to Hume's project of humbling the ambitions of rational man to demonstrate, contrary to Locke, that much of what we naturally believe cannot satisfy the Lockean requirements of rational belief. The striking conclusion that emerges out of Hume's account of the origins of our natural beliefs is that the Lockean rationalistic theory of human nature falls short of the standard of philosophical piety: by failing to acknowledge the limits of our rationality, and in particular by presuming that it is possible to be both rational and a Christian theist, Locke invites rather than prevents abstruse metaphysical speculation, a development that, Hume contends, poses an insidious threat to human well-being. Hence, by showing the narrow limits of Lockean reason and the superior power that our nonrational nature holds over us, Hume thinks he can elicit from his Enlightenment readers a greater share of self-knowledge and humility. Essentially, Hume will argue that Lockeans, such as Cleanthes, both overestimate the power of human reason and underestimate the destructive character of Christian faith.

I have concentrated thus far on Hume's opposition to Locke's conception of rationality. Against Locke, Hume maintains that reason has only a limited authority in generating and governing our beliefs. For Hume, our natural beliefs are held involuntarily, are produced in us through nonrational mechanisms, and ultimately are not amenable to rational justification in the sense of being based on reason.[39] Yet while Hume wants to show that these natural beliefs are nonrational, he nevertheless offers in the first *Enquiry* a kind of rational justification for them. In a sense, for Hume our holding natural beliefs is reasonable even though such beliefs are not rational in the strict evidentialist sense. Hume argues that, given our human nature, it is appropriate for us to hold some of our beliefs on the basis of instinct and custom. We would in effect misuse our cognitive faculties if we attempted to doubt our instinctual, natural beliefs, simply because we cannot justify them on the basis of reason alone.

In developing this subtle outlook, Hume separates his own version of skepticism from radical, ancient Pyrrhonism, and further illuminates the role of humility in the activity of true philosophy. In the final section of the first *Enquiry*, Hume defends natural beliefs, beliefs for which we are unable to provide a Lockean rational justification, on what are basically pragmatic grounds. Hume argues that Pyrrhonian efforts to doubt our natural beliefs are unsuited to our human nature and thus manifest a lack of self-knowledge. Hume does not believe that the Pyrrhonist's doubts about nonevident realities can be refuted by any appeal to evidential reason. Yet he still insists that these doubts are absurd in the context of human thought and action. First, he observes that the Pyrrhonist's efforts to suspend belief in all things nonevident cannot sustain itself against the superior power of our nonrational human nature. "Nature is always too strong for principle," Hume declares, and while the skeptic's reasonings may throw us "into a momentary amazement and confusion," human nature will inevitably reclaim nature's authority as we return to common life and find ourselves assenting to those very beliefs we cannot rationally justify.[40] Here Hume offers a pragmatic argument based on what it is humanly possible for us to doubt. He thinks that, in a way similar to the erroneous views of Locke, the Pyrrhonist misunderstands the authority of evidential reasoning in governing our beliefs. Just as Locke overestimates the authority of reason, the Pyrrhonist overestimates the significance of the lack of rational justification for some of our most important beliefs. The fact that we cannot disarm the Pyrrhonist with rational arguments, Hume notes, does not mean that we will, as a consequence of recognizing this fact, be able to modify our assent and withhold judgment concerning our natural beliefs; we cannot withhold our assent in just those cases where our instinctual composition compels us to believe independently of the presence or absence of evidence. Ultimately for Hume both the Lockean and the Pyrrhonian underestimate the power of human instinct.

39. For Hume's conception of natural belief, see David Fate Norton, *David Hume: Common-Sense Moralist and Sceptical Metaphysician* (Princeton, NJ: Princeton University Press, 1982), 192–238; and Stanley Tweyman, *Skepticism and Belief in Hume's Dialogues Concerning Natural Religion* (Dordrecht: Martinus Nijhoff, 1986), esp. 7–19.

40. Hume, *Enquiry*, sec. 12, p. 160.

But Hume's defense of these common life beliefs against the threat of excessive intellectual skepticism goes beyond simply endorsing them on the grounds that our nature compels us to assent to them. Hume contends, in addition, that it is indeed a good and fortunate thing that we are so constituted as to believe in a limited number of unseen things despite the lack of proper evidence to justify believing in them. That "no durable good" can ever result from the Pyrrhonist's way of doubt, Hume declares, is the "chief and most confounding objection" against it.[41] Here Hume's point is that human well-being, both individual and social, depends on our holding certain basic, nonrational beliefs, and the Pyrrhonist who recommends suspense of judgment as a way to attain mental tranquility is, in effect, recommending a way of life that is not only unlivable but also contrary to our needs as active agents. To some it might seem improper that Hume rejects a philosophical position merely because of its undesirable ethical consequences. Certainly, one might protest, a position is not false just because it entails consequences we find unpalatable. But Hume is not guilty here of confusing truth with utility. Hume is not saying that the skeptical arguments of the Pyrrhonian, arguments to the effect that we have no rational basis for our beliefs about realities outside of our impressions, are themselves fallacious because they lead to undesirable results. Rather than refute the specific skeptical arguments of Pyrrhonism as bad arguments, Hume condemns the overall Pyrrhonian perspective regarding the importance of such arguments. For Hume, given our human nature, Pyrrhonism falsely conceives of the proper role philosophical arguments should play in human life. The province of the true philosopher, for Hume, is to protect the social order by fixing the limits of reason and establishing the authority of our natural beliefs. In so doing, the philosopher promotes philosophical reflection as a pragmatic activity useful for society as a whole. And Hume wants true philosophy to afford the restoration of the self for the individual philosopher as well. For Hume, true philosophy guards us against two forms of philosophical despair: one arising out of the dogmatic philosopher's frustration of seeking to know what we cannot know, and the other arising out of the radical skeptic's melancholy and anxiety resulting from trying to doubt what we by nature are compelled to believe. Basically, the Pyrrhonist violates human nature instead of teaching us how to reconcile ourselves to it. That no durable good can come from such excessive doubt is a valid ground for refutation, if we accept Hume's vision of both human nature and the fundamental purpose of the philosophical enterprise.

To be reconciled to our human condition, Hume thinks that we must gain the self-knowledge of our nonrational selves. The key error of both the Lockean and the Pyrrhonian is that they falsify the human condition by exaggerating, in quite different ways, the proper place of the human intellect. Locke does so by

41. Ibid., sec. 12, p. 159.

insisting that we govern our beliefs according to the standards of evidentialist reason. The Pyrrhonist goes too far in estimating the role intellectual doubt ought to play in human life. Hence, both fall short of the Humean standard of true philosophy. In essence, Hume opposes the excessive rationalist and excessive skeptic by situating human life between the two extremes of doubt and dogmatism: to be human is to be unable to succeed either in the Pyrrhonist project or the Lockean rationalist one. Having neither certainty on matters unseen nor the ability to doubt the existence of what lies beyond empirical and logical evidence, humans are best advised, Hume believes, to accept our nonrational makeup and pursue the way of the mitigated skeptic. But what are the essential characteristics of Hume's mitigated skeptic?

By promoting this moderate perspective lying midway between Lockean dogmatic assertion and Pyrrhonian withdrawal, the Humean mitigated skeptic endeavors to restrain the philosophical tendency to become alienated from our common life beliefs and practices. Hume's sage advice—"Be a philosopher; but amidst all your philosophy be still a man"[42]—serves to reinforce his basic point that philosophy must not be allowed to claim for itself an authority beyond what is warranted by the narrow limits of human reason. And it is just this concern to keep philosophy from usurping its rightful place in the lives of beings seeking happiness and avoiding distress that underlies Hume's insistence that true philosophy must not form an alliance with faith and indulge in speculations or make definite commitments concerning the ultimate principles of reality. Hume endorses leading the examined life and cautions us against relying excessively on the powers of human reason; at the same time, he is adamant about imposing severe anti-theistic limits on the subject matter for proper human reflection. Hume's anti-theistic stance will be examined in detail in the following chapter. For now, I will confine my analysis of this aspect of Humean skepticism to a most revealing remark Hume makes in his closing words on the outlook of mitigated skepticism in section 12 of the *Enquiry*. Here, curiously, Hume justifies confining the philosopher to a naturalistic account of common life on the grounds that so doing is a reasonable extension of his general principle that human philosophers must not presume to know what they do not know. In delineating the character of the humbled mitigated skeptic, Hume remarks:

> Those who have a propensity to philosophy, will still continue their researches; because they reflect, that, besides the immediate pleasure, attending such an occupation, philosophical decisions are nothing but the reflections of common life, methodized and corrected. But they will never be tempted to go beyond common life, so long as they consider the imperfection of the faculties they employ, their narrow reach, and their inaccurate operations. While we cannot give a satisfactory reason, why we believe, after a thousand experiments, that

42. Ibid., sec. 12, p. 9.

a stone will fall, or fire burn; can we ever satisfy ourselves concerning any determination, which we may form, with regard to the origin of worlds, and the
situation of nature, from, and to eternity?[43]

The structure of Hume's reasoning here is the following: Hume reminds the
reader of one of the most significant findings of his *Enquiry*, that human
reason is incapable of providing a satisfactory rational account of certain everyday features of our lives, such as belief in the existence of physical objects
and natural causes. Based on this limitation, Hume then infers that the wise
philosophical skeptic, knowing so little about everyday life, would certainly not
seek to go beyond this arena to speculate or inquire into those metaphysical
subjects that lie beyond the boundaries of our secular experience. As we shall
see clearly in our later examination of Hume's case against belief in miracles
in the first *Enquiry*, it is clear that Hume means here to exclude theistic questions and commitments from the arena of common life and philosophical
reflection. In fact, likely above all else, Hume wishes to convince us that the
whole realm of theistic religious beliefs and concepts should be dismissed as
being "beyond common life," and thus unworthy of consideration by the wise
and humbled inquirer.

Now, again, Hume's rationale for reaching his anti-theistic conclusion in
the above passage appears to be this: insofar as our human faculties are too
imperfect to make sense of everyday occurrences, they can hardly be suited
for investigating matters pertaining to the supernatural and transcendent,
matters even more obscure to us than those beyond the purview of reason in
our ordinary, natural lives. It is not clear, however, that Hume's exclusion of
theistic concerns from philosophical reflection on the basis of this purportedly prudent move is justified. For one thing, given the fact that Hume himself
admits that we are justified in holding our natural beliefs even though they defy
rational (evidential) justification, as they serve us well in the tasks of ordinary
living, why should the philosopher necessarily be averse to holding definite
beliefs about the sort of issues of concern to traditional theists simply on the
grounds that these religious matters even more radically transcend the limits
of our human reasoning? What Hume seems to imply in this passage is that
going outside the boundaries of secular common life would amount to a failure of humility on our part regarding our human faculties. Hume's properly
humbled, mitigated skeptic would not affirm any religious creed because he or
she believes that doing so would be an act of unjustified arrogance. But why
could one not instead most reasonably regard the fact of our limited human
rational faculties, and especially the fact that, as Hume shows us, humanity
cannot live by evidential reason alone, as pointing us to a profound religious
insight that we are not meant to guide our lives merely on the basis of our own

43. Ibid., sec. 12, p. 162.

resources? Why not take Hume's case concerning the limits of our reason as showing that we have a very good reason to look beyond our natural resources in conducting our lives? Why not, in other words, see the intractable limits of human reason as a sort of natural sign of our need for God?

Hume might have been more persuasive in his case against human religious arrogance if he were merely attacking the modern philosophical view that human reason can, through evidential reasoning, determine crucial truths about the existence and nature of the divine. If Hume were merely arguing against a well-known tenet of Enlightenment philosophical theology, promoted as we have seen by such thinkers as Locke or Cleanthes (in the *Dialogues*)—a tenet that purports to have discovered evidential knowledge of God based on a rational, causal proof for the existence of God—Hume might well have made a compelling case. For if Hume is right about the strict limits of causal reasoning, then perhaps the effort to prove God's existence on the basis of certain empirical facts exhibits a dangerous lack of self-knowledge and lack of humility about our rational limits. Yet in the *Enquiry* Hume extends his antipathy to theism further than simply to advise us that it is presumptuous to claim to know through evidential reasoning crucial propositions about God. As we shall see, especially in his analysis of miracles, Hume's stance is that the true philosopher must avoid believing any account concerning the actions or character of a transcendent deity. But why is this attitude of religious and metaphysical agnosticism the most appropriate humble response to our human condition? Could not one plausibly argue the reverse point of view, that awareness of our frailties should lead us passionately to inquire into questions of religious meaning and even perhaps to accept our profound need for God? Perhaps the awareness of our inability to guide our secular lives by Lockean reason should persuade us to look for a transcendent source of meaning for our lives as a whole. It is not at all obvious why Hume's naturalistic, mitigated skeptic has the only, or even the greatest, claim on humility. As we shall see later, Hume does have an array of other, more formidable arguments that if successful would justify his anti-theistic stance. For now, though, I would like to make two points with respect to Hume's skeptical strategy: first, that Hume provides an ingenious Socratic critique of the standard Enlightenment doctrine of autonomous reason and, second, that Hume must show us why his own version of Socratic humility precludes religious belief. For now, let us simply acknowledge that in a manner both like and unlike Socrates, Hume calls his contemporaries to a humbled life of self-examination, a life lived wisely within the intractable limits of our mortal reason.

And yet, as I intend to argue, Hume never adequately justifies his aversion to Christian faith. Before considering Hume's reasons for his antipathy to Christian faith in more depth, however, let us look further into how one might reason from a "Humean" recognition of the limits of evidential reason to a most un-Humean, religious outlook. It will be instructive at this point to consider the place of a Socratic kind of humility in two other Socratic philosophers, Augustine and Pascal. Specifically, I propose that we now look at the meaning of humility in Augustine's doctrine of "loving reason" and in Pascal's understanding of reason and the heart. Interestingly enough, both Augustine and Pascal share Hume's recognition of the limits of strict, evidential reason. At the same time, they clearly also would argue against Hume, insofar as they believe that recognizing the merit of possessing humility about our human intellectual capacities should lead us, on reflection, to see our need for faith in a God of love. On what grounds, though, do Augustine and Pascal fundamentally disagree with Hume concerning the legitimacy of religious belief? Furthermore, is there any rational way to adjudicate the fundamental disagreement among these three Socratic thinkers concerning the proper relationship of philosophical humility and religious faith? I will seek to provide some answer to both questions in the remaining space of this chapter.

Saint Augustine: Gadfly of Hippo

Let us turn our investigation to considering the place of both humility and faith in the philosophy of Augustine. Central to Augustine's theory of reason and faith is his conviction that our reasoning about how to live well as humans ought to be directed and molded by our needs and desires as feeling agents who are fundamentally, and above all else, lovers. The centrality of love in Augustine's thinking underlies his affirmation of the priority, at least in one sense, of belief over rational understanding. Understanding why Augustine gives priority to belief in turn requires appreciating the importance of love in his thought. As Gilson, in his classic work *The Christian Philosophy of Saint Augustine*, remarks, "The more a doctrine tends to be built around charity the more Augustinian it is."[44] But what exactly does it mean to build an entire philosophy around *caritas*? And how does such a philosophy offer an alternative to Humean skepticism without itself succumbing to blind authoritarianism?

To comprehend the place of love in Augustine's philosophy, let us begin by noting how Augustine conceives of the interdependence of belief and rational understanding in human life in general. Having done this, we can better appreciate why, for Augustine, we cannot understand ultimate truths about human life unless we first begin in faith. When Augustine wishes to distinguish reason (*ratio*) from belief (*fides* or *credere*), he typically draws on the basic distinction of firsthand versus secondhand experience. So, for example, in the

---

44. Etienne Gilson, *The Christian Philosophy of Saint Augustine* (London: Victor Gollancz, 1961), 238. Gilson characterizes the relation of true philosophy and wisdom in Augustine as follows: "On this score the mark of Augustinianism is its refusal to count as 'true philosophy' any doctrine which shows what must be done but fails to provide the power to do it. For this reason Christian wisdom alone deserves the name 'philosophy' because it alone makes it possible to translate the vision of contemplation into action" (242).

Enchiridion, where he seeks to answer Laurentius's query about the role of reason in the life of faith, Augustine distinguishes two sources of truth: reason and authority. What one knows through reason, on the one hand, must be grounded in one's own immediate and direct conscious experience of some reality. Augustine regards both sensory experience and the kind of rational insights gained in mathematics and logic as instances of beliefs based on reason. So, for example, one might through reason, according to Augustine, determine the visual qualities of a physical object by actually observing it. Thus I know by my own reason that my daughter Nadia caught her first fish out of Lake Eva in Tennessee in the summer of 1998 because I saw her catch it there at that time. Similarly, one might learn one of the truths of mathematics rationally by seeing for oneself how a theorem derives from intuitively obvious mental perceptions. For example, I might know through my own reason the validity of the Pythagorean theorem, if I am able to grasp all the steps necessary to demonstrate it. To know a truth by reason, then, is basically a matter of seeing it, either through sensory perception or mental conception, for oneself.

With many important things in life, Augustine goes on to show, it may be inconvenient, hard-hearted, or simply impossible to know something for oneself through one's own reason. At times it is reasonable, Augustine says, to believe some truth even when one has not "seen it for oneself." In fact, in order to gain access to truth at all through our own reason, we must rely, at least implicitly, on the testimony of others. In every area of human life, in addition, there are times when it is reasonable that we believe not because we ourselves can confirm the truth of what we believe, but out of a personal trust in what another person tells us. Unless we are willing to believe in the authority of others, that is, we could never even begin to reason.

In *De Utilitate Credendi*, Augustine specifies two such crucial areas of human life in which one is fully justified in assenting to a truth based on another's testimony: friendship and the filial bond of children to their parents.[45] It is significant that in both of these spheres of human life, the justification for believing in what one cannot see for oneself is bound up with the goodness of personal relationships. It is good for friends to love one another, as it is good for children to trust their parents. In the latter case, Augustine points out that children typically believe on the basis of their parents' testimony alone that their parents are who they say they are; it would be ludicrous, Augustine says, for children to suspend belief that their parents are their real parents until they are provided with independent evidence confirming the testimony of their parents. In the case of children, Augustine argues that it is good for children generally to love their parents and submit themselves to their authority. But children can develop these filial virtues only if they trust their parents

---

45. Augustine, *The Advantage of Believing*, trans. Luanne Meagher, vol. 4 of *The Fathers of the Church* (New York: CIMA, 1947), 9.22–12.27.

about things that they cannot see on their own. In other words, as a general rule, children violate no proper epistemic duty and use their cognitive faculties properly when they accept the authority of their parents and trust that what they say is true. Augustine defends the claim that children are justified in believing in their parents' authority on the basis of the ethical role of and importance of trust in a child's moral development.

Augustine's case for the propriety of trust between friends resembles that for the justification of children trusting their parents, but it does not hinge on the same principle of hierarchical dependence and moral development. Yet here as well Augustine holds that the very possibility of the enjoyment of a human good requires a willingness to trust another in matters one cannot see for oneself. The kind of person who refuses to trust a friend without independent confirmation of everything he or she says is unduly suspicious, "for there is also no friendship at all unless something is believed which cannot be demonstrated by positive reasoning."[46] In his discussion, Augustine acknowledges that a person could go too far and be excessive in his or her willingness to believe what a friend says. One should be duly cautious, and not be one of those who can "be fooled all of the time." But our enjoyment of personal relationships both in childhood and as adults depends on our willingness to take risks and believe some of the things that others say, because we trust that they are the sort of persons who would not deceive us. Our will to believe others, then, signifies our trust in the goodness of others. For children such a disposition to trust the goodness of one's parents is typically natural and unreflective; for true friends the willingness to believe and trust one's friend is rooted in an act of will, in an act of loving another person and thereby affirming that they possess such worth that one is willing to risk being deceived in trusting them. Children exhibit this trust in their parents naturally without consciously knowing very much of the risks involved; adult friends may, and at times should, be well aware of the risks they take.

Augustine's account of the importance of trusting one's parents and one's friends reveals his overarching concern with human nature and specifically with our proper functioning and the ethical requirements for our communal welfare. It is a basic premise of Augustine's psychology that all people by nature pursue their own happiness. Essential to the realization of this aim on Augustine's view is the need to cultivate the classic moral virtues, such as prudence, courage, temperance, and justice, all of which must in turn be informed by charity. All people share this fundamental desire for happiness, but they often differ in their conception of both the particular nature of and the correct path to their genuine happiness. Augustine's defense in *De Utilitate Credendi* of the reasonableness of believing what we cannot confirm by our own reason is best understood against the background of his teleological

46. Augustine, *Advantage of Believing*, 10.24.

conception of people; we realize our natural place in the order of creatures only through our growth in the virtues. Augustine thinks that we must be willing to trust certain people, because unless we do so we will fail to develop and promote the virtues rooted in charity. So it is not surprising that after discussing both instances of reasonable belief, Augustine extends the scope of his case to include all of our social existence: Augustine takes it as a general truth that throughout our lives we must be willing to believe in order to live at all successfully in community with others. We cannot see directly into the souls of other people, and yet we would at times treat them unjustly if we were the sort of people who refused in principle to believe what others say. Indeed, to refuse in principle to trust others would lead us to continual violations of the obligations of justice, for rendering to others what is their due often necessitates trusting in their testimony. Thus near the end of his analysis in *De Utilitate Credendi* of the importance of believing, Augustine observes that "many examples can be cited which show that absolutely nothing would remain intact in human society if we should determine to believe only what we can grasp by perception."[47] The willingness to believe, for Augustine, is no less than a necessary condition for civil community and the cultivation of the virtues of character. Hence, the justification and rationality of belief, for Augustine, is grounded in a teleology of human life.

So far we have seen how Augustine defends the disposition to believe as rooted in our responsibilities toward others. As we will see, Augustine also recognizes that we can be unreasonable not only by refusing to believe others when we ought to do so, but, just as important, by being too willing to believe others when we should withhold assent and be less credulous about what they say. One can, in other words, be too willing to believe. For his position to be philosophically coherent and defensible, Augustine needs to provide a criterion of reasonable belief. It is clear that Augustine never intends to defend blind obedience to all socially established authority. If belief must at times precede reason, it is equally true for Augustine that our reason must aid us in discernment so as to moderate our tendency to accept what others tell us. We will return to this problem of discernment when we examine how Augustine addresses the question, in the context of religious belief, of whose authority we should be willing to accept. It is certainly unwise, Augustine says, to embrace any and all religious authority. A wise person will accept the call to believe, but not uncritically so. For Augustine, some religious belief is rational, but not all religious belief is rational. Augustine's treatment of this problem of which religious authority to believe in will provide the key for appreciating how Augustine would respond to the accusation that he endorses blind authoritarianism. But before we consider that serious issue in detail, we must look more specifically at how Augustine conceives of faith and reason.

47. Ibid., 12.26.

We will see how Augustine's doctrine of faith and reason builds on his overall defense of the willingness to believe.

Augustine envisions human life as a journey of faith. In its ideal form, human life is a journey beginning in faith (*fides*) and ending in that fully completed state of understanding that Augustine calls wisdom (*sapientia*). In Augustine's view, the starting point, faith, and the ultimate *telos*, wisdom, serve as the ideal alpha and omega stages of Christian discipleship. In a classic formulation of this essential component of his philosophy, Augustine remarks, "Faith seeks, understanding finds; whence the prophet says, 'Unless ye believe, ye shall not understand.' "[48] The contrast to Hume here is unmistakable. To see faith and reason as Augustine does is to proceed in a strikingly un-Humean fashion. Whereas Hume finds faith subversive to reason, Augustine envisions faith as effecting the crucial transformation of the whole person, preparing and equipping him or her for reason's fulfillment. What faith starts, in other words, reason completes. And indeed, reason alone, without the power of faith, cannot achieve the goal of understanding. Let us note here that Augustine basically asserts two claims about the nature of faith: first, that faith seeks and, second, that the faith that seeks is a necessary precondition for religious understanding. Both aspects of faith are decisive for comprehending how Augustine conceives of the rationality of faith.

As Augustine envisions the human condition, we are all inescapably born into a most serious game of blindman's bluff. The target we all seek in this life is self-knowledge and real happiness. We seek to know ourselves, to fulfill our nature, to find true peace and joy. Yet because "man is a great deep,"[49] because the most important truths about our lives are never fully transparent to us in this life, we lack the power, Augustine insists, simply to remove our blindfolds to see the way to true fulfillment. Furthermore, while we wander about seeking our goal, the authoritative voices around us provide conflicting advice on where we should step and in which direction we should turn. Given our predicament as pilgrims who never see fully, for Augustine we as mortal humans will never fully understand our own selves, and as a consequence will never in this life fully enjoy real happiness. For Augustine, in addition, faith alone does not end our strivings, as if faith by itself would remove our blindfolds and lead us directly home. Faith may be said to "save us," but not in the sense that faith in and of itself makes us whole. Rather, in an Augustinian view, faith is more an act of trust enabling us slowly to gain in self-understanding and see through the veil of our limited comprehension.

To have faith in God, for Augustine, is thus to trust a personal God who reveals to us the path for reaching our final end without entirely revealing to us

48. Augustine, *On the Trinity*, trans. Arthur Hadden and William Shedd, vol. 8 of *A Select Library of Nicene and Post-Nicene Fathers of the Christian Church*, ed. Philip Schaff (Grand Rapids: Eerdmans, 1956), 15.2.2.

49. Augustine, *Confessions*, trans. F. J. Sheed (Indianapolis: Hackett, 1993), 4.14.

any of the truths we would need to grasp in order to stop our seeking. Hence to have faith in God necessarily means that we must trust in what God tells us rather than fully and directly see the truth for ourselves. In sum, religious faith essentially seeks the very thing it lacks—namely, a complete and final communion with, and enjoyment of, God. Like Socrates, Augustine's person of faith is a seeker, and not a possessor, of complete self-knowledge.

Let us look now more closely at how Augustine understands the nature of faith in God. For Augustine, to have faith in the Christian God definitely requires believing certain truths, such as that God exists and that God has acted in history to redeem humanity in the life and death of Jesus of Nazareth. Part of the nature of faith is thus a matter of *believing that* certain propositions are true. But genuine faith in Augustine's view also means *believing in* God as the ultimate good and end of all human yearning and aspiration. It is crucial to appreciate how for Augustine faith is a disposition requiring a commitment of the "whole person" and not just a trusting, partial apprehension of truths about a divine reality. Augustine explains this point especially clearly in his commentary on the Gospel of John, *In Evangelium Johannis Tractatus*:

> Dost thou wish to understand? BelieveFor God has said by the prophet: "Except ye believe, ye shall not understand." To the same purpose what the Lord here also added as He went on—"If any man is willing to do His will, he shall know concerning the doctrine, whether it be of God, or whether I speak from myself." What is the meaning of this, "If any man be willing to do His will"? But I had said, if any man believe; and I gave this counsel: If thou hast not understood, said I, believe. For understanding is the reward of faith. Therefore, do not seek to understand in order to believe, but believe that thou mayest understand; since, "except ye believe, ye shall not understand." . . . But the Lord Himself says openly in another place: "This is the work of God, that ye believe on Him whom He has sent." "That ye believe on Him," not that ye believe Him. But if ye believe *on* Him, ye believe Him; yet he that believes Him does not necessarily believe *on* Him. For even the devils believed Him, but they did not believe *on* Him. Again, moreover, of his apostles we can say, we believe Paul; but not, we believe on Paul: we believe Peter; but not, we believe on Peter. For, "to him that believeth on him that justifieth the ungodly, his faith is counted unto him for righteousness." What then is "to believe on Him"? By believing to love Him, by believing to esteem highly, by believing to go into Him and to be incorporated in His members. It is faith itself then that God exacts from us: and He finds not that which He exacts, unless He has bestowed what He may find. What faith, but that which the apostle has most amply defined in another place, saying "Neither circumcision availeth anything, nor uncircumcision, but faith that worketh by love"? Not any faith of what kind soever, but "faith that worketh by love": let this faith be in thee, and thou shalt understand concerning the doctrine.[50]

50. Augustine, *Homilies on the Gospel of John*, trans. John Gibb, vol. 7 of *A Select Library of Nicene and Post-Nicene Fathers of the Christian Church*, ed. Philip Schaff (Grand Rapids: Eerdmans, 1956), 29.6.

It is clear in this passage that, for Augustine, believing in God is from the point of view of human agency as much a matter of the human will as it is of the human intellect. The human will for Augustine is both the faculty of choice and the seat of love. From an Augustinian point of view one performs an act willingly insofar as one freely chooses to pursue it; in addition, one wills an object as one's highest good when one desires it above all else for its own sake and seeks to enjoy it, to cling to it, forever.[51] It is the latter sense of willing something as the ultimate good in one's life that we must keep in mind here. To believe "on God," as Augustine expresses it, involves the will because it expresses two key aspects of loving God as one's highest good: first, acknowledging God's worth, and second, desiring intimate communion with him. It is of fundamental importance not to overlook how Augustine envisions a form of *amor*, ordinate love or *caritas*, as informing faith because merely "believing that" God possesses certain attributes, without feeling or affirming God's beauty in the manner of love, is certainly far from what Augustine understands to constitute the nature of faith. Indeed, we would miss Augustine's point entirely if we interpreted him to be saying merely that true faith requires believing not only that God exists but also that God is good, as if such belief made no demands on one's emotions or desires. Given Augustine's conviction that, from a psychological view, all people naturally seek their own happiness, it would really make no sense to Augustine for a person honestly to assert, "Well, yes, God is very good, indeed God is the highest good, but so what?" A person could, of course, utter those words but, if Augustine is correct, not in all sincerity. From the Augustinian perspective, the devils who believe that God exists but reject God do not really believe that God is the highest good; they cannot, that is, believe that God is *their* highest good, for rational beings by nature love rather than abhor what they believe to be their ultimate good. Thus the devils' "belief that God exists" profits them nothing precisely because it is not informed by charity. "Now what shall I say of love?" Augustine queries in the *Enchiridion*, to which he replies: "Without it, faith profits nothing; and in its absence, hope cannot exist."[52] Belief in God, for Augustine, draws its very life from the loving affirmation of God's goodness and thus essentially expresses an act of the will.

If it is a serious error to think that faith works without love, so is it wrong, Augustine says, to believe that one can possess true faith simply by feeling a "love" for God and desiring to serve one's neighbors without grounding these attitudes in definite beliefs about who God is and how God has acted in human history. Augustine does not believe that, because the essence of faith is charity,

51. For Augustine on the will's love of the supreme good, see *Advantage of Believing* 16.34; *On the Trinity* 8.7.10; *Eighty-Three Different Questions* 35.1–2; *On Christian Doctrine* 1.4.4; *City of God* 14.6–7; *On Free Choice of the Will* 1.14.99–116.

52. Augustine, *Enchiridion*, in *The Essential Augustine*, ed. Vernon Bourke (Indianapolis: Hackett, 1974), 172.

we can thereby simply dispense with the cognitive aspect of "belief that" God exists or that God is good. Rather, Augustine should be read as espousing his own version of the doctrine of the unity of the virtues. Apart from charity, all the natural virtues are corrupted by pride, and faith and hope, as virtues endowed by grace, also fall short of being meritorious without charity. In addition, even a nascent form of charity must not be completely blind, for it must affirm the reality and goodness of what it seeks. Without such belief, charity lacks an object and amounts to the love of nothing (or, perhaps, a narcissistic love of one's own loving).

I have emphasized love's contribution to faith in our discussion to show how Augustine's reading of Scripture requires that faith precludes neutrality of the will. This means, Augustine says, that insofar as one truly believes "on God," one must both judge that God is the highest good and yearn to be united with him; thus the believer cannot be an indifferent spectator. It should be clear that the person of faith must be committed or biased, given that Augustine thinks that to have faith, one must trust in God as one's highest authority and as the only complete source of happiness. Thus a faithful believer is no more capable of being neutral than an impassioned erotic lover would be. Consider how being neutral toward another person would appear to entail one of two attitudes. The first is a kind of ethical indifference in which one neither approves of nor cares for the other person's being: "She exists but who cares?" The second might be a slightly less unethical sort of indifference that declares, "I would not wish her ill, but I have no desire to be with her, let alone to wish her well or help her." For Augustine, either form of neutrality toward any rational creature, let alone the Highest One, would be a failure of charity and a violation of justice.

To appreciate this point, consider the difference between believing in God as the true God and believing that some proposition—say, "roses are red"—is true. Now it does seem intelligible to conceive of one believing that roses are red in abstraction from any evaluative attitude on one's part regarding the worth of roses. The mere belief that "roses are red" would seem neutral, then, because one could be said to have the belief without approving of, or even having any noticeable feeling toward, the object of one's belief. We could, for example, imagine a roomful of people all deliberately beholding the same vase of roses. Granted, this shared activity would not normally occur in everyday life, but one could imagine it taking place in a special session of the American Philosophical Association. Let us allow that all the people viewing the roses share the same basic belief that "the roses are red"; we may further suppose that, as individuals, they would likely experience diverse feelings about the roses and might even, as a group, exhibit a wide spectrum of emotions toward these roses, ranging from intense pleasure to indifference or even annoyance. One could thus reasonably abstract the belief that "roses are red" from this whole spectrum of emotional responses and regard the mere belief itself as a purely intellectual affair. (Though, of course, the act of believing would still involve some component of willing.) What the members of the group share in terms of belief is still real: it is the mere belief in itself apart from any evaluative component. We might in academic discussions regard our common belief that roses are red as possessing a neutral intellectual component or perhaps even as a neutral intellectual act.

In contrast to our case with the roses, when Augustine speaks of *belief on God*, neutrality is categorically ruled out; in this case, one who is not moved to seek God is one who has not yet esteemed God in the right way, in the way essential to genuine "faith that worketh by charity." The demand of charity on faith is, for Augustine, twofold: charity requires both our loving God as our highest good and our loving our neighbors as ourselves. In *De Doctrina Christiana*, Augustine explains how the two great commandments of Matthew 22 serve as the core of Scripture:

> To this warning that we must beware not to take figurative or transferred expressions as though they were literal, a further warning must be added lest we wish to take literal expressions as though they were figurative. Therefore a method of determining whether a locution is literal or figurative must be established. And generally this method consists in this: that whatever appears in the divine Word that does not literally pertain to virtuous behavior or to the truth of faith you must take to be figurative. Virtuous behavior pertains to the love of God and of one's neighbor; the truth of faith pertains to knowledge of God and of one's neighbor. . . . But Scripture teaches nothing but charity, nor condemns anything except cupidity, and in this way shapes the minds of men.[53]

Because he understands that the fundamental purpose of Scripture is to teach us how to grow in charity, Augustine proceeds to make the principle of charity into the fundamental interpretative principle for the reading of Scripture:

> Thus when the tyranny of cupidity has been overthrown, charity reigns with its most just laws of love for God for the sake of God and of one's self and of one's neighbor for the sake of God. Therefore in the consideration of figurative expressions a rule such as this will serve, that what is read should be subjected to diligent scrutiny until an interpretation contributing to the reign of charity is produced. If this result appears literal in the text, the expression being considered is not figurative.[54]

Charity is thus for Augustine the essential wellspring of faith and the standard for education in the Scriptures. Not surprisingly, it is also for Augustine of fundamental importance for the growth and perfection of reason.

53. Augustine, *On Christian Doctrine*, trans. D. W. Robertson (Indianapolis: Bobbs-Merrill, 1958), 3.10.
54. Ibid., 3.15.

When he turns to instructing his reader on the close kinship of faith and reason, and the importance of charity in both, Augustine often relies on two passages of Scripture: 2 Corinthians 5:7—"for we walk by faith, not by sight"—and 1 Corinthians 13:12—"For now we see in a mirror, dimly, but then we will see face to face."[55] Both texts inform Augustine's basic conception of faith and wisdom. To have faith is to trust God, to love God, or at least to yearn to love him as our greatest good. The possessor of faith, however, still seeks rather than fully enjoys, as one who feels hunger rather than satiation. The experience of faith for Augustine includes both the joy of being found and the unrest of being unable to enjoy full communion with the One who has found us. Because the faithful do not yet fully abide in God, their love suffers the limitation of unfulfilled desire, and the people of faith, being pilgrims, naturally "walk" rather than "sit back" complacently and "take it easy." Now, if faith is this state of charity in an unfulfilled and imperfect form, wisdom, the perfection of our rational nature, is faith transformed into fullness, because wisdom for Augustine is that final and complete union with God sought after in faith. Only in wisdom does the possessor of faith find what he or she seeks. To have this wisdom is to know the highest good and "cling to the truth."[56]

While it is true for Augustine that wisdom is a state of "seeing" the highest good, it also, like faith, cannot be a matter of neutrality, of some sort of "seeing from afar." Rather, for Augustine the wise person not only sees but also tastes. Such a person both sees God face-to-face and enjoys the beauty of God's person. As in the case of Augustinian faith, Augustinian wisdom involves a union of intellect and will, but now in a way that completes what faith initiated. So, as Augustine remarks, understanding (*intellectus*) is "the reward of faith."[57] Here we encounter a crucial aspect of the fundamental Augustinian doctrine of the harmony of reason and faith. While their misuse can certainly lead to conflict and mutual antagonism, in their natural and proper expression, jointly rooted in charity, the growth of faith and the growth of reason regarding ultimate reality are inseparable. For Augustine, the perfection of reason in wisdom alone affords the yearning of faith its satisfaction. Of course, he insists as well in his account of the religious life on the impossibility of attaining wisdom without beginning in faith. Thus we find that for Augustine love is as essential for understanding God as it is for believing in him. Neither belief in God nor a real understanding of God in Augustine's universe could be available to a skeptic who insists on remaining a neutral spectator until sufficient evidence

---

55. For Augustine on 2 Cor. 5:7, see *Enchiridion*, 1.37.41; *Eighty-Three Different Questions* 61.7.65; *Homilies on the Gospel of John*, 75; *Confessions XIII*, 14. Augustine affirms the teaching of 1 Cor. 13:12 in *Enchiridion*, 1.13.31; 2.8.11; 2.12.17; *Letter* 120; *Confessions* 8.1; 10.1; 10.5; *Homilies on the Gospel of John*, 101, 102; *On the Trinity* 15.11; *City of God* 29.29. Neither list comes close to being complete.

56. Augustine, *Advantage of Believing*, 16.34.

57. Augustine, *Homilies on the Gospel of John*, 29.6.

is found. The path to true understanding or wisdom is thus available only for those who, responding first in trust and affirming with their will the authority of the highest good, seek through their love to see more clearly and fully the God in whom they already believe. To declare with Augustine that one must first believe in order to understand does indeed sound quite strange, if not ludicrous, if one presupposes that understanding or wisdom is nothing more than a combination of "believing that such and such is the case" and having evidence to support it. But then, wisdom for Augustine is not merely justified true belief, but rational love in its full realization.

To accord the principle "*credo ut intellegam*" its proper rank in Augustine's thought, it is crucial to look even more closely at this doctrine of rational love. We encounter one of Augustine's most far-reaching reflections on this doctrine in *De Diversis Quaestionibus LXXXIII*:

> However, as for a good which is not loved, no one can possess it or have it perfectly. For who can know to what extent something is good when he does not enjoy it? But he does not enjoy it if he does not love it, nor therefore does he who does not love it possess what is to be loved, even if he who does not possess it could love it. Therefore no one knows the happy life and is wretched, because if it should be loved (and it should be), then to know the happy life is the same as to possess it.
>
> Since these things are so, what else is it to live happily but to possess an eternal object through knowing it? For the eternal is that in which alone one can rightly place his confidence, it is that which cannot be taken away from the one who loves it, and it is that very thing which one possesses solely by knowing it. For of all things, the most excellent is what is eternal, and therefore we cannot possess it except by that part of ourselves in which lies our excellence, i.e., by our mind. But whatever is possessed by the mind is had by knowing, and no good is completely known which is not completely loved. Nor is it the case, since the mind alone can know, that thus it alone can love. For love is a kind of desire, and we can see that desire is also present in other parts of the soul. If this desire is in accord with the mind and reason, it will be possible for the mind to contemplate what is eternal in great peace and tranquility. Therefore the soul ought to love with its other parts as well this magnificent object which must be known by the mind. And since that which is loved necessarily affects with itself that which loves, it follows that what is eternal, loved in this way, affects the soul with eternity. Wherefore, strictly speaking, it is eternal life which is the happy life. However, what else but God is that eternal object which affects the soul with eternity?[58]

Augustine speaks here of a kind of love peculiar to reason, arguing, in a way reminiscent of Plato, that the rational mind cannot know the good without

---

58. Augustine, *Eighty-Three Different Questions*, trans. David Mosher, vol. 70 of *The Fathers of the Church* (Washington, DC: Catholic University of America Press, 1982), 35.1–2.

loving it.[59] But how exactly does Augustine justify the claim that "no good is completely known which is not completely loved"? In essence, he does so by specifying the role of love as crucial both for the function of reason and the nature of wisdom. Probably most contemporary readers, having become so accustomed to the modern philosophical dichotomy between reason and passion, will find Augustine's more Platonic conception of reason rather foreign. But it is not unreasonable to conceive of reason in Augustinian terms once we consider that reasoning is an activity of rational agents pursuing some end. The pursuit of any end for Augustine involves the will, for it is the will by which rational agents choose among alternatives and seek to satisfy some desire. What Augustine refers to here as reason is not reason thought of as a mere blind machine, indifferently processing data, but reason as seeking an end and thus as being passionate and desiring. Reason in this latter sense never acts merely as a piece of heartless technology. Perhaps a better way to put this point would be to note that Augustine here views reason as an active faculty with its own proper end and desire. He does not regard reason as a passive tool like a calculator, which someone might use either for good or ill. Augustinian reasoning is not a neutral technological process but is an ethical and teleological activity. As Augustine states, reason by its very nature seeks to know and thus possess and enjoy the good. Reason's desire to know the good seeks not only to understand its full nature but also to possess it in a striking sense. We possess an object of love by uniting our wills to it and grasping its nature intellectually. Wisdom is thus a matter of both seeing and possessing. Furthermore, in describing this fulfillment of rational love, Augustine echoes Plato by including the element of imitation in the nature of knowing the good: the soul's communion with the highest good transforms the soul into an image or likeness of its object. The eternal good thus delivers to the soul something of its own nature, as the creature participates in the eternity of the divine nature.

Since Augustine regards the proper function of reason to be the intimate sharing of God's glory, and not just the intellectual apprehension of facts, his theory of rationality is certainly not theologically neutral in the more familiar modern sense. His theory of what it means to be rational is no more neutral than is his metaphysical vision of reality as a hierarchical order of inherently good, created beings. In fact, the two are intimately connected, for the Augustinian rational person employs reason neither to master nature nor simply to see why things are as they are, but to become the sort of person whose internal order enables him or her, by God's grace, to find his or her proper place in the order of creation. Only such a divinely transformed person has the power to be fully united in heart and mind to the mind of God. Thus it is this fullness

---

59. I argue for the inseparability of love and knowledge in Plato's thought in "Reason and Passion in Plato's *Republic*," *Ancient Philosophy* 9 (Fall 1989): 173–87.

of being with God, of both seeing God face-to-face and being able to rejoice fully in submission to God, that Augustine has in mind when he speaks of wisdom. The process of gaining wisdom ends not in intellectual vision alone, but in the full completion of the rational soul; the road to wisdom ends for the Augustinian seeker in the *imitatio Dei*.

Given the psychic holism of reason and passion central to Augustine's understanding of wisdom, it should not be surprising to find him refusing to accord reason autonomy from the life of faith. To have wisdom, one must fully realize one's natural capacity of reason in three ways: (1) seeing the nature of the good; (2) loving it completely; and (3) abiding with it and taking on its character. Hence the completion of rational nature is as much a way of feeling and willing as it is one of intellectual apprehension. We can appropriately speak of Augustine's doctrine of *sapientia* as "holistic" for the reason that none of these functions of wisdom are really capable of existing in isolation. Seeing God as supremely good, as Augustine argues in *De Diversis Quaestionibus LXXXIII*, involves the proper response of love. To know God as the Good, in other words, requires the purity of heart to love God as God—that is, as the only good we should love absolutely and unequivocally for his own sake, as the only being truly Good in and of himself. Without this full assent of the intellect and will, one does not know God, just as from an Augustinian perspective we could say that we cannot know other people as human without affirming their dignity as free rational agents loved by the supreme being. In a very important sense, Augustine's proper practice of philosophy fuses our capacity for reason with our feelings and desires.

Consider, for example, the ethical implications of Augustine's view of treating another person merely as an occasion for corporate profit or personal pleasure: by acting in such a way that one reduces another human self to a mere commodity, a person offends the moral order on the level both of willing and of believing. By treating another person merely as a thing, one fails to acknowledge the other person's equal worth; such an error of acknowledgment entails both a disordered willing and a disordered thinking. Failing to acknowledge the independent worth of the other person means choosing to will, think, and act toward the other in a way that violates the proper order of goodness. Augustine envisions the truly rational person as properly acknowledging—not just abstractly thinking about— the world as it "really is." Thus the questions of how one feels toward others, how one affirms or denies their worth, and how one thinks about them—Is this person actually my neighbor?—all converge into one interconnected, complex way of being in the world. For Augustine, the only truly wise way of being human is to acknowledge and affirm the proper order of things: "He lives in justice and sanctity who is an unprejudiced assessor of the intrinsic value of things. He is a man who has ordinate love."[60]

60. Augustine, *Eighty-Three Different Questions*, 1.27.

It is perhaps this deep connection between wisdom and ordinate love more than anything else that underlies Augustine's declaration that "one must believe in order to understand." So Augustine explains the significance of *"credo ut intellegam"* in his *Letter to Consentius*:

> God forbid that He should hate in us that faculty by which He made us superior to all other living beings. Therefore we must refuse so to believe not as to receive or seek a reason for our belief, since we could not believe at all if we did not have rational souls. So, then, in some points that bear on the doctrine of salvation, which we are not yet able to grasp by reason—but we shall be able to sometime—let faith precede reason, and let the heart be cleansed by faith so as to receive and bear the great light of reason; this is indeed reasonable. Therefore the Prophet said with reason: "If you will not believe, you will not understand"; thereby he undoubtedly made a distinction between these two things and advised us to believe first so as to be able to understand whatever we believe. It is, then, a reasonable requirement that faith precede reason, for, if this requirement is not reasonable, then it is contrary to reason, which God forbid. But, if it is reasonable that faith precede a certain great reason which cannot yet be grasped, there is no doubt that, however slight the reason which proves this, it does precede faith.[61]

As this passage indicates, those who seek wisdom must begin in faith, because wisdom is a matter of the heart, and people cannot use their hearts well without believing in things they cannot yet see. The heart must be "cleansed by faith so as to receive and bear the great light of reason." That faith serves to purify the heart and purge it of its inordinate love of self is a theme that runs throughout Augustine's writings.[62] Augustine tends to emphasize two particular ways in which the human spirit suffers from disordered love. First, without God's grace the human heart suffers from the malady of pride in both its treatment of other humans and its relationship to God. To fulfill the two great commandments of charity, pride must give way to humility. But Augustine does not believe that people can cure themselves or that they will ever succeed in reorienting their hearts through their own efforts. To learn how to be genuinely humble in our loves, we need a cure for our own disordered love of self that only a divine physician can provide. And, as Augustine understands the process of sanctification, of being made into a living image of God, the

61. Augustine, *Letter* 120, vol. 2 of *Letters*, trans. Sister Wilfrid Parsons, vol. 18 of *The Fathers of the Church* (New York: Fathers of the Church, 1953).

62. Augustine speaks of the role of faith in both purifying the mind and the purging of inordinate love by means of charity. For Augustine, these are simply two descriptions of the same process of spiritual healing. See, for example: *On the Trinity* 1.1.3; 8.4.6; 8.20.21; 15.26.24; *Advantage of Believing* 16.34; *On Christian Doctrine* 1.10.10; 2.7.9–11; *Eighty-Three Different Questions* 36; *Of True Religion* 3.3; *Letter* 120; *Soliloquies* 1.6.12; *On Free Choice of the Will* 1.15.113; 3.24.249–50; *City of God* 10.32.

human patient cannot fully recover except over a lifetime. We are not simply and immediately remade by divine grace into unselfish, humble lovers the moment we begin our life of faith. Rather, as Augustine shows us in his own autobiography, the road to wisdom is a slow and inevitably difficult process of a pilgrim's progress and regress. Finally, faith is essentially a gift of grace working in the human heart and transforming us into the sort of persons who will be able to love well and judge reasonably.

Thus a healthy human life must embody a mutual dependence between reason and faith. Just as it is the case that reason must await the healing power of faith in order to possess the truth, it is also true that humans must believe reasonably and not carelessly pledge their loyalty to a false authority. Rather, to have genuine faith one must completely and single-mindedly put one's trust only in God's grace. Thus we face the crucial problem regarding our need to believe in some authority: how does one reasonably choose in which authority to place one's trust? As we see in the autobiographical narrative in the *Confessiones* where Augustine details the drama of his own false commitments, it makes all the difference in the world how and where one begins on the road to wisdom. Starting off on the wrong foot or with the wrong frame of mind can be ruinous. Hence blind faith must be ruled out as an act of folly and a counterfeit form of genuine faith. But, we might fairly ask, how is one then even to begin? The answer lies in a stance we might well term "reasonable faith." We have seen already that Augustine believes it is reasonable to trust in the integrity of others when we cannot see fully and directly into their hearts. So we might ask the following questions: Under what circumstances and in whom is it reasonable to place our trust? In whom, if anyone, is it reasonable to place our ultimate trust? Wherein lies the difference between reasonable trust in authority and blind authoritarianism?

Augustine's answers, not surprisingly, reflect his understanding of our natural place in God's order. The authority in whom we may reasonably put our ultimate trust must be that of the only one who can provide the proper cure for our spiritual disorder and serve as our true Good. As I have noted, the basic nature of our spiritual disorder for Augustine is inordinate love, and the root of such disorder is, in one form or another, excessive pride. A related and second manifestation of this spiritual unhealth for Augustine is our preoccupation with and excessive, possessive love of temporal goods. Both kinds of inordinate love prove to be obstacles in the quest for wisdom. If we are to know the highest good fully and so both love and possess it, then both forms of spiritual disease must be cured. For Augustine, the remedy for both kinds of disorder comes to us not by means of our own devices, but only through God's grace. Faith in God serves as the medicine of the soul by which these unhealthy forms of affection are transformed into genuine love. To the question, "Which ultimate authority is it reasonable to trust?" Augustine responds that it is reasonable to trust as one's highest authority only the authority of the One who is the True Physician. The rationality of belief in God, then, which is essentially the rationality of trusting in the proper authority, is, quite astonishingly for a modern reader, a matter of the rationality of choosing the right physician. Hence the Augustinian canons for justified religious belief, far from being merely a matter of epistemology, are bound up with such questions as, "What are people for?" and even "Why are people so unhappy?"

If we accept this Augustinian scheme of the order of being and acknowledge our own self-centeredness and lust for finite goods, then we can see how it is rational to believe on the God who alone offers effective grace to sinners. We see that making sense of when it is reasonable to submit to authority requires a basic understanding of the human condition, of both what we yearn for and of why we fall short of attaining it. Similarly, children are generally reasonable in trusting their parents, as they need both the love and guidance their parents can provide. Likewise, friends may be reasonable in trusting one another insofar as friendship is crucial for our well-being. Thus in all cases of trusting in some other person, the rationality of our believing is embedded in the context of what it means to be a human pilgrim. Augustine insists on the priority of faith over understanding because he views all people in terms of the drama of human sinfulness and redemption. If he is right about both our spiritual sickness and the requisite nature of the cure, then he can make a good case for the reasonableness of faith in God's authority. In essence, we come back to the crucial point that the question of whom it is reasonable to believe in hinges on the question of who we really are: epistemology, metaphysics, and even psychopathology—to push the point—are thus inextricably interconnected in Augustine's thought.

For us as inheritors of the modern Enlightenment conception of autonomous reason, however, Augustine's approach to rational belief will likely seem strikingly unfamiliar, if not unintelligible. But on an everyday level, most of us at least implicitly understand that in many cases what is reasonable for a healthy person, whether in the physical or spiritual sense, is folly for the sick. We understand as well that determining the rationality of a proposed medical treatment or course of bodily exercise will require an account of the condition of the patient and the nature of good health. We might well say that one's beliefs are the exercises and treatments of the soul. In Augustine's view, our natural human goal is, of course, to grow into the blessedness of good health. Faith in the God of grace, we might then say, will appear reasonable to those pilgrims who acknowledge that they cannot make it home, cannot attain full health, on their own. So, indeed, Augustine explains the relation of faith, authority, and reason in *De Vera Religione*:

> The treatment of the soul, which God's providence and ineffable loving-kindness administers, is most beautiful in its steps and stages. There are two different methods, authority and reason. Authority demands belief and prepares man for reason.

Reason leads to understanding and knowledge. But reason is not entirely absent from authority, for we have got to consider whom we have to believe, and the highest authority belongs to truth when it is clearly known. But because we dwell among temporal things, and love of them is an obstacle to our reaching eternal things, a kind of temporal medicine, calling not those who know but those who believe back to health, has priority by the order, not of nature or its inherent excellence, but of time. Wherever a man falls there he must lie until he is raised up.[63]

Note that on this account reason and authority are not at odds, because they serve the same basic purpose: to cultivate the virtues of will and intellect that will make it possible for the self to enjoy God's perfect nature. Yet faith must be the starting point for this cultivation of human character, for faith in God's authority is necessary if we are to develop the skills of discernment and affection necessary for enjoying God fully without being impaired by inordinate love. The faith that makes this enjoyment possible and thus heals our fallen nature is not a blind faith, just as the appeal to authority in Augustine is not a species of authoritarianism. On the contrary, in one sense Augustine allows that reason must precede faith by discerning what authority is worthy of a person's absolute trust. No human authority deserves such allegiance, for the obvious reason that no human power alone can heal the human heart.[64] Thus it appears that an Augustinian can make a case just as strong, if not stronger, against submission to tyrannical human authority as even the doughtiest of Enlightenment rationalists or Humean skeptics. As we have seen, complete trust in Divine grace is rational on Augustine's view. To be sure, Augustine's case will not be compelling to anyone who feels no need of such grace; yet if Augustine is right about the proper function of reason in human reason, allowing for this qualification still means that faith in God is in fact rational for every person, whether or not he or she affirms that it is.

I have argued thus far that Augustine's thesis, "one must believe in order to understand," is intelligible only within the larger context of his beliefs

63. Augustine, *Of True Religion*, trans. and ed. John Burleigh, vol. 6 of *Augustine: Earlier Writings*, Library of Christian Classics (London: SCM, 1953), 24.45.

64. Cf. Augustine's reconciliation of reason and authority in Sermon 43:

And so, beloved, that other man too whom I set up against myself, calling in the prophet as referee because of the argument that arose between us, he too isn't saying just nothing when he says, "Let me understand, in order to believe." Of course, what I am now saying, I am saying to help those people believe who do not yet believe. And yet, unless they understand what I am saying, they cannot believe. So what this person says is partly true—"Let me understand, in order to believe"; and I on my side, when I say, just as the prophet says, "On the contrary, believe, in order to understand," am speaking the truth. Let's come to an agreement, then. So: understand, in order to believe; believe, in order to understand. I'll put it in a nutshell, how we can accept both without argument: Understand, in order to believe, my word; believe, in order to understand, the word of God. (*Sermons*, trans. Edmund Hill, vol. 2 of *The Works of Saint Augustine*, ed. John E. Rotelle [Brooklyn, NY: New City, 1990])

about human nature and human health. According to Augustine, the individual who possesses faith has responded to God in love. To love God means that one affirms who God is rather than simply posits that God exists. To affirm God is to esteem him as the highest good and to desire communion with him. The latter element of desire is crucial because it expresses the absolutely fundamental importance of humility in Augustine's thought. When Augustine recounts his own conversion in *Confessiones* 8, he tells a story of a seeker after truth who has come to acknowledge that only through God's grace does he have the power to love the truth as he should. In affirming God in Christ, Augustine confesses that he cannot attain God and draw near to him except through divine grace. His affirmation of God thus expresses a crucial moment of self-understanding of his own imperfection. Indeed, as Augustine describes his conversion, it is at once a self-surrender and self-enlightenment: in turning to God in faith, Augustine confesses that he could never have done so through his will alone. In renouncing his own autonomous power even to embrace God's grace, Augustine finds himself filled with that love he sought unknowingly for so long: "Late have I loved Thee, O Beauty so ancient and so new, late have I loved Thee! And behold, thou wert within and I was without."[65]

In relating his experience of coming to faith in God, Augustine provides in a narrative form a Socratic defense of his faith. His faith in God makes sense of the reality of what, in looking back on his life, Augustine sees as a deep longing for communion with the God of love. In the *Confessiones*, it is the Christian message that explains for Augustine the meaning of the struggle he has experienced in his lifelong quest for wisdom; it is only in the context of his yearning for wisdom and his continual experience of failure that Augustine's conversion makes rational sense to us. Augustine writes not to prove to anyone who reads his account that there really is a God of love, but to make sense of his own experiences and to instruct those who have similarly felt the need for God or experienced the power of God's grace. It is because of his humble encounter with divine love that Augustine can recommend faith as the true remedy for a longing soul. The story of his conversion in the *Confessiones* delivers to us in narrative form the very conception of faith and reason that Augustine recommends through explicit statement in the works we have been considering. In the *Confessiones* we hear the story of the philosophical seeker becoming the Christian believer. Augustine's story is a narrative demonstration of the failure of autonomous reason and the transformation of the human heart by divine love. And it is a narrative account of the reasonableness of faith, since only through faith can we hope to complete the rational journey toward wisdom. Despite its conclusion, the story of the *Confessiones* is told from the perspective of a pilgrim still seeking after the face of God.

65. Augustine, *Confessions*, 10.27.

In this way, the *Confessiones* shows rather than tells the Augustinian drama of rational love.

Augustine well knows that the potential his personal narrative possesses for persuading his readers is seriously limited: if the reader does not share Augustine's longing and has not also experienced inner failure and the longing for divine love, then Augustine's remedy will not seem especially rational. In assessing the reasonableness of faith in God, then, one must believe in order to understand, because understanding the rationality of faith requires being the sort of person for whom faith makes sense. To return to the initial theme of this book, we can appreciate how, for Augustine, the rational integrity of faith can be defended only from the particular perspective of a philosophical restoration of self. If one tries instead to bracket out one's needs and engage in a disinterested rational inquiry, how could one possibly defend what Augustine means by rational belief in God?

We might pause at this point to note how Augustine's own teleological conception of "loving reason" or "rational love" is decidedly biased and firmly rooted in a particular, historical, teleological tradition, so much so that this conception would lose both its identity and its coherence if it were extracted from the metaphysical system within which it resides. It is perhaps here in particular that we come upon one of the most fundamental differences between Hume and Augustine. For Hume, the principles of ethical evaluation are grounded not in reason but in the nonrational moral sentiments. Reason, in Hume's view, really has no direct role in the estimation of the value of things, for the manner in which we approve and disapprove of things reflects the internal nature of our sentiments, not the external order of things. The proper function of Humean reason is to grasp the necessary connections among perceptions and to discern the probability of events based on past experience. In the ethical sphere this reason plays a crucial role in clarifying the nature of the facts relevant to our moral sentiments. In all these offices, reason operates in a world devoid of intrinsic value. Humean reason renders judgments on the relations of valueless facts. The estimation of the worth of things is for Hume the concern of nonrational sentiments, with reason playing only an instrumental role. It seems reasonable to suppose that if one views reality merely as such a world of valueless facts, then very likely a Humean-type account of rationality will make the most sense.

But, of course, such a conception of reason would not make good sense in an Augustinian universe where reality itself is, as Gerard Manley Hopkins put it, "charged with the grandeur of God"[66] and where the function of reason itself is to lead us to full possession of, and participation in, this grandeur. Consider that whatever is real for Augustine possesses its own value and contributes in

---

66. "God's Grandeur," in *Poems and Prose of Gerard Manley Hopkins*, ed. W. H. Gardner (Harmondsworth: Penguin, 1963), 27.

some measure to the holistic goodness of the totality of beings. In addition, for Augustine, since it is the place of reason to discern the nature of things, reason can be neither neutral nor indifferent. Reason cannot simply serve to trace the relations of valueless facts, because in an Augustinian universe such "facts" simply do not exist. In Augustine's view, to be is to possess goodness. The reality of any being possesses an inherent beauty that radiates inwardly through its own unity and outwardly through its conjunction with the totality of what is. Thus if I am to know the reality of other humans, for example, I must acknowledge their inherent goodness, for that worth is essential to who they are. I might certainly encounter a person who is not good qua human. In shaking the hand of Adolf Hitler, one would not be shaking the hand of a good man, but the action would nevertheless be an exchange with a being whose reality is profoundly good—that is to say, inherently good, even though corrupted. Hitler was a morally wretched person, but he was human, not a mere fact. It is the nature of charity to love the person despite his or her sins, even if those sins are horrendous. And it is the nature of Augustinian reason not only to perceive, but also to assent to the goodness of all things.

On this account, then, when reason functions properly, discerning and affirming the reality of things, reason fulfills its purpose and finds its own proper place, reflecting the goodness in the order of things. Reason must also make this discernment according to the proper standard—that is, not in terms of anthropocentric utility, but in reference to the ultimate purpose each created being has to glorify God. In a final sense, then, a person cannot have true knowledge of any reality without possessing the wisdom that comes from knowing God. Since all things, in other words, are knowable only insofar as we discern their goodness, even knowledge of created things can be attained only when one sees in the light of Goodness itself. Put another way, we can now see how the question of the reasonableness of belief in God for Augustine cannot be separated from Augustine's conception of the function of reason in realizing the end of achieving wisdom. The wise person properly acknowledges the intrinsic value of all things in how he or she thinks, feels, and acts. But only through faith in God can one become the sort of person who can properly acknowledge the inherent goodness of beings in the world; thus faith in God is rational insofar as faith is a necessary condition for realizing the proper function of our reason.

Before turning to consider how Pascal may be seen as a deeply Augustinian thinker, I would like to explore one further aspect of Augustine's conception of rationality. To hold, as Augustine does, that faith precedes understanding is to conceive of the philosophical project in a Socratic rather than Cartesian sense. That is to say that, like Socrates, Augustine is a dialectical thinker. According to Augustine, the purpose of philosophy is to gain self-knowledge, yet the nature of human theorizing always leaves us falling short of our ultimate aim. The best human philosophy can achieve is to make sense of and defend one's core beliefs. Philosophy, in other words, is always a matter of faith seeking understanding. This dialectical conception of philosophy is evident throughout Augustine's works. In what follows, I will consider an especially clear illustration of a dialectical Augustinian text, his classic work *De Libero Arbitrio*.

In this treatise, Augustine attempts to clarify and to some extent justify the nature of his own Christian philosophy by citing as prophetic authority the Septuagint's translation of Isaiah 7:9, "Unless you believe, you shall not understand."[67] The central problem faced by the work's two interlocutors, Evodius and Augustine, is that of reconciling the Christian doctrine of God with the existence of evil. Evodius offers a series of dialectical objections and questions that occasion some of Augustine's most impressive accounts of free will, foreknowledge, and the goodness of God that pervades all reality. Were it not for Augustine's explicit reminder that one cannot understand without first believing, the reader might easily view the work as a piece of purely "rational" theology carried out independently from faith. But it is precisely this notion of autonomous understanding that Augustine goes on to reject:

> Our Lord Himself, by His words and deeds, first urged those whom He called to salvation to believe. Afterwards, when He spoke about the gift He was to give to those who believed, He did not say, "This is life eternal so that they may believe." Instead He said, "This is life eternal that they may know Thee, the one true God and Him whom Thou didst send, Jesus Christ." . . . Therefore, in obedience to the teachings of our Lord, let us seek earnestly. That which we seek at God's bidding we shall find when He Himself shows us—as far as it can be found in this life and by such men as we are. We must believe that these things are seen and grasped more clearly and fully by better men even while they dwell in this world, and surely by all good and devout men after this life. So we must hope and, disdaining worldly and human things, must love and desire divine things.[68]

Let us note first how Augustine portrays understanding as the fulfillment of belief. The person who believes trusts in God and yet does not see God face-to-face. It is fundamental to faith for Augustine that faith is a loving assent to him who is neither fully seen nor fully possessed. Faith thus implies incompleteness; the faithful are pilgrims seeking their home and hoping to attain it. The final goal of the believer is to attain wisdom, "the truth in which the highest good is discerned and held."[69] It is this wisdom, a final state of blessed union of heart and mind to the highest Good, that is in the fullest sense what Augustine means by "understanding." As he makes clear in the above passage,

67. See Augustine, *On Free Choice of the Will*, 1.2 and 2.2.4–6.
68. Augustine, *On Free Choice of the Will*, trans. Anna S. Benjamin and L. H. Hackstaff (Indianapolis: Bobbs-Merrill, 1964), 2.2.17–19.
    69. Ibid., 2.9.

such wisdom is unattainable through human efforts alone; complete wisdom, the state of harmonious communion of intellect and will with God, is a gift of grace that comes to us only as God provides it.

Yet while wisdom is ultimately a gift bestowed freely by God, Augustine also holds that it is right and good for believers to seek whatever degree of understanding is attainable through faithful reflection and philosophical inquiry. The particular sort of understanding sought after in his dialogue with Evodius is a matter of being able to defend one's core of faith against skeptical criticism. Augustine seeks through dialectical investigation to offer a Socratic *logos* of what he most deeply believes. Being rational in this Socratic context requires an attitude of honest confrontation with dialectical challenges to one's fundamental moral beliefs and a response to the challenges consistent with those beliefs. As we have noted earlier, both requirements are integral to the Socratic method. My contention is that for Augustine, the model of rational inquiry for seekers is Socratic in the sense that the inquirer both acknowledges that ultimate wisdom is unattainable by human efforts and seeks nevertheless to articulate the most plausible case possible for the moral ideals one affirms. It is especially crucial to understand just why the Socratic model of rationality differs markedly from the modern foundationalist's. For Socrates, rational inquiry is not a deductive process of deriving conclusions from undeniable first premises. On the contrary, the starting points for Socratic inquiry are a person's fundamental moral convictions, and these are not at all clearly indubitable in and of themselves. Further, the whole purpose of *elenchus* is not to achieve certainty by establishing infallible starting points, but to gain self-knowledge by learning how to state and defend one's core beliefs dialectically. On the Socratic model, one begins with a set of fundamental commitments and then seeks not to prove them but to make the best sense one can of them. My claim is that Augustinian rationality in an inquiry such as *De Libero Arbitrio* is Socratic in just this respect. Given Augustine's conception of the necessity of belief in general, one who engages in rational inquiry already is situated in a particular moral universe whether or not one happens to live in a Christian one. For those, however, who do live by faith and hope in a Christian worldview, the purpose of inquiry is to articulate, test, and defend dialectically the basic commitments of faith in God.

If we conceive of rational justification not according to the Lockean or Cartesian linear model of proof, but as a Socratic process of giving a *logos* from within the framework of one's beliefs, attitudes, and commitments, we can grasp a further crucial aspect of the significance of Augustine's position. As we have noted, Socratic philosophy can take many different possible forms. But insofar as they all share the basic dialectical method of Socratic inquiry, and all see the nature of philosophy as the quest for greater self-knowledge rather than the acquisition of final certainty, every variant of Socratic philosophy upholds the thesis that one must believe in order to understand. We can see why Socratic thought has this feature by recalling the basically ad hominem dimension of the method of *elenchus*. On the Socratic view one cannot help but stand on one's prereflective beliefs and experiences if one seeks to make progress in rational inquiry. How could one seek to know oneself and test the coherence of one's whole self without starting off with those fundamental beliefs and values that define who one is? The purpose of rational inquiry in this context is not to determine a set of indubitable starting points from which to conduct one's life, but to clarify first of all just what one really believes and then test whether one's fundamental beliefs can function coherently in the context of one's other beliefs as well as in one's life. The rationality one seeks is inevitably shaped by the character of the person whose life is being examined, since it is always a particular person, with his or her particular views and preferences, who does the seeking. In this respect the Augustinian seeker is unique only in terms of the kind of faith and love that characterizes who he or she is. Every Socratic thinker must believe in something, must stand for something, or else he or she possesses no self to understand critically, let alone to confront through dialectical inquiry. Socratic philosophy may well posit final knowledge as an ideal, but the method of self-examination is invariably fallibilistic.

Our analysis of the Socratic dimension of Augustine's thought serves to help us see how an Augustinian would respond to the kind of charge a modern evidentialist might well make against Augustine's faith-based epistemology. Let us consider an evidentialist accusation made by the quintessentially modern skeptical philosopher Bertrand Russell against the Augustinian dimension of the philosophy of Thomas Aquinas. Interestingly enough, what Russell objects to in the Thomistic philosophy—that it begins its process of rational inquiry already committed to certain truths in faith—would from a Socratic viewpoint simply be the unavoidable limitation of all human philosophy. Russell contends:

> There is little of the true philosophic spirit in Aquinas. He does not, like the Platonic Socrates, set out to follow wherever the argument may lead. He is not engaged in an inquiry, the result of which it is impossible to know in advance. Before he begins to philosophize, he already knows the truth; it is declared in the Catholic faith. If he can find apparently rational arguments for some parts of the faith, so much the better; if he cannot, he need only fall back on revelation. The finding of arguments for a conclusion given in advance is not philosophy, but special pleading. I cannot, therefore, feel that he deserves to be put on a level with the best philosophers either of Greece or of modern times.[70]

The Socratic and Augustinian reply to Russell would be to call him to greater self-knowledge about the role of special pleading in all philosophical discourses—an element rather evident, at least to some readers, in Russell's own

---

70. Bertrand Russell, *A History of Western Philosophy* (New York: Simon & Schuster, 1945), 463.

works. The reply, in other words, would be to note how each and every instance of philosophical thinking, from a Socratic perspective, involves some form of "special pleading." The factor that makes all the difference for assessing the rational integrity of the varieties of philosophical argumentation is not the presence or absence of special pleading, but the willingness or openness on the part of those presenting their arguments to examine their own presuppositions. Hence while Russell may well be justified in protesting against a religious, blind faith that abhors the probing light of reason, his insistence that philosophical inquiry from the beginning put aside all faith is itself from a Socratic perspective a naive and entirely unreasonable philosophical stance. Ironically, in making such a charge against Thomas Aquinas, Russell exhibits unfortunate ignorance not only of the conditions of rational thought in general, but also of the inevitably uncertain commitments guiding his own methodology. In essence, from a Socratic perspective, Russell's modern skeptical objection amounts to a violation of the Delphic Oracle: in making such a protest, Russell exhibits his lack of *sophrosune*.

In my analysis thus far, I have sought to explain the meaning of two fundamental tenets of Augustinianism: "*credo ut intellegam*" (I believe in order to understand) and "*fides quaerens intellectum*" (faith seeking understanding). I have focused on these aspects of Augustine's thought both because of their fundamental importance for Augustine's conception of faith and reason and because I wish to show that it is in precisely these two respects that Pascal should be seen as an Augustinian. Spelling out in detail just what it means to understand the *Pensées* as a work within the Augustinian tradition will be my primary task in chapters 3 and 4. For now, I would like to provide an introductory sketch of the basic contours of Pascal's Augustinian commitments.

Blaise Pascal: Gadfly of Port Royal

Following Augustine, Pascal insists that to attain a rational understanding of God, one must first turn to God in loving faith. The Augustinian declaration "*credo ut intellegam*" envisions a form of rationality in which cognition and affection—or put more precisely, intellectual perception and unselfish love—are inseparable. In Pascal's thinking, this Augustinian fusion of intellect and love is most evident in his doctrine of the heart as the proper faculty for a genuine apprehension of God. Speaking of the heart as the source of love, Pascal remarks:

> I say that it is natural for the heart to love the universal being or itself, according to its allegiance, and it hardens itself against either as it chooses. You have rejected one and kept the other. Is it reason that makes you love yourself?[71]

71. Blaise Pascal, *Pensées*, trans. A. J. Krailsheimer (Harmondsworth: Penguin, 1966), frg. 423.

It is the heart which perceives God and not the reason. That is what faith is:
God perceived by the heart, not by the reason.[72]

As Augustine did before him, Pascal portrays his faith not as the conclusion of
an argument but as a loving response to God. One no more comes to love God
through a process of rational proof than one pursues self-interest only after
reasoning that it is prudent to do so. As we shall see, in denying that love of
self or of God is the logical conclusion of an argument based on reason, Pascal
does not mean to suggest that faith is irrational or that reasoning about one's
faith is improper. Rather Pascal wishes to clarify that faith must be a response
of approval and desire, of affirmation and love, which is as much a matter of
what one feels as what one thinks. Thus it is that Pascal reasons in an extended
reflection on the difference between the two orders of knowledge—derivative
knowledge acquired by reasoning and knowledge of first principles grasped
through the heart—that "principles are felt, propositions are proved."[73] We
feel first principles inasmuch as we find ourselves either drawn to them or actually believing them involuntarily. We believe in space and motion naturally
rather than as the result of rational artifice. We pursue our own self-interest
so naturally that we often find it difficult not to, even if we reason that we
should not do so. Similarly, Pascal thinks that under certain circumstances,
one will naturally find oneself passionately drawn to embrace God. While
belief in God is neither universal nor entirely involuntary for Pascal, it is still
natural and rational. How Pascal defends this thesis further reveals the deeply
Augustinian orientation of his thinking.

Let us at this point consider how Pascal characterizes the paradoxical condition of human life: to be human, he contends, is to yearn naturally for a
self-unity that we cannot achieve through our meager faculties. The greatness
of human nature lies in our self-consciousness and in our capacity to project
the perfect ideals of goodness, knowledge, and true happiness. But while our
nature bears these marks of greatness, it utterly fails on its own to carry us
to their fulfillment. Ironically, our wretchedness is the natural shadow of our
greatness; we suffer only because we are great enough to become wretched.
Pascal's case for faith hinges on this portrayal of human life. Pascal hopes
that those who can be brought to acknowledge the paradoxical nature of our
existence can be brought to a loving and rational faith in Christ, for, like Augustine, Pascal envisions faith as the rational remedy for our basic existential
affliction. In a sense, Pascal's paradox argument is a detailed articulation of
the vision of faith and reason inherent in Augustine's narrative of conversion. For Augustine, conversion to faith makes sense only as one sees the
affliction for which grace is the remedy. Similarly, Pascal will make his case

72. Ibid., frg. 424.
73. Ibid., frg. 110.

for the reasonableness of faith contingent on his own account of our human brokenness. Yet Pascal no more thinks that he is constructing an intellectual proof compelling to all thinkers than does Augustine; instead, Pascal seeks to bring about in his reader the prior awareness of our paradoxical nature, without which one will not see the reasonableness of Pascal's case for faith. For Pascal, in order to understand why faith makes sense in one's life, one must humbly acknowledge one's need to be healed. But acknowledging this need becomes fully possible only as one confronts the message of Christ; the true understanding of why faith in Christ makes sense comes only as one feels drawn to Christ in love. The heart is necessary for faith because it is through our hearts that we acknowledge our plight and our need for divine healing. Thus, as with Augustine, in order to understand one must first believe.

It is no coincidence that both Augustine and Pascal react with hostility to purely philosophical efforts to know God. Augustine attacks the Manichees and Neoplatonists essentially for the same reason: he comes to believe that both schools of thought are guilty of intellectual pride, of seeking through reason alone—apart from grace—the goal of salvation. Of his previous interest with the rationalism of the Manichees, Augustine writes in *De Utilitate Credendi* (1.2):

> It is then my purpose to prove to you, if I can, that the Manichees profanely and rashly inveigh against those who following the authority of the Catholic Faith, before they are able to gaze upon the Truth, which the pure mind beholds, are by believing forearmed, and prepared for God Who is about to give them light. For you know, Honoratus, that for no other reason we fell in with such men, than because they used to say that, apart from all terror of authority, by pure and simple reason, they would lead within to God, and set free from all error those who were willing to be their hearers. For what else constrained me, during nearly nine years, spurning the religion which had been set in me from a child by my parents, to be a follower and diligent hearer of those men, save that they said that we are alarmed by superstition, and are commanded to have faith before reason, but that they urge no one to have faith without having first discussed and made clear the truth?[74]

In a similar vein, Augustine rejects Neoplatonism. In a classic statement of his rejection of Neoplatonism because of its presumption to attain the highest good through human efforts alone, Augustine says:

> Now that I had read the books of the Platonists and had been set by them towards the search for a truth that is incorporeal, I came to see Your invisible things which are understood by the things that are made. I was at a standstill, yet I felt what through the darkness of my mind I was not able actually to see; I was certain that You are and that You are infinite, but not as being diffused through

---

74. *Advantage of Believing*, in Bourke, *The Essential Augustine*, 28–29.

space whether finite or infinite: that You truly are and are ever the same, not in any part or by any motion different or otherwise; and I knew that all other things are from You from the simple fact that they are at all. Of these things I was utterly certain, yet I had not the strength to enjoy You. I talked away as if I knew a great deal; but if I had not sought the way to You in Christ our Saviour, I would have come not to instruction but to destruction. For I had begun to wish to appear wise, and this indeed was the fullness of my punishment; and I did not weep for my state, but was badly puffed up with my knowledge. Where was that charity which builds us up on the foundation of humility, which is Christ Jesus? Or when would those books have taught me that? Yet I think it was Your will that I should come upon these books before I had made study of the Scriptures, that it might be impressed on my memory how they had affected me: so that, when I later should have become responsive to You through Your Books with my wounds healed by the care of Your fingers, I might be able to discern the difference that there is between presumption and confession, between those who see what the goal is but do not see the way, and [those who see] the Way, which leads to that country of blessedness, which we are meant not only to know but to dwell in.[75]

Both passages reveal Augustine the Christian philosopher looking back on his pre-Christian intellectual experience. What he sees in Manicheism and Neoplatonism reflects what he perceives in his own personal odyssey: a soul in unrest unable to find healing because of its proud refusal to see the limits of reason. Essentially, for Augustine pure reason alone will not bring us to the goal philosophy seeks, because reason alone cannot heal the pride inherent in an errant, selfish will. What Augustine rejects, of course, is not the goodness of reason per se, but the proud exercise of reason apart from faith. Augustine attacks such philosophical arrogance in much the same way that Pascal rejects modern proofs for the existence of God as "useless and sterile."[76] Contrasting the God of the philosophers with the God of Scripture, Pascal remarks:

The Christian's God does not consist merely of a God who is the author of mathematical truths and the order of the elements. . . . But the God of Abraham, the God of Isaac, the God of Jacob, the God of the Christians is a God of love

75. Augustine, *Confessions*, 7.20.

76. Pascal, *Pensées*, frg. 449. It is worth noting here the current position of the so-called reformed epistemologists, such as Plantinga, that theistic belief is properly basic is essentially Augustinian. One might go so far as to describe modern evidentialists as guilty of "Manicheism." At least it is clear in Augustine's discussion above that he is well aware of the evidentialist strategy and that he opposes it on the grounds that it reverses the proper priority of faith and reason. Augustine attacks this reversed priority not simply because it indicates an epistemic confusion, but because what underlies it is a prideful ignorance of our need for grace. In making this spiritual diagnosis of those who wish to attain God through reason apart from faith, Augustine draws on his own spiritual journey for perfection that led him through successive phases of Manicheism, skepticism, and Platonism. For Augustine's own confession of pride inherent in his "Platonic" quest for wisdom, see *Confessions*, 7.20 and *City of God*, 19.4.

and consolation; he is a God who fills the soul and the heart of those whom he possesses; he is a God who makes them inwardly aware of their wretchedness and his infinite mercy: who unites himself with them in the depths of their soul: who fills it with humility, joy, confidence, and love: who makes them incapable of having any other end but him.[77]

People cannot come to God through "reason alone," Pascal insists, because knowledge of the true God requires a loving affirmation of God and his plan for salvation; as a result, Pascal condemns the modern philosophical enterprise of proving the existence of God on purely rational foundations, which set aside matters of the heart, and presuming to reach God through a dispassionate meditation on clear and distinct ideas. In opposing Descartes in particular on this matter, Pascal means not to defend a Christian version of fideism—the view, as Penelhum says, that faith and reason "are so disparate that faith is not undermined, but strengthened, if we judge that reason can give it no support"—but to object, on Augustinian grounds, to a philosophical form of apologetics that divorces rationality from affection and the dispositions of the will.[78] For Pascal as for Augustine, rational understanding of God cannot precede the assent of

77. Ibid.
78. The characterization of Christian fideism I have quoted here is from Penelhum (*God and Skepticism*, ix). It is with respect to the question of Pascal's fideism that I find myself in disagreement with Penelhum's fine analysis. According to Penelhum, Pascal embraces the fideistic position that the spheres of faith and reason are separate; Pascal is a Christian fideist, Penelhum contends, insofar as he sees the skeptical attack on reason, and especially on natural theology, as playing a very positive role in establishing the authority of faith. We grasp the proper authority of faith, in other words, precisely when we see that it needs no support or assistance from reason at all. As Penelhum observes, "The insistence that faith needs no justification from reason, but is the judge of reason and its pretensions, is usually called Fideism" (ibid., 1). For a further discussion of Pascal and fideism, see chapter 4.
I do not think that it is helpful to portray Pascal as a fideist per se because it suggests misleadingly that Pascal is not committed to the project of showing in some sense how Christian faith is profoundly rational. It is true that Pascal speaks disparagingly of one kind of rational attempt to support faith—namely modern natural theology. But here Pascal is primarily seeking to expose the folly of trying to find God apart from a loving surrender of the heart (see *Pensées*, frgs. 449 and 781). Pascal's quarrel is not with those who seek to make a rational case for faith but with those who seek to know God as a philosophical abstraction rather than a loving and forgiving God of grace. Furthermore, Pascal does not think that faith needs the support of natural theology in order to be rational. He suggests that those who think so lack self-knowledge. Penelhum certainly does not overlook Pascal's insistence on the place of the heart in knowing God. So he writes, "It is Pascal's passionate contention that an honest understanding of man's predicament can only come from the standpoint that God's grace makes available to us in faith" (*God and Skepticism*, 63). I think that it is more illuminating to place Pascal in the Augustinian tradition that holds that one must first believe in order to understand. The key advantage to doing so is that here we can more easily appreciate how Pascal could attack the efforts of the abstract philosophers and nevertheless seek to show the rational integrity and superiority of faith over skepticism. Put simply, Pascal rejects the modern evidentialist stance that assumes that one must first understand (on the basis of evidential reasoning) in order to believe, but accepts the

faith, because without the love and humility that accompany genuine faith one lacks those very conditions necessary for the growth of understanding.

Augustine and Pascal share not only a common faith but, more important for this discussion, also a similar commitment to a doctrine of reason in which love plays an indispensable role. Both thinkers defend what we might term "love's reason" or "rational love." They envision a kind of understanding in which reason is not unmoved and love is not blind. As Augustine remarks in *De Diversis Quaestionibus LXXXIII*, "no good is completely known which is not completely loved," so Pascal can say, "Truth is so obscured nowadays and lies so well established that unless we love the truth we shall never recognize it."[79]

Yet before we can make sense of Pascal's conception of rational love, we must develop our analysis of Pascal's views on reason, doubt, and faith by observing how in the *Pensées* Pascal sets before his readers the paradoxical nature of our most fundamental and basic beliefs.[80] All people, he contends, naturally and inevitably affirm a number of first principles that we can neither establish as luminously self-certifying nor actually doubt, even though we may on intellectual grounds perceive their uncertainty.[81] For Pascal as for Hume, the recognition that we must assent to fundamental principles that we cannot render certain affords us an essential insight into our human nature, one that

---

Augustinian call of "faith seeking understanding." Pascal is not a fideist, then, because he in no way recommends a life of faith opposed to all rational inquiry and argumentation.

79. Pascal, *Pensées*, frg. 739. Of the essential spirit of Augustine's philosophy, Gilson remarks:

> Saint Augustine's interest in the philosophical life was awakened by his reading of the *Hortensius*, a dialogue of Cicero which has since been lost. From that day on, he was consumed with the love of wisdom, and as time went on, he thought of this discovery as his first step on the way of sorrows which was to lead him to God. This is a point of prime importance if we are to understand Augustine, for in his doctrine wisdom, the object of philosophy, is always identified with happiness. He wants to find the kind of good whose possession will satisfy every desire and ensure peace. Such thorough-going Eudaemonism can be explained by the fact that Augustine always regarded philosophy as something quite different from the speculative pursuit of a knowledge of nature. He was concerned most of all with the problem of his own destiny. For him, the important thing was to strive for self-knowledge and to learn what must be done in order to be better and, if possible, to be happy. (*The Christian Philosophy of Saint Augustine*, 3)

As a description of why humans ought to philosophize, Gilson's fine statement would apply equally well to Pascal.

80. My understanding of Pascal's thought owes a great debt to Penelhum's *God and Skepticism* (see esp. 62–87). I have also benefited from the following studies: Diogenes Allen, *Three Outsiders* (Cambridge, MA: Cowley, 1983), 15–51; J. H. Broome, *Pascal* (London: Edward Arnold, 1965), 134–201; Roger Hazelton, *Blaise Pascal* (Philadelphia: Westminster, 1974), 110–45; Peter Kreeft, *Christianity for Modern Pagans: Pascal's Pensées—Edited, Outlined, and Explained* (San Francisco: Ignatius, 1993); and Thomas V. Morris, *Making Sense of It All: Pascal and the Meaning of Life* (Grand Rapids: Eerdmans, 1992).

81. Pascal, *Pensées*, frgs. 110, 131.

both the Cartesian foundationalist and the Pyrrhonist obfuscate. The position Pascal endorses requires us to see how the conflict between the skeptic and the Cartesian leads us beyond both these alternatives to the resolution of faith. Faith, for Pascal, plays a role both in our natural believing and in our more specifically religious believing in a transcendent, loving God. More importantly, these two levels of faith for Pascal are themselves intimately related, for it is by grasping our natural state of holding certain fundamental beliefs in faith that Pascal thinks we are prepared to see the reasonableness of—and then can honestly seek—higher faith in God. Basically, then, Pascal's case for theistic belief proceeds on three levels. First, Pascal shows what is wrong with both the Cartesian and Pyrrhonist strategies; second, he describes how people must live by a kind of natural faith; and third, as a consequence of having worked through these prior two levels, he seeks to lead his readers to the affirmation of Christian faith. Let us now turn to examining more closely each step in this argumentative progression.

The first level of apologetic argument for Pascal centers on the debate between Cartesianism and Pyrrhonism. Pascal intends to teach us how each philosophical position is unsustainable, since in fact each succumbs to the dialectical refutation presented by the other. Thus Pascal hopes to lead us dialectically to a third position, one that can explain both why the original two philosophical stances had to fail and how, in contrast, this position is not susceptible to their mutually opposing refutations. Concerning the dialectical standoff between the Cartesian and the skeptic, Pascal remarks: "I pause at the dogmatist's only strong point, which is that we cannot doubt natural principles if we speak sincerely and in all good faith. To which the sceptics reply, in a word, that uncertainty as to our origin entails uncertainty as to our nature. The dogmatists have been trying to answer that ever since the world began."[82]

With elegant clarity this passage sums up Pascal's dissatisfaction with the classic conflict between radical ancient skepticism and philosophical dogmatism—which is to say, the view that reason can lead us to final, certain knowledge. First of all, Pascal rejects the dogmatist project, and in particular the Cartesian form of this project, which seeks to establish an indubitable set of first principles. The Cartesian project cannot succeed, Pascal notes, because, as the ancient Pyrrhonists have observed, once we raise doubts concerning the origin of reason itself, there is no indubitable authority or criterion available to us to guarantee the veracity of reason's own intuitive principles. Since "there is no certainty apart from faith as to whether man was created by a good God, an evil demon, or just by chance," Pascal asserts, "it is a matter of doubt, depending on our origin, whether these innate principles are true, false, or uncertain."[83] In one crucial respect, however, Pascal finds the Cartesian

---

82. Pascal, *Pensées*, frg. 131.
83. Ibid.

outlook to have merit. While Pascal denies that any of our first principles are beyond all possible rational doubt, he insists that on a practical level we cannot suspend our belief in them and voluntarily remain in a state of cognitive neutrality. Pressing this point against the Pyrrhonian side, Pascal says, "No one can go that far, and I maintain that a perfectly genuine sceptic has never existed. Nature backs up helpless reason and stops it going so wildly astray."[84] Here we see one of the most striking similarities between Pascal's and Hume's theories of belief. Both thinkers emphasize that what preserves us against the excesses of extreme intellectual doubt is not reason's discovery of indubitable truths, but our nonrational propensity to hold certain basic, nonderivative convictions about ourselves and the world we inhabit. (Here, of course, "nonrational" means "not derived from reason"; it does not mean "irrational.") For Pascal, this discovery of our nonrational self leads to the formulation of the doctrine of the heart as the source of legitimate faith. It is the place of the heart that Pascal thinks has been overlooked by both Cartesian and Pyrrhonian stances. Indeed, that "the heart has its reasons, of which reason knows nothing"[85] proves to be Pascal's essential insight leading us, he hopes, to rethink in an even more radical way the terms of the quarrel between dogmatist and skeptic. To appreciate how this is so, we must turn our focus to Pascal's account of natural faith.

According to Pascal, people hold a wide array of beliefs through a kind of natural faith. At least some of these beliefs we hold by faith are essential for our continued survival as natural beings. For example, Pascal thinks that our self-awareness as to whether we are sleeping or awake is rooted in a natural faith rather than in some process of experiential reasoning: "[N]o one can be sure, apart from faith, whether he is sleeping or waking, because when we are asleep we are just as firmly convinced that we are awake as we are now."[86] As Pascal goes on to add, it is logically possible that what we experience as being awake may only be "another sleep slightly different from the first." To this extent the skeptic is right in denying that we can have certain knowledge that our waking experiences are true rather than illusory. Yet we will by nature, Pascal believes, persist in interpreting our waking perceptions as prima facie veridical. Our attitude of implicit trust in them cannot be rationally justified by means of evidential reason without relying on the evidence of our waking perceptions in the first place. That we must trust in faith what we cannot prove beyond doubt to be reliable is simply a basic fact of our human nature.

We might note one crucial difference between Pascal's doctrine of natural faith and Hume's doctrine of natural beliefs. Unlike Hume, Pascal wishes to treat our nonrational nature as a source of knowledge, though not, of

---

84. Ibid.
85. Ibid., frg. 423.
86. Ibid., frg. 131.

course, the sort of absolute knowledge sought after by Descartes. Pascal says:

> We know the truth not only through our reason but also through our heart. It is through the latter that we know first principles, and reason which has nothing to do with it, tries in vain to refute them. . . . We know that we are not dreaming, but, however unable we may be to prove it rationally, our inability proves nothing but the weakness of our reason, and not the uncertainty of all our knowledge, as they maintain. For knowledge of first principles, like space, time, motion, number, is as solid as any derived through reason, and it is on such knowledge coming from the heart and instinct, that reason has to depend and base all its arguments.[87]

In Pascal's view, then, we know both through reason and through the heart. What we know through reason is the result of what we have demonstrated on the basis of underived, first principles. The first principles mentioned in this passage all appear to be fundamental presuppositions for our everyday experience of physical reality: we naturally interpret our waking sensory experiences as informing us of a spatial-temporal plurality of objects capable of motion. Since all our empirical reasoning relies on this framework, insofar as the framework provides us with a context of interpretation for all of our sensory experience, our rationally derived, empirical conclusions can be no more certain than those principles of natural faith that provide their context. Thus to the extent that we have knowledge of physical reality at all, it is perfectly appropriate to speak of knowing these first principles, even though reason cannot provide more basic evidence to justify them. So for Pascal the heart is actually a legitimate source of knowledge. More importantly, that "the heart has its reasons of which reason knows nothing" means in this context that the heart has its own "rationality." Whereas Hume insists, at least in the first *Enquiry*, on maintaining a sharp division between the judgments of reason and those of our nonrational nature, Pascal wishes to call attention to the essential explanatory role played by our first principles. Although we hold these through faith rather than with certainty, we can affirm that they make possible the everyday judgments on which we depend for our basic natural existence. And insofar as we rely on these principles of the heart in order to act and think as humans, Pascal accords them the status of being proper objects of human knowledge. Just as he thinks that our first principles are proper objects of knowledge, Pascal holds that our first principles are rationally justified, in the sense that we are not misusing our cognitive faculties in holding them, even though they are not generated through any process of evidential reasoning—the cognitive activity Pascal typically refers to as "reason." Thus for Pascal it is both natural and rational to hold certain beliefs in faith. Having come to this

---

87. Ibid., frg. 110.

moment of self-understanding, we are at the brink of a self-transformation, which Pascal sees as an indispensable preparation for the affirmation of Christian faith. But what is it about the discovery of the place of the heart in human believing that has the power to transform our innermost lives?

Pascal's answer is that our progress through the classical struggle between dogmatic philosophy and Pyrrhonism to the recognition of the authority of the heart should lead us to the further recognition of the essential paradox of our human condition. As an initial step, he notes that the peculiar quarrel between Cartesianism and skepticism reveals our own fundamental inadequacy to control our lives and attain our own happiness through our natural abilities to reason or doubt. Consider how, albeit in radically different ways, both the philosophical dogmatist and the extreme skeptic seek to secure a way of life where the individual inquirer through his or her own powers can achieve fulfillment. For the Cartesian, the path must be one of solitary, individual meditation on one's private, clear, and distinct ideas. For the Pyrrhonist, one labors toward *ataraxia*, a state of inner freedom from mental unrest and suffering achieved through an individual process of the private suspense of judgment regarding all questions of ultimate truth. In starkest contrast, Pascal seeks to help us discern a human existence suspended precariously between what the heart yearns for and what our human powers alone permit us to achieve. Rather than gain access to truth or psychic health through our own faculties, we instead experience the discomforting truth that we are caught between the ideal happiness, knowledge, and goodness we desire, ideals legitimately yearned for by the Cartesian outlook, and the limited and inadequate resources we actually possess for reaching them.[88] Pascal thinks that our encounter with this disunified self ought to perplex us and bring us to an acute sense of our suffering rather than of our prospects for autonomous contentment. Setting us before ourselves as we really are, as "dual creatures," Pascal declares, "What sort of freak then is man! How novel, how monstrous, how chaotic, how paradoxical, how prodigious! Judge of all things, feeble earthworm, repository of truth, sink of doubt and error, glory and refuse of the universe."[89] Like Hume, Pascal here connects true self-knowledge with awareness of our imperfections. In a markedly un-Humean manner, however, Pascal insists that our humbled assessment of our own faculties produces a greater sense of disharmony and perplexity: we see in ourselves a riddle with no natural solution. In this respect, our self-knowledge reveals both our limits and our heart's deepest longing to transcend them. Yet if Pascal is right, we cannot without self-deception deny either our limits or our heart's yearning to transcend them. According to Pascal, what we most fundamentally do not understand is ourselves.

88. For Pascal's presentation of this aspect of our "dual humanity," see esp. ibid., frgs. 131, 148, 149, 429–431, and 446–450.
89. Ibid., frg. 131.

For Pascal, the pursuit of self-knowledge has both a negative and a positive aspect. What makes this pursuit negative is that it throws us into self-perplexity and can often cause pain and frustration. But just as with the Socratic art of exposing inconsistency within one's innermost beliefs, Pascal's conception of self-examination is positive as well as negative. The two aspects are bound together. Pascal thinks that the positive result can be achieved only through the negative experience of one's own incompleteness. Our agonizing moment of self-discovery occasions our further admission of our need for some divine answer to our paradoxical existence. To confess this need, to acknowledge our own inability to complete ourselves, is to humble our proud determination to live as autonomous persons. According to Pascal, it is only through the renouncing of our self-centeredness and our intellectual pride that we can find a genuine solution to our paradoxical condition. So Pascal remarks, "Know then, proud man, what a paradox you are to yourself. Be humble, impotent reason! Be silent, feeble nature! Learn that man infinitely transcends man, hear from your master your own true condition, which is unknown to you. Listen to God."[90] On this description of the road to theistic faith, we find God through a suffering awareness of our own wretchedness; we turn to God not through a rational proof but through the heart's desire for a satisfactory resolution to our existential predicament.

Pascal defends Christian faith by leading his reader to the recognition of the intelligibility and attractiveness of the basic Christian teaching of our inevitable misery apart from God. As a Christian apologist, Pascal describes the underlying strategy of his evangelical program as follows:

> Order: Men despise religion. They hate it and are afraid it may be true. The cure for this is first to show that religion is not contrary to reason, but worthy of reverence and respect.
>
> Next, make it attractive, make good men wish it were true, and then show that it is.
>
> Worthy of reverence because it really understands human nature.
>
> Attractive because it promises true good.[91]

This passage is especially significant in illuminating the subtle interrelationship in Pascal's thought between reason and faith. Pascal begins by observing that many people abhor religion and that at least part of their opposition to it is that they would simply prefer it not to be true. For Pascal, this natural aversion to faith is part of our wretched condition that needs an effective response. But an effective restoration of self, one that will bring about a genuine cure, cannot ignore the rational side of our nature and appeal only to our heart's desire for a final good that offers us the fulfillment we cannot find in the lesser

90. Ibid.
91. Ibid., frg. 12.

goods of earthly lives. To show how communion with a God of love would be an attractive option is certainly part of Pascal's program. But Pascal insists as well that a valid religious solution to human life must agree with reason in two respects. First, its teaching must not be rationally incoherent; it must not be "contrary to reason." Second, it must provide an account of human existence that makes rational sense of our basic predicament; it must be worthy of "reverence." We might well say that what Pascal demands is neither a rational proof nor a blind faith, but a religious solution that properly appeals to the whole person, to reason as well as to the heart. Let us note here that for Pascal faith is eminently rational even though it goes beyond reason. Faith is beyond reason in the evidential sense that it is not a conclusion derived from a neutral evidential basis of logical or empirical premises. Yet faith in God is rational in the sense that it provides the best explanation of our human condition and enables us to become the kind of creatures we are designed to be, to realize our nature as God's rational creatures.

Despite the rational cogency of faith, Pascal thinks humans spend an immense portion of their lives fleeing from rather than facing honestly their inner awareness of inadequacy and distress.[92] To make the Christian story appealing, Pascal must first effect in his audience the recognition of our inner condition and in particular demonstrate our natural incapacity to heal our own discomfort. The message of grace will not appear attractive and worthy of reverence until the hearer has the self-knowledge necessary to grasp his or her paradoxical condition. But this self-knowledge itself requires a certain humility that comes from the heart—namely, the humble acknowledgment that one really cannot make straight the crooked reality of one's psyche. Thus it is that Pascal's apologetic strategy cannot simply appeal to a set of premises that we should expect to be acknowledged as indubitable by all rational people. On the contrary, Pascal's hearer must become a certain kind of person, a person who honestly and humbly acknowledges his or her inadequacy in order to be able to perceive the truth and goodness of the Christian message.

If Pascal's rendering of the human condition is correct, it follows that we can know ourselves only through the heart. To understand how the heart makes self-knowledge possible, we need to attend both to the object of self-knowledge, to the truth about ourselves that Pascal is concerned to reveal, and to how we gain access to this truth, where the issue is not the object of knowledge but the state of apprehension in which we come to perceive it. The fundamental truth of our humanity is what Pascal often refers to as our duality, that state of yearning to possess certain ideals—in particular, goodness and knowledge—without the natural means to attain them. Being in this mode of having and not having causes us inner agony and makes the heart feel a deep sense of lack and dissatisfaction. But it is always possible

92. Ibid., frgs. 132–39.

and often more pleasurable, Pascal thinks, to hide from ourselves our true condition. Thus we tend to conceal the natural unrest of our hearts and divert our self-conscious gaze to any number of external matters, because the revelation of our inner suffering forces us to acknowledge ourselves as flawed and unhappy. To look at ourselves truly, then, is more than just to perceive some neutral set of properties. A Cartesian, introspective gaze over the field of our supposedly clear and distinct ideas is clearly not what Pascal would consider as self-knowledge. Indeed, Pascal's analysis of the paradoxical self is undoubtedly intended in part as a serious critique of Descartes's purely intellectual account of self-awareness. What Pascal requires for successful self-inquiry is the acknowledgment of one's troubled psyche; this admission of one's inner reality is certainly neither dispassionate nor morally neutral. To admit one's psychic disorder requires that one see the facts of one's psyche with a particular disposition of the heart—namely, humility. Only a truly humble response to the self one observes introspectively allows us to interpret who we are truthfully. Through pride we can escape the painful awareness of our duality and either ignore our unrest or refuse to accept that alone we are incapable of healing it. The point is that what we see inside ourselves depends in part not on the data we encounter but on the prior orientation of our heart to interpret what the data means.

Finally, by appreciating the role humility plays in Pascal's account of self-knowledge, we can understand why Pascal thinks that it is natural for people to embrace faith. Our humble acknowledgment of our own inadequacy prepares our hearts to respond to the Christian story with the necessary humility. Pascal believes that only those who realize their need for healing are ready to make a loving assent to God's call for reconciliation. Just as our hearts make it possible to relate truthfully to ourselves, so it is through humility that the heart can respond truthfully to God in love. It is only through acknowledging our own need for healing that we can see how a message of grace makes sense. Our proper response to the Christian witness of grace is to love God in return for the love he offers in Christ. So Pascal, again in a radically un-Cartesian manner, states, "It is the heart which perceives God and not the reason. That is what faith is: God perceived by the heart, not by the reason."[93] Faith comes from the heart because the heart is the source of our love and it is natural for us, Pascal says, to love God once we realize so forcefully why our lives are miserable without him. At the same time, for Pascal, as for Augustine, humans lack the power to love God adequately—that is, without the perverse presence of human selfishness. Faith in God is natural, but we can attain it finally only by receiving faith and love as gifts of grace.

In asserting that faith must come from the heart rather than reason, Pascal insists that any purely abstract and theoretical assent to God's existence

93. Ibid., frg. 424.

is not true faith; rather, true faith is a loving acknowledgment of God as the only effective source of our heart's fulfillment and cure of our heart's distress. Knowing God becomes possible only through knowing oneself as the kind of creature who needs grace; in both these forms of knowing, the way in which one becomes capable of knowing is a function in part of the heart of the knower. According to Pascal, finally, without humility with respect to ourselves and the love of God, we remain unknowers.

Hume, Pascal, and the Humility of Reason

Let me now summarize Pascal's Augustinian and radically un-Cartesian conception of passionate reason. Following Augustine, Pascal regards the question of what it means to be rational as unanswerable apart from a teleological understanding of the function of human life:

1. To answer the question "What does it mean to be rational?" we must ask the question, "What is the function, or what are the functions, of reason?" Put simply, one thinks or acts rationally when one believes or acts in a way that promotes the proper function of reason.

2. Although the specific functions of reason may well differ markedly depending on the sphere of life in which reason is operating—for example, reasoning in a chemistry experiment may differ in important ways from reasoning in poetry—the general function of reason is to bring us in touch with what is real. This, of course, is a "biased" account of the nature of rationality. That is to say, it is certainly not a neutral description, but instead is one that reflects a teleological conception of what it means to be rational thinkers committed to understanding the nature of an objective reality similar to the one we find defended, for example, in book 4 of Aristotle's *Metaphysics*.

3. In the context of reasoning about the nature of the self and about the reality of human life, we cannot get in touch with or apprehend the truth about what is real without understanding what is the overall *telos* or function of human life. The question "What is the function of reason?" is inseparable from the question "What are people for?"

4. We cannot answer the question "What are people for?"—that is, we cannot understand the *telos* or function of human life—apart from intuitions about ourselves that are available to us only through two basic affections of the heart: humility and love.

5. From the perspective of an honest human inquirer, the humble recognition of the human condition should serve to help us discover that we ultimately desire to know God and abide with God, that it is life with God that alone can afford us our true happiness. Furthermore, our

humble recognition of our own deficiencies should convince us that we cannot through our own efforts alone satisfy our "God-directed" desire. To get in touch with the truth about ourselves—that is, to make sense of ourselves and to become what we yearn to be—we must receive God's grace by which power alone we can realize our proper function.

6. From this humble perspective on the human condition, it is rational to believe an account of the human story that both makes sense of our lives and gives us the power to overcome the human paradox and become fully ourselves. Believing such an account is rational insofar as it enables us to be in touch with what is real, to apprehend the truth about ourselves, and thus fulfill the proper function of our reason.

7. It is thus rational for people seeking to understand the meaning of human life to acknowledge the limits of human evidential reason alone, to seek to receive God's grace by faith, and to believe in God.

On this account of the nature of rationality, the rational person cannot be dispassionate, and his or her reasoning will never be autonomous. This basic conception of passionate reason is central to the philosophies of both Augustine and Pascal and warrants our serious consideration. My overarching goal in this study is to make a convincing case that this Pascalian and Augustinian conception of passionate reason offers a viable cure for our postmodern condition of cultural and intellectual disembeddedness. In defending a Pascalian understanding that the function of human life is to grow in love by believing and abiding in the God of love, I certainly make no pretense to presenting a "purely objective" analysis. The Humean apologist, for example, will find a great deal that is unwise in the position I wish to defend. In fact, the radical differences between the Humean and Pascalian outlooks now appear so deep and far-reaching that it might well seem to us impossible to conceive of any nonarbitrary way to rationally negotiate the disagreements between them. Yet I think one may, with due caution, assess the rational virtues and vices of these two fundamentally opposed outlooks without simply begging the question in favor of one or the other. While one will not be able to rest such a case on any incorrigible proofs, one can evaluate the Pascalian and Humean outlooks Socratically.

When we compare the philosophies of Hume and Pascal, one contrast is unmistakable. For Hume, the self-enlightenment of the moderate philosopher involves rejecting as unwise that very confession of faith in a transcendent, personal God that is essential to Pascal's description of self-enlightenment. It is curious that these two philosophers, equally committed to the virtues of self-knowledge and humility, should come to such radically incompatible conclusions about how to realize these virtues in human life. As we have seen, for both Augustine and Pascal, the question of what it is rational to believe about human life cannot be answered apart from a teleological conception of the proper function both of human life and of human reason within the various spheres of human life. Put simply, Augustine and Pascal think that we cannot answer the question "What is rational to believe?" without wedding such a question to the broader question of "What are people for?" In this way, both the Augustinian and the Pascalian refuse to separate epistemology from metaphysics. Their defense of the rationality of Christian faith turns on three basic convictions: first, that all people naturally seek their fulfillment and completion as humans; second, that the most important function of reason in human life is to help us by means of questioning and critical reflection to attain our natural end, which is to love God, neighbor, and self in proper order; and third, that apart from the cross by which we gain access to God's power and grace, reason cannot fulfill its proper function. Based on these crucial beliefs, both Augustine and Pascal conclude that it is "reasonable to go beyond reason."[94]

As I have argued in this chapter, a very significant part of what makes Hume and Pascal dialectical in their thinking is found in their shared understanding of what it means to do philosophy. Philosophy for both Pascal and Hume must find its proper place if it is to serve our fallible human nature rather than violate it. Pascal and Hume insist that we are by nature beings who must believe but who cannot be certain. Of these beliefs that are essential to our well-being, only some can be shown to be based on "reason." For Hume, beliefs are based on reason when they are either immediate reports of, or inferences directly inferable from, our impressions. For Pascal, only beliefs inferred from more basic logical or sensory intuitions can be said to derive from "reason." Both thinkers basically agree that only beliefs that are supported by hard evidence

94. To avoid confusion, I should clarify that my account of Socratic rationality is not intended to answer the important epistemological question of what constitutes justification of our beliefs in general. The Socratic conception of rationality is best seen as articulating the intellectual virtue of being rational in the practice of *elenchus*. Socrates clearly seems to hold that every capable adult ought to spend some time engaging in serious reflection on the nature of human excellence. But the Socratic method itself presupposes that some of our beliefs are justified in the more general epistemological sense of being well-formed, true beliefs. The Socratic view certainly does not claim, then, that our beliefs themselves are justified only when we are able to give a rigorous account of them in the face of dialectical scrutiny: we do not, in other words, need to be able to show we are justified in holding a given belief in order to be justified in holding it. Nevertheless, for Socrates we must be able to give an account of the nature of the virtues if we claim to know that certain actions are virtuous. To claim to know instances of virtuous actions is to claim to have more than just a well-formed belief; to claim to know what is virtuous is to presume to be the sort of person who can both clarify and defend one's core moral beliefs. Put simply, Socrates' primary concern is with the rationality of people, rather than with the rationality of specific beliefs in isolation from the person who holds them. To that extent, the Socratic account of the virtue of rationality seems more compatible with an externalist than an internalist epistemology. For a fine analysis of the difference between internalism and externalism in epistemology, see William Alston, "Knowledge of God," in *Faith, Reason, and Skepticism*, ed. Marcus Hester (Philadelphia: Temple University Press, 1992), 17–28.

can be said to derive from evidential reason. And they agree that it would be both foolish and impossible to try to conduct one's life solely on the basis of the beliefs supplied to us by finite "reason."

It is especially important to appreciate, however, how both Hume and Pascal work with a second and much more subtle conception of being rational. Both Pascal and Hume employ what is essentially a functional account of human believing, an account that they regard as basic both to human nature and to the proper practice of philosophy. On this less restrictive view of rationality, certain fundamental beliefs can be said to be rational insofar as they permit people to attain their proper *telos*. Pascal and Hume recognize that we must hold certain basic beliefs about ourselves and the world in order to function well as humans. Though both Pascal and Hume often speak of "reason" in a narrow, evidentialist sense, and employ such a restricted conception of reason in a number of their arguments, they make use of a second and more subtle understanding of "being rational" in their arguments about the proper role of philosophy in human life.

Following Socrates, Pascal and Hume contend that the basic purpose of philosophy is to achieve a special form of self-knowledge—a knowledge of who we are that allows us to live wisely a moderate life between the extremes of rational hubris and skeptical indifference. What this means, among other things, is that we recognize the role of the passions in forming our characters and in revealing to us the goods of human life. In discovering this truth about ourselves, we also see how limited is the authority and role of evidential reason in determining our core beliefs. A rational person is one who has attained sufficient self-understanding to see that the end of philosophy is to serve the proper ends of human life. To be rational in this sense is to conform our beliefs not merely to the evidence of our external senses or the deliverances of the logical intellect, but to an inner awareness of the ends and limits of human living. It is by means of this conception of rationality that Pascal defends the Christian faith as "rational" and Hume the "rationality" of the life of the mitigated skeptic in the *Enquiry* and the philosophical theist in the *Natural History*. Despite the significant differences between their stances, both thinkers share a distinctive vision of philosophy as serving the ends of human life. To be wise is to see how reason serves within a larger complex world of desires and passions. The proper office of reason in this sense is to serve as an integral and pivotal part of this whole and not always, so to speak, to rule. Philosophical reason is reflective and critical but not autocratic. It is even at times meant to serve the passions.

In a classic statement of his vision of critical and yet modest rationality, Hume remarks:

> Man is a reasonable being; and as such, receives from science his proper food and nourishment. But so narrow are the bounds of human understanding, that

little satisfaction can be hoped for in this particular, either from the extent or security of his acquisitions. Man is a sociable, no less than a reasonable being: But neither can he always enjoy company agreeable and amusing, or preserve the proper relish for them. Man is also an active being; and from that disposition, as well as from the various necessities of human life, must submit to business and occupation. But the mind requires some relaxation, and cannot always support its bent to care and industry. It seems, then, that nature has pointed out a mixed kind of life as most suitable to the human race, and secretly admonished them to allow none of these biases to *draw* too much, so as to incapacitate them for other occupations and entertainments. Indulge your passion for science, says she, but let your science be human, and such as may have a direct reference to action and society. Abstruse thought and profound researches I prohibit, and will severely punish, by the pensive melancholy which they introduce, by the endless uncertainty in which they involve you, and by the cold reception which your pretended discoveries shall meet with, when communicated. Be a philosopher; but, amidst all your philosophy, be still a man.[95]

Hume speaks here to his eighteenth-century intellectual audience in something of the same way that Socrates does to his Athenian jurors. For both, the life of critical self-reflection is essential. The examined life of the philosopher helps to clarify the circumstances of our ethical problems, to check the passions, and to scrutinize our basic beliefs. But such rational activity must serve the practical ends of life, rather than alienate us from our common humanity. To keep our philosophizing within its proper bounds, we must recognize the severe limits of reason and avoid the sin of excessive pride in the power of reason to achieve knowledge of ultimate matters. For Hume, reason must submit in practical affairs to the authority of our passions; reason must in a sense become passion's slave, lest reason seek to govern human life through its own resources. For Socrates, such language as "reason's slavery" would be quite foreign. But Socrates stresses with the same vehemence as does Hume the need for rational humility.

Indeed, Socrates would not speak of reason's enslavement, but not because he rejects the counsels of the heart. Rather, he would not do so because his own conception of reason is very unmodern. For Socrates, rationality is first and foremost a human virtue, not a property of specific beliefs. To appreciate why this is the case for Socrates, we need to recognize that finally Socratic questioning tests not one or more beliefs, but the whole life of the person who holds these beliefs. Being rational in the Socratic sense is fundamentally a matter of how one lives; one's beliefs are or are not rational in a derivative sense. That rationality is better regarded as a human virtue than as a property of beliefs seems plausible insofar as an adequate account of the content of any particular belief would seem to require tracing the relations of that belief to

95. Hume, *Enquiry*, sec. 1, pp. 8–9.

the attitudes and other beliefs of the person who holds it. This is to say that a belief is rational or irrational not in isolation but in relation to certain key features of the whole person who holds that belief.[96]

A rational person, for Socrates, lives his or her life with intellectual humility and pursues a self-understanding that he or she confesses to be fallible. Here the end of reason is to live well as a rational being who cannot really know with certainty. The proper activity of reasoning is not deductive but circular: the practice of the *elenchus* is to test one's beliefs, desires, feelings, and actions with the aim of becoming a unified, coherent person. In ethics in particular, the primary form of reasoning, then, is recollection, a clarification and trans-formation of what one already believes rather than a demonstration of ethical truths based on some universally agreed upon premises. Unlike Hume, Socrates does not oppose reason to sentiment in such a way that reason itself is inert, for Socratic reason, functioning properly, governs our actions and decisions. Likewise, the Socratic thinker employs reason not to establish proofs or discern the relations of matters of fact, but to subject one's beliefs to the challenge of *elenchus*, in a way that enables one to recollect one's real self. Despite these fundamentally significant contrasts, however, it remains essential for both Socrates and Hume that the philosopher engages in rational reflection in a manner that steers a middle course between the Scylla of autonomous reason and the Charybdis of antiphilosophical skepticism.

Another way to characterize the convergence of Humean and Socratic conceptions of the nature of philosophy would be to note how both thinkers recommend a life of reason situated within the whole of the human psyche, within a complex matrix of beliefs and feelings shaped by one's place in the social order. This inherited, prephilosophical social arena of common life provides the raw material for philosophical reflection. The province of reason is not to step outside this inheritance in order to establish an autonomous system; it is, rather, to clarify, modify, and correct various components of the whole in order to achieve a coherent, stable, and fulfilled life. As I have argued already, such a conception of the proper exercise of reason is essential as well for the Pascalian defense of Christian faith. Like Hume, Pascal argues for a philosophical life that acknowledges the limits of reason and the dependence

---

96. Clearly my remarks in defense of the thesis that we ought to think of rationality pri-marily as a quality of persons, as a kind of epistemic virtue rather than as a property of beliefs, are cursory and unsatisfactory. I am not sure how to defend this view, even though it seems intuitively right to me. Perhaps one could even show, following Aristotle's lead, that beliefs are rational when they are held by rational agents, not that agents are rational when they hold ra-tional beliefs. But I am unsure at present how to construct a good case for such a view. Nothing in my assessment of Hume and Pascal hinges on how we finally conceive of the relationship of the rationality of people and the rationality of their beliefs. For a fine example of virtue-based epistemology, see Linda Zagzebski, "Religious Knowledge and the Virtues of Mind," in *Rational Faith: Catholic Responses to Reformed Epistemology*, ed. Linda Zagzebski (Notre Dame, IN: University of Notre Dame Press, 1993).

of reason on the life of the passions. Both Pascal and Hume contend that philosophical reflection serves the final good of living well according to our real human nature. That they differ so strikingly on the validity of Christian theism, while agreeing so substantially on the proper place of philosophy in human life, should lead us to ask why. The answer to this question, or at least my own best account of the answer, will be the subject of the following three chapters. My account begins with Hume's case against Christian belief. As we shall see, Hume's case against Christianity is as complex and subtle as his conception of philosophical reason.

2

HUME'S SKEPTICISM AND THE WISDOM OF THE HEART

In my discussion of Hume's mitigated skepticism in chapter 1, I argued that Hume must supply an additional premise in order to argue validly that because human reasoning is narrowly confined in matters of fact, true philosophers ought not to inquire into ultimate questions concerning the nature of God or the origin of the universe. At this point, a serious problem confronts Hume in the first *Enquiry*, for Hume recognizes that people cannot, and indeed should not even attempt to, conform their believing to the narrow standard of evidentialist rationality associated with modern foundationalism. In essence, Hume holds that in order to survive, let alone function well in the world, people must hold certain natural beliefs that are rationally insupportable. If people cannot and should not conform their beliefs to the restrictive canons of "scientific," Lockean rationality, can Hume consistently proceed to reject theistic beliefs simply on the grounds that they fail to satisfy such "scientific," rational norms? The mere fact that theists cannot provide sufficient evidential grounding of their religious convictions cannot for Hume justify denying them a legitimate place in human life. To justify his rejection of theistic belief, Hume needs a justified ethics of belief that serves to clarify why rationally unjustifiable *natural* beliefs are permissible, whereas rationally unjustifiable *theistic* ones are not.

To appreciate why Hume refuses to treat theistic beliefs on a par with nonrational, natural beliefs, we need to grasp that Hume, in fact, employs

two criteria in building his case against theistic beliefs. The first is basically an epistemic criterion, stipulating that it is unwise to assent to any
metaphysical beliefs—beliefs, that is, about what really exists—that either
cannot be rationally justified on the basis of empirical evidence or are not
the result of a universal, involuntary mechanism such as those that generate
our natural beliefs. I will designate this one as Hume's epistemic criterion
of metaphysical minimalism. The second criterion is more psychological
than the first: people must especially avoid those unnecessary metaphysical
beliefs that can be shown to create psychic unrest and social turmoil. To say
that a specific metaphysical belief is unnecessary means that it cannot be
inferred from empirical matters of fact and is not an involuntary belief, such
as our natural belief in causal powers or the existence of external objects.
Typically, Hume makes independent use of these two criteria in opposing
theism. In the *Enquiry Concerning Human Understanding*, Hume presupposes the epistemic criterion in assessing the credentials of theistic faith.
In *The Natural History of Religion*, Hume develops a psychopathology
of theistic faith clearly utilizing his psychological criterion. I will argue in
what follows that taken on its own, Hume's epistemic criterion is defective, because it makes rational sense to rely on it only if one has already
presupposed a secular, nontheistic outlook. This defect can be partially
remedied if one accepts Hume's second criterion and also endorses Hume's
diagnosis of the psychological dynamics of faith. In this respect, Hume's
second criterion is both more fundamental and more decisive. I will argue,
however, that Hume's diagnosis of faith in *The Natural History of Religion*
is woefully unsympathetic and narrow-minded. In the final section before
the conclusion of this chapter, I will clarify what is at the heart of Hume's
misdiagnosis of the rationality of theism. Essentially, what Hume overlooks
is the Augustinian conception of the crucial interconnectedness of rationality and love. Both in his diagnosis of the fruits of theism and in his overall
analysis of the relationship between reason and faith Hume fails to perceive
the primacy of love.

Hume's Epistemological Refutation of Theism

> The common man thinks a miracle can just be *seen* to be reported. Quite the
> contrary. One has to be, I was discovering, reasonably sophisticated even to
> perceive the miraculous. It takes experience; otherwise, more miracles would
> be encountered.
>
>   Loren Eiseley, "The Innocent Fox"[1]

1. Loren Eiseley, "The Innocent Fox," in *The Star Thrower* (San Diego: Harcourt Brace,
1978), 57–58.

In the first *Enquiry* Hume relies on an epistemic criterion, one that embraces a preference for "metaphysical minimalism." He does so both in his essay against belief in miracles in section 10 and in his apology for Epicurus in section 11. In each of these discourses, Hume attacks an essential component of traditional Christian theism. Hume's strategy in each essay is basically the same: Christian theism purports to believe in certain transcendent occurrences or facts for which, according to Hume, there is not sufficient empirical evidence. More importantly, Hume argues, since these theistic beliefs lack hard evidence, they are rationally unsupported and should be dismissed. Curiously, Hume appears to see no irony, given his own aversion to Enlightenment rationalism, in promoting this style of anti-theistic reasoning. Consider, for example, how Hume succinctly recounts one of his skeptical arguments opposing belief in miracles:

> Upon the whole, then, it appears, that no testimony for any kind of miracles has ever amounted to a probability, much less a proof; and that, even supposing that it amounted to a proof, it would be opposed by another proof; derived from the very nature of the fact, which it would endeavor to establish. It is experience only, which gives authority to human testimony; and it is the same experience, which assures us of the laws of nature. When, therefore these two kinds of experience are contrary, we have nothing to do but subtract the one from the other, and embrace an opinion, either on the one side or the other, with that assurance which arises from the remainder. But, according to the principle here explained, this subtraction, with regard to all popular religions, amounts to an entire annihilation; and therefore we may establish it as a maxim, that no human testimony can have such force as to prove a miracle, and make it a just foundation for any system of religion.[2]

In assessing the merits of belief in miracles, Hume appears in this passage to rely on the very kind of evidentialist reasoning he unequivocally rejects, as contrary to our human nature, in the context of his defense of our natural beliefs. How do we make sense of Hume's rejection of religious beliefs because we cannot justify them on the basis of empirical evidence, yet also make sense of his defense of nonreligious, natural beliefs despite our inability to justify them by the same kind of evidence? Later, at the close of his essay "Of Miracles," Hume offers the following overall assessment of the rationality of Christian belief:

> So that upon the whole, we may conclude, that the *Christian Religion* not only was at first attended with miracles, but even at this day cannot be believed by any reasonable person without one. Mere reason is insufficient to convince us of its veracity: And whoever is moved by *Faith* to assent to it, is conscious of a continued miracle in his own person, which subverts all the principles of his

2. Hume, *Enquiry*, sec. 10, p. 127.

understanding, and gives him a determination to believe what is most contrary to custom and experience.[3]

It is surely curious that Hume appears in this skeptical assault to be wearing the hat—or perhaps the habit—of the Lockean rationalist who cautions us to proportion our beliefs to the evidence. In constructing his refutation of revealed theology, Hume argues that the "wise man"—by which Hume means a properly functioning human reasoner—"proportions his belief to the evidence."[4] Hume declares that when the rational person confronts putative testimony to a miracle, he or she must adhere to the basic, rational principle of conforming his or her assent and dissent to the weight of the evidence. Can this really be the same Hume, the cautious theist might well ask, who brilliantly undermines the Lockean evidentialist position and defends natural beliefs despite their nonrational status?

The same question arises in the context of section 11, where Hume seeks to undermine the theist's conviction in a benevolent, providential God. Here, especially, Hume condemns as "mere conjecture and hypothesis" the attribution of any characteristics to the divine being that cannot be justified on the basis of empirical evidence.[5] How unlike his attitude to natural beliefs, once again, is his stance with respect to doctrines of theistic belief that extend beyond the firm foundation of empirical evidence:

> Thus I bring the dispute, O Athenians, to a short issue with my antagonists. The course of nature lies open to my contemplation as well as theirs. The experienced train of events is the great standard by which we regulate our conduct. Nothing else can be appealed to in the field, or in the Senate. Nothing else ought to be heard in the school, or in the closet. In vain would our limited understanding break through those boundaries, which are too narrow for our fond imagination. While we argue from the course of nature, and infer a particular intelligent cause, which first bestowed, and still preserves order in the universe, we embrace a principle which is both uncertain and useless.[6]

For the sake of argument, let us grant with Hume that neither firsthand historical evidence nor secondhand testimony can prove that certain miracles have occurred and, furthermore, that the order and regularity of natural events does not provide sufficient evidence to prove the existence of the traditional God of theism. Even granting these premises, we might well ask what follows. Certainly it follows that we have to disagree with those, like Locke, who purport to establish their religious system of theism through causal reasoning regard-

3. Ibid., 131.
4. Ibid., 110.
5. Ibid., sec. 11, p. 145.
6. Ibid., 142.

ing the reports of miracles or the order of nature. Recall that in the *Essay*, Locke defines faith as assenting to a proposition on the grounds that God has revealed it. Yet for Locke, in order to be rational, such faith must not contradict the self-evident truths of reason and must be based on evidence that God has indeed revealed the truth held by faith. So Locke states, "Whatever God hath revealed is certainly true: no doubt can be made of it. This is the proper object of faith: but whether it be divine revelation or no, reason must judge; which can never permit the mind to reject a greater evidence to embrace what is less evident."[7] In this way, Locke holds that a rational person may believe by faith that God has performed particular miraculous actions, but only under two conditions: first, that the person has rational grounds for believing in God's existence, and second, that the person has rational grounds in the form of historical evidence for believing that God has revealed himself through a miracle. The Humean arguments against theistic belief would thus appear to have disastrous consequences for the Lockean believer, since, if Hume is right, historical evidence does not conclusively support the occurrence of a miracle, and there are no empirical grounds for belief in God in the first place. If Hume is right, then the whole project of Lockean theology is doomed. Locke's theist would be unable to establish any rational proofs of God's existence and thus would be barred from believing in any specific divine interventions in human history. Obviously from the perspective of the skeptical arguments of the first *Enquiry*, not to mention the critique of natural theology in the *Dialogues*, the prospects for Lockean, rational theism are not promising.[8]

Yet, as I have argued, Hume rejects the strict Lockean criterion of believing only in accordance with evidence when Hume is defending our nonreligious, natural beliefs. So we need to ask again, "How does Hume justify drawing his conclusion that Christian believers are wrong in accepting the scriptural witness of God's miraculous interventions?" I think Hume's best answer, but one that is only implicit in these passages from the first *Enquiry*, rests with his doctrine of metaphysical minimalism, which states that we should hold metaphysical beliefs only if either immediate evidence or natural beliefs compel us to do so. As a philosopher of common life, Hume sanctions only those metaphysical convictions genuinely essential to our natural existence; fortunately for us, Hume notes, these are the very beliefs that nature enforces through sentiment rather than through reason. And these are not beliefs that make any positive claims about supernatural reality. From the point of view of

7. Locke, *Essay*, 4.18.10.
8. It might be worth noting here how Hume's ethics of belief and subsequent rejection of traditional Christian theism bear a remarkable resemblance to the stance of many later nineteenth- and twentieth-century biblical critics, from David Strauss and Rudolf Bultmann to Van Harvey. For a penetrating and lucid assessment of the philosophical difficulties inherent in modern biblical criticism, see C. Stephen Evans, *The Historical Christ and the Jesus of Faith* (Oxford: Clarendon, 1996).

a metaphysical minimalist, there are, most significantly, two crucial differences between natural beliefs, such as our belief in natural causes, and supernatural beliefs, such as the Christian belief in a God who acts within history.[9] Natural beliefs are held involuntarily and are essential for our well-being in a merely natural order. Belief in miracles, according to Hume, falls into neither category. In fact, he argues, belief in miracles conflicts with the proper use of our customary belief in the uniformity of nature. In this way, Hume's philosopher of common life seeks to remain a skeptic about metaphysical concerns to the extent that our complex human nature allows. And thus while Hume opposes Pyrrhonism, he reflects its spirit in his preference for suspending judgment whenever such a state of doubt is possible. For Hume, in other words, one is unjustified in believing in any matter of fact, unless one's belief reports immediate experience, can be inferred from the principle of experience, or is the result of a natural, involuntary sentiment. In delineating the ethics of belief in this way, Hume's criterion of metaphysical minimalism—what we might also term Hume's criterion of "mitigated skepticism," that one ought to govern one's metaphysical beliefs by a rational assessment of hard evidence unless one is naturally compelled to believe—serves both to warrant his unequal treatment of natural and religious beliefs and to exonerate him from the charge of inconsistency.

Three Answers from the *Enquiry*

But why, we might well ask, should anyone adopt Hume's metaphysical minimalism in the first place? Basically, Hume recommends that we presume all metaphysical beliefs guilty until proven innocent. His presumption looks very much like that of the Lockean, except that Hume insists we judge such beliefs before the bar of nature as well as that of strict, rational evidence. The Christian theist will want to know why Hume closes his domain of common life to other sources of belief, which would permit us to believe in God and even in certain accounts of miracles. Three arguments in the *Enquiry* alone bear directly on this question. First of all, for Hume religious metaphysical beliefs, in particular, are suspect because of the past record of intolerance and violence rooted in religious superstition and prejudice. It is no coincidence that Hume sets the stage for his discussion of miracles by purporting to have found a decisive argument for safeguarding true philosophy from the deceitful and pernicious influences of superstitious religious zealots.[10] From the opening

---

9. On the crucial differences between natural and religious beliefs, see Terence Penelhum, "Hume's Skepticism and the Dialogues," in *McGill Hume Studies,* ed. David Norton, Nicholas Capaldi, and Wade Robison (San Diego: Austin Hill, 1979), 253–78; and Tweyman, *Skepticism and Belief in Hume's Dialogues,* 7–19.

10. Hume, *Enquiry,* sec. 10, p. 110.

pages of the *Enquiry* to its conclusion, this concern to free philosophy from the corruptions of religious superstition is fundamental to Hume's overall project. By showing the limits of human reason, Hume endeavors to confine philosophical thinking to the boundaries of common life, to cure metaphysics of "its rash arrogance, its lofty pretensions, and its superstitious credulity."[11] Thus while common life requires that we have some metaphysical beliefs, Hume argues that we should nevertheless presume that religious beliefs are guilty until proven innocent. This line of argument is, however, of limited forcefulness. Surely the thoughtful theist might share Hume's disgust for, or at least be disappointed in, the pretentious and proud dogmatism of those who presume to know more about God than they have any right to. And the theist can certainly heed Hume's call for humility, and yet still defend the legitimacy of religious conviction in general, in a way that Hume's skeptic will not allow.

In one respect, the cautious theist—say a follower of Aquinas—might even prefer the Humean view of reason and faith to that of Locke. To appreciate this point, let us look briefly at Philo's response to Cleanthes's theology in the *Dialogues*. In the *Dialogues*, Cleanthes's service to the cause of faith is highly questionable, because he insists on endorsing faith only when it satisfies the canons of rational belief rooted firmly in scientific evidence. Philo sets out from the beginning of the *Dialogues* on a sort of Socratic mission—namely, to cure Cleanthes of his impious pretensions and to effect in him the self-knowledge that the human intellect cannot have firm, scientific knowledge of the divine. From the standpoint of at least some Christian theists, Philo might appear to stand on firm theological footing when he cautions Cleanthes against the attitudes of self-reliance and autonomy that so naturally spring from an exalted sense of the powers of human reason. Cleanthes, however, appears unaware of the potentially dangerous implications of his particular form of rationalism.

In part 1 of the *Dialogues*, Cleanthes endorses the Lockean theory that the realm of faith should be treated in no way differently from the other sciences; rational persons, Cleanthes says, "proportion their assent to the precise degree of evidence" in all circumstances.[12] Now a cautious theist might respond to Cleanthes as follows: on the Christian view, in order to have faith, to believe in God, one must trust in God, seek to obey God's will, and persevere even in the face of suffering and uncertainty. In characterizing the virtue of faith, Hebrews 11 begins with the declaration that "faith is the assurance of things hoped for, the conviction of things not seen." In this chapter, the writer of Hebrews wishes to emphasize both the importance and the basic nature of faith. Faith is important because it is that firm and loving trust in God that

11. Ibid., sec. 5, p. 41.
12. Hume, *Dialogues*, 137–38.

God especially desires. The faithful are God's followers who, like Abraham, are willing to risk all out of their assurance that God is good and possesses the power to carry out his promises. To have faith thus entails both the firm belief that God exists and the steadfast commitment to act in accordance with God's will; to have faith demands trust even in the face of overwhelming evidence of the folly of acting faithfully, whatever the cost.

As Aquinas observes, faith is virtuous precisely because it involves the assent of a trusting and loving will that is not compelled to assent based on clear evidence.[13] Interestingly, in this key respect, Philo seems closer to Aquinas and to the author of Hebrews than does Cleanthes, insofar as Philo suspects from the very beginning that Cleanthes's demand for definitive proof for religious belief will have ruinous consequences for faith. Note, in contrast to Philo, that Cleanthes insists on believing only to the precise degree warranted by scientific evidence. Thus for Cleanthes a legitimate faith would require a very solid evidential proof, to the degree that it would not be at all reasonable to expect even from a successful argument from design. How, we might ask, could the order of the cosmos, apart from revelation, teach us enough about God to reorient our lives and seek to live in harmony with God's will? How could the order of nature alone teach us about God's unconditional love for humanity, our alienation from God's love, and our need for a redeemer? Here Aquinas's position shows greater wisdom from the point of view of Christian theism than does Cleanthes's Lockean view: although Aquinas endorses a version of the design argument, he also insists that the conclusion of any such argument provides only one of the preambles to, rather than the substance of, genuine

---

13. For Aquinas's theory of faith as uncoerced assent of a loving will, see *Summa Theologiae,* IIaIIae 2–6. For an excellent analysis of Aquinas and Calvin on the role of evidence in faith, see Kenneth Konyndyk, "Faith and Evidentialism," in *Rationality, Religious Belief, and Moral Commitment,* ed. Robert Audi and William J. Wainwright (Ithaca, NY: Cornell University Press, 1986), 82–108. My references to Hebrews 11 and to Aquinas as promoting nonevidentialist accounts of faith are indebted to Konyndyk's essay. Konyndyk characterizes Hume as a descriptive rather than normative evidentialist. By this he means that Hume recognizes that our natural beliefs lack evidence but also sees the folly of believing we have an obligation to withhold our assent to them. Insofar as our belief system contains nonrational natural beliefs, it is structurally irrational, though from this it does not follow that we have a duty to stop having these natural beliefs. As I will argue later, Hume works with more than one sense of rational. For Hume our natural beliefs are irrational according to the Lockean criterion but may properly be called rational insofar as they "accord" with human nature and can be justified from the perspective of common life. Beliefs that are irrational in this wider Humean sense, such as Christian beliefs in a providential deity, are irrational and dangerous, according to Hume, and should be rejected. Hence, as a common life thinker, Hume's criterion of rationality is normative and not merely descriptive. With some hesitation, I would add that Hume in the end implies that we have a kind of duty to reject the Lockean criterion—it is, however, a peculiar duty in the sense that everyone cannot but reject it, at least in life, if not in philosophical theory. Holding the Lockean criterion in theory indicates a lack of self-knowledge. As humans, we ought not to hold theories that falsify our human nature. In other words, philosophers have a duty to remember who they are. In this respect, Hume aligns himself with the Socratic tradition.

faith in the living God. For Aquinas, even though the principle of sufficient reason leads us, via the "Five Ways," to posit an intelligent author of the natural world, this naturally acquired knowledge falls far short of the divinely bestowed knowledge of God's nature and providence requisite for redeeming human life and enabling us to live by faith, hope, and love.[14] Returning then to Hume's opposition to rational pretentiousness, my point is that the cautious theist, seeing clearly the danger inherent in the view of those theists like Cleanthes who overlook the need for epistemic humility, might well welcome a Humean skeptic, in this one respect, as more of a friend to the faith than are its Lockean defenders.

Ironically, then, Hume's first argument based on the danger of human arrogance on metaphysical matters fails to justify its conclusion that we should hold as few metaphysical beliefs as possible and certainly not hold any theistic beliefs. Indeed, a cautious theist might in contradistinction to Hume offer a critique of the overall strategy of Hume's *Dialogues* in the following manner. The cautious theist might find himself or herself substantially in agreement with much of Hume's skepticism concerning the apologetic efforts of modern theologians such as the Lockean Cleanthes. Our cautious theist might especially agree with Philo when he calls into question the Lockean position, represented by Cleanthes, in which Christian belief may be embraced only insofar as it can be justified on the basis of unambiguous, hard evidence. For, as Hebrews 11 reminds us, the great heroes of Christian faith are meritorious precisely because of their willingness to believe in the face of uncertainty and inadequate evidence. Such stalwarts of the faith as Abraham and Noah remained steadfast and trusted God even when their circumstances made their commitment seem to many around them to be unreasonable. These great heroes are held up for our esteem just to the extent that they walked courageously by faith in the absence of concrete evidence confirming the wisdom of their calling. Yet Cleanthes, given his commitment to weighing the evidence at all costs, and to believing only on the basis of evidence, would have to condemn such heroes as "unenlightened enthusiasts." In the end, Cleanthes's doctrine of rationality thus becomes something he may well never have intended—namely, a rigid barrier against trust in God. Cleanthes's ethics of rational belief forces him finally to choose either to obey reason or to obey God. Put another way, Cleanthes thinks in essence that he can obey two masters, both his own autonomous reason and the God of Abraham; if Philo is right, as a cautious theist has good reason to think he is, then it turns out that Cleanthes is deeply self-deceived. From the standpoint of a cautious theist, Cleanthes's absolute reliance on his own power of reason—of evidential

---

14. For Aquinas's teaching on the limits of our natural knowledge of God, see *Summa Contra Gentiles*, 3.37–59.

reason—turns out to be excessive self-reliance, and Philo is right to warn him of the inherent pride and arrogance of his philosophical position.

Now if Hume's point were merely to accuse some of his Christian opponents, represented in the *Dialogues* by the character of Cleanthes, of betraying the real spirit of religious humility, he would no doubt be justified. But citing inconsistencies between theory and practice within a tradition does not by itself provide persuasive grounds for rejecting the fundamental beliefs of that tradition; so, also, noting the dogmatism or self-deception associated with some parts of a theistic tradition does not, without further argument, warrant rejecting that tradition in its entirety. The circumspect theist might share much of Hume's suspicion about modern efforts to demonstrate the scientific credentials of faith but conclude that what is needed in human life is not the absence of faith but the presence of humbled faith.

In all fairness to Hume, we should note two further arguments he offers in the *Enquiry* that might serve to support his metaphysical minimalism. As we noted in chapter 1, in section 12 of the *Enquiry* Hume also argues against theistic belief as a consequence of reason's inability to provide a sufficient explanation of natural causes. For Hume, the true philosopher must acknowledge that it is, so to speak, only through the "grace of nature," rather than the "merits of reason," that the human philosophical inquirer is preserved from nihilistic doubt in the face of Pyrrhonian attacks on our natural beliefs. As a mitigated skeptic, Hume's post-Pyrrhonian believer comes to recognize the power of sentiment over reason, and subsequently he or she resolves not to proceed beyond the boundaries of common life. So, Hume argues: "But they will never be tempted to go beyond common life, so long as they consider the imperfection of the faculties they employ, their narrow reach, and their inaccurate operations. While we cannot give a satisfactory reason, why we believe, after a thousand experiments, that a stone will fall, or fire burn; can we ever satisfy ourselves concerning any determination, which we may form, with regard to the origin of worlds, and the situation of nature, from, and to eternity?"[15]

As we have noted, the premises of this argument echo the skeptical conclusions of sections 4 and 5 concerning the limits of reason in our everyday causal judgments. There Hume argues that we cannot rationally justify such natural beliefs as our belief in the uniformity of nature. He observes further that our scientific formulations of the general causal principles of gravity and elasticity describe only *how* bodies behave and do not ultimately explain *why* they behave in the manner they do. So, Hume declares, even our most rigorous and sophisticated scientific laws merely "stave off ignorance a little longer."[16] Based on such evidence of our ignorance of the inner workings of natural

15. Hume, *Enquiry*, sec. 12, p. 162.
16. Ibid., sec. 4, p. 31.

processes, Hume recommends that we should not presume to know anything about supernatural truths, given that these truths are even more remote to us than are the empirical laws of science. Now, this advice might look and sound like common sense. If we cannot fully understand the mechanisms and forces pertaining to the parts of the universe we do perceive, then surely we ought not to presume fully to understand the nature and actions of a divine reality beyond our perceptions. But the truth of this reasonable proposition regarding our human limits is really not what Hume is trying to establish. Hume means to argue that we should limit ourselves in our philosophical inquiries and in our beliefs to secular matters pertaining to our natural, common lives. More importantly, this more extreme Humean proposition rejects as unwise and unreasonable all theistic beliefs regardless of whether, like Cleanthes, one presumes to establish their truthfulness on the basis of empirical evidence. Clearly, the "hold no beliefs beyond common life" policy of Hume's skeptic, if rationally justified, would provide Hume with the sound footing for his metaphysical minimalism we have been seeking.

Yet whether Hume's policy of "hold no beliefs beyond common life"—and thus "hold no theistic beliefs at all"—provides us with a reasonable directive for governing our beliefs is far from obvious. Might not someone sympathetic to many of Hume's insights on the strict limits of human evidential reason regard our cognitive limits not as a barrier to faith but as religiously symbolic, as signifying our dependent status as creatures who, being formed by God, are utterly dependent on him? At least the fact that we have rational certainty about very little, if anything, should serve to remind us that there is no neutral, safe ground for a prudent skeptic on which one can stand without the risk of being in error.

Granted that there is no arena of life free from the danger of false commitment, might not our cautious theist once again bypass Hume's skeptical conclusion by interpreting the meaning of our intractable human ignorance in a theistic light? If we are indeed meant by our Creator to rely on him rather than on our own powers, might not our cognitive limitations be intended by God as an incarnate symbol of our deep need for grace? In a sense, such a point of view is not that far from Hume's own perspective, in which our human limits serve as a sign of our need to rely on Nature and not just on pure reason. The cautious theist and Hume could, in fact, agree that modern intellectuals in particular must be warned against the lure of rational autonomy, against the lure of a life committed to a rational self-rule, in which one submits to no authority except one's own reason.

Now the mere recognition of our intractable human ignorance does not, of course, in and of itself confirm or prove theism, but it fits well with those theistic convictions that uphold our deep need for grace and for a life guided not by rational sight alone but by faith in an authority higher than ourselves. Why not, we might now wonder, follow Pascal and interpret our cognitive finitude as an aspect of our existential paradox, one that beckons us to acknowledge our need to trust in the power of a supreme being? Admittedly, Pascal's interpretation of our finite condition is no more self-evidently true than is Hume's, and would, from a Socratic standpoint, finally need to be defended rather than simply accepted blindly. In chapters 3 and 4 I will defend Pascal's analysis of our human limits. For now, my intention is simply to clarify why Hume's move from the recognition of our inherent ignorance to the thesis of metaphysical minimalism is once again inconclusive.

In sum, to justify his rejection of nonrational theistic beliefs, Hume still needs some nonarbitrary criterion by reference to which he can defend his metaphysical minimalism. A third and final place we might look in the first *Enquiry* for such a criterion is in Hume's argument against believing in miracles. Let me begin by explaining how the case against miracles fits into the overall skeptical project of the *Enquiry*. In fact, it is in his attack on belief in miracles that Hume in the *Enquiry* provides his most formidable defense of metaphysical minimalism.

As we have seen, in his *Enquiry* Hume articulates and defends a theory of human nature in which the virtue of practical wisdom is embodied in the outlook of the mitigated skeptic. Briefly to review, it is essential to this form of skepticism that we recognize that people cannot live by reason alone. In support of this conception of the limits of human reason, Hume demonstrates that a basic feature of our human nature is that we cannot function properly without relying on instinctual, natural beliefs that neither originate in reason nor are justifiable by rational argument. Unlike the radical Pyrrhonists of the ancient world, Hume thinks that we should not withhold our assent to all those beliefs about the real world that cannot be supported by compelling rational argument. And yet, while Hume is willing to walk the path of moderation when it comes to being skeptical about our beliefs regarding the natural world, the same cannot be said of his attitude to beliefs regarding the supernatural world. When it comes to beliefs about the divine, particularly those beliefs about the divine that are central to Christianity, Hume shows nothing less than an unrelenting and unmitigated skepticism.

In his essay "Of Miracles" in particular, Hume seeks to convince us of the irrational character of traditional Christian theism. Hume's strategy in this essay is straightforward: as Hume understands Christian teaching, the authority of Christian theism stands or falls on the authority of beliefs in the providential, miraculous actions of a transcendent God. But, Hume says, there is insufficient empirical evidence to justify believing in such miracles. And since Christian theistic beliefs lack evidential support, and thereby violate the proper epistemic canons of rational belief, Hume contends that respectable rational beings should have nothing to do with them. In sum, a wise person cannot embrace Christian teaching, because the central, authoritative beliefs of this teaching are irrational.

Surprisingly, once again Hume appears to see no irony in such an evidentialist method of anti-Christian deconstruction in the first *Enquiry*. The irony is that Hume's strategy for rejecting Christian belief in God's miraculous works in human history, for example, would seem significantly to conflict with one of the most central lessons of the first *Enquiry*: we as humans must accept our rational limits and acknowledge that some of our most basic beliefs about ourselves and the natural world are also nonrational. Recall that, for Hume, the mere fact that our natural beliefs are not rationally justified is not a sufficient reason to reject them. Hume thinks that we are justified in holding these beliefs—and thus in a sense we might say that we are "rational" in doing so—even in the absence of adequate evidential justification. The problem Hume faces is that his case against miracles appears to be inconsistent with what is arguably the most fundamental component of his theory of human nature. If Hume himself is quite willing to admit that humans, even enlightened modern citizens living in the eighteenth century, should not try to live by evidential reason alone, why is he unwilling to make the same allowance for those who wish to uphold the doctrines of the Christian faith?

In my critique of Hume's case against belief in miracles, I will first show how we can read Hume charitably in such a way as to remove the apparent inconsistency in Hume's stance toward natural beliefs that are not rationally supportable, on the one hand, and religious beliefs that, according to Hume, also lack rational support, on the other. My basic strategy here will be to show how Hume can, in fact, be exonerated from the charge of inconsistency, if his case against miracles given in section 10 of the *Enquiry* is rationally compelling. Having presented Hume's aversion to Christian theism in as charitable a light as I can, I will then show two crucial reasons why, in fact, Hume's case against belief in miracles is not rationally compelling. I will argue specifically that Hume's infamous case against miracles suffers two significant flaws. First, Hume seriously misrepresents the nature of the miraculous. Second, subsequent to this misdescription, Hume's case against miracles turns out to be logically flawed insofar as it simply begs the question by assuming a naturalistic point of view. I will end my inquiry by showing how a study of Hume's argument against miracles can nevertheless help us to understand more clearly the significance of miracles in Christian faith.

Let us begin by recalling two passages in which Hume adeptly summarizes his skeptical argument opposing belief in miracles. Hume writes:

Upon the whole, then, it appears, that no testimony for any kind of miracles has ever amounted to a probability, much less a proof; and that, even supposing that it amounted to a proof, it would be opposed by another proof; derived from the very nature of the fact, which it would endeavor to establish. It is experience only, which gives authority to human testimony; and it is the same experience, which assures us of the laws of nature. When, therefore these two kinds of experience are contrary, we have nothing to do but subtract the one from the other, and embrace an opinion, either on the one side or the other, with that assurance which arises from the remainder. But, according to the principle here explained, this subtraction, with regard to all popular religions, amounts to an entire annihilation; and therefore we may establish it as a maxim, that no human testimony can have such force as to prove a miracle, and make it a just foundation for any system of religion.[17]

Hume tells us here in no uncertain terms that the historical testimony of miracles cannot rationally establish the veracity of Christian belief. At the close of his essay, Hume goes a step further, accusing all those who accept the testimony of miraculous occurrences of being irrational. As Hume puts it:

So that upon the whole, we may conclude, that the *Christian Religion* not only was at first attended with miracles, but even at this day cannot be believed by any reasonable person without one. Mere reason is insufficient to convince us of its veracity: And whoever is moved by *Faith* to assent to it, is conscious of a continued miracle in his own person, which subverts all the principles of his understanding, and gives him a determination to believe what is most contrary to custom and experience.[18]

As we have already noted, it is a curious fact that Hume appears in this skeptical assault to resemble the Lockean rationalist who cautions us to proportion our beliefs to the evidence. After all, it is this rationalist who holds, first, that people have an absolute duty to assent only to beliefs that are rational and, second, that beliefs are rational only if they are based on logical or empirical hard evidence. In a rather Lockean fashion, in constructing his refutation of revealed theology, Hume states quite candidly that the "wise man proportions his belief to the evidence."[19] According to Hume, it follows that when the rational person confronts some putative testimony to a miracle, he or she must adhere to this obligatory, rational principle, conforming his or her assent to the weight of the empirical evidence.

In arguing in this way, Hume exemplifies the suspicion of superstition and religious enthusiasm characteristic of the Enlightenment. Recalling the Humean problem we have been examining, we might find ourselves once again perplexed by Hume's procedure and ask, "Can this really be the same Hume who, having undermined the Lockean evidentialist position by showing our dependence on the nonrational side of our human nature, now tells us that in the case of Christian beliefs we must follow the straight and narrow road and believe only when empirical evidence and rational inference can justify our beliefs?"

17. Ibid., sec. 10, p. 127.
18. Ibid., 131.
19. Ibid., 110.

To make sense of Hume's position, I have argued that Hume seems to presuppose in the first *Enquiry* a principle of metaphysical minimalism, that we should presume all metaphysical beliefs guilty until proven innocent. Though this presumption looks very much like that of the Lockean, Hume intends that we judge all metaphysical beliefs before the bar of nonrational nature as well as that of reason. Again, a thoughtful Christian theist might well respond to Hume by asking him to justify his metaphysical minimalism. The theist might query, "Why should I adopt your metaphysical minimalism since it seems tailor-made to dismiss the supernatural as a valid source of belief?"

When challenged in this way, it would seem that, in order to justify his stance, Hume requires some nonarbitrary criterion by reference to which he can answer the thoughtful theist. I propose that whether or not Hume intended this consequence, such a criterion would be established if he were successful in his argument against belief in miraculous events. Basically, what Hume attempts to demonstrate in this argument is that when the Christian assents to some testimony of miracles, such as that Christ rose from the dead, the Christian not only assents to a belief that is *nonrational*, but he or she also *subverts* the essential experiential principle governing empirical reasoning and thereby believes *irrationally*. If Hume's line of reasoning here stands up to rational scrutiny, then Hume could respond to the charge of inconsistency by saying that natural beliefs are fundamentally unlike theistic beliefs, the latter alone being beliefs founded on the purported occurrences of miracles. Although our natural beliefs are not rationally justifiable, according to Hume, neither are they irrational. To believe in the uniformity of nature or the existence of external objects, two crucial Humean natural beliefs, is to believe beyond what any actual empirical evidence warrants. But for Hume the status of theistic beliefs referring to or dependent on the occurrence of miracles is entirely different: whereas natural beliefs are nonrational, theistic beliefs founded on the idea of a personal God acting supernaturally in history are irrational. Put another way, our natural beliefs aid us in interacting with the world and significantly supplement the limited resources of our rationality. Theistic beliefs of the sort held by Christians, however, set us against our rational nature by requiring us to believe contrary to the weight of the evidence. In this respect, theistic beliefs place us in opposition to ourselves and, in Hume's words, subvert "all the principles of [our] understanding" and give us "a determination to believe what is most contrary to custom and experience."[20]

Hume's Attack on and Misunderstanding of Miracles

I have tried up to this point to defend Hume's skeptical attack on theism by extending to him a degree of interpretive charity. I intend in the rest of my

20. Ibid., 131.

discussion to deliver to Hume something of the justice that I think his case against miracles deserves.

Suppose, Hume says, that we confront—presumably either in person or through historical documents—the claim of someone to have witnessed a miracle. Is it reasonable or unreasonable, Hume queries, to accept this testimony? Hume means to argue that it can never be reasonable to accept such testimony. In constructing this case, Hume makes the crucial assumption that in order for an event to be miraculous, it must be a *violation of a law of nature*; unfortunately, Hume says very little about what a law of nature is and how we establish what is, and is not, a genuine law. Hume's most detailed description of the nature of the miraculous is as follows: "A miracle may be accurately defined, *a transgression of a law of nature by a particular volition of the Deity, or by the interposition of some invisible agent.* . . . A miracle may be either discoverable by men or not. This alters not its nature and essence."[21] There is no doubt, I think, that here Hume could have defined the nature of the miraculous with much more care and precision. For one thing, Hume does not tell us very clearly what constitutes a law of nature. Hume also seems to overlook the crucial purpose of God's miraculous actions—namely, to reveal some important truth about God's benevolent purposes toward humans. A "miracle" performed by God in private (in the absence of any human witnesses) reveals nothing to people, all of whom desperately need God's help. Suppose, for example, that last night for two hours God made the water in the Chattahoochee River running through Atlanta completely pristine and unpolluted. Suppose, furthermore, that no mortal was present to witness this extraordinary occurrence. For Hume, such an occurrence would still count as a miracle. I would call it an impressive and extraordinary event, a supernatural act of God, but not a miracle. Contrary to Hume, I would argue, based on the New Testament account of miracles, that if "a miracle falls in a forest and no one is there to see it, then a genuine miracle just did not occur."

Hume seems to misunderstand here that miracles, at least those of the sort recounted in Scripture, are essentially meant to instruct a wayward people and to reveal something important about God's nature or will to a human audience. Thus an unwitnessed miracle would not be a genuine miracle, because it would not serve God's purpose in performing miracles. Putting aside these shortcomings in Hume's case for now, however, we can acknowledge that Hume's basic point still seems correct—namely, that miraculous events by definition are exceptions to the "usual course of nature."[22] I do think that Hume is right to note that miracles are extraordinary events that "interrupt" the normal sequence of events and are the result, as Hume rightly notes, of divine action rather than simply of natural causes. Certainly classic instances

21. Ibid., 115 (italics in the original).
22. Ibid., 127.

of the miraculous, such as Christ's resurrection or the turning of Cana's water into wine, are both extraordinary events and manifestations of God's direct causal agency. Yet although Hume is correct on these aspects of the miraculous, he is quite mistaken to define miracles as *violations of natural laws*. I shall argue in what follows that precisely this mistaken characterization of the nature of the miraculous as a "violation" leads Hume to conclude erroneously that assenting to the occurrence of miracles is *irrational*.

Let us begin by examining more closely how, according to Hume, we should regard reports of such miracles as that of the resurrection of Christ. First of all, Hume argues, to assess rationally any secondhand testimony concerning events we have not ourselves witnessed we must rely on the "principle of experience." We must, in other words, evaluate the probability of the truth of the person's report by reasoning from past experience. To do so, we need to judge the evidence of the person's character as reliable or dubious, as well as the independent likelihood of what the person reports to have taken place. In the particular case of miracles, Hume contends that we must weigh the positive evidence, if any, of the person's veracity *against* the negative evidence regarding the occurrence of the extraordinary event. Now, by definition, according to Hume, a miracle is a violation of a law of nature. To call some occurrence miraculous, then, one must presume that all past experience up to this event provides a uniform and constant regularity that the purported miracle violates. So Hume reasons that the negative evidence against a miracle occurring is our accumulated uniform past experience of a natural regularity. In the particular case of the resurrection, we note our uniform past experience that dead persons do not return to life. Here Hume thinks we have the strongest probable evidence—the uniformity of past experience—we can ever have, and this evidence clearly weighs against the miraculous event. The evidence in favor of the miracle, however, turns on the reliability of the witness giving testimony. But, Hume adds, even if the person's character is known by us to be totally trustworthy, it could never outweigh the contrary evidence of uniform past experience. Since we judge the person's character by the same rule of past experience we use in judging the likelihood of the event itself, we cannot have better evidence *for* the veracity of our witness than we have *against* the occurrence of any event that conflicts with our uniform past experience.

At best, Hume observes, in assessing the trustworthiness of someone's testimony to have witnessed a miracle, we are confronted with equal evidence for and against the actual occurrence of the reported miracle. Since it is the mark of a rational person in reasoning about matters of fact not to assent contrary to the preponderance of the evidence, and since the evidence is at best inconclusive, the rational person can go no further toward belief than to suspend judgment. Rational people will therefore never actually accept the testimony of miracles. Hume has no doubt that a person cannot be a Christian without believing that some miracles have happened. Thus having argued that it is never rational to accept the testimony of a witness to a miraculous occurrence, he concludes that a rational person cannot be a Christian.

In assessing the merits of Hume's case, let us first consider how Hume argues from his account of what we understand another person to mean when he or she reports that a miracle has occurred to his conclusion that it is always irrational to assent to this testimony. Basically, Hume infers that in order to deem a particular event to be a miracle, we must assume that prior human experience has been uniform and thus supports the operation of a law of nature up to the time of the conflicting testimony. Furthermore, once this uniformity of experience resulting from a law of nature is granted, we see, if we are rational, that the evidence supporting the testimony to a miracle could never outweigh the prior contrary evidence of the uniformity of nature we presuppose in describing the reported event as a miracle in the first place. Contrary to what Hume thinks, however, neither of these inferences seems very reasonable. First, the fact that certain people refer to an event as a miracle surely does not require that they assume, on pain of incoherence, that nature has been uniform for all people up to the time at which this reported miracle was supposed to have taken place. What Hume ought to say here is that those who believe that some miracle has occurred must believe that God has acted in history and performed some extraordinary act that indeed runs counter to the ordinary course of nature. Note that saying this is not the same as saying that the event violates a law of nature; "runs counter to" simply means that the event is out of the ordinary, that it swims upstream, so to speak, from the usual course of nature, and that it could not happen by natural forces alone. But there is no reason here to require, as Hume does, that in order for some miracle to occur it must be the case that the regularity to which this miracle is an exception has been uniformly experienced, without exception, prior to the occurrence of this miracle. Hume's position entails the seemingly absurd thesis that no more than one instance of any species of miracle could ever occur and be reported, since once the regularity in question has been "violated," we no longer have the uniformity of experience necessary, by definition, for a miracle to take place.

By insisting that any genuine occurrence of a miracle presupposes a context of past seamless uniformity of cause and effect, Hume places an unreasonable restriction on the traditional understanding of God's providence. Surely if God wills he can perform the same species of miracle at different times even before the same witnesses. Consider, for example, the sequence of encounters with the risen Christ reported in John 20:24–29. After Mary Magdalene and others have seen the risen Christ, we learn that Thomas was skeptical and suspended belief in a good Humean fashion. He proclaims that he will believe only when he is presented with decisive empirical evidence: "Unless I see the mark of the nails in his hands, and put my finger in the mark of the nails and my hand in his side, I will not believe" (v. 25). When Thomas later acknowledges Christ's divinity, declaring "My Lord and my God," he assents to a miracle even though he knows very well that by assenting to it he no longer has reason to doubt the earlier testimony of the others that he had previously rejected. In this case, Thomas, if asked, would presumably say, if the Humean restriction were put to him, that he certainly has witnessed an astounding miracle, even though others before him witnessed the same miracle and encountered the risen Lord. In other words, Thomas has no need to posit that until his encounter with Jesus, nature has been uniform and all prior human experience has supported the principle that the dead remain dead. On the Humean view, Thomas's encounter with the risen Lord could not be described as witnessing a real miracle because other individuals had experienced this "violation of the law of nature" before him. Here Hume's view certainly appears outrageous.

Now a Humean might respond to my criticism here by rejecting my counterexample as misleading. I have argued that granting the testimony in the Gospel of John, Thomas clearly did witness a miracle. Yet Thomas was not the first to encounter the risen Christ. We know that others before him had seen the risen Christ and witnessed the same miracle. Thus it would seem to follow that Hume's definition of the nature of the miraculous is simply too restrictive. "On the contrary," the Humean might retort, "your supposed counterexample shows only that various persons may over a period of time be witnesses to the same miracle." The supposed multiplicity of witnesses to the resurrection of Christ demonstrates only how many individuals could in principle witness the same miracle. The point still remains that prior to this collective experience of the resurrection, dead people have remained dead. The resurrection is an extraordinary event that is unprecedented; it remains the case that no similar resurrection had occurred up to this one. Here the Humean may well be right in one respect—namely that the resurrection of Christ is indeed an entirely unique event that never has and never will be repeated in human history. Still it remains the case, contrary to Hume, that a person who assents to the occurrence of a miracle need only believe that an extraordinary event caused by God has occurred, not that nature has been entirely uniform up to the time of the miraculous event. If my example of Thomas above does not make this point sufficiently persuasive, consider a clearer counterexample to Hume's definition.

Since the resurrection of Christ is indeed an unprecedented event in which the incarnate Son of God returns from the dead and takes on a unique bodily existence, let us consider instead the other examples recorded in the New Testament of dead persons being brought back to life. Two examples are Christ's breathing life back into Lazarus and his raising of the widow's son in Nain. Now if Hume were correct, anyone who witnessed the widow's son in Nain being brought back to life by the supernatural agency of Jesus could not coherently describe the raising of Lazarus as miraculous as well. But this latter position is surely unwarranted; if Jesus can intervene once on behalf of

Lazarus, clearly Jesus has the power to raise others if he so wills. Even granting, then, that the resurrected body of Christ had powers not possessed by Lazarus's body, and thus Jesus's resurrected body differs substantially from Lazarus's "raised" body, the point remains that, according to the Scriptures, God has acted more than once in history to bring persons back from the dead. Hence, just as different persons may over time come to witness the same miraculous "being raised from the dead," so too different persons over time may be eye-witnesses of different instances of the same kind of miracle. So in the case of Lazarus and the widow's son in Nain, different individuals were witnesses to the same basic kind of miracle occurring more than once by God's grace. The key point here is that we have no reason to agree with Hume that the mere fact that some people term an event miraculous provides solid evidence, or logically requires us to believe, that no similar events—no similar miracles, that is—have occurred in the past. Hume is right to recognize that miracles are extraordinary events; he errs in articulating this extraordinary aspect of the miraculous in terms of it being a violation of some uniform, seamless law of nature. And as I shall argue below, while Hume properly recognizes that miracles are not simply natural events resulting merely from the powers of natural bodies, he fails to distinguish a divine causal agency that transcends the order of natural causes from one that violates such a natural order.

There is an additional and more significant reason for thinking that Hume's initial characterization of miracles as violations of natural laws is misleading. Even if we grant that in some instances a particular sort of miracle occurs in an unprecedented manner and conflicts with the uniform past experience of humankind, that conflict alone should not lead us to think of the anomalous miracle as *violating* a prior natural regularity. Here I think it is essential to understand that, contrary to Hume's account, one could typically accept someone's testimony of a miracle without holding that any of the earlier human experiences of nature's uniformity were erroneous.

Let us now, for the sake of argument, take up once again the example of Christ's resurrection. My point is that accepting that Christ rose from the dead does not entail that any of the earlier experiences of humans remaining dead and not being resurrected are false. The testimony of Christ's resurrection conflicts with the earlier data only if one takes the past data necessarily to be evidence for a universal, entirely uniform law of nature—as Hume puts it—that dead people remain dead. But it is misleading to think, as Hume seems to, that interpreting the past data in this way is somehow rationally obligatory or even epistemically neutral with respect to the question of believing in miracles. One might well look at the earlier data in a different way: one might see the more or less uniform empirical data as evidence for a divinely willed regularity that in certain cases, and, more importantly, in one supreme case, God has chosen for good reason to suspend in a remarkable way. Hume supposes that there is only one way to interpret the general uniformity of experience that dead people stay dead—that is, as evidence of a law of nature purporting that in *all circumstances* the dead will always remain dead.

A theist who exhibits a modest caution regarding the claim of other persons to have experienced miracles could suppose instead that there is a natural law, stemming from God's will, that holds that under *normal circumstances*— that is, under natural circumstances in which God does not supplement the natural powers of created objects—dead people will not come back to life. When a miracle occurs, however, the theist would say that we no longer are under normal circumstances in which physical objects are determined solely by their God-given natural powers. Because a miracle suspends the limitations of natural powers and involves a special kind of supernatural intervention of God in human history, accepting someone's report of a miracle violates no past experience or prior regularity of nature.[23] Thus to regard uniform past experience in the way that Hume does—as evidence for a seamless law describing what happens to dead bodies in all cases—is unjustified. The most Hume ought to say is that past experience of the natural world provides evidence for a natural law describing what happens to dead bodies when the only powers affecting them are natural and physical.[24]

23. My critique of Hume's case against belief in miracles is especially indebted to the work of Keith Yandell, *Hume's Inexplicable Mystery* (Philadelphia: Temple University Press, 1990), 315–38; and Morris, *Making Sense of It All*, 168–71.

24. I find a penetrating and highly provocative response to the Humean outlook in the writings of Flannery O'Connor. In a letter dated September 6, 1955, O'Connor states:

> To see Christ as God and man is probably no more difficult today than it has always been, even if today there seem to be more reasons to doubt. For you it may be a matter of not being able to accept what you call a suspension of the laws of flesh and the physical, but for my part I think that when I know what the laws of the flesh and the physical really are, then I will know what God is. We know them as we see them, not as God sees them. For me it is the virgin birth, the Incarnation, the resurrection which are the true laws of the flesh and the physical. Death, decay, destruction are the suspension of these laws. I am always astonished at the emphasis the Church puts on the body. It is not the soul she says will rise, but the body, glorified. I have always thought that purity was the most mysterious of the virtues, but it occurs to me that it would never have entered the human consciousness to conceive of purity if we were not to look forward to a resurrection of the body, which will be flesh and spirit united in peace, in the way they were in Christ. The resurrection of Christ seems the high point in the law of nature. (Flannery O'Connor, *The Habit of Being*, ed. Sally Fitzgerald [New York: Farrar, Straus and Giroux, 1979], 100)

In essence, O'Connor hoists the Humean-style skeptic on his own petard: she argues that miracles should not be seen as violating Nature because Nature, in fact, realizes its true identity only when miracles break through the succession of ordinary events, lifting Nature beyond its accustomed limits of decay and corruption. Apart from God's direct presence revealed in miracles, Nature is not fully itself. In this letter, O'Connor shows how the concept of nature involves an interpretation of the data of natural events and is not simply given in the mere sequence of events. Whether miracles violate the order of nature depends on how one interprets the significance of natural events. Hume regards them "naturalistically," while O'Connor views them through the lens of theism; neither standpoint is religiously or epistemically neutral.

Thus far I have argued against Hume on the grounds that he misrepresents the true nature of the miraculous and misdescribes the way in which miracles relate to natural regularities. Now I propose to argue that, based on these two misunderstandings, Hume's case against belief in miracles ultimately just begs the question. Basically, Hume merely takes for granted that past observations of natural regularities should be interpreted naturalistically rather than theistically. Without making this assumption, Hume cannot oppose uniform past experience to the testimony of miracles and speak as if the latter contradicts the former. From a theistic perspective, there need be no conflict in believing both that the natural order behaves in certain uniform ways and that God can, if he so chooses, supplement the natural, created powers he sustains by his creative agency and bring about extraordinary events. The theist will say that God's miraculous interventions *supplement* rather than *violate* the natural powers and capacities of created bodies. Thus we need to recognize that Hume's argument succeeds only if one initially insists on interpreting the data of uniform (or near uniform) past experience in a naturalistic or nontheistic way. The naturalist upholds the metaphysical stance that nature is all that exists, has existed, and will exist. For the naturalist there are no supernatural beings or events of any kind; there is no reality beyond the natural. If one merely assumes the truth of naturalism at the outset, one rules out in principle the possibility of circumstances in which a supernatural agency supplements the powers of natural bodies. And if there is no possibility of such supernatural activity, then one could infer from the claim that "dead people remain dead under natural circumstances" the stronger claim, crucial to the success of Hume's argument, that "dead people remain dead under all circumstances." But interpreting the past uniformities of nature "naturalistically" in assessing the rationality of belief in miracles simply begs the question against theism: this move assumes, of course, that there is no God sustaining the universe. Only by begging the question in this manner, that is, in favor of a naturalistic point of view, is Hume able to present his case that belief in miracles *contradicts* our past experiences.

My objection to Hume's line of reasoning can be summarized as follows. In assessing the case for and against believing in miraculous events, such as the resurrection of Jesus Christ, Hume argues in this manner:

1. In reasoning about matters of fact, the rational person will not hold beliefs that are contrary to the preponderance of the evidence.
2. It has been the uniform past experience of humans that dead people remain dead.
3. The uniform past experience that dead people remain dead provides us with the strongest kind of evidence available to humans that there is a law of nature that tells us that, under all circumstances, it is impossible for dead people to come back to life. Let us call this law "ODAD" ("once dead always dead").

4. The testimony of the so-called eyewitnesses to the resurrection of Jesus Christ violates the ODAD law of nature.
5. Even the strongest evidence in favor of the veracity of the witnesses reporting the resurrection of Jesus Christ cannot outweigh the contrary evidence in favor of the ODAD law of nature.
6. Therefore, a rational person may not believe that the miracle of the resurrection of Jesus Christ did in fact occur.

My response to Hume is that step 3 simply begs the question: it assumes the principle of naturalism. Furthermore, both steps 4 and 5 misrepresent the true relationship between miracles and natural laws, for we are justified in saying that the miracle of Christ's resurrection violates the ODAD law of nature only if we assume the principle of naturalism (PN): "There can be no supernatural agency that has the power to supplement the powers of merely created, natural entities and that could thereby cause certain extraordinary events to happen in our world. The only causes of events in our world are natural." Of course, once we assume this principle, there is little point in carrying out Hume's argument to its final conclusion. PN simply begs the question against the theist.

It is important to note that in response to Hume, the cautious but thoughtful theist need not in turn beg the question against Hume. I mean that the theist need not beg the question against Hume by assuming in advance that miracles have in fact occurred; the theist needs to insist only that miracles resulting from supernatural agency *are possible*. Since Hume himself explicitly states in his essay on miracles that he does not mean to rule out the *possibility* of miracles, let us call the thoughtful theist's principle "Hume's Admission" (HA): "It is *possible* that there is a supernatural agency that has the power to supplement the mere powers of created natural entities and that could thereby cause certain extraordinary events to happen in our world. It is *possible* that some causes of events in our world are supernatural rather than natural." It is crucial to see here that unless Hume opts to beg the question against the theist, he must allow HA, as he does at one point very clearly in his essay on miracles. Acknowledging the possibility of miracles, Hume candidly states, "I beg the limitations here made may be remarked, when I say that a miracle can never be proved, so as to be the foundation of a system of religion. For I own, that otherwise, there may possibly be miracles, or violations of the usual course of nature, of such a kind as to admit proof from human testimony."[25] But if, with Hume's own stated approval, at least as indicated in this one passage, we grant HA, then we must revise steps 3, 4, and 5 in Hume's original argument in the following way:

First, the third premise that originally read:

25. Hume, *Enquiry*, sec. 10, p. 127.

3. The uniform past experience that dead people remain dead provides us with the strongest kind of evidence available to humans that there is a law of nature that tells us that, under all circumstances, it is impossible for dead people to come back to life. Let us call this law "ODAD" ("once dead always dead"),

must be revised to read as follows:

3a. The uniform past experience that dead people remain dead provides us with the strongest kind of evidence available to humans that there is a law of nature to the effect that it is naturally impossible for dead people to come back to life. This law of nature tells us that *under those circumstances in which only the natural powers of physical bodies are at work*, it is impossible for dead people to come back to life. Let us call this law "ODAND" ("once dead always *naturally* dead").

Second, the fourth premise originally read:

4. The testimony of the so-called eyewitnesses to the resurrection of Jesus Christ violates the ODAD law of nature.

This must in turn be revised as follows:

4a. The testimony of the so-called eyewitnesses to the resurrection of Jesus Christ *agrees with the ODAND law of nature and yet posits the occurrence of an extraordinary event brought about by God's supernatural agency.*

Finally, the fifth premise originally read:

5. Even the strongest evidence in favor of the veracity of the witnesses reporting the resurrection of Jesus Christ cannot outweigh the contrary evidence in favor of the ODAD law of nature.

This must be revised as well:

5a. If there is testimonial evidence in favor of the veracity of the witnesses reporting the resurrection of Jesus Christ, *that evidence does not in principle conflict with the natural evidence in favor of the ODAND law of nature.*

Clearly, once Hume's case is revised by substituting steps 3a, 4a, and 5a for their original counterparts, in order to avoid simply assuming the principle of naturalism, PN, Hume's skeptical conclusion (step 6) no longer follows. Here is what is left of Hume's case now that we have corrected steps 3, 4, and 5:

1. In reasoning about matters of fact, the rational person will not hold beliefs that are contrary to the preponderance of the evidence.
2. It has been the uniform past experience of humans that dead people remain dead.
3a. The uniform past experience that dead people remain dead provides us with the strongest kind of evidence available to humans that there is a law of nature to the effect that it is naturally impossible for dead people to come back to life. This law of nature tells us that *under those circumstances in which only the natural powers of physical bodies are at work*, it is impossible for dead people to come back to life. Let us call this law "ODAND" ("once dead always *naturally* dead").
4a. The testimony of the so-called eyewitnesses to the resurrection of Jesus Christ *agrees with the ODAND law of nature and yet posits the occurrence of an extraordinary event brought about by God's supernatural agency.*
5a. If there is testimonial evidence in favor of the veracity of the witnesses reporting the resurrection of Jesus Christ, *that evidence does not in principle conflict with the natural evidence in favor of the ODAND law of nature.*
6a. Therefore, it does not follow that insofar as any rational person does believe in the ODAND law of nature, he or she would ipso facto be irrational to believe that the miracle of the resurrection of Jesus Christ did in fact occur. There is, in other words, no incompatibility in principle—as a great Scottish skeptic once seemed to think—between believing in ODAND and believing in the resurrection of Jesus Christ.

Admittedly, this rendering of Hume's case suffers one sorry defect in comparison with the original: my revised version lacks that sense of dénouement that makes Hume's original argument so dramatically arresting. Indeed, we might now wonder what significant conclusion, if any, follows from Hume's revised argument. For, rather than throw down the skeptical gauntlet and dare the theist to admit his or her epistemic guilt, our revised argument almost extends a hand of reconciliation. Our corrected Humean premises clearly leave open the possibility of harmony between Athens and Jerusalem, even if we grant that the revised version of the Humean argument says nothing about how one would rationally come to believe that the resurrection did occur.

Of course, we must also acknowledge that our revised Humean argument certainly does not confirm either that any miracles have occurred or even that we are reasonable in believing any reports of miracles as found, say, in the Scriptures. Nevertheless, our revised Humean argument does leave open the possibility that a wise person might rationally come to believe in miracles and might do so in a way that changes that person's whole life. Given the flaws in his original rendering of the case against miracles, we should conclude that Hume's skeptical, wise man who will not even consider assenting to the occurrence of miracles is the one who is irrational: in rejecting the scriptural testimony of miracles simply on the basis of the principle of experience, Hume's anti-Christian skeptic proportions his beliefs in a manner that simply begs the question against theism.

Now, a plausible Humean rejoinder to my criticism might be to challenge the theist's own grounds for adopting a theistic outlook rather than a naturalistic one. Or, to put the issue in slightly different terms, a Humean might well recall the very challenge Hume articulates in part 2 of his essay "Of Miracles." In this section, Hume offers his most damaging argument against religious rationalists who tout their tradition's testimony of unique miracles as confirming evidence for their own particular religious tradition. It is here that Hume pits one evidentialist theistic tradition against another, concludes that such competing perspectives are mutually antagonistic, and finally opts for the classic skeptical resolution of suspending judgment in the face of antinomic points of view. Hume sets up this Pyrrhonian-style opposition of perspectives by contending that rival religious traditions affirm in their creedal formulas the existence of specific, unique miracles. Moreover, Hume reasons that to accept one tradition's account of the miraculous is, in effect, to accept one or more miracles as confirming evidence for that particular tradition's being the one true religion. In Hume's view, in other words, if I accept the Christian account of the resurrection of Christ, I must accept this miracle as proof for the veracity of Christian faith and thus as disproof of all rival, competing, non-Christian traditions.

Here it is worth emphasizing one key feature of Hume's skeptical position—namely, that Hume's primary concern in part 2 of his essay on miracles is with religious systems that regard the historical testimony of miracles as rational confirmation of their own particular tradition. As Terence Penelhum has noted about Hume's line of criticism in part 2, "Hume is arguing against those who appeal to the alleged historical occurrence of miracles in order to establish the authority of a religious system. He is attacking the attempt to base the credentials of revelation upon historical evidence."[26] Very significantly, whether Hume himself realized it, Hume is not posing a threat to those believers who do not regard miracles as an evidential basis, and indeed as confirming evidence, for their particular set of theistic beliefs. Rather, he aims his sights on that pervasive Enlightenment mentality, defended by Locke among many others, that holds that a person can have a rational faith in miracles only if that faith is supported

26. Terence Penelhum, *Hume* (London: Macmillan, 1975), 175.

by clear rational evidence that God has indeed acted miraculously at certain specific moments in history.

As a critique of Enlightenment apologists who regarded faith as rational only if it is supported by some clear, external confirmation that God is really speaking to us and revealing certain truths for our instruction, Hume's refutation in part 2 may well be decisive. To carry out his strategy, however, Hume must assume that the evidence for any particular miracle cited by one religious tradition is basically no better or worse than that for any other miracle used as evidence by different religious traditions. Now, there may be very good grounds for holding that the reports of miracles in one religious tradition are more credible than those in other rival traditions. But whether Hume is right in presuming otherwise is not my real concern.

It is crucial to note here that Hume portrays the project of comparing the credibility of various religious traditions too simplistically. To assess the rationality of accepting a particular religion's testimony of the occurrence of divine agency in human history, one would need to raise a number of questions that would range from those regarding the character of the witnesses, to the coherence of the miraculous testimony in the context of the overall faith, and, ultimately, to the overall coherence of the faith for diagnosing and redeeming the human condition. So, for instance, the testimony to God's miraculous activity in a religion that denies the inveterate nature of human self-centeredness strikes me as lacking credibility, insofar as any religion that overlooks or denies human sinfulness fails to offer a truthful diagnosis of human life. One thing Hume overlooks is that when assessing the rationality of a given religious tradition, one must look first and foremost to the intelligibility of the core of its message. Insofar as any religious account of human life seeks essentially to diagnose and offer a remedy for human unhappiness and suffering and to provide an account of a path to enlightenment or salvation, we should judge the rationality of that account in terms of its success as a teleological outlook. For the purposes of evaluating Hume's position on miracles, the important point is that the historical testimony of miracles is not simply a matter of judging the empirical likelihood of the events or the evidence for or against the reliability of the witnesses. Rather, one should believe or disbelieve such testimony in the larger context of the message of salvation this testimony is meant to affirm. Put simply, whether it is rational to accept any of the miracle stories found in the New Testament, for instance, is not a question one can properly answer independently from assessing the coherence and efficacy of the gospel itself.

Hume, in contrast, presumes that the project of rationally comparing rival religions involves treating the testimony of miraculous occurrences in each religion as empirical evidence for the truthfulness of the religion as a whole. He regards the various narratives of miraculous events in each tradition as serving the function of providing confirming evidence for their faith. Here I think that Hume misrepresents the proper epistemic status of the accounts of miracles in theistic perspectives. Genuine miracles are not what the Humean wise skeptic thinks they are. They are not meant to be neutral evidence concocted by the Supreme Being to confirm the authenticity of a certain prophet or savior-figure. Miracles are not, in other words, supposed to be extraordinary data serving to confirm some theistic hypothesis.

On the contrary, miracles, at least in the biblical accounts, function as signs, as manifestations, of God's providence. The purpose of these signs is not to provide evidence for neutral spectators but to lead, inform, and speak to those individuals who are willing to acknowledge their own fallen state and need for God's love. At least from a New Testament perspective, a wise person must first see clearly with the "eyes of one's heart" that he or she needs God before miracles can be understood correctly. Only such a person, one who is humble and receptive to Jesus Christ, can read the miraculous sign correctly as indicating the way to redemption. That Christ performs miracles makes sense to such a rational person because he or she finds plausible Christ's message of human sin and the need for divine grace. Those who respond to Christ, as Pascal would say, with a loving response can be taught by the miracle stories and can defend them as rational within the larger context of the Christian message. Hume's oversight is a matter of applying the wrong model of rational justification to the miracle stories. By taking the narratives of miraculous events as the foundation for a religious system, Hume turns the edifice of faith upside down. The true epistemic foundation of a theistic system is its diagnosis and remedy for human incompleteness and sinful rebellion; the narratives of miracles within the Christian tradition serve as signs to those who are open to following that religion's path for salvation. If these miracle stories make sense to us, they do so within the whole narrative of salvation, not by serving as its evidential foundation.[27]

Jesus's Warnings to the Miracle Seekers

To clarify the difference between regarding miracles as signs and regarding them as proofs, it may be instructive to look briefly at some of the New Testament accounts of Christ's warnings against those who sought miracles. If Hume were right in thinking that rational persons should regard miracles as proofs, it becomes difficult to understand the sort of ambivalence Christ exhibits regarding faith and miracles. Why, especially, would Christ respond with loving remonstrance to Thomas's confession of belief after Thomas has finally seen for himself the risen Lord? Rather than congratulate Thomas for

27. For two especially helpful studies of Hume and the problem of miracles, see C. S. Lewis, *Miracles* (New York: Macmillan, 1960); and Richard Swinburne, *The Concept of Miracle* (London: St. Martin's Press, 1970).

his rational integrity as a good Humean skeptic—and for not being susceptible to enthusiastic emotion—Christ uses this occasion for teaching Thomas
about true faith. Christ says to Thomas: "You believe because you have seen
me. Blessed are those who have not seen and yet believe" (John 20:29 NEB).[28]
Here Christ seems to warn against the very thing that Hume assumes is necessary for any rational assessment of theistic faith—namely the demand for
evidence prior to faith and the taking of the occurrence of miracles to be the
foundation of one's belief in God. From the perspective of Christ's teaching to
Thomas, Hume appears to be wrong about the proper attitude the wise person should adopt toward miracle stories. A Humean could reply that perhaps
Christ is calling on Thomas to choose between wisdom and blessedness. But
is Christ really teaching Thomas that he must choose between being faithful
and being wise? Is it not clear that Christ simply rejects as unwise the Humean approach to miracles, which is exemplified in Thomas, given Thomas's
profound need for grace? That the scriptural stance on miracles simply makes
no sense on a Humean account would seem to be indicated as well by the first
great commandment, "Love the Lord your God with all your mind," and on
those other scriptural occasions where Christ speaks to the spiritual dangers
of "seeking for signs."

In the Synoptic Gospels, Jesus repeatedly warns the Pharisees and Sadducees,
as well as the multitudes, against "seeking" for miraculous signs. So in Luke
11:29–31, Jesus condemns the crowd's eagerness for signs because their attitude
shows that they are a proud generation who would wish to see signs for the
wrong reasons: for entertainment or for the sake of worldly power. They fail
to see that Jesus's miraculous signs are meant to lead people to repentance and
to reliance on God. Jesus condemns those who "seek after signs" because they
relish the display of divine power without acknowledging their own brokenness and need for redemption. To seek after signs simply for entertainment,
self-aggrandizement, or nationalistic pride is to seek for God's power for the
wrong reasons. In his striking ambivalence toward performing miracles, Jesus
distinguishes, in effect, two crucially different attitudes toward miracles. As
Jesus reminds the crowd gathered around him, his miracles are meant as signs,
like the sign of Jonah, to call people to repentance. Jesus's miracles testify to
the authority of the Son of Man, who has come to call his people back to right
relationship with God. So the many miracles recorded in Luke—for example,
the curing of the paralytic man (5:17–26), the curing of the centurion's servant
(7:1–10), and the raising of the widow's son in Nain (7:11–17)—testify to the
authority of Jesus: Jesus is the incarnate Son of God who has a power unique
to the human race to forgive sins and to heal the broken. Thus the witness of
Jesus, on which all his teaching and miracles converge, is that he has come to

---

28. Compare Jesus's warning against the Pharisees and Saducees: "An evil and adulterous
generation asks for a sign" (Matt. 16:4).

restore sinners to true life in communion with God. Hence Jesus's miracles are not meant to serve the Enlightenment epistemological purpose of providing evidence for neutral spectators; his miracles serve instead the spiritual and ethical purposes of testifying to the divine authority of Jesus and bringing people to repent of their hard-heartedness. The miracles are thus meant as signs for those who are willing to ask for God's forgiveness; in contrast, those who were disposed to be proud and self-satisfied historically resisted the call and did not internalize the message of Jesus's miracles. Merely seeing the evidence of God's extraordinary power is not what is important from a scriptural perspective. The purpose of miracles is moral transformation, not epistemological verification. Only those witnesses who are already open to confessing their need for God can read Jesus's signs correctly. Desiring to partake of God's miraculous power in order to be on "the winning side" or to "get what one wants" is to display an inordinate love of miracles. Unfortunately, it is this perverse and inordinate love of God's signs, in one form or another, to which the church has, all too often in its history, succumbed.

Consider next how Jesus responds in Matthew 16:2–4 to the Scribes and Pharisees who desire to test him:

> He answered them, "When it is evening you say, 'It will be fair weather; for the sky is red.' And in the morning, 'It will be stormy today, for the sky is red and threatening.' You know how to interpret the appearance of the sky, but you cannot interpret the signs of the times. An evil and adulterous generation asks for a sign, but no sign shall be given to it except the sign of Jonah."

Here Jesus condemns the Scribes' and Pharisees' request for a sign, for he reads their request as itself a sign, in this case as a sign of their inner hard-heartedness. Jesus refuses to perform miracles either to entertain the multitude or for those who are unwilling to repent. Although Jesus performs many signs, he will not display them at the request of those whose hearts are unwilling to hear his real message. Clearly what is at issue here relates to the purpose of miracles in Jesus's ministry. Jesus refuses to provide miracles as neutral evidence or as ammunition for those who are proud and unrepentant. For such individuals, even believing that the miracles have occurred and that they provide evidence of supernatural power would not generate what Jesus intends—namely a humble and repentant turning to God. Certain forms of human pride, as found unfortunately throughout history in some of God's own "followers," shackle God's power to the service of human ambition and self-centeredness. Indeed, powerful figures representing God's authority have all too often perverted the reality of God's supernatural agency, turning it into an instrument for their own status and self-importance. No doubt, all people, whether powerful or not, are prone to treat God as their valet or servant in the pursuit of their own priorities and self-interest, rather than as the supreme moral authority under whom they are to serve and grow out of their habits of self-centeredness.

Jesus does not perform miracles to convince neutral Humean spectators because, from his point of view, no such persons even exist. Behind that kind of request for a sign, for visible evidence of Jesus's authority, is a person who lacks an openness to faith. For Jesus, the "name of the game" in performing miracles is *not* to provide evidence for intellectual scrutiny; the purpose of miracles is to help those who are willing to acknowledge their sinfulness and their need for God's healing. So in the case of Thomas, the evidence of Jesus's resurrected body serves to strengthen Thomas's faith. Thomas's response is not the intellectual act of a Humean skeptic declaring, "So you do in fact exist!" It is the spiritual act of a repentant servant confessing, "My Lord and my God." As the New Testament repeatedly shows, even the eyewitness experience of miracles often did not change people's rebellious hearts.[29] Here, once again, we see a serious misunderstanding in the basic approach Hume adopts in investigating the question of miracles.

Pascal's View: Miracles Are for the Poor in Spirit

Now, if in contrast to the Humean approach we follow Pascal's account of faith and rationality, it is quite apparent why Christ warns against an excessive concern with external evidence of God's power. According to Pascal, true faith involves a recognition, not of external evidence in favor of God's existence so much as of the internal evidence of one's inner need for redemption. For Pascal, faith means turning to God out of a loving recognition that one needs the saving grace that Christ offers. One problem with Hume's whole account of faith and miracles is that Hume envisions the wrong kind of priority between faith in God's redemptive providence and belief in miracles. Not surprisingly, Pascal offers a radically un-Humean perspective on the evidential role of miracles in the life of faith:

> "If I had seen a miracle," they say, "I should be converted." How can they be positive that they would do what they know nothing about? They imagine that such a conversion consists in a worship of God conducted, as they picture it, like some exchange or conversation. True conversion consists in self-annihilation before the universal being whom we have so often vexed and who is perfectly entitled to destroy us at any moment, in recognizing that we can do nothing without him and that we have deserved nothing but his disfavour. It consists in knowing that there is an irreconcilable opposition between God and us, and that without a mediator there can be no exchange.[30]

29. See also three passages in the Gospel of John—9:13–41; 10:25–30; and 11:45–57. Those who truly know and love the Father will recognize the authority of his Son (John 6:45; 8:47).

30. Pascal, *Pensées*, frg. 378.

And elsewhere:

> The prophecies, even the miracles and proofs of our religion, are not of such a kind that they can be said to be absolutely convincing, but they are at the same time such that it cannot be said to be unreasonable to believe in them. There is thus evidence and obscurity, to enlighten some and obfuscate others. But the evidence is such as to exceed, or at least equal, the evidence to the contrary, so that it cannot be reason that decides us against following it, and can therefore only be concupiscence and wickedness of heart. Thus, there is enough evidence to condemn and not enough to convince, so that it should be apparent that those who follow it are prompted to do so by grace and not by reason, and those who evade it are prompted by concupiscence and not by reason.[31]

As Pascal recognizes, a fundamental ground or basis for accepting God's word is our own sense of emptiness and wretchedness apart from God. On Pascal's account, it is only through such humility that we can be open to God's gift of faith. Miracles serve, then, not to confirm faith, but rather as signs or manifestations of God's character as just and loving, and of our own need for redemption. This is to say that miracles are meant not to prove God's existence or some aspect of God's character to an unbelieving observer, but rather to reveal something of God's nature or communicate an aspect of God's will for those willing to trust in God. And if we affirm that it is true that we need God's grace, that our own wills and intellects alone cannot procure for us the good we yearn for, then it should make sense to us that God would at particular moments supplement our limited understanding and lead us back to him. On this view, divine revelations serve not to provide us with objective proof, but to instruct us regarding the fullness of life God desires for us. So, for example, Christ's resurrection functions as God's sign that Christ is truly the savior he claims to be. On this account, we do not regard the story of the resurrection as confirming evidence because true faith does not need such external confirmation. The rationality of faith hinges in part on the question of its power to heal us and to make sense of our wretchedness. Only those who see clearly within themselves their own need for redemption can apprehend the external signs of God's miracles for what they truly are.[32]

31. Ibid., frg. 835.

32. Pascal argues in fragment 835 specifically against the view that miracles serve as empirical evidence by which reason can judge independently of the inclinations of the heart. For Pascal's account of God's hiddenness and the role of humility in perceiving God's presence, see esp. *Pensées*, 18, "foundations" (frgs. 223–44). Pascal argues in fragment 234 that God remains partially hidden, not to compel the mind to believe but to leave room for the assent of the heart. In this respect, Pascal's account of the relation of external evidence to faith resembles that of Aquinas. For Aquinas's analysis of the merit of faith, see *Summa Theologiae* IIaIIae 2.9–10. Terence Penelhum provides an excellent analysis of Aquinas's doctrine of faith in his essay, "The Analysis of Faith in St. Thomas Aquinas," in *Faith*, ed. Terence Penelhum (New York: Macmillan, 1989), 113–33.

Hume's Case against Miracles: A Summary

Let me now summarize my refutation of Hume's case against miracles. If Hume were successful in showing how belief in miracles is irrational, he would be on solid ground in his effort to drive a wedge between natural beliefs and theistic beliefs. But the case Hume constructs against belief in miracles both begs the question in defining miracles as violations of natural laws and simply assumes that rational theistic traditions should rely on miracle stories as proofs for their faith. Thus while the Lockean evidentialist may have much to be vexed about in Hume's line of reasoning, those theists who understand faith and miracles along the lines presented by Pascal have little cause for anxiety. For the Pascalian, at least, it remains unclear how Hume can reasonably justify his use of the "Humean wedge."

Finally, I suspect that Hume is averse to theistic metaphysical commitments because he simply presupposes a naturalistic framework in his philosophical inquiries. Consider how in section 5 of the first *Enquiry* Hume makes a curious claim about his skeptical philosophy. In his defense of limiting inquiry to the realm of common life, Hume asserts that the sole passion underlying the skeptic's "epistemic reserve"—that is, supporting the skeptic's commitment to metaphysical minimalism—is the love of truth.[33] To some extent, this claim seems justified. In restricting the skeptic's metaphysical arsenal to the fewest possible beliefs, he or she may avoid that human temptation to indulge that characteristically gnostic appetite for secret enlightenment available only to the intellectually elite. But, then again, if we refuse to take any risks in the direction of theism, what are we presupposing about this love of truth? Clearly, if it is love of truth that fires our inquiries, we shall want to hold as many true beliefs as possible, rather than hold only those we are simply compelled to hold. Suppose now that there is a God and that our happiness is dependent on him. If this God values faith, as the writer of Hebrews teaches, it would make sense that he would not compel us through evidence to believe in him. Trusting another person, whether human or divine, presupposes that we do not have absolutely firm evidence that the person is reliable. If I know, in the sense of believing with certainty based on evidence, that another person will keep a promise, for instance, there is no room for trusting that person. Trust in someone is an act as well as a disposition that affirms the other's self-worth; because I trust this person I accept the risk of being rejected, disappointed, or deceived by that person. When we trust a friend, we in effect declare that this person is of such worth to us that we are willing to risk being deceived or disappointed by that person. We open ourselves to risks because the person is worth it. Without the willingness to accept this kind of risk, trust is impossible. Ironically, the element of risk persists even if we refuse to be vulnerable

---

33. Hume, *Enquiry*, sec. 5, p. 41.

to others and resolve instead to trust nobody. The individual who is unwilling to trust anyone as a friend loses the benefits of companionship and friendship. What kind of wholeness and fulfillment can we hope to attain without the intimacy of friendship?

From a human point of view, God's call to us to be faithful challenges us to face these opposing risks of trusting and not trusting. Apparently, God desires deeply for our own sakes that we be willing to risk our futures on the prospect of God's goodness and mercy. Now, if God does indeed place a supreme value on trust, we risk both error and misery if we consider adopting Hume's miserly stance toward metaphysical convictions. Given the possibility that God may exist and may be calling us to faith, how is it that the love of truth recommends Hume's religious skepticism over the theist's faith? Put another way, if we cannot prove that God either exists or does not exist, should not our natural passion for truth lead us to be open to the *possibility* that God may be calling us to walk by faith? Once again, it appears that Hume's conception of the love of truth is viable and coherent only if one presupposes that we live in a naturalistic universe.

It is illuminating in this context to recall one place in the *Enquiry* where Hume speculates about why we are determined through sentiment to infer future events from past associations. In section 5 of the *Enquiry*, Hume sketches a purely naturalistic account of how our habits of belief have been implanted in us by the "wisdom" of nature. A fortunate kind of preestablished harmony, he observes, exists between the order of nature and the nonrational, customary operations of the mind.[34] Note here how Hume speculates about the utility of our beliefs in such phenomena as causes and effects. He suggests that our instinctual propensity to connect cause and effect has survival value in a real universe governed by mechanistic laws, in a universe that, as Hume says later, "is regulated by principles and maxims very different from ours."[35] Obviously, Hume does not presume to be certain about the correlation between the realm of actual experience and the realm of nature beyond our impressions. Yet given that we do believe in causal relations, Hume offers one account illuminating why it makes good sense that we do. Hume refrains from claiming to know the truth of his speculative hypothesis, just as he refrains from claiming to know that our natural beliefs are true.

Now, one might press Hume here to defend why his speculation about the fortunate harmony between nature and custom is not a violation of Hume's metaphysical minimalism. Clearly Hume's speculation regarding this "pre-established harmony" ventures beyond the realm of mere natural beliefs and

34. Ibid., pp. 54–55. For a helpful analysis of Hume's naturalized theory of preestablished harmony, see Joao-Paulo Montiero, "Hume, Induction and Natural Selection," in *McGill Hume Studies*, ed. David Norton, Nicholas Capaldi, and Wade Robison (San Diego: Austin Hill, 1979), 291–308.

35. Hume, *Enquiry*, sec. 11, p. 146.

posits an ultimate, metaphysical account for human experience. Setting aside this lapse, we might grant Hume that if we share his naturalism and take it as the starting point for our philosophical inquiries, we might proclaim Hume's metaphysical minimalism to be the true heir of the love of truth. But we cannot do so, at least not without some further argument, if we allow that theism may be true. Again, it appears that the wary and cautious theist might well applaud many of Hume's skeptical arguments without sharing Hume's thoroughgoing suspicion against religious commitment.

Before we dismiss Hume's anti-theistic views in the first *Enquiry* as unfounded, however, we need to examine his unflattering diagnosis of theistic faith found in *The Natural History of Religion*. Here Hume reveals what may well be his final and perhaps most devastating weapon against theism. Indeed, if Hume's psychological assessment of theistic psyche in his *Natural History* is sound, then Hume has a final and perhaps decisive move to make in support of his anti-theistic stance. The success of Hume's lengthy apology for mitigated skepticism in the first *Enquiry* ultimately hinges not simply on his epistemological presuppositions and arguments, which I think are unjustified and unsuccessful, but also on his detailed, psychological perspective on human life. It is in Hume's exposition in the *Natural History* concerning how we may live virtuously within the limits imposed on us by our ignorance of ultimate matters that we encounter his strongest reasons for opposing Christian theism. In other words, Hume's decisive weapon against faith in God is rooted in his psychology—or perhaps, more accurately put, in his *psychopathology*—of religious belief.

Hume's Psychological Refutation of Theism

I turn now to examine Hume's psychopathology of theism, for it is in his colorful analysis of the disordered and disordering character of traditional theistic belief that he comes closest to giving us his fundamental justification for his aversion to theism; without it, he cannot establish his conclusion that people should not venture into the realm of theistic speculation and inquiry. This is to say that Hume's psychopathology of theism provides us with the crucial missing premise that we have been seeking and that will justify his insistence on erecting a rigid barrier against theistic belief and practice. This premise, spelled out in Hume's psychology of religious consciousness, has two parts: Hume holds, first, that people naturally seek their own happiness, a happiness that requires striving to the greatest possible extent for a life free from inner psychic turmoil and conflict and, second, that Christian faith, as well as all other popular varieties of theism, does not lead to our happiness but causes in its followers immense inner distress and psychic disorder. If one then adds to Hume's missing premise the basic Humean dictum of the first *Enquiry* that the true philosopher should engage in philosophy only insofar as it positively impacts our human nature, it would follow that the true philosopher should shun all popular forms of theism, including Christianity.

In the first *Enquiry*, Hume takes for granted that liberating philosophy from the influences of religion is a good and necessary activity. While Hume does not explicitly condemn theism on psychological grounds in the first *Enquiry*, he does offer an in-depth psychopathology of theistic faiths in *The Natural History of Religion*, and his account of faith in this work provides just the sort of transitional ground Hume needs to support his thoroughgoing rejection of theism in the *Enquiry Concerning Human Understanding*. My contention is that, assuming his diagnosis is accurate, the negative diagnosis of theistic faith in the *Natural History* provides Hume with just the additional premises he needs to complete his case that the mitigated skeptic is wise to avoid all theistic speculations and concerns. Put simply, if Hume's diagnosis of theistic faith in the *Natural History* is accurate, then he can easily justify his unequal treatment of natural and religious beliefs. The first *Enquiry* makes it quite clear that Hume perceives theistic belief as a threat to human well-being. The *Natural History* undergirds Hume's antipathy to theism by offering a detailed diagnosis showing just how theism threatens the stability and unity of the human psyche.

My analysis of Hume's "missing premise" will proceed as follows. First, I will characterize the basic features of Hume's diagnosis of faith in the *Natural History*; second, I will present two compelling reasons that suggest Hume's diagnosis is seriously defective. In a nutshell, then, I maintain that Hume's grim diagnosis concerning theistic faith fails to provide a rationally credible teleological assessment of human well-being.

Hume sets out in *The Natural History of Religion* to bring to light the psychological origins and springs of religious belief—to provide, as the title indicates, a natural history of man's religious practices and convictions. To comprehend the truths inherent in our many-channeled religious heritage, Hume argues that we need to recognize a fundamental distinction between rational and nonrational forms of theism. Concerning the foundations of religion in human nature, Hume remarks:

> There are two questions in particular that challenge our attention, to wit, that concerning its origin in human reason and that concerning its origin in human nature. Happily, the first question, which is the most important, admits of the most obvious, at least, the clearest, solution. The whole frame of nature bespeaks an intelligent author; and no rational inquirer can, after serious reflection, suspend his belief a moment with regard to the primary principles of genuine Theism and Religion. But the other question, concerning the origin of religion in human nature, is exposed to some more difficulty.[36]

36. David Hume, *The Natural History of Religion*, ed. H. E. Root (Stanford, CA: Stanford University Press, 1956), 31.

Against the background of Philo's devastating criticisms in the *Dialogues* of the argument from design, and indeed of Hume's well-known rejection of there being any rational grounds for belief in God, Hume's affirmation here of a rational belief in an intelligent author might seem so out of character for Hume that one might suspect he is simply being disingenuous. But as Hume subsequently analyzes religious beliefs, he continues to reassert this claim that belief in an ultimate designer is hardwired into our rational nature, so we cannot simply dismiss what Hume says as mere skeptical irony. On a close reading of Hume's views in the *Natural History*, it becomes clear both that Hume is not at all endorsing the dubious kind of Lockean rational apologetics attacked by Philo and that, with some careful qualification, what he really means to say about "rational" religious belief fits quite harmoniously into the overall Humean conception of our passionate and rational nature as humans. As I will try to show, in the *Natural History* Hume has not actually changed his attitude toward theism or toward his conception of rationality in the *Enquiry*, even if he does employ a vocabulary of rationality in the *Natural History* that is not entirely of a piece with his "official position" in the *Enquiry*.

Let us note, first, that for Hume "genuine theism" is rational, but it is not rational in the sense that it satisfies the strict evidentialist canons of rationality or those presupposing a modern foundationalist criterion. On the strict evidentialist rendering, our belief in the design of the cosmos could be called rational only if it were based on an empirical proof, in the form of a deductive argument, establishing the existence of a supreme intelligence as the designer of the cosmos. In contrast, Hume's argument endorsing rational theism in the *Natural History* conceives of what we might call a psychological rationality rather than a strictly empirical or logical rationality. As I will argue, Hume's account of the rationality of theism closely resembles his defense of natural beliefs: neither genuine theism nor natural beliefs are rational in the sense of being derived from evidential reason.

Hume clarifies this non-Lockean conception of the rationality of religious belief in the following characterization of the imaginative basis of rational theism: "All things in the universe are evidently of a piece. Everything is adjusted to everything. One design prevails throughout the whole. And this uniformity leads the mind to acknowledge one author; because the conception of different authors, without any distinction of attributes or operations, serves only to give perplexity to the imagination, without bestowing any satisfaction on the understanding."[37] The rationality of this brand of theism is decidedly Humean rather than Lockean. According to Hume, the human mind settles on the monotheistic hypothesis for basically two psychological reasons. The first reflects Hume's general conviction that the human mind seeks tranquility: the human mind is drawn to account for the order of nature by inferring a

37. Ibid., 26.

single deity, because this thesis allows us to avoid the perplexity that confronts us with the polytheistic hypothesis—the perplexity that results because we have no rational method for either differentiating between, or limiting the number of, such deities. Second, the monotheistic hypothesis is more natural for us insofar as it arises, according to Hume, from a natural propensity in people to posit a single intelligence as the source of the uniform operations of nature. So Hume notes:

> Though the stupidity of men, barbarous and uninstructed, be so great, that they may not see a sovereign author in the more obvious works of nature, to which they are so much familiarized; yet it scarcely seems possible, that anyone of good understanding should reject that idea, when once it is suggested to him. A purpose, an intention, a design is so evident in every thing; and when our comprehension is so far enlarged as to contemplate the first rise of this visible system, we must adopt, with the strongest conviction, the idea of some intelligent cause or author. The uniform maxims, too, which prevail throughout the whole frame of the universe, naturally, if not necessarily, lead us to conceive this intelligence as single and undivided, where the prejudices of education oppose not so reasonable a theory.[38]

Clearly, in defending this doctrine of rational theism, Hume is certainly not offering a traditional proof for a supreme being of the traditional form deconstructed by Philo in the *Dialogues*. Instead, Hume describes the predominately involuntary psychological mechanisms by which fairly sophisticated observers of nature are drawn to believe in some kind of ultimate intelligent author of the cosmos. Through the observation of the uniformities of nature, such people naturally seek a cause proportioned to the effect: the conception of one author for the entire universe more neatly squares with the uniformity of natural laws. We seek a unified cause for the systematic order of nature, Hume says, not because it is empirically necessary but because it offers a basic satisfaction to human understanding. It is thus because of our sentimental and imaginative human nature rather than because of any "pure reason" that the mind finds rational comfort in a monotheistic framework.[39] As we will

38. Ibid., 74.

39. Here Hume embraces a much more definite religious hypothesis than Philo does when he contends in the *Dialogues* that the idea of divinity is so empty that the quarrel between atheist and theist is merely verbal. At least in the *Natural History*, Hume says that it is natural for people to posit a single intelligence as the source of natural order. Philo, on the contrary, insists that the analogy between the ultimate cause of nature and the human mind is so remote as to make any positive description of it essentially vacuous. Nevertheless, one should not overlook the clear point of agreement between these two Humean texts: both the *Dialogues* and the *Natural History* argue that it is contrary to reason to attribute any personal or moral qualities to the divinity. The crux of Hume's argument (articulated by Philo in part 7) is the following: (1) human moral judgments, and in particular our assessment of praiseworthy moral qualities, is based not on pure reason but on human moral sentiments; (2) a supreme being would have

see, Hume's deity in the *Natural History* lacks moral attributes and would be unfit to serve as a recipient of anything like worship or petitionary prayer. Indeed, Hume remains unequivocally opposed in the *Natural History* to any form of theism that attributes personal characteristics, such as love or moral virtue, to the ultimate cause. Nevertheless, the Humean "theist" prefers one conception of the divine nature, monotheism, to the less satisfying doctrine of polytheism. Devoid of moral qualities though it is, Hume's deity still remains an intelligence whose work bears the mark of rational intention. "Even the contrarieties of nature," Hume remarks, "by discovering themselves every-where, become proofs of some consistent plan, and establish one single purpose or intention, however inexplicable and incomprehensible."[40]

It is worth noting at this point how Hume's genuine theism harmonizes, albeit with some tension, with his portrait in the first *Enquiry* of the passionate, mitigated skeptic who accepts philosophy's essential office as being counselor to the person of common life. According to the Hume of the first *Enquiry*, since the purpose of philosophy is to help us live as humans, philosophical reason must acknowledge its dependence on human sentiments and basic needs. The philosopher who overlooks our complex nature as reasoning and sentimental beings will be unable to provide us with a philosophy capable of guiding us in living well within our cognitive limits. Good philosophers, in other words, must be attuned to our sentiments and not forget how largely our beliefs and actions are formed and sustained by imagination and affection. Genuine theism, Hume now tells us in the *Natural History*, is a sound, philosophical form of religious belief since it offers basic satisfaction to the sentimental foundation of human reasoning. Further, genuine theism provides a speculative systematic wholeness that coheres harmoniously with the rest of our natural beliefs; as people desiring a systematic understanding, we find such theism "cognitively" satisfying. So we see how Hume's case for genuine theism incorporates his general emphasis on the sentiments and affections governing human affairs and extends it in a fascinating way into the realm of our natural religious consciousness. There is a key difference, though, between the *Enquiry*'s portrait of the true skeptic and Hume's account of the rational theist. In the *Enquiry*, Hume

---

to be very unlike human beings; (3) so it is unreasonable to hold that a supreme being would possess either human sentiments or sentiments significantly resembling human sentiments. Therefore, (4) it is unreasonable to hold that a supreme being would share any of those moral qualities that humans consider praiseworthy. The proper theistic response would be to deny that point 3 follows from points 1 and 2, or to accept the validity of inferring point 3 and deny that points 1 through 3 entail point 4. That God is very unlike us certainly does not entail that God cannot also be like us in certain crucial respects. Indeed, one would expect there to be deep affinities between God and humans if we are created in his image. For a concise refutation of the skeptical thesis that God is totally unlike all creatures, see Thomas V. Morris, *Our Idea of God* (Notre Dame, IN: University of Notre Dame Press, 1991), 16–23.

40. Hume, *Natural History*, 74.

is a hard-line agnostic; he closes off common life to all metaphysical and religious beliefs not grounded in natural beliefs or in rational evidence. In contrast, the *Natural History* envisions a more complex set of sentiments bound up with our believing nature and working in conjunction with our empirical reasoning to generate our beliefs. Hume identifies a rational propensity and a rational desire, both of which serve to unify our beliefs about natural processes under the idea of an intelligent designer; they are parts of a natural psychological disposition directing our philosophical reflections. As Hume puts it, philosophical theism arises from this mechanism and is rational because it realizes the implicit aim of scientific theorizing—to satisfy our natural curiosity about the universe. Hume now justifies a very attenuated theism on the grounds that it originates in a healthy natural disposition and fulfills the rational desire to perceive coherence.

For Hume's genuine theist, the satisfaction we experience in beholding the order of nature is the initial seed of satisfaction that grows through our natural constitution into a philosophical pleasure of beholding unity and coherence in the world order. As with our natural beliefs, the genuine theist's belief in a divine architect posits a metaphysical being whose nature eludes our limited grasp. Unlike our natural beliefs concerning the physical world, the rational theistic hypothesis of genuine theism, Hume carefully observes, is neither universal nor uniform for all people. Not all people embrace genuine theism, presumably because many are too ignorant to marvel at the beautiful contrivances of nature, and because the propensity to systematize does not, in conjunction with other natural propensities, produce the same specific conception of deity in all those in whom it operates. One wonders whether Hume believes here that there might be denominational divides among deists. Nevertheless, Hume is now willing to call this general deistic form of religious belief rational.

In so doing Hume does not really betray his commitment in the first *Enquiry* to mitigated skepticism. The mitigated skeptic in the first *Enquiry* recognizes the need to believe beyond rational evidence. In the *Natural History*, Hume simply employs a less restrictive conception of rationality and permissible belief than he does in the first *Enquiry*: in the *Natural History*, those beliefs about the ultimate causes of the world order, generated from our natural propensity to make sense of nature, are now accorded the status of being rational. They are rational in the sense that they satisfy our distinctively human desire to understand. To summarize Hume's stance, we might say that genuine theism for Hume is rational in something of the same way that Christian belief is rational for Augustine and Pascal: a religious belief is rational insofar as it makes sense of our experience and arises properly out of our sentiments. Put another way, religious belief can be rational if it is grounded in the proper functioning of our complex cognitive nature. Yet in the *Natural History* Hume is far from being an Augustinian, for he is unequivocally clear that this new openness to the rationality of a certain kind of religious belief does not extend to the religious beliefs of the Christian believer. Such a person's foundation for belief, according to Hume, is not reason, even reason in the sense of a belief-forming mechanism rooted in a sentimental propensity to believe in a unifying cause of the natural order. Christian theism, and popular theism in general, arises out of a human emotion of the most pernicious character. In other words, even allowing for his more generous perspective on religious belief, Hume remains committed in the *Natural History* to the very exclusion of traditional Christian theism so essential to his vision of the mitigated skeptic in the first *Enquiry*.

According to Hume's diagnosis, Christian theism, as a variant of popular theistic belief in a divine author with personal and moral qualities, is the culmination of a religious history whose seeds are the anxious fears and trembling hopes of the earliest forms of polytheism. Primitive religious minds found the divine presence not in the regularity and order of nature, Hume says, but in their own ignorant and pathetic aspirations to control the forces of tempest and disease that continually haunted their precarious existence. The primitive motives of worship are the desire to flatter and ingratiate oneself with "higher" powers who control our destinies. How different from those of the philosophical theist, Hume remarks, are the original springs of popular religion. Hume states that the first religious beliefs of man were born of "the anxious concern for happiness, the dread of future misery, the terror of death, the thirst of revenge, the appetite for food, and other necessities. Agitated by hopes and fears of this nature, especially the latter, men scrutinize, with trembling curiosity, the course of future causes, and examine the various and contrary events of human life. And in this disordered scene, with eyes still more disordered and astonished, they see the first obscure traces of divinity."[41]

This account reveals one important respect in which popular theism for Hume differs so substantially from philosophical theism: the root state of mind of popular theism is thoroughly irrational. Primitive religious worship, the first historical stage of popular religious consciousness, originates out of ignorance of the natural causes of everyday events. As we shall see, popular religion, being born of ignorance, only perpetrates ignorance and irrationality as it takes hold of human life. After identifying the passionate motives of this original theism, Hume goes on to enrich his analysis by identifying the basic natural propensities by which primitive man sought relief from his anxious self-concern. Humans have basic propensities to project an invisible intelligent power in nature, to anthropomorphize—that is, to personify the powers responsible for natural events—to form our beliefs about nature into a coherent system, and to focus our attention on visible objects as the sources

41. Ibid., 28.

responsible for natural events.[42] Together with the passionate springs of fear and dread, and the desire to seek the favor of intelligent powers through adulation and worship, these propensities issue in various forms of polytheistic belief. In time, the disposition to appease or flatter the "wrathful" gods led primitive minds to ascribe greater and greater perfection to a single power. Eventually by their most determined efforts, these frightened worshippers reached the notion of a single, all-powerful God. This psychological root of self-interested adulation runs very deep and, indeed for Hume, continues to be one of the predominant sources for Christian faith in a single God. Such monotheistic believers, as Hume envisions them, "endeavor, by an affected ravishment and devotion, to ingratiate themselves" with their deity.[43] On this account of Christian life, worship, praise, service, and devotion all serve to curry favor with and merit the approval of an Almighty Judge. Furthermore, these forms of religious activity exhibit a common concern and methodology: the concern, on the one hand, being the entirely self-centered desire to secure

42. For Hume's account of these specific propensities, see *Natural History*, 26, 29, 38–41, 74–75. Yandell offers an excellent detailed analysis of these religious propensities in *Hume's Inexplicable Mystery*, 9–44, 114–17. Yandell provides a thorough and comprehensive account of the range of propensities delineated in Hume's study of popular theism. My discussion of Humean religious propensities is certainly not meant to be more than a brief overview. In his analysis of Hume's account of the origins of polytheism, Yandell notes that, for Hume, polytheism is rooted in "a propensity in human nature, which leads into a system, that gives some satisfaction" (Hume, *Natural History*, 29). Yandell clarifies how this propensity "which leads into a system" is best understood as a second-order propensity:

> The propensity to understand, under appropriate circumstances, often gives rise to, and is instantiated in, the operation of one or more of the set of first-order propensities mentioned above, [propensities to posit intelligent power, to anthropomorphize, to attend to observables, and to offer endless adulation] in the way that the capacity to perform motor skills, under appropriate circumstances, gives rise to and is instantiated in, walking across a room. (*Hume's Inexplicable Mystery*, 12)

So, according to Yandell, it makes perfect sense for Hume to say that the second-order propensity to understand gives rise to the first-order propensity to anthropomorphize. Yandell's reading of Hume's propensity "which leads into a system" is also supported by what Hume says earlier regarding philosophical theism. The observation of the uniformity of nature leads the mind to monotheism, Hume notes, because the less systematic polytheistic hypothesis "serves only to give perplexity to the imagination, without bestowing any satisfaction on the understanding" (*Natural History*, 26). In this passage Hume's tactic is clearly to uncover a basic human disposition to satisfy the understanding by achieving systematic coherence among one's beliefs. Later, where Hume has trained his sights on exposing the origins of polytheism, he cites the same psychological propensity and need for a system: like rational monotheists, polytheists seek a system that will offer satisfaction to their understanding (ibid., 29). The difference simply is that polytheists seek to find this satisfaction through what for Hume is a much more primitive and unstable framework—that is, through myriad personified natural forces. Yandell does not call attention to this common thread—the need for satisfaction of human understanding—in Hume's analysis of the origins of both genuine and popular theism. If my interpretation is correct, Hume recognizes that there is at least one shared rational propensity underlying both rational and popular forms of theism.

43. Hume, *Natural History*, 45.

one's future, to guarantee one's personal happiness; the method, on the other, is the submissive and hypocritical exchange of flattery for special privileges.

Out of the materials of popular theism's psychological origins, Hume completes his grim portrait by emphasizing how such a religious mind quite plausibly must continually suffer disorder and unrest. The monotheist, activated by fear of divine retribution, seeks to pay homage with the most sincere efforts of praise and adulation. But given his root conception of God as susceptible to flattery and prone to jealousy, the monotheist must secretly feel that repulsion and resentment of the slave toward his master. Thus the monotheist must seek to quiet his doubts and overlook his own sense of contradiction. Such dissimulation, however, never completely succeeds; as the believer vacillates between the opposing states of guilt and resentment, the inner spirit suffers pain and is tortured by an implicit awareness that he cannot succeed in believing what he must confess.[44] Hume also describes the believer's psychic disorder in terms of the two underlying religious propensities to ascribe visible causes to natural phenomena and to posit a single supreme intelligence as the ultimate cause of the universe. Try as they might, Hume observes, popular theists cannot remain firm in their focus on an immaterial, pure spirit, but they inevitably succumb to the temptation to think of God in corporeal, idolatrous terms.[45] In this species of conflict, the mind again cannot find satisfaction. Although the mechanism is slightly different here, the net result—a mind torn between incompatible urges—is the same as in the case of the unbelieving flatterer. As one could only expect, such a duplicitous and unhealthy spirit could hardly bear good fruit. Hume drives this point home with uncompromising clarity:

> The greatest crimes have been found, in many instances, compatible with a superstitious piety and devotion. Hence, it is justly regarded as unsafe to draw any certain inference in favour of a man's morals, from the fervor or strictness of his religious exercises, even though he himself believes them to be sincere. . . . *Those who undertake the most criminal and most dangerous enterprizes are commonly the most superstitious.* . . . To which we may add, that, after the commission of crimes, there arise remorses and secret horrors, which give no rest to the mind, but make it have recourse to religious rites and ceremonies, as expiations of its offences.[46]

To see why traditional theism on Hume's account is so contrary to the aims of good philosophy, we must recognize the existence of a clear causal connection between popular religion's inner agony, on the one hand, and its external manifestation, religious intolerance and immorality, on the other. Part of the self-torture experienced by the devoted monotheist stems from the

44. Ibid., 67.
45. Ibid., 46–48.
46. Ibid., 72–73 (italics in the original).

determined effort to hide the truth of unbelief and unrest. There is for such a person always the threat of external criticism, the best remedy for which is conformity and intolerance. In addition, the desire to flatter may lead to the most outrageous acts of murder, torture, and barbarism. "Perhaps," reasons the agonizing theist, "if I perform an act no one would ever do for normal motives, I will finally prove my loyalty to God and earn my spiritual peace." The fruits of Christian theism, Hume clearly implies, are the utter opposites of what the New Testament envisions as the fruits of the Spirit—love, joy, peace, kindness, gentleness, and self-control (see Gal. 5:22–23).

We might note here how Hume's attack on psychological grounds against Christian belief parallels his pragmatic case against the Pyrrhonist. If Hume is right, Christian faith and human nature are utterly incompatible. First, it is impossible in Hume's view for the Christian to deceive himself or herself so totally that the inner absurdities of Christian belief do not echo in his or her consciousness, and do not assert themselves in the Christian's inner thoughts. Second, being a Christian is not only impossible in practice, but it threatens as well the basic good and necessary stability of human society. This story Hume tells repeatedly in the *History of England*, a history, as Hume recalls it, rampant with examples of religious warfare, intolerance, and social injustice.[47] Unfortunately, in contrast with Pyrrhonism, Christianity and popular monotheism in general actually are able to subvert the forces of nature and retain their hold on their devotees. Compared to Christianity, Pyrrhonism is, relatively speaking, an innocent, harmless mistake of philosophers who, like the Lockean rationalist of the Enlightenment, fail to appreciate the power of nonrational mechanisms of belief-formation. Pyrrhonists may well cast themselves into intellectual despair for some time, but such fits of hubristic skepticism are inevitably short-lived. Christianity, in Hume's rendering, does not let its victims escape so easily or let itself get off as lightly; its conflict with human nature is not so eradicable, its sins not so private and transient. Nonetheless, Hume's strategy for dealing with both aberrations is similar. Pyrrhonism and Christianity make people unfit for common life; they are irrational in the fundamental sense that they violate crucial natural propensities in us and are thus inhuman.

Yet it should be overwhelmingly evident to anyone who is even mildly sympathetic to the Christian tradition that what Hume provides in the *Natural History* is not a critique of genuine Christian faith. Instead, Hume uncovers, with devastating accuracy and courageous honesty, the perverse and unfortunate nature of theistic hypocrisy. Admittedly, there are many forms of

---

47. Hume vividly portrays the factious and destructive influences of Christian enthusiasm in his account of the downfall of Charles I and the subsequent reign of Cromwell. For Hume's treatment of the role of religious frenzy in the drama of Charles I, see esp. *The History of England*, ed. William Todd (Indianapolis: Liberty Classics, 1983), 5:210–13, 441–546. Hume reflects on the role of "gloomy enthusiasm" in the era of Cromwell in ibid., 4:140–45.

religious hypocrisy, so to avoid confusion let me specify the particular species of hypocrisy I have in mind. From beginning to end, Hume's popular mono-theists have no higher sense of worship than bribery. Their spiritual existence, fueled predominantly by fear, is all petition and no benediction. But of what exactly are Humean Christian zealots afraid? What accounts for their fear? To respond we must emphasize two facts, both central to the psychological description Hume develops. As Hume characterizes them, theistic believers pursue acts of flattery because they want release from a life of uncertainty and pain. Quite naturally, they seek their own happiness. They engage in flattery because they think that God demands it in exchange for bestowing the blessings they desire. As they envision him, God is fundamentally and predominately a God of despotic power, a God who issues inexplicable commands and then punishes those who disobey. As Hume explains, there is no more basic reason to account for obedience than that it is a self-protective measure taken against an all-powerful ruler. Worship is thus merely a means to a natural end; it is basically an insurance policy paid to a very tough institution. One might well conclude that, for Hume, religious faithfulness is similar to Glauconian jus-tice in book 2 of Plato's *Republic*: faithfulness, like justice, is not something desirable in itself but is a second-best compromise in a world where security depends on paying a price.

But this fear-based manifestation of "faith," while it may occur much more often than we might like, is, from a Christian perspective, not faith but hypoc-risy. For the Christian, worship is an end in itself, since it is a loving fellowship with a loving God, not a relationship built on fear and bribery. Let me explain, then, what I take to be the essential limitation of Hume's diagnosis. The root malady of popular religious consciousness—at least of what Hume thinks is popular religious consciousness—is that it lacks the essential reality of love. But consider that when Jesus is questioned in Matthew 22 on the greatest commandment in the law, he responds not just with one but with two com-mandments, two that quite clearly he understands to be inseparable. We are first commanded, Jesus says, to love the Lord our God with our whole selves, and second, to love our neighbor as ourselves (Matt. 22:37–39). As Jesus goes on to assert, these commandments play a fundamental role in the true life of faithfulness, since all other religious precepts and teaching of the prophets depend on them and make sense only insofar as they are understood as rooted in these supreme commandments (Matt. 22:40). *Agape* love, in other words, is the inner life and necessary foundation for the believers' relationship to God. Indeed, love is the key to understanding the essential difference between Humean and New Testament models of religious belief. In explaining how this is so, I will be especially concerned to focus on two fundamental points of difference—the first regarding the character of the one to whom obedience is offered, and the second regarding the crucial difference the character of God makes in the nature of worship. Taken together, these differences clarify why it is the case that fear-based Humean popular theism is, from a Christian perspective, a fraudulent and virulent perversion—an expression not of true faith but of religious hypocrisy.

How is it, first of all, that *agape* love is the foundation of the believer's relationship to God as well as to other people? Perhaps no passage from the New Testament more powerfully addresses this question than 1 John 4:7–12:

> Beloved, let us love one another, because love is of God; everyone who loves is born of God and knows God. Whoever does not love does not know God, for God is love. God's love was revealed among us in this way: God sent his only Son into the world so that we might live through him. In this is love, not that we loved God but that he loved us and sent his Son to be the atoning sacrifice for our sins. Beloved, since God loved us so much, we also ought to love one another. No one has ever seen God; if we love one another, God lives in us, and his love is perfected in us.

In this account of *agape* love, we encounter the decisive priority of God's love for people. It is God's love that is primary and original; human love for God is a response, not a causal antecedent, to the love of God. Indeed, God loves his people so profoundly, the writer of 1 John says, that despite our continual refusal to love God, he manifests his love for us through the ultimate sacrifice of the cross. The cross demonstrates that the character of God's love is unconditional; it is not a reward for good behavior but a remedy for a loveless race. Divine love calls us out of our natural self-centeredness, and it presents Christ's sacrifice as a reparation for humanity's rejection of God. Now, to accept God in Christ means in part that we affirm God's nature as perfect love and acknowledge our own thirst and hunger for this love. But in calling us out of alienation from his love, God can free us only by transforming us into the image of Christ. God's offer of grace frees us from having to attain or doubt our self-worth, since we now realize that our worth is rooted in God's unconditional love. At the same time, we cannot accept God's grace exclusively for ourselves. Since unmerited grace is offered to all and since none in any way merit it, we can accept this gift of grace only if we acknowledge that we are no more worthy of it than our irksome colleague or next-door neighbor. Hence, if we refuse to love our fellow human, we set ourselves against God's love and separate ourselves from God's Spirit. But it is just this separation that God has sought to overcome for our own sakes; unless we respond to God's love for us by loving others as God loves them—that is, unconditionally—we oppose the grace that God offers. Put another way, as God's love for us affirms our worth, and can be embraced only with humility and gratitude, we celebrate it by rejoicing in it and loving one another. Unconditional love either is accepted unconditionally—that is, with the acknowledgment and affirmation that such love is offered universally to all of humanity—or is not accepted at all.

Clearly, the emphasis in our passage from 1 John is not on placating a wrathful God, but on abiding or participating in God's nature as perfect *agape*.[48] So the writer of 1 John goes on to say, "There is no fear in love, but perfect love casts out fear; for fear has to do with punishment, and whoever fears has not reached perfection in love. We love because he first loved us. Those who say, 'I love God,' and hate their brother or sisters are liars" (4:18–20). These verses draw a significant contrast between two radically opposed relationships to God. On the one hand, it allows that we might obey God out of fear, out of a sense of self-interested avoidance of getting on God's "bad side." But if such fear alone is our root motivation for worship, our response to God does not affirm who God is and what he has revealed through the cross. To be perfected in God's love is to grow closer to God and to overcome our mistrust and fear that God is unreliable or a mere cosmic tyrant. Grounding belief in God in fear, in this sense, could result from a natural hesitation to believe that the God of the whole universe could really love us. Then again, it might stem from our anxiety about trusting in a God who truly loves all people, for we are well aware of the risks and possible humiliation that often result from loving others unconditionally. Mere common sense informs us these dangers

---

48. I do not mean to imply in my analysis of *agape* love that because God loves his human creation there can be no meaningful and coherent sense in which humans in their rejection of God incur God's wrath. My quarrel lies exclusively with Hume's distorted analysis of the role of fear and anxiety in his psychology of theistic belief. For Hume, believers turn to God and obey God only because they fear the consequences of not doing so. What such believers lack is any affirmation of God as good and any recognition of God's love that could inspire genuine gratitude. My rejoinder to Hume is simply that such people as Hume characterizes do not really believe *in* God. Rather than trust in God, they seek only to flatter and manipulate an object of terror. My case against Hume thus leaves open the issue of just how Christ's life and death serve as atonement for our sinning against God. Nothing in my argument here is intended to entail the rejection of the New Testament understanding of the cross as a propitiation for sin (see John 1:29; 3:14–16; 11:51–52; Rom. 3:25; Col. 1:13; Heb. 9; and 1 John 1:2; 4:10). The question, in particular, of what it means for Christ's sacrifice to be a propitiatory act accomplishing the reconciliation of God and sinful humanity is of crucial importance for an understanding of Christian faith but lies beyond the scope of my argument. Any plausible account of the meaning of Christ's propitiation for sin must focus on an analysis of how sin renders people guilty and places them in a state of moral indebtedness to God. One fundamental matter of debate among Christian thinkers is whether Christ's paying back to God what people are no longer able to repay is necessary primarily because of God's just nature (so thinks Anselm) or because of our need as sinners to be healed (so argues Aquinas). On the Anselmian view, the atonement is necessary insofar as it would be unjust for God to forgive humans without God's honor being restored. For Aquinas, God could have forgiven us without the work of Christ on the cross, but doing so would not have helped us to be restored to proper harmony with him. For two excellent accounts of the atonement along the lines of Thomas Aquinas's position, see Eleonore Stump, "Atonement According to Aquinas," in *Philosophy and the Christian Faith*, ed. Thomas V. Morris (Notre Dame, IN: University of Notre Dame Press, 1988), 61–91; and Richard Swinburne, "The Christian Scheme of Salvation," in Morris, *Philosophy and the Christian Faith*, 15–30. Anselm offers his account of the atonement in *Cur Deus Homo*. For Aquinas's view see *Summa Theologiae* IIIa 46–48.

are involved in heeding the call of a God who loves us so radically as to send into our world his only begotten Son.

With due respect to Hume, we might note that the historical church has often acted with more worldly common sense than true faith. True faith, built on real love, is obviously a lofty and discomforting ideal. Still, we do not even begin to attain this ideal of new life if our belief stems from mere fear of divine retribution rather than from love of God for who God is. For if our deepest motive for worship of God is fear of God's brute power, as Hume himself argues, then it turns out that in worship we are fundamentally concerned only for ourselves and are seeking, through flattery, merely to avoid punishment. To affirm who God is, and to focus not exclusively or obsessively on our imperfections but on God's excellence, we must accept God's love for us, since love is God's nature. To accept this love involves, in part, recognizing its worth and seeking to participate in it. Moreover, by uniting ourselves to this love, by abiding in it, we know God not from a distance but in fellowship. To obey God merely out of fear implies a denial of God's nature and the exercise of a faith, if one wants to deem it such, that exhibits the very self-centeredness we are called to reject. In responding to God merely out of fear for ourselves we remain bound up with our own desires and needs. True faith, in contrast, responds to the original and primary divine love by loving God and one's neighbor, or at least by yearning to love God and one's neighbor. True faith, according to 1 John, is rooted in a true understanding of whom we are to obey. True obedience, properly understood, is founded on this love of a God who is supremely good and beautiful. To reverse the priority of love and obedience, to try to love God as the highest good merely to avoid his wrath, is to try to affirm God's being and become unselfish and loving for purely selfish, unloving motives. Surely Hume is right to charge such a religious outlook with dissimulation.[49]

I would like to make one further point in this context. I think it is undeniable that what Hume criticizes in the *Natural History* is repeatedly acknowledged in the New Testament as a live option and tempting alternative to genuine faith. Hume is not, in other words, entirely off the mark in his analysis of religious natural history. Indeed, Hume's psychopathology of fear-based religious belief might well be taken as an in-depth elucidation of Paul's warning to the church in Corinth: "If I have all faith, so as to remove mountains, but do not have love,

---

49. In contrasting the place of love and fear in the life of faith, I do not mean to deny that there is a kind of fear of God, in the sense of respect and awe in the face of God's majesty and moral perfection, which is a legitimate, if not essential, aspect of a healthy Christian life. The "fear" that is the beginning of wisdom, for example, is just such a healthy sense of respect and awe in the face of God's authority and grandeur. I do not mean to imply, moreover, that a God of love would not feel wrath toward human injustice and would never resort to punishing his people. I am arguing that fear of God's power alone, apart from love of God and awareness of God's amazing grace, has no legitimate place in the life of the Christian believer.

I am nothing" (1 Cor. 13:2). The early church in Corinth appears, from what Paul teaches throughout his letter, to have been mired in unloving dissension and discord. Paul diagnoses a root problem of the Corinthian church to be a failure of love and an excess of self-centeredness, and Paul explicitly counsels the Corinthian Christians not to be ignorant of the crucial truth that the ideal of a shared, Christian life is to live together in harmony and love as the body of Christ. The unity of this body is love, essentially that love of Christ for the individual members who must follow him by being committed to one another's individual good as well as to the corporate good of the whole body. The work of love is to unify the community, to oppose our natural egoism, and to seek the benefit of others and not just of our private selves. In love we, so to speak, take on a new, corporate identity; we recognize that our individual good is bound up with the greater good of the Christian community. Paul's warning in his letter emphasizes the essential interconnection between love and true faith. True faith, as trust in God, seeks to mirror the self-giving and other-centered quality of God's love for humanity. Divorced from this love, religious practice centers on the self, typically lacks the power to oppose the temptations of inordinate love, and engenders competition and disharmony. In 1 Corinthians, Paul recognizes the actuality of such egoistic, loveless faith, but in no uncertain terms does he declare to the Corinthians that such perverse faith is not real faith at all.

My criticism of Hume's argument from religious psychopathology hinges on the insight that Hume oversimplifies the psychology of religious belief. Faced with the question of what people should believe about God, Hume reduces our options to either a barbarous, dishonest, religious hypocrisy or an impersonal, merely intellectual, deistic theism. Because of the way Hume narrows the alternatives, it is quite reasonable for Hume to conclude at the end of the *Natural History* that the whole of religion is "a riddle, an enigma, an inexplicable mystery."[50] "Indeed," the Christian theist might well reply, "so it seems when popular, traditional religious life is grasped only through its darkest expressions." And not surprisingly, at the decisive conclusion of his polemic, Hume himself flees to the calm refuge of philosophy, where one may go only so far as to assent to an impersonal deity, whose existence offers no practical guidance, makes no radical demands on our lives, and merely offers to the intellectual elite a pleasant degree of tranquility for their understanding. But if, in contradistinction to Hume, we avoid such a theological reductionism and entertain that a religious faith rooted in *agape* love is possible—and certainly Hume never shows that it is not—then there is a third choice between the Humean dichotomy of minimal theism and barbaric, fear-based religion. Then it is far from clear that Hume's choice of minimal theism is the only, or even the most, reasonable choice for us to make.

50. Hume, *Natural History*, 76.

It is clear that throughout his writings Hume seeks to offer civilized humans a remedy against pernicious and unhealthy ways of life, and he certainly presents compelling criticisms of bad faith. Like Socrates, Hume essentially seeks to cure what he considers to be a malady of religious sentiments rooted in destructive passions and self-ignorance. For Hume in the *Natural History*, all traditional forms of religion that involve belief in personal deities or in a single all-powerful deity are condemned as severely unhealthy. But as an exercise in accurately diagnosing the various forms of the religious life and in recommending only the most minimal theism as compatible with a sound philosophical restoration of self, Hume's effort falls seriously short. In essence, his tactic is to expose an unhealthy perversion of faith and misrepresent it as the genuine article. But to do so is irrational when much evidence to the contrary is readily available in culture and in historical documents.

No doubt the parameters of Hume's historical study of religion are in part determined by the social and political dynamics of modern European religious warfare. Our final verdict on Hume's *Natural History* ought thus to depend in part on how we answer an important historical question: how accurately or inaccurately did Hume diagnose the actual religious spirit of his eighteenth-century contemporaries?[51] Unfortunately, this is not a very easy

---

51. David Norton argues convincingly that Hume's skepticism concerning the moral benefits of popular theism responds to the moral imperative for theism inherent in the very influential tradition of Protestant natural law philosophy from Hugo Grotius and Samuel von Pufendorf to John Locke. (See Norton, "Hume, Atheism, and the Autonomy of Morals," in *Hume's Philosophy of Religion*, ed. Anthony Flew [Winston-Salem, NC: Wake Forest University Press, 1985], 97–144.) This modern apologetic tradition may well have provided for Hume one of the most illustrative examples of unhealthy Christian ethical philosophy. If so, Hume's antagonism is understandable. Despite their differences, the key figures in modern, prudential, natural law philosophy agree that a prudential form of theism is a fundamental presupposition for a coherent theory of morality. In particular, these thinkers characteristically maintain that belief in divine judgment is absolutely necessary for securing public morality. So Locke declares in the *Letter Concerning Toleration*, "Those are not at all to be tolerated who deny the being of a God. Promises, covenants, and oaths, which are the bonds of human society, can have no hold upon the atheist" (quoted in Norton, "Hume, Atheism, and the Autonomy of Morals," 98). It is not especially clear whether Locke means this as a psychological or logical entailment. Perhaps the atheist could, even though he had no ultimately sufficient reason to, be true to his oaths. Whether or not Locke allows for the possibility of a morally decent collection of atheistic intellectuals, he firmly believes, as do Grotius and Pufendorf, that atheism for the great majority of common men could lead only to anarchy and moral decadence. Their reasoning might well have laid much of the groundwork for Hume's reaction to religious morality. Most importantly, at least as Hume understands them, they contend that without the threat of divine punishments, most people will find the temptations of injustice, and of immorality in general, too attractive to withstand. But for Hume, if these natural law proponents are correct, then the ironic quip attributed to Mark Twain, "I wrestled with my conscience and I won," would aptly predict the course of human history in every religious age. For Hume, in other words, the prudential, modern, natural law tradition cannot sustain a stable moral social order. As Norton shows, Hume takes on this powerful modern natural law consensus, reverses the implied entailment, and argues in the *Natural History* that everyday religion and morality are thoroughly incompatible. It is also

question to answer, for it requires us not only to examine historical events, but also to penetrate into the souls of Hume's contemporaries. Assessing the inner spirituality of others is never easy, especially as we can never be fully assured of our own integrity and objectivity. Ironically, *The Natural History of Religion* demonstrates that how we interpret any sphere of human action—that is, how we construct our social narratives—will unavoidably reflect our own principles of value and, in particular, reflect what we as interpreters believe to be rational and irrational. Our theories of rationality, in turn, are not generated ex nihilo but emerge and evolve out of what we experience and how we understand the nature of the world. Indeed, if we read Hume's *Enquiry* and *Natural History* against the background of Cartesian and Lockean foundationalism, this lesson about the nature of rationality should strike us as one of the most fundamental lessons to be learned from Hume's philosophy of religion.

As we have seen, Hume's philosophy of common life insists that our theory of rationality must ground itself in an inquiry about human nature. According to the *Enquiry*, it is permissible, and in one sense "rational," from the point of

---

worth noting how Hume represents this modern natural law position in the person of Cleanthes in the *Dialogues*. Consider Cleanthes's very modern defense of religious morality: "Religion, however corrupted, is still better than no religion at all. The doctrine of the future state is so strong and necessary a security to morals, that we never ought to abandon or neglect it. For if finite and temporary rewards and punishments have so great an effect, as we daily find: How much greater must be expected from such as are infinite and eternal?" (*Dialogues*, 12.82).

Philo subjects Cleanthes's position to a devastating series of criticisms, many of which correspond to those against popular theism found in the *Natural History*. Philo rightly objects, for example, to the double-minded prudentialism implicit in Cleanthes's religious viewpoint. In essence, Philo notes, Cleanthes's religious morality reduces to nothing more than "a narrow, contracted selfishness." On Cleanthes's view, the masses need religion not to overcome their egoism, which presumably he thinks impossible, but to scare them into external compliance with moral rules. This sounds very much like saying that if we cannot make the majority of everyday folks into true gentlemen and ladies, we can at least mold them into decent hypocrites. So Cleanthes's strategy for defending the faith plays right into the hands of Hume the critic in the *Natural History*. Philo certainly perceives with more penetration than Cleanthes, and his final contribution to the dialogue dwells on the inherent perversity of Cleanthes's apologetics, for in Cleanthes's view the common person only pretends to be moral: the common person wears the covering of the lamb, but only because he or she thinks it pays to do so. In response, Philo predicts that such persons will continually need to dissemble and confront their unbelief with a constant inflaming of hypocritical enthusiasm. And how much greater the hypocrisy when their dissimulation employs the language of faith and love. If we take Cleanthes as a reasonable exponent of this modern, prudential, natural law position, then we can understand Philo's vehemence and appreciate as well the timeliness if not complete accuracy of Hume's antagonism to Christianity.

Whether or not Hume fairly represents this modern natural law tradition in the figure of Cleanthes, it is worth recalling that it is Cleanthes who objects in the beginning of the *Dialogues* to Philo's pairing of skepticism and religious faith as useful allies. Against Philo, Cleanthes cites the worthy name of John Locke as the first thinker to appreciate so clearly that faith is simply another species of reason to be judged and defended according to evidentialist credentials. It is no coincidence that Philo, having devastated the epistemological basis of Lockean evidentialism, continues at the very end of the *Dialogues* to undermine another component of Locke's position.

view of human nature to hold natural beliefs even though they compel us to believe beyond clear evidence and even though the concepts central to them, such as that of causal power and material object, are neither clear nor distinct. As I have argued, Hume explicitly extends the boundaries of rational belief in the *Natural History* to embrace in a very attenuated form the belief in a divine being. For Hume, this philosophical theism is rational. It is rational even though it is not the conclusion of any valid evidential reasoning. Hume calls such theism rational because it fulfills our need as human thinkers to achieve a coherent system of beliefs, to attain systematic rather than fragmentary knowledge. In this respect, Hume's justification of his philosophical theism has much more affinity to an Augustinian analysis of the rationality of faith than it does to the foundationalist method of Descartes and Locke. Unlike his foundationalist predecessors, Hume connects what is rational to believe with an account of the crucial facts of our human nature, and especially with the operations of human sentiment. So Hume justifies rational theism through a self-reflective inquiry into the roots of the human pursuit of knowledge, the conclusions of which can be justified only through reflection on experience, not by an evidential proof. Essentially, in the *Natural History* Hume examines the human practice of seeking to understand the regularities of nature, sifts out its psychological foundations, and accepts as rational the form of theism that, he thinks, so naturally affords the mind the fulfillment it desires. But due to his failure to distinguish corrupt from genuine forms of traditional Christian faith, Hume never considers the possibility of a truly Christian life being rational in something of the same way as is Hume's genuine theism. This is to say that Hume never really comes to terms with the Augustinian strategy for reconciling faith and reason. It is Pascal, not Hume, who understands Augustine's confessional defense of the rationality of faith. Not surprisingly, for both Augustine and Pascal, such a defense makes no sense at all apart from love.

Hume versus Augustine (and Pascal): Opposing Rationalities in Conflict

I turn now to developing a second line of criticism against Hume's overwhelmingly negative regard for theistic faith. Whereas in the previous argument I took issue with Hume's psychological description of the inner life of true Christian faith, in this part of my investigation I will contend that Hume's general understanding of faith and reason is seriously deficient. The crux of my argument is that in his characteristic attacks on the rational credibility of traditional faith, Hume oversimplifies the question of the rationality of faith and fails to reckon with the conception of rationality essential to the Augustinian tradition. For Augustine, as well as for Pascal, who is a deeply Augustinian thinker, the question of the rationality of faith has nothing to do with whether one can infer the existence of God or prove that God has acted in human history on the basis of some set of empirical or logical propositions that would be rationally compelling to any disinterested person. Instead, for the Christian, belief in God functions not as the conclusion of such an argument or as a derivative principle to be supported by epistemically prior evidence, but as a necessary ethical starting point, an ethical first principle, on the basis of which alone one can make sense of oneself and thus defend the rationality of faith. Whereas Hume wants to say that in matters of personal, theistic faith the wise person will proportion his or her belief to the evidence, Augustine argues that unless he or she first becomes transformed into a person of faith, a person who experiences the transforming power of God's love—or is the kind of person who sees that he or she needs divine healing and yearns for the power of this love—then he or she lacks the "inner evidence" necessary for appreciating the rationality of faith and for growing in wisdom. Both Augustine and Pascal argue in similar ways that it is only through the heart that a person who lacks faith in God can begin to appreciate its rationality as a solution for human life, and conversely it is only through the heart that a person who possesses faith can articulate why his or her faith is rational. To whatever degree one comprehends the rationality of faith, whether as a non-believer coming to see how faith makes sense, or as a faithful pilgrim seeking to grow deeper in faith and love, one must be guided by the directives of the human heart, and in particular by the passion of love, to grasp the rationality of faith. It is this conception of faith and rationality that is expressed in Augustine's classic proclamation "*credo ut intellegam*" ("I believe in order to understand"). Hume, in seeking to expose in both the *Dialogues* and the first *Enquiry* the rational deficiency of Christian faith, assumes in effect the reverse, that one must first understand in order to believe.

The crux of my critique of Hume's dramatic analysis of the rationality of faith is this: when Hume sets out, particularly in the *Dialogues* and the first *Enquiry*, to challenge the rational credentials of theistic faith, he works within the confines of the doctrine of rationality derived from modern foundationalism and entirely overlooks the more ancient Augustinian account of reason and faith. But it is precisely this alternative view that Hume ought to consider, for at least two reasons: first, because the Augustinian doctrine fits more naturally than its Enlightenment counterpart with the outlook on faith and evidence present in the New Testament; and second, because it represents a long-standing tradition within Christian thought—beginning with Augustine and running through Anselm and Aquinas to Pascal—against which Hume's classic, and ingenious, refutations of theism are basically beside the point.

Before proceeding, let me review the key features of Hume's anti-theistic strategy. According to Hume in the first *Enquiry* and the *Dialogues*, to show that religious belief is in fact rational one would have to show that there are scientific—which is to say empirical—or logical foundations that from the point of view of the disinterested observer would provide either certain or probable evidence for the existence of God. Belief that God exists is thus rational, on Hume's general view, if and only if such rational foundations exist on which religious belief can be supported. Contrary to the apologetic efforts of many Enlightenment defenders of theism, Hume contends, of course, that such foundations cannot be found because they simply do not exist. So it is that Hume attacks the rationality of accepting the historical testimony of miracles and his skeptical character Philo seeks in the *Dialogues* to subvert the project of natural theology; all of Philo's skeptical arguments converge on the key assertion that our evidence of nature's uniformity does not provide sufficient evidence for theism. In sum, Hume's critical writings on the rationality of faith contend overall that the neutral standards of rational evidence required for establishing the rational credibility of theism simply cannot be found. In the *Natural History*, Hume relaxes his prohibitions against religious belief only to the extent that one may intellectually assent to the existence of an intelligent designer whose being has absolutely no influence on one's conduct and morals. If Hume is right, certainly the Enlightenment project of Christian apologetics attempted by philosophers such as Locke simply fails. The Lockean apologist will never succeed, Hume concludes, in showing how theistic belief is rationally justified on the basis of any appropriately neutral empirical evidence. Moreover, in his attack on belief in miracles, Hume insists that "we may establish it as a maxim, that no human testimony can have such force as to prove a miracle, and make it a just foundation for any such system of religion."[52] In essence, what Hume argues is that no historical testimony serves as a rational foundation for a particular religious tradition. Thus any religious system founded on such testimony is irrational.

Clearly in all these discourses on religion Hume endeavors to persuade us that Christian religious belief is irrational, because there are no rational, evidential grounds for historical Christian belief. As Hume explicitly tells us in his essay "Of Miracles," since the wise man "proportions his belief to the evidence,"[53] he will not embrace belief in God because such belief subverts his reason. This is to say that, for Hume, religious belief results from the malfunctioning of our cognitive apparatus. Now, whether or not one finally agrees with Hume's negative assessment both of the evidential status of belief in miracles and of the proofs of God's existence based on the order of the cosmos, the curious fact remains that Hume's offensive forays here against the rationality of faith never confront the kind of opposing stance on the relation of faith and reason found in Augustine and Pascal. Hume overlooks that what is essential to Pascal's account of faith is an Augustinian conception of rationality. Simply put, Hume presumes that Christian belief in God is

52. Hume, *Enquiry*, sec. 10, p. 110.
53. Ibid.

rational if and only if there is either empirical or logical evidence to support it; Hume thus presupposes that the rational inquirer ought to begin in a state of suspended belief and embrace faith only insofar as he or she can find rational confirmation of God's existence in the data of empirical observation or logical deduction. For the Augustinian, however, the order of discovery is exactly the reverse: on the Augustinian view, first one must respond to God in faith, in an act of assent that expresses humility and love; only after this initial act of believing in God does one have sustained access to the sort of "evidence" one really needs to show how belief in God is rational. From an Augustinian point of view, both the believer and the nonbeliever must in some respect exhibit a humble and loving attitude toward the message of God's grace in order to grasp its rationality. In other words, Augustine contends that even our initial and least robust access to the rationality of faith requires a preparation of our hearts that enables us initially to see and feel how faith makes sense of our human condition.

Whereas Hume in effect requires that we secure the evidence before we believe, Augustine insists that, unless one believes, unless one trusts in certain truths that one cannot yet fully see, one will suffer from a combined disorder of both the intellect and the will: one will be unable to affirm the rationality of faith because one will be unable to access the kind of evidence needed to make rational sense of faith. For Augustine, what is at issue here is not a matter of endorsing fideistic irrationalism—the view that believers ought to oppose reason out of their loyalty to faith—but is instead a firm conviction in the doctrine of reason's dependence on the heart, and specifically of reason's need to be directed by a proper, ordered love, *caritas*, in order for reason to fulfill its own purpose. In effect, Augustine exhibits an insight here that is often heralded as the achievement of postmodernism—the recognition, namely, that reason cannot function autonomously and solve fundamental problems of human life independently of particular commitments and loyalties. As I shall argue, one certainly does not need to be a radical postmodernist to realize that all of the exercises of our human reason are "biased" or rooted in human interests. In saying that "I must believe in order to understand" (*"credo ut intellegam"*), Augustine means to say that true understanding will always be "biased" since it depends on a heart purified by a faith that "worketh by love." Unlike Hume, then, Augustine conceives of a type of rationality in which the rational justification for religious belief is unavailable to those who remain neutral spectators, because such individuals cut themselves off from access to the very evidence needed to make the case seem reasonable. On Augustine's view, in fact, the very conception of autonomous rationality is itself a tragic illusion—it is an illusion insofar as reason can never overcome the "prejudices of the heart," and it is tragic because philosophers who suffer this illusion are themselves failing to be rational about the nature of reason.

As we have seen, Hume is, of course, well aware of reason's lack of complete autonomy in human life. As Hume notes in the first *Enquiry*, some of our most fundamental beliefs neither originate in nor can be justified by logical or empirical reasoning. When it comes to natural beliefs about physical objects and the regularity of nature, Hume does in effect affirm that one must first "believe" in order to understand. But in the sphere of religious experience, Hume does not practice this epistemic generosity. Given what he regards as the clear psychological and social maladies perpetrated by theistic religious beliefs, Hume draws the line and will endorse stepping out in faith only if a sufficient, evidentialist case can be presented to confirm it. The real issue, then, between Augustine and Hume is not a question of reason's overall lack of autonomy and dependence on belief. The crucial point over which Augustine and Hume differ is on the wisdom of assenting to religious belief before seeing clearly undeniable rational evidence confirming its truth. In declaring that one must first believe in order to gain an understanding of God, Augustine holds the exact opposite view of Hume: for Augustine, it is wise for a person to trust in God before being able to see clearly the evidence that "proves the case." The stand Augustine takes here would likely strike Hume and many other moderns as an unfortunate example of medieval authoritarianism—it is as if Augustine were saying that the proper place of the human creature is to obey blindly and submit one's reason without question to the divine power and authority. In this respect, Augustine would seem vulnerable to the charge of medieval anti-intellectualism put forth strikingly by the twentieth-century philosopher Bertrand Russell against Augustine's heir, Thomas Aquinas. Let us recall the passage we discussed earlier in which Russell attacks Aquinas for medieval anti-intellectualism. Russell writes:

> There is little of the true philosophic spirit in Aquinas. He does not, like the Platonic Socrates, set out to follow wherever the argument may lead. He is not engaged in an inquiry, the result of which it is impossible to know in advance. Before he begins to philosophize, he already knows the truth; it is declared in the Catholic faith. If he can find apparently rational arguments for some parts of the faith, so much the better; if he cannot, he need only fall back on revelation. The finding of arguments for a conclusion given in advance is not philosophy, but special pleading. I cannot, therefore, feel that he deserves to be put on a level with the best philosophers either of Greece or of modern times.[54]

In rendering this judgment, Russell sounds a great deal like Hume. Certainly Russell makes it clear that philosophers of the first rank must set aside their prior religious commitments, if they are so unfortunate to have any, in order to heed the voice of reason. Similarly, in his treatment of miracles Hume argues that true philosophers must avoid the snares of credulity and must believe

54. Russell, *History of Western Philosophy*, 463.

only what accords with rational evidence. Both Russell and Hume would concur that for a philosopher to begin his or her thinking in faith would be unbecoming, for a truly wise philosopher necessarily eschews the dangers of dogmatic, blind obedience to authority. But, of course, in asserting that *"credo ut intellegam,"* Augustine does not sanction either blind faith or unquestioning submission (and neither, of course, does Aquinas). Instead, what Augustine really means to say is something that neither Hume nor Russell appear to have understood—namely, that our reasoning about how to live is directed and molded by our experience as feeling agents who are fundamentally, and above all else, lovers.

Let us note again a serious weakness in Hume's assessment of Christian faith. It may well be the case that Hume succeeds in exposing the errors and pretensions of that tradition of modern philosophical apologetics that sought to justify religious belief according to the directives of modern foundationalism. But this is a victory of only limited significance. Unfortunately, what Hume fails to comprehend is the Augustinian approach to the problem of faith and reason. Curiously, just as Hume fails in his *Natural History* to see how true faith must be rooted in love, so in his other works on faith and reason Hume overlooks a form of the rational justification of belief that insists that the fundamental ethical commitments one views as rational will depend in great part on what one most deeply loves. As we have seen, for an Augustinian, *"credo ut intellegam"* is the spiritual equivalent of *"amo ut intellegam."* Yet when Hume takes on modern defenders of the faith, he limits himself to attacking those who seek to rest faith on some type of "pure" evidence. Both Hume and the modern apologists he so skillfully disarms are inheritors of the Enlightenment. How totally different is that tradition whose founder could say "Love knoweth it. O truth who art Eternity."[55]

Conclusion

Before proceeding to the next chapter, it may be useful to review what I have argued thus far. Fundamentally, I have sought to clarify how both Pascal and Hume are philosophers of human nature who call us to be reconciled to our limited and imperfect human faculties. For Pascal, in whose work there are many echoes of Augustine's teachings on the strivings of the human heart, our awareness of our limits should lead us naturally to an affirmation of divine

---

55. Augustine, *Confessions*, 8.10.16. Part of what I am calling an Augustinian outlook contends that how we understand the moral character of ourselves and the world depends in part on our wills and thus on our feelings or affections. A dispassionate outlook does not see the world truthfully because it fails to respond in a rationally appropriate way to what is good. For a contemporary, but not specifically Augustinian, argument in defense of such an account of human moral understanding, see Taylor, *Sources of the Self*, 3–24.

grace. Hume, in contrast, rejects religious faith, including and especially Christian faith, as both psychologically destructive and rationally insupportable. I have argued that Hume's negative diagnosis of Christian faith is defective. Hume fails to understand the inner life of a faith that is animated by love rather than anxiety and ignorance. Furthermore, Hume's powerful criticisms of the Lockean reconciliation of faith and reason simply do not extend far enough even to challenge the radically dissimilar outlook on faith and reason characteristic of the Augustinian tradition.

I do not presume in this chapter satisfactorily to have constructed a positive case for the kind of Christian skepticism found in Pascal; obviously, if my description of the character of Socratic teleological philosophy is correct, there is no reason to think that anyone could prove to every rational person's satisfaction that a specific account of human health and disorder is true. Yet given the current state of philosophical humility in the academy about who is rational and who is not, and about what it even means to be rational, it seems that the Socratic model has much to recommend it. Much more argument will need to be provided, of course, to show how Pascal's own version of Socratic Christianity is itself reasonable according to this Socratic model. To conclude, let us recall that those committed to the Socratic enterprise are obligated to try to achieve coherent self-knowledge of their own way of being and to open themselves up to external criticism. They also have an obligation to attend carefully to the forms of life they wish to condemn as unhealthy or unsuitable for humans. Despite his many merits as social critic and religious skeptic, Hume falls seriously short of fulfilling this latter obligation in his treatment of Christian faith. In this context, Hume may well be charged with malpractice.

3

PASCAL, PARADOX, AND THE WISDOM OF THE HEART

Arguments and teachings surely do not influence everyone, but the soul of the student needs to have been prepared by habits for enjoying and hating finely, like ground that is to nourish seed. For someone whose life follows his feelings would not even listen to an argument turning him away, or comprehend it [if he did listen]; and in that state how could he be persuaded to change? And in general feelings seem to yield to force, not to argument.

Hence we must already in some way have a character suitable for virtue, fond of what is fine and objecting to what is shameful.

Aristotle, *Nicomachean Ethics*[1]

Not only do we only know God through Jesus Christ, but we only know ourselves through Jesus Christ; we only know life and death through Jesus Christ. Apart from Jesus Christ we cannot know the meaning of our life or our death, of God or of ourselves.

Thus without Scripture, whose only object is Christ, we know nothing, and can see nothing but obscurity and confusion in the nature of God and in nature itself.

Pascal, *Pensées*[2]

1. Aristotle, *Nicomachean Ethics*, 10.9.1179b20–30, trans. Terence Irwin (Indianapolis: Hackett, 1985), 292.
2. Pascal, *Pensées*, frg. 417.

In the last chapter, I challenged Hume's opposition to Christian faith by arguing, in effect, that as a religious critic Hume lacks subtlety. This is not to say
that Hume's criticisms of theistic traditions entirely misrepresent the varied
histories of these traditions. On the contrary, Hume shows powerful insight
in his attacks on the Lockean school of Christian apologetics. Furthermore,
Hume is clearly right in claiming that religious devotion can be rooted in
harmful motives and sentiments. But scoring with these two blows does not
give Hume the final victory. It obviously does not do so if, as I have argued with
respect to Christian theism, what Hume attacks are the church's weakened
and disoriented flanks.

Let me explain further why I characterize Hume's victory in such compromised terms. First, Hume is to be credited with providing a decisive series
of devastating blows to the Enlightenment project of apologetics rooted in
the writings of John Locke. Yet while the Lockean account of rational faith
is impressive in its analytical rigor, it is woefully limited in the two respects
we have already noted. For one thing, the Lockean project represents only
one distinctively modern solution to the problem of faith and reason. The
fact that Hume succeeds in exposing its inadequacy, which I grant, certainly
does not show that faith cannot be reconciled to reason in some other manner. Second, the Lockean project is itself internally defective, insofar as the
"scientific" canons of rationality that it employs are themselves rationally
untenable. According to Locke, to be rational a belief must be supported by
the evidence of sensory ideas, incorrigible mental perceptions, or the necessary relations of ideas. But this account of what it means to be rational, in
and of itself, cannot be justified on the basis of these restricted sources of
evidence; since the Lockean standard of rationality nullifies itself, it is irrational. Insofar as the Lockean conception of rationality is seriously deficient,
the post-Enlightenment theist need not be too forlorn over Locke's demise at
the hands of a perceptive Humean critic; the theist might, in fact, feel a debt
of gratitude to Hume for his relentless clarity. More importantly, however,
the post-Enlightenment theist should see that in Hume's effort to combat the
influence of the modern church in politics and culture, he entirely overlooks
the Augustinian tradition that embraces rational inquiry but nevertheless
insists on faith, in one form or another, as a necessary starting point for
self-understanding. Hume also overlooks the possibility of a faith rooted in
love rather than flattery. In these two fundamentally important ways, then,
Hume's diagnosis of religious theism falls short, since it simply fails to be
"proportioned to the evidence."

In Pascal, on the contrary, we encounter a richer and deeper understanding of the nature of Christian faith and of the mutual interrelationship of
faith and reason. Thus far in my inquiry I have offered no sustained defense
of the Pascalian view. As I have argued already, the alternative to Humean
skepticism that Pascal espouses upholds the Augustinian tenet that self-

understanding is impossible apart from faith. Since for both Augustine and Pascal true faith must be rooted in love, from their perspective "*fides quaerens intellectum*" can be reformulated as "*caritas quaerens intellectum.*" Thus far in my inquiry I have challenged Hume's diagnosis of Christian faith as irrational and unhealthy. I would now like to proceed to evaluate the rational integrity of Pascal's assessment of the human condition. How defensible is Pascal's diagnosis of human frailty and the need for grace? What, if anything, can be said in favor of Pascal's essentially Augustinian epistemology? In the remaining chapters of this book, I intend to clarify and defend this Augustinian outlook on faith and understanding as it is embodied in Pascal's *Pensées*. I shall strive to argue my case in a Socratic spirit, with the aim of clarifying and defending without presuming to say the final word.

In chapter 4 I shall argue that Pascal's outlook offers a more coherent account of human life than does the outlook of the secular postmodernist. But before I defend Pascal over against postmodernism, I would like to look in more detail at how Pascal makes his case for the rationality of Christian faith. I shall argue that Pascal's defense of Christian faith as rational depends both on a particularly Augustinian conception of rationality and on a controversial but compelling diagnosis of the human condition. My assessment of Pascal's merits as existential diagnostician and defender of faith will focus on his paradox argument. I shall contend that while Pascal defends Christian faith as rationally justified, his defense will not seem persuasive to those who do not share certain key intuitions. Such a limitation in Pascal's paradox argument, however, should not be seen as a serious defect. Rather, the fact that Pascal's paradox argument will seem compelling only for those already disposed in their hearts to accept it is just what one should expect given the epistemology of the Augustinian position. For Pascal, to comprehend how faith in Christ provides the best answer to the problem of human existence requires an act of self-understanding. Like all efforts at self-understanding, our ability to achieve this understanding presupposes that we can be brought to see our lives through a crucial intuitive disposition of our hearts. That Pascal does not try to "prove" the validity of his own faith to all possible persons no matter what their sentiments is no defect at all in his argument; on the contrary, Pascal's limited defense of faith reveals just how well he understands the inherent limitations of an Augustinian defense of any account of the human good. More importantly, that Pascal's paradox argument depends for its success on the heart of its reader shows Pascal's own depth of self-understanding. In other words, the very fact that Pascal constructs a major argument for Christian faith that never presumes to be a universal, neutral proof testifies to Pascal's Socratic self-knowledge concerning the limits of human reasoning.

Pascal and the Rationality of Faith

The heart has its reasons of which reason knows nothing.[3]

No one can go that far, and I maintain that a perfectly genuine sceptic has never existed. Nature backs up helpless reason and stops it going wildly astray.[4]

As I shall argue, Pascal's defense of the rationality of faith should be understood in the context of his awareness of both the greatness and wretchedness of human rationality. Pascal is deeply skeptical about the prospect of trying to make adequate sense of our lives by relying solely on our own natural faculties apart from the help of God's grace. Yet it is within such a skeptical outlook about human reason in particular that Pascal also wants to show why faith in God's grace made possible through the person of Jesus Christ is eminently rational. But just what kind of skeptic is Pascal?

Let us consider some difficulties associated with skepticism in general. First of all, we can observe how philosophical attempts to prove either the validity or invalidity of reason certainly seem paradoxical. Attempting to prove the validity of reason by constructing a compelling deductive proof showing how reason reliably leads us to truth opens one up to the skeptical charge that one has begged the question. How, the skeptic queries, can the philosopher argue cogently in favor of reason without presupposing the trustworthiness of reason in the first place?[5] But if using reason to prove its own reliability is problematic, as the skeptic may well insist, is it not also the case that using reason, as the skeptic might use it, to establish the unreliability of reason is equally paradoxical if not incoherent? How can the skeptic argue persuasively against reason unless the skeptic relies on the very faculty he or she contends is untrustworthy? A key problem for the skeptic is this: if the skeptic really purports *to argue* in favor of his or her position, then the skeptic must use that very organ of reason he or she condemns, in order to support the conclusion the skeptic embraces. Paradoxically, then, it seems that one can argue neither for nor against the integrity of reason as a faculty—or set of functional skills— for attaining the truth. The defender of the reliability of reason, on the one

---

3. Ibid., frg. 423.
4. Ibid., frg. 131.
5. One might cite as the classic articulation of the first of these paradoxes Antoine Arnauld's objection against Descartes that his *Meditations* were guilty of circular reasoning. At least on Arnauld's reading, Descartes attempts in *Meditation Three* to prove the reliability of clear and distinct ideas by constructing a proof for the existence of a perfect divinity. As Arnauld observed, however, the proof relies on clear and distinct ideas for the articulation of its premises. For Arnauld's famous objection to Descartes's proof of the veracity of clear and distinct ideas, see the "Fourth Set of Objections," in René Descartes, *The Philosophical Writings of Descartes*, trans. John Cottingham, Robert Stoothoff, and Dugald Murdoch (Cambridge: Cambridge University Press, 1984), 2:150.

hand, appears to have no recourse but to beg the question by presupposing the very conclusion he or she seeks to demonstrate. The doubter of the reliability of reason, on the other hand, seems caught in the absurdity of presupposing the reliability of the very practice he or she seeks to condemn.

Yet this paradox of skepticism may be less formidable than it appears. What the paradox shows is how certain strategies for either defending or attacking the validity of reason are doomed to self-refutation. The philosophical defender of reason cannot successfully refute the skeptic by deductively proving the validity of reason, and the skeptical critic of reason cannot successfully call into question the authority of reason simply by arguing that reason is untrustworthy. In the history of the quarrel between skeptics and defenders of reason, there are more subtle and sophisticated strategies on both sides. Pyrrhonian skepticism is one particularly ingenious attempt to debunk the authority of philosophical reason without self-referential absurdity. A fine example of a non-question-begging defense of reason is Aristotle's dialectical refutation of the radical skeptic in book 4 of the *Metaphysics*. In its own unique fashion, Pascal's *Pensées* also seeks to resolve the ancient dispute between reason and skepticism by appealing to faith. To appreciate the subtle nature of all three perspectives on the authority of reason, we must first recognize how they avoid the kind of dilemma proposed by our paradox. The ingenious nature of Pyrrhonism, for example, becomes evident once we see that the Pyrrhonist solution of suspending judgment is not intended as the conclusion of an argument at all, but is rather proposed as the psychological outcome of the repeated frustration that comes in discovering the antinomic nature of philosophical arguments. While I think that both Hume and Pascal offer compelling arguments against this clever Pyrrhonist strategy, it is nevertheless a highly subtle strategy that does not in and of itself succumb to our paradox of reason and skepticism. What I hope to do in this chapter is to show how Pascal's moderate skepticism about the authority of reason exhibits its own subtlety of argumentation and is not just a species of self-defeating religious irrationalism. Three questions are particularly relevant to such a task. First, what does Pascal mean in his famous declaration that "the heart has its reasons of which reason knows nothing"? Second, how does Pascal avoid falling prey himself to a Christian version of fideistic irrationalism? Finally, why is Pascal not being an irrationalist skeptic when he proclaims that faith is accessible only through the heart and not through reason? All three questions serve to emphasize an intriguing feature of Pascal's apologetic strategy: Pascal seeks to defend the rationality of faith by arguing that faith is beyond reason.

Before we turn to Pascal's nuanced doctrine of the proper relationship of faith and reason, let us return briefly to the subtlety of the Socratic conception of reason by which Aristotle refutes the radical skeptic. In book 4 of the *Metaphysics*, Aristotle proposes to defend reason against the skeptic by defending the principle of noncontradiction as a fundamental first principle of coherent thought.[6] As Aristotle notes, whereas one cannot demonstrate the truth of the principle of noncontradiction without relying on it in one's reasoning, one can defend the principle dialectically—*elenchi*—by showing how any coherent skeptical claim the skeptic makes against the principle of noncontradiction implicitly presupposes the very principle itself. To refute the skeptic effectively, Aristotle argues not deductively but Socratically. Aristotle argues as follows: For the skeptic, or anyone else for that matter, to make any kind of intelligible assertion of the form S is P, the skeptic must conceive both of some subject S and of some predicate or characteristic P. But to think coherently of S, one must in thought distinguish this S from what is not-S. Similarly, to attribute P to this subject, one must intend some characteristic P that is not the same as not-P. As Aristotle observes, insofar as the person making this assertion intends some definite S and some definite P, he or she must presuppose some identity of S and P that separates them from what they are not. But S and P can have their own definitive identity only if to be S is not to be not-S, and to be P is not to be not-P. In other words, unless the principle of noncontradiction applies to the skeptic's assertion of S is P, whatever content this assertion might have, the skeptic simply fails to utter a claim susceptible to philosophical examination. That is, if the skeptic means nothing at all determinate or definite in saying "S is P," then he or she is not offering an intelligible challenge to the authority of reason.

Now, of course, as Aristotle notes, the skeptic could respond to Aristotle here by declaring that in denying the authority of the principle of noncontradiction, he or she means to say simply that S is P and that S is not-P. The skeptic thus means in a determinate way to assert a contradiction and to stand by it. Aristotle's counter reply is that such a skeptical pairing of assertions is philosophically challenging only if in uttering this contradiction the skeptic means the same thing by "S" and "P" in both parts of his or her declaration that S is P and S is not-P. If this were not the case, then the two statements would not be in logical conflict. That is, if either the S in the first assertion is not the same S as in the second, or the P in the first is not the same P as in the second, there simply is no contradiction being asserted, and the skeptic would have failed to offer any radical denial of the principle of noncontradiction. If, however, the skeptic digs in his or her heels and insists on affirming two contradictory claims as really contradictory, so that the same subject both has and does not have the same attribute, the skeptic must still assume the persistent identity of S and P as the same S and P in both contradictory assertions, and thus he or she must first presuppose the principle of noncontradiction in order to negate it. Yet even here Aristotle realizes that the skeptic has one final possible skeptical option. The skeptic could simply acknowledge his or her own inconsistency, insist, in fact, that he or she openly both affirms and denies the principle of noncontradiction, and thus claim that while one must presuppose first that S *is*

6. Aristotle, *Metaphysics*, 4.4.1006a1–1009a5.

not not-S and P *is not* not-P to assert his or her contradictory claims, the skeptic also holds that S *is* not-S and P *is* not-P. In other words, the skeptic can simply accept the inconsistency as an expression of his or her radical rejection of reason. But then, as Aristotle wryly concludes, the extreme skeptic ultimately fails to challenge the authority of reason since he or she in effect says both nothing and everything. For if every time the skeptic says anything determinate, he or she then retracts the claim and asserts the opposite, nothing the skeptic says can be challenged successfully because the skeptic sets down nothing "challengeable." At the same time, because the skeptic now openly denies every assertion he or she makes, the skeptic in another sense says everything precisely because he or she denies nothing. Thus the skeptic can successfully elude refutation, but only by paying dearly for this immunity to dialectical testing, for to have no position open to refutation is, Aristotle notes, in effect, to have no rational consciousness. Put another way, insofar as the skeptic avoids being refuted by having nothing to say, on the one hand, and saying everything, on the other, the skeptic is for all practical purposes no more than an intellectual vegetable (*to phuton*).

Aristotle's refutation of the extreme skeptic is an ingenious extension of the Socratic method.[7] As we have seen, at the heart of the Socratic method is the goal of challenging a respondent's most basic beliefs. More importantly, Socrates tests a person's core beliefs not by demanding a deductive proof for them, but by challenging the person to defend them in the face of successive questions and objections. In the early dialogues, for example, Socrates does not seek a proof for a person's notion of *arête*, since one's conception of *arête* serves as a first principle for one's moral outlook and cannot simply be proven. There are no more basic premises, that is, by which one could logically establish the true nature of the virtues. But for Socrates one's account of one's first principles can be tested in terms of both the internal coherence of those principles and their epistemic and ethical consequences. This is to say that while it is unreasonable from a Socratic perspective to demand a deductive proof for one's fundamental moral beliefs, it is eminently reasonable to require one to show how these beliefs are the foundation for a coherent set of beliefs, and indeed for a coherent psyche possessing a complex range of beliefs, desires, and emotions. For Socrates, moral first principles are tested dialectically by a series of questions designed to reveal whether one has the self-knowledge needed to show how one's most basic ethical beliefs function within a coherent, defensible human life.

Now, in his confrontation with the skeptic Aristotle proceeds to disarm his opponent in a similar dialectical manner. Aristotle acknowledges that it would be foolish to proffer the skeptic a proof of the principle of noncontradiction; one mark of the wise person for Aristotle is for that person to know when

---

7. Terence Irwin offers an in-depth and perceptive account of Aristotle's dialectical method in *Aristotle's First Principles* (Oxford: Clarendon, 1988). For a general account of Aristotle's dialectical approach to justifying first principles, see chapters 1–3. A brief and elegant analysis of Aristotle's refutation of the skeptic can be found on pages 181–98.

rational proof is appropriate and when it is not. It is clearly not appropriate to attempt to construct a proof, Aristotle says, when we are seeking to defend in ethics or metaphysics our fundamental first principles. For Aristotle, what is especially significant about the principle of noncontradiction is that it is a necessary presupposition for all coherent discourse and thought, whether ethical, scientific, metaphysical, or logical. Yet even though Aristotle recognizes the futility of demonstrating this first of all first principles, he argues that our acceptance of it is not just arbitrary. On the contrary, we can defend this "supraprinciple" precisely and rigorously by showing how any attempt on the part of the skeptic to deny it must first presuppose it. Once Aristotle brings the skeptic to this moment of self-discovery, the skeptic still may or may not choose to affirm the principle and acknowledge the folly of skepticism. If the skeptic chooses to affirm it upon acknowledging the force of Aristotle's negative proof (*elenchi*), he or she thereby returns to the ranks of the nonskeptics. If the skeptic instead insists on both affirming and yet denying this principle, and indeed every other assertion he or she makes, then the skeptic renders himself or herself no more cognitively endowed than a vegetable.

It is very much worth noting how craftily Aristotle carries out this version of a Socratic refutation. In the end, he must admit that it is possible for the skeptic to refuse to relent from the original position. But for a person to try to do so is itself, for Aristotle, a profound contradiction. In Aristotle's view, since all people naturally have a desire to know—that is, to seek to understand themselves and their world, not merely as a means by which to produce some concrete commodity, but as something intrinsically desirable—the skeptic cannot violate the conditions of intelligible thought without denying his or her own nature. In this respect, Aristotle's whole strategy has a strikingly ad hominem character. We can grasp how his refutation succeeds, finally, only if we keep in mind that it is presented to a person whose natural form is directed toward intelligibility. Granting Aristotle's thesis that the desire to know is part of what it means to be fully human, the skeptic who refuses to relent thereby denies his or her own humanity. But everyone, even the skeptic, according to Aristotle, has an innate wish (*boulesis*) to become fully human and thus achieve the human *telos*. Thus the skeptic who steadfastly adheres to his or her original position suffers from a special sort of incoherence, the teleological incoherence of professing to believe in a way contrary to who one really is. In the end, according to Aristotle, the persistent skeptic refutes himself or herself. In a Socratic sense, the failure of the radical skeptic is self-generated.

Pascal's Dialectical Defense of Faith

I have presented Aristotle's refutation of the skeptic in order to characterize a feature of dialectical argumentation that I think is central as well to Pascal's defense of faith. As does Aristotle, Pascal recognizes, first of all, that first principles cannot be defended by appeal to more basic beliefs. In other words, we cannot defend these principles by means of a deductive or demonstrative proof. Nor are these first principles self-evident in the Cartesian sense of being beyond any possible, rational doubt. Insofar as our most fundamental beliefs cannot be justified either deductively or as self-evident, Pascal concludes that they are not knowable through our reason. So, Pascal notes, "We know the truth not only through our reason but also through our heart. It is through the latter that we know first principles, and reason which has nothing to do with it, tries in vain to refute them."[8] In stating that first principles are not known through reason, Pascal clearly does not mean to imply that we violate some epistemic duty, or that our beliefs in first principles are "unjustified," violating some rational standard concerning how we must govern our beliefs when we hold first principles through the heart. While our fundamental beliefs cannot be justified by "reason," Pascal never means to imply that we are at all irrational in holding them. For Pascal we are eminently reasonable, and we use our cognitive faculties of reflection and argumentation properly, when we believe in certain first principles that are beyond reason. The fact that our first principles are not based on "reason" means only that we cannot support them through logical or empirical reasoning. Our first principles are rational even though "reason . . . has nothing to do with [them]."

Now, before we turn specifically to the logic of the paradox argument, let us recall that, for Pascal, when we rely on the first principles of the heart in order to reason, we can legitimately be said to *know* these first principles. We know, in other words, in a way that is both necessary and natural the basic intuitions of our hearts. So Pascal argues: "We know that we are not dreaming, but, however unable we may be to prove it rationally, our inability proves nothing but the weakness of our reason, and not the uncertainty of all our knowledge, as they [the skeptics] maintain. For knowledge of first principles, like space, time, motion, number, is as solid as any derived through reason, and it is on such knowledge coming from the heart and instinct, that reason has to depend and base all its arguments."[9] In essence, Pascal defends these first principles in terms of their cognitive function in human life. In this passage he claims that it is natural for humans to reason about space, time, motion, and number. He then argues that our natural reasoning about the physical realm itself depends on our having certain basic beliefs. Without these basic beliefs our natural reason would lack the initial presuppositions required to derive empirical conclusions. Pascal justifies our holding these basic beliefs in natural first principles not by basing them on other beliefs that provide evidence for them, but by showing how they serve as the necessary presuppositions for our natural reasoning about evidence in

8. Pascal, *Pensées*, frg. 110.
9. Ibid.

the first place. In a way similar to Aristotle, Pascal defends these specific first principles—what we might term the first principles of empirical reasoning—by clarifying how we as humans must rely on them if we are to carry out our natural function of evidential reasoning. Thus our knowing certain truths through the heart in no way entails that we are being irrational in doing so. Putting this point another way, we could say that for Pascal it is unreasonable to assert that we should hold only those beliefs that can be supported on the basis of empirical or logical evidence. It would be unreasonable, that is, to propose that we believe only on the basis of what evidential reason can validate. Indeed, insofar as our beliefs in crucial first principles make derivative, empirical knowledge possible in the first place, and are held naturally by all of us, it is irrational and even sheer folly for any person to try to doubt them: "No one can go that far, and I maintain that a perfectly genuine sceptic has never existed. Nature backs up helpless reason and stops it going wildly astray."[10]

In one respect, Pascal's account of first principles would appear to differ substantially from Aristotle's. Nowhere in Aristotle's writings do we find Aristotle defending the vision of our "nature" protecting our otherwise helpless human reason from paralyzing skepticism. And nowhere do we find Aristotle contending that it is by the heart alone that we can refute the radical skeptic who demands rational justification of our basic beliefs. Whereas in the *Metaphysics* Aristotle refutes the radical skeptic through a dialectical exercise of reason, we might think that Pascal seems to abandon reason as inadequate to combat skepticism and that, as a result, Pascal seems to embrace not reason but the authority of a nonrational, instinctual Nature. So it would seem that Pascal has unequivocally abandoned the rational *eudaimonism* of Aristotle with its fundamental commitment to the ideal of the full human life as the fully rational life of the virtues and the life of complete rational flourishing. And yet to oppose these two thinkers in this manner is to be misled by the surface of Pascal's vocabulary. It is not the Aristotelian vision of the rational person of moral and intellectual virtue that Pascal means to reject when he appeals to the authority of nature over against that of "reason." Pascal's adversary is the Cartesian rational philosopher who presumes to combat skepticism and to grasp reality through self-evident clear and distinct ideas. Indeed, it is against this modern vision of the Cartesian rationalist, and not against that of a dialectical defender of our rationality, that Pascal means to articulate his refutation by showing the dependence of our reasoning on our nonrational nature. Thus Pascal defends the role of the heart by insisting that the first principles implicit in exercises of reasoning are not absolutely certain and are not themselves the offspring of our reason. The skeptic, Pascal notes, can undermine the Cartesian dogmatist project simply by demanding evidence for relying on reason in the first place. As does Aristotle, Pascal sees the

10. Ibid., frg. 131.

pointlessness of combating skeptical attacks on first principles by constructing deductive arguments. Concerning those first principles that we cannot as humans naturally doubt, Pascal remarks: "I pause at the dogmatist's only strong point, which is that we cannot doubt natural principles if we speak sincerely and in all good faith. To which the sceptics reply, in a word, that uncertainty as to our origin entails uncertainty as to our nature. The dogmatists have been trying to answer that ever since the world began."[11]

Here let us note that Pascal is not attacking Aristotelian reason. Instead, Pascal attacks a distinctively modern conception of reason in his refutation of dogmatism. What he primarily objects to is the dogmatist's claim to rest the whole of our reasoned set of beliefs on a bedrock of rationally self-evident intuitions. This is to say that what Pascal means in saying that reason cannot defend our first principles is that *Cartesian* reason cannot validate such principles. Pascal himself thinks that some of our beliefs are indeed basic and fundamental and that the objects of these beliefs, our first principles, are grasped immediately by an intuitive faculty. But he insists, nevertheless, that these basic beliefs are not luminously self-evident. Rather, we know our first principles insofar as our nature in a sense moves us involuntarily to assent to them. On a philosophical level, we can recognize not only that these principles are not known to us through some Cartesian faculty of reason, but also that these principles afford us the fundamental starting points we need to reason at all. So it is that Pascal opposes nature to reason. In doing so, he certainly does not conceive of nature as blind or arbitrary. The beliefs provided for us by nature are not themselves blind or arbitrary. And they are certainly not irrational beliefs.

Pascal's nuanced and subtle understanding of the difference between following "reason" and being "rational" is evident as well in the following two fragments.

There is nothing so consistent with reason as this denial of reason.

Two excesses: to exclude reason, to admit nothing but reason.[12]

As does Socrates, Pascal argues that in recognizing the limits of reason we gain wisdom of ourselves. Part of that wisdom, for Pascal, lies in our grasping that reason and the heart are interdependent sources of belief. Only as we see the limits of reason do we understand the proper function of reason in our lives. And only as we see the limits of reason do we grasp the proper cognitive function of our hearts. Someone who understands what it means to be rational, then, embraces the paradox that it is eminently rational to believe what is

11. Ibid.
12. Ibid., frgs. 182, 183.

beyond reason. Now, our understanding of our limits as reasoners becomes especially important for Pascal when we turn to the question of how we can come to know God and how faith in God makes rational sense of our lives. Essentially, Pascal argues that our knowledge of God through Christ serves as the supreme first principle for knowing both the nature of the human self and the nature of the world. More importantly, however, we cannot attain this knowledge of the truth about ourselves if we adopt the point of view of a dispassionate spectator. On the contrary, our capacity to know God hinges on our willingness to humble ourselves, accept our limits as rational humans, and acknowledge our need for God. Bringing us to this recognition of the inadequacy of our natural powers and awakening in us a yearning for God's grace in our lives are the two fundamental goals of Pascal's paradox argument. This kind of humble acknowledgment of God's proper place in our lives is essentially what Pascal means by saying that we can know God only through our hearts.

For Pascal, the heart makes possible both natural knowledge of the universe and ethical or spiritual knowledge of the human condition. As Augustine conceives of the mind as both cognitive and passionate, so Pascal conceives of the heart as a unity of both cognition and will. Just as in the sphere of our natural reasoning, so in the case of understanding ourselves, we must rely on the basic beliefs of the heart, as we are naturally moved to assent to them. That we rely on the first principles known through the heart is eminently rational, for in so doing we properly exercise the cognitive function of our hearts, which in turn makes possible the proper functioning of our reasoning, whether we are reasoning about the physical world or ourselves.

Once we see just what Pascal means by "reason," namely a modified Cartesian notion of reason, we can appreciate the subtlety of Pascal's skeptical doctrine of the heart. Pascal modifies the Cartesian conception of reason in the following ways: (1) contrary to Descartes's view, Pascal thinks that reason lacks the power to supply us with luminously self-certifying first principles; and (2) in accordance with Descartes's account, Pascal thinks that reason still possesses the function of inference, of drawing well-grounded conclusions based on sound evidence. Pascal is a skeptic of reason insofar as he insists on our recognizing the limits of reason, and insofar as he rejects Descartes's claim to have uncovered a set of indubitable, purely rational starting points through rational self-reflection. Pascal rejects this Cartesian vision because Pascal is convinced that Descartes misunderstands the status of first principles and thus overestimates the power of reason.

For Pascal the most serious danger associated with the Cartesian misunderstanding is that such a misunderstanding tempts us to a kind of philosophical pride in which we lose sight of our cognitive limitations and ultimately may even think that we can solve our most pressing problems through our own resources. In attacking the dogmatist's faith in reason, Pascal attacks not the use of reason to grasp truth but the presumption that we can establish reason's autonomy from the rest of human nature. In an effort to combat this "Cartesian heresy," Pascal actually works out his own subtle defense of the rationality of our intuitive beliefs. As we have seen, Pascal argues that our beliefs in first principles are rational not because these principles are impervious to all possible skeptical doubt, as Descartes holds, but because the heart has its own form of rationality that is not threatened by mere abstract, skeptical arguments. Furthermore, Pascal notes that anyone who engages in empirical reasoning and so employs reason in one of its own proper functions must, in order to reason at all, depend on the wisdom of the heart. In effect, the skeptic who boasts of doubting even our first principles fails to realize that as a human he or she will never be able to sustain such doubt. Here we see Pascal arguing against the radical skeptic in a manner quite similar to Aristotle. As Aristotle did before him, Pascal ultimately challenges the skeptic to acknowledge and accept his or her fallible humanity. The skeptic's final maneuver to avoid refutation, which Aristotle describes in terms of a metamorphosis into "vegetablehood," Pascal dismisses as unnatural and finally unsustainable.

Thus both Aristotle and Pascal believe that fundamental first principles are essential in all coherent human thinking. Moreover, both refute the skeptic not with a neutral deductive proof but with a dialectical, ad hominem argument that challenges the skeptic to acknowledge that first principles are already implicitly at work in his or her living and thinking as a human. If the skeptic refuses to assent to the latter point, the skeptic fails to be true to himself or herself. The key move, then, for both thinkers is to argue in such a way as to bring the skeptic to a more enlightened state of self-knowledge.

By assimilating Pascal's refutation of skepticism to that of Aristotle, I intend especially to stress the point that for Pascal the doctrine of the heart entails no flight into irrationality. As I have argued, we must keep in mind that the conception of reason Pascal sets his sights against is distinctively Cartesian. It would be a serious error, for instance, to assume that, by attacking reason, Pascal sets himself in opposition to any or all alternative conceptions of rationality. Indeed, one could argue truthfully that with his recognition of the role of the heart in human thinking, Pascal is much nearer to Aristotle than is Descartes. At least such a stance seems reasonable if we compare Aristotle's conception of ethical reasoning with Pascal's general epistemology. In the *Nicomachean Ethics*, Aristotle cautions his audience against expecting too great a rigor from an inquiry into the human good. Ethical inquiry will inevitably lack the rigor of an exact science, according to Aristotle, for two basic reasons. First, ethical deliberation requires perception of particulars, and there can be no exact science showing us how to succeed in such perceptual apprehension. Second, in defending an account of the human good, Aristotle acknowledges that his account will be persuasive only to those who have already developed the proper ethical habits. It is, in fact, one of the primary functions of the polis as moral community to engender those habits that will shape an individual's emotions, desires, and beliefs about what is good and bad. Individual reason on its own lacks the power to enable us to make rational judgments concerning the attainment of the virtues.

Why is it that for Aristotle moral reflection cannot lead to truth without the prior training of human character? Part of Aristotle's answer is basically that moral reflection lacks self-evident principles on which to base its conclusions. The fundamental *arche* of moral reasoning, for Aristotle, is a conception of the nature of the human good. The highest first principle in ethics is the nature of the final cause in human life. So, Aristotle writes: "For excellence and vice respectively preserve and destroy the first principle, and in actions that for the sake of which is the first principle, as the hypotheses are in mathematics; neither in that case is it reason that teaches the first principles, nor is it so here—excellence either natural or produced by habituation is what teaches right opinion about the first principle."[13] For Aristotle, at the center of this human good lies our practical reason that expresses itself in how we think about and act in order to achieve the overall set of goods that are constitutive of human flourishing. In other words, the basic human good for Aristotle is the life of reason coherently displayed in the various spheres of activity of human life. To excel rationally, a person must develop the rational capacity to determine what is just, what is temperate, how to share life with friends, and so on. Yet Aristotle knows very well that his own account of the human good conflicts with various other accounts, such as the Homeric outlook in its extolling of honor above reason. To be convinced of Aristotle's account over any of his competitors', one must have the sort of character that already appreciates the worth and pleasure of rational activity. Arguments alone, apart from the formation of character, cannot convince a person about the nature of the highest good.

Consider how, near the end of the *Nicomachean Ethics*, Aristotle relates moral reasoning to the habits of character:

> Some think it is nature that makes people good; some think it is habit; some that it is teaching.
>
> The [contribution] of nature clearly is not up to us, but results from some divine cause in those who have it, who are the truly fortunate ones.
>
> Arguments and teachings surely do not influence everyone, but the soul of the student needs to have been prepared by habits for enjoying and hating finely, like ground that is to nourish seed. For someone whose life follows his feelings would not even listen to an argument turning him away, or comprehend it [if he did listen]; and in that state how could he be persuaded to change? And in general feelings seem to yield to force, not to argument.
>
> Hence we must already in some way have a character suitable for virtue, fond of what is fine and objecting to what is shameful.[14]

13. Aristotle, *Nicomachean Ethics*, 7.8.1151a14–19.
14. Ibid., 10.9.1179b20–30.

Aristotle's perspective in this passage on the role of character in moral thinking is certainly much nearer to Pascal's view of the heart than to the Enlightenment doctrine of a disembedded, autonomous reason. Aristotle is quite clear that moral philosophy is powerless to convert souls misshapen by the forces of bad habits. Yet if his own account of the good life, of a life in which essential human capacities are fully realized, were self-evident in the basic Cartesian or Enlightenment sense, Aristotle could genuinely hope to convince any person regardless of his or her values and moral experience. But for Aristotle, moral philosophy is dialectical not demonstrative. We test moral theories, Aristotle says, by judging them over against moral appearances, the *phainomena*, of reputable human experience. Insofar as these appearances are largely a matter of our ordinary moral responses and opinions, however, moral philosophy is not an exact science. And since moral philosophy is not an exact science, the best way available to us for justifying our view of the human good is by assessing its merits with respect to our various particular moral as well as metaphysical beliefs. Rather than try to prove an account of the human good deductively, Aristotle shows how his own account of *eudaimonia* accords with his basic metaphysical teleology and the basic moral intuitions of well-formed, fourth-century Greeks, whom Aristotle appears to have regarded as representative of well-formed humans generally. Neither the first principles of moral philosophy itself nor the particular beliefs it is supposed to make sense of and harmonize with are beyond possible future revision. On the contrary, in an Aristotelian view, moral thinking concerning the good life operates out of a communally rooted world of preexisting loyalties, beliefs, and habits. Apart from these preexisting elements that make up a person's character, there is no way to justify dialectically any particular conception of human flourishing. Making these concessions concerning the limits of reason, however, certainly does not commit Aristotle to any version of irrationalism. We might well say, nevertheless, that Aristotle does not endorse a rationalistic ethics pressed from a Cartesian mold. If we wanted to make this point emphatically we would say that for Aristotle the first principles of moral thinking are not knowable by reason—which is to say, by reason in Descartes's sense.

But it would obviously be most misleading to cite Aristotle as an opponent of reason. Rather, Aristotle envisions a form of reasoning that develops out of the Socratic method of *elenchus*. In Aristotle, the Socratic challenge to state, clarify, and defend one's view of *arête* is transformed by being wedded to a sophisticated metaphysical teleology of form, essence, and actuality. If by "reasoning" we mean something akin to Aristotle's method of ethical justification—akin, that is, to a dialectical process of testing one's overall conception of human fulfillment, which seeks coherence rather than certainty—then we may describe Pascal's defense of faith similarly as an effort of reasoning and not as an appeal to the irrational authority of the heart. I think that such a case can be made specifically with reference to Pascal's paradox argument.

Although he is certainly not a metaphysician of Aristotle's depth or subtlety, Pascal upholds a teleological conception of human life. And, like Aristotle, Pascal recognizes that a dialectical justification of his own account of this *telos* must make rational sense of human life by appealing to the whole person. "It is the heart which perceives God," Pascal reminds us, "and not the reason."[15]

Pascal's Teleological Apologetics

I propose to argue in what follows that, in a way akin to Aristotle and deeply reminiscent of Augustine, Pascal practices a form of "teleological dialectic" in his defense of faith. Before proceeding, let me contrast the view I wish to articulate to another, rather widespread, characterization of Pascal's basic strategy. The fact that Pascal so passionately insists on the limits of reason can easily make him appear to be an advocate for irrationalism. Thus Richard Popkin remarks that "Pascal's total immersion in religion made him end up basically anti-philosophical and anti-rational, although he was still brilliant in using rational, philosophical arguments to demolish opponents like the Jesuits and to develop the skeptical implications involved in the human search for truth."[16] Here Popkin portrays Pascal's skepticism in a way that closely parallels Penelhum's description of Pascal, discussed in chapter 1, as a modern Christian fideist. According to Penelhum, Pascal basically regards reason and faith as incompatible sources of authority. To defend faith, Pascal resorts to the skeptical fideistic strategy of undermining the authority of reason in order to establish the opposing authority of faith. In Penelhum's view, Pascal upholds a tradition of theistic apologetics that maintains "that faith and reason are so disparate that faith is not undermined, but strengthened, if we judge that reason can give it no support."[17]

Penelhum's interpretation of Pascal's project of skeptical fideism would seem to offer a quite plausible account of two key components of Pascal's thinking. First, it would clarify why Pascal finds Pyrrhonism an ally in the defense of faith. Penelhum cites three reasons in particular for why Pascal believes that the Pyrrhonist's undermining reason serves to recommend faith.[18] First, the skeptic advances the fideistic cause of unmasking the pretentious ambitions of the dogmatic philosophers who seek to prove the existence of God through reason alone. Second, through their strategy of undermining these philosophical claims, the Pyrrhonists help to reveal to us the essential hiddenness of God. Finally, Penelhum notes, the Pyrrhonist inadvertently paves the

15. Pascal, *Pensées*, frg. 424.
16. See Blaise Pascal, *Blaise Pascal: Selections*, ed. Richard H. Popkin (New York: Macmillan, 1989), 16.
17. Penelhum, *God and Skepticism*, ix.
18. Ibid., 88.

way for the conversion to faith through the very failure of skepticism to offer us an antidote to the distress and unhappiness of our uncertain condition. As Penelhum remarks, this very failure, however, should spur us to recognize that human nature has resources other than reason which enable us to conduct our secular affairs in spite of our uncertainties. It should also help open us to divine grace and so prepare the way for faith. In this way it will help us indirectly toward the assurance that we have been mistakenly seeking through the exercise of reason.[19] In portraying Pascal in such terms, Penelhum, like Popkin, stresses Pascal's antagonism to reason. Both perceive Pascal essentially to be hostile to reason. What Popkin describes as an irrationalist posture of using skeptical tools to discredit the dogmatist's claim to have found truth, Penelhum describes as a Christian form of skeptical fideism. While Penelhum develops this reading of Pascal with impressive clarity and grace, the reading does not fairly or accurately portray Pascal's real position on the relationship of faith and reason.

More importantly, it is unhelpful to portray Pascal as a fideist per se because such a characterization suggests misleadingly that Pascal is not committed to the project of showing how Christian faith is both beyond reason and yet profoundly rational. It is true that Pascal speaks disparagingly of one kind of rational attempt—namely that of the modern natural theologians, such as Descartes—to support faith on the basis of reason. But in this context Pascal is primarily seeking to expose the folly of trying to find God apart from a loving surrender of the heart. Pascal's quarrel is not with those who seek to make a rational case for faith, but with those who seek to know God as a philosophical abstraction or theoretical entity, rather than as the loving and forgiving God of grace. So Pascal contrasts genuine faith rooted in the heart with an abstract, merely intellectual belief in God:

> And that is why I shall not undertake here to prove by reasons from nature either the existence of God, or the Trinity or the immorality of the soul, or anything of the kind: not just because I should not feel competent to find in nature arguments which would convince hardened atheists, but also because such knowledge, without Christ, is useless and sterile. Even if someone were convinced that the proportions between numbers are immaterial, eternal truths, depending on a first truth in which they subsist, called God, I should not consider that he had made much progress towards his salvation.
>
> The Christian's God does not consist merely of a God who is the author of mathematical truths and the order of the elements. That is the portion of the heathen and Epicureans. He does not consist merely of a God who extends his providence over the life and property of men so as to grant a happy span of years to those who worship him. That is the portion of the Jews. But the God of Abraham, the God of Isaac, the God of Jacob, the God of the Christians

19. Ibid.

is a God of love and consolation: he is a God who fills the soul and heart of those whom he possesses: he is a God who makes them inwardly aware of their wretchedness and his infinite mercy: who unites himself with them in the depths of their soul: who fills it with humility, joy, confidence, and love: who makes them incapable of having any other end but him.

All those who seek God apart from Christ, and who go no further than nature, either find no light to satisfy them or come to devise a means of knowing and serving God without a mediator, thus falling into either atheism or deism, two things almost equally abhorrent to Christianity.[20]

Here Pascal condemns a mathematical, abstract approach to knowledge of God because he perceives it as "useless and sterile." True knowledge of God is not a matter of "knowing" that there is a divine being, but a matter of uniting with God in love and humility. Knowing God requires knowing that God is the true end of human life and that without God humans are destined to be unhappy and unfulfilled. Moreover, this knowledge of God must affirm that God is the ultimate good for human life. Such an awareness of God's goodness is, for Pascal, inseparable from the self-awareness of human wretchedness and misery. Unless one seeks to know God with humility and with the longing to be filled with God's love and to share in God's grace, one is not approaching God in a way that truly *affirms* God. Thus, from Pascal's perspective, it is spiritually useless, if not dangerous, to demonstrate rationally that a "perfect substance" exists without grounding one's reasoning in a humble state of mind that acknowledges our wretchedness and need for healing. It is useless because, according to Pascal, true knowledge of God is meant to provide not satisfaction of mere intellectual curiosity, but passionate union with our true good. Given such a spiritual understanding of what "knowing God as God" involves, it is not surprising that Pascal is suspicious of the purely rational project of modern natural theologians such as Descartes to ground knowledge of self and world in a merely theoretical knowledge of the existence of a perfect being. The danger inherent in such an enterprise is that it has the potential to lure us into thinking that God is approachable through reason alone rather than through an awareness of our fundamental disorder and brokenness apart from God's grace.

To appreciate further Pascal's contrast between these two ways of knowing God, consider how differently Pascal and Descartes conceive of human "certainty." In an effort, no doubt, to emphasize his disagreement with the Cartesian method of knowing God through clear and distinct ideas alone, Pascal declares that "it is the heart which perceives God and not the reason."[21] In saying this, Pascal means to emphasize that knowledge of God is not inferred from any set of premises. We do not, in Pascal's view, acquire our knowledge of God through

20. Pascal, *Pensées*, frg. 449.
21. Ibid., frg. 424.

a process of deductive or inductive reasoning. Instead, knowledge of God is a starting point, a fundamental first principle, that we must grasp intuitively as a response to our own desperate, dual state of greatness and wretchedness. Let us recall again that the source of all of our intuitive beliefs, for Pascal, is not a Cartesian faculty that offers us absolute rational certainty. By asserting that first principles are grasped intuitively by the heart rather than by reason, Pascal calls attention to how these principles are not absolutely certain in the sense that no one could possibly doubt them by means of some skeptical argument. Unlike Descartes, Pascal does not endow his basic intuitions with impregnable self-evidence or incorrigibility. Yet Pascal also holds that our intuitive beliefs possess a felt certainty in that we find ourselves drawn to assent to them despite the fact that we can, if we wish, entertain skeptical grounds for calling the very reliability of our cognitive faculties into question. One primary reason that Pascal identifies the heart as the source of our fundamental beliefs is to emphasize how these beliefs are humanly certain even though they are ultimately philosophically uncertain. Hence, Pascalian intuitions resemble Cartesian rationally indubitable clear and distinct perceptions in the respect that we cannot, in any immediately voluntary way, simply by an act of will, choose to affirm or deny them. In the case of our intuitions, Pascal thinks that we do not so much choose to believe as we are moved to believe. Yet in the case of our knowing God, how we are moved to belief depends in part on how we regard ourselves and even on how we feel and what we desire.

Thus, in a way contrary to Descartes, Pascal insists that the intuitions we feel are nevertheless susceptible to skeptical criticism. Clarifying the psychologically "certain" nature of these first principles, Pascal writes:

> We know the truth not only through reason but also through the heart. It is through the latter that we know first principles, and reason, which has nothing to do with it, tries in vain to refute them. . . . Principles are felt and propositions are proved, and both with certainty though by different means. It is just as pointless and absurd for reason to demand proof of first principles from the heart before agreeing to accept them as it would be absurd for the heart to demand an intuition of all the propositions demonstrated by reason before agreeing to accept them.[22]

In this passage Pascal accords a kind of certainty to both reasoned and intuited beliefs. The latter, however, are "certain" not because they are rationally indubitable, but because we naturally "feel" them to be true. To say that our first principles are felt does not mean, to be sure, that they are therefore merely subjective or noncognitive. We feel first principles not blindly—as if they were mere objects of feeling—but intelligently, by a nondeductive, but cognitive, natural endowment.

22. Ibid., frg. 110.

Let us note again that, in speaking of our intuitions as certain, Pascal does not mean "certain" in the Cartesian sense of being beyond any possible, coherent doubt. As we have already seen in this respect, Pascal sides with the Pyrrhonists:

> The strongest of the skeptics' arguments, to say nothing of minor points, is that we cannot be sure that these principles are true (faith and revelation apart) except by some natural intuition. Now this natural intuition affords no convincing proof that they are true. There is no certainty, apart from faith, as to whether man was created by a good God, an evil demon, or just by chance, and so it is a matter of doubt, depending on our origin, whether these innate principles are true, false, or uncertain.[23]

Note here that Pascal refers specifically to Descartes's strategy of validating reason by proving the existence of a perfect God who could not deceive us by equipping us with a defective faculty for discerning the truth. In Pascal's view, Descartes was indeed justified on one key point. Descartes was right to conclude that until we can know for sure the narrative story of how our human cognitive faculties came into being, the skeptic holds the upper hand in the debate over the reliability of reason. For until we can know with certainty that our rational faculties were given to us by a fully trustworthy source, the skeptic is right to insist that we cannot know for sure that the psychologically compelling dictates of our rational faculties are indeed trustworthy. Now, of course, Pascal also holds that the Pyrrhonist stance is finally humanly impossible to maintain, so it is also clear that he is not proposing that we try to suspend belief regarding our natural intuitions. What Pascal does argue here is that, apart from some kind of faith, we have no satisfactory response to the skeptic.

Granted the theist's faith in a good God, it makes sense to trust our natural intuitions. But for Pascal, our knowledge of God comes only through faith and is not absolutely certain. Thus since our defense of our natural intuitions against radical skepticism depends on faith in God, which is itself an intuition of the heart, the only certainty we can ever acquire in this life is ultimately rooted in faith. In other words, on Pascal's account, our intuitions are "certain" in that we naturally and immediately, under the right circumstances, are inclined to embrace them. And we are reasonable in doing so, insofar as we use our cognitive abilities properly when we hold some of our beliefs intuitively through the heart. To be sure, it is simply unreasonable for anyone to demand rational proof for what is prior to, and presupposed by, all efforts to construct compelling proofs. Nevertheless, Pascal insists, none of our beliefs are beyond the intellectual scope of the skeptic's abstract doubt. For Pascal, our intuitions are "certain" for us as humans but are not "certain"

23. Ibid., frg. 131.

in the sense of being beyond skeptical doubt for any rational being thinking abstractly apart from faith.

Let us now return to investigate further what knowing God means for Pascal. In declaring that it is through the heart that we know God,[24] and that only through surrender and love can we know God,[25] Pascal has more in mind than that knowledge of God serves as a fundamental cognitive first principle and is not derived from evidential reasoning. For as we saw in chapter 1, knowing God for Pascal begins with, and is essentially rooted in, an act of love. We might well describe the contrast between Cartesian and Pascalian knowledge of the divine as that between a neutral, propositional knowledge—that God exists—and an intuitive, passionate knowledge—of God as one's highest object of love. The latter, unlike the former, involves not only moral affirmation, the acknowledgment of God as the Supreme Good, but an element of loving desire or need. Knowing God has its roots in a needful, appreciative love. Both aspects, appreciative love of God and desperate need for God's grace, are inherent in what Pascal envisions as genuine knowledge of God.

But what does it mean to say that knowing God through the heart requires moral acknowledgment and affirmation? Consider again how Pascal contrasts the Christian conception of knowing God with that of the Epicurean:

> The Christian's God does not consist merely of a God who is the author of mathematical truths and the order of the elements. That is the portion of the heathen and Epicureans. He does not consist merely of a God who extends his providence over the life and property of men so as to grant a happy span of years to those who worship him. That is the portion of the Jews. But the God of Abraham, the God of Isaac, the God of Jacob, the God of the Christians is a God of love and consolation: he is a God who fills the soul and heart of those whom he possesses: he is a God who makes them inwardly aware of their wretchedness and his infinite mercy: who unites himself with them in the depths of their soul: who fills it with humility, joy, confidence, and love: who makes them incapable of having any other end but him.
>
> All those who seek God apart from Christ, and who go no further than nature, either find no light to satisfy them or come to devise a means of knowing and serving God without a mediator, thus falling into either atheism or deism, two things almost equally abhorrent to Christianity.[26]

According to Pascal, knowing God entails loving God as God, as the supremely good being, and also entails surrendering to God one's supposed autonomous claim to being one's own highest authority. That knowing God requires loving God is rooted in the fact that to know God is to judge and affirm that God alone is the ultimate good for human life. As Pascal expresses this point, by

24. Ibid., frg. 424.
25. Ibid., frg. 449.
26. Ibid.

relating to God in love we become "incapable of having any other end but him."[27] In fragment 449 Pascal seeks to illuminate the character of this knowing by contrasting it to a distant and merely theoretical belief about God as held by the Epicureans. For the Epicureans, the fact of divine existence has virtually no impact on human life, since divine beings exist solely unto themselves and are indifferent to human striving. The only impact such religious belief has for the Epicurean is to show the irrelevance of the divine for human affairs. That is, from an Epicurean standpoint the sole ethical significance of knowledge of the divine is the knowledge that the divine has no interest in, and is basically irrelevant for, mortal human life. What the Epicureans know about the divine, in other words, will not aid us in our quest for salvation if, as Pascal thinks, our natural resources alone cannot offer us lasting peace, and yet our hearts continually yearn for God's affection. In other words, the Christian God, Pascal insists, cannot be known from the perspective of a neutral, disinterested observer precisely because God's love is essential for our wholeness as humans. For Pascal, knowing God means not just recognizing God's goodness as a property of a perfect substance, but genuinely loving God as that good that completes human life. Thus one way to articulate the nature of this loving knowledge is to describe it as a state of affirming God as the good that alone can satisfy human longing.

Thus far we have considered one volitional aspect of Pascal's conception of knowing God. But this aspect of assenting to God as God, of esteeming God as the highest good, also involves an element of desire and need. Affirming God as one's ultimate good means that one acknowledges one's need for God. This act of affirmation does not just assert a fact of existence, "God exists," or even a moral fact, "God is good," as it goes beyond assertion, and even estimation, to desire. As a person gripped by the paradox of human duality, one cannot reasonably and honestly say, "I love God," yet feel no need for God. That one cannot reasonably do so follows both from the nature of personal erotic love in general and from the peculiar nature of an appreciative and desiring love of God. On the level of personal, erotic love, feeling neither longing for another person in that person's absence nor joy in that person's presence is simply an external sign that one does not genuinely love that person—or at least does not love him or her as a person on whom one deeply depends for one's happiness.

Thus when Pascal speaks of knowing God, he has in mind a unique form of *personal knowing*—of knowing a specific person as good, as opposed to knowing just that some being or entity exists. To know another person as worthwhile, as being inherently good as a person, necessitates affirming that person as inherently good and worthwhile, and not merely as useful for achieving some private end. To affirm a person as worthwhile would seem,

27. Ibid.

in addition, to require some positive feeling toward that person. If one takes no pleasure in seeing another person live well, can one be said really to affirm him or her as a person? If one feels no displeasure in witnessing another being deeply harmed, can one, again, be said to affirm that individual as a person? It would seem that we cannot know another person even as our neighbor—that is, as a being possessing dignity and deserving of respect—without caring for that person and desiring his or her well-being. The same is true, but to a much greater degree, when Pascal speaks of knowing God and caring for what God, in His perfect wisdom and love, cares for. The kind of knowledge Pascal refers to when he speaks of knowing God reflects in an analogous way two aspects of personal knowing of other human persons: caring for the other person's well-being and acknowledging that person's intrinsic goodness as a creature reflecting God's beauty and goodness. In many contexts, no doubt, the act of knowing a being does not entail that the subject care for the object he or she knows. But there is a valid and familiar sense of "knowledge," bound up with a conception of knowing other persons as possessing moral worth, where "knowing" requires moral affirmation. He who looks upon me as a mere commodity, as something valuable only as a function of his own personal desires, does not know who I am.

More importantly, when Pascal speaks of knowing God he conceives of God as the supreme good, the most perfect of persons, with whom our union is essential for our human happiness. That is to say that we cannot, from Pascal's perspective, really know God at all without affirming that human life is wretched apart from God's love. We must come to our knowledge of God through the gospel of Jesus Christ, Pascal insists, as it is through this gospel that we finally clearly see both the beauty of God's love for us and our own brokenness and selfishness as creatures who need to be healed, not through any knowledge of God we can acquire on our own, but through God's own revelation through the life, death, and resurrection of Jesus Christ. So, Pascal says:

> The metaphysical proofs for the existence of God are so remote from human reasoning and so involved that they make little impact, and, even if they did help some people, it would only be for the moment during which they watched the demonstration, because an hour later they would be afraid they had made a mistake.
>
> *What they gained through curiosity they lost through pride.* (St. Augustine, *Sermons*, CXLI)
>
> That is the result of knowing God without Christ, in other words communicating without a mediator with a God known without a mediator.
>
> Whereas those who have known God through a mediator know their own wretchedness.[28]

28. Ibid., frg. 190 (italics in the original).

For Pascal, knowing God requires acknowledging God's supremacy and confessing our own human powerlessness to embrace God through our own resources alone. Put another way, our acknowledging of God must be accompanied by our own admission of our deep need for God's grace, for a divine healing of our paradoxical condition of being rebels against the very good we most deeply need and desire.

Now, of course, not all cases of "personal knowing" need involve a desire to be intimate with and in communion with the person one knows. Whereas I might acknowledge the goodness of my neighbor without desiring to be close to my neighbor, for Pascal I cannot acknowledge who God really is without yearning or desiring to be united to and intimate with God. As a general rule, one cannot love the highest good in one's life, whatever it is, and remain indifferent to it when it appears to be present. Given that God is a very unique kind of ultimate good for Pascal, namely a personal God of love, we see all the more that we cannot affirm this highest good without loving him. To affirm this God whose nature is love requires that one relate to God by responding in love both to God and to those whom God loves. Not to love God and one's neighbor in response to God's love would be to deny that God is perfect love and is indeed that good that one longs for and needs to be united with in order to find human fulfillment. In other words, not to love God, but still to posit that there is a God, is, in the end, not really to affirm God but only to affirm an abstract fact. When Pascal condemns those who seek to reach God through reason alone, he is thus insisting on the role of love in knowing God. If, as Descartes does, we understand by "reason" a faculty merely for seeing theoretical truths (through direct insight or inference), for intellectually assenting to what is true, rather than affirming and loving the truth, Pascal's opposition to the project of natural theology stems from his conviction that God cannot be known merely by being "seen," and thus that reason alone, as a merely disinterested faculty for demonstrating theoretical truth, cannot bring us to knowledge of God.

Pascal: Faith Is Rational but Beyond Reason

Granted that Pascal rejects any merely theoretical conception of knowing God, how is it that our assent to faith in God is nevertheless rational on Pascal's view? To see why faith is rational without being "based on reason," let us recall the three-tiered structure of Pascal's paradox argument. First of all, in this argument Pascal pits the rationalist and Pyrrhonist strategies against each other to reveal the inadequacy of both. The paradox argument shows how each opponent succumbs to the critical refutation of the other. To overcome this outcome of mutual destruction, Pascal sets forth as a resolution his theory of the heart as a natural source of certain basic, intuitive beliefs. Like

Hume, Pascal contends that we naturally hold specific beliefs about what is real beyond our immediate perceptions, even though we cannot absolutely verify them. Yet unlike Hume, Pascal believes that once we acknowledge our humbled status as finite thinkers committed to metaphysical beliefs of which we cannot be certain, we are in the right cognitive and affectional condition to grasp how our nature yearns beyond its own meager resources for a knowledge and goodness it cannot attain on its own. In grasping our dual condition as beings who yearn for more than we can obtain through our human resources, we become the sort of persons for whom the gospel message of grace can make profound rational sense. But just what sort of persons must we become to appreciate Pascal's Augustinian solution of grace supplying what the human will and human reason cannot? We must be the sort of self-reflective beings who can acknowledge our limits. More specifically, to feel the burden of our fragmented existence, and as a result yearn to be healed, we have to possess, to some degree, a specific kind of humility. To make progress in searching for God, we must have that crucial humility rooted in the awareness that we are incapable of curing ourselves. Unless we can openly acknowledge to ourselves that our very lives defy our own comprehension, that the knowledge and goodness our nature seeks cannot be naturally acquired, and that this state of disunity repels us, we will not be in a position to comprehend the rationality of grace. In other words, to grasp that God's revelation of grace is worthy of reverence and respect, and thus that the good news of Jesus Christ completes our rational yearning for wholeness, we must first become the sort of people who can admit that our lives are mired in an inescapable perplexity and thus are in need of a radical solution we cannot provide.

Pascal reacts so harshly to the philosophical project of proving the existence of God because the seeker after God must have humility in order to encounter a God who fills the soul rather than simply explains the arrangement of the universe. As we have seen, the fundamental problem with natural theology for Pascal does not lie within the proofs themselves. It is rather the way certain modern philosophers employ these arguments to which Pascal objects. In fragment 781 in particular, Pascal explains why it is deeply misguided to employ theoretical arguments for God's existence, as he supposes some natural theologians do, as a means to cure disbelievers of their unbelief. Such a strategy is misguided, Pascal argues, because God will remain hidden to those who do not seek him with the proper moral attitudes of humility and yearning; as a result, those without faith will not encounter God through these proofs and will instead often become discouraged and skeptical about having any rational grounds at all for believing. Curiously enough, Pascal thinks that these arguments could play a legitimate role if they were used not to convince unbelievers but to instruct and edify those who already believe. Speaking to this matter of the proper versus the improper employment of the theoretical proofs of God's existence, Pascal says:

I marvel at the boldness with which these people presume to speak of God. In addressing their arguments to unbelievers, their first chapter is the proof of the existence of God from the works of nature. Their enterprise would cause me no surprise if they were addressing their arguments to the faithful, for those with living faith in their hearts can certainly see at once that everything that exists is entirely the work of the God they worship. But for those in whom this light has gone out and in whom we are trying to rekindle it, people deprived of faith and grace, examining with such light as they have everything they see in nature that might lead them to this knowledge, but finding only obscurity and darkness; to tell them, I say, that they have only to look at the least thing around them and they will see in it God plainly revealed; to give them no other proof of this great and weighty matter than the course of the moon and the planets; to claim to have completed the proof with such an argument; are indeed feeble, and reason and experience tell me that nothing is more likely to bring it into contempt in their eyes. This is not how Scripture speaks, with its better knowledge of the things of God. On the contrary it says that God is a hidden God, and that since nature was corrupted he has left men to their blindness, from which they can escape only through Jesus Christ, without whom all communication with God is broken off. *Neither knoweth any man the Father save the Son, and he to whomsoever the Son will reveal him.*

This is what Scripture shows us when it says in so many places that those who seek God shall find him. This is not the light of which we speak as of the noonday sun. We do not say that those who seek the sun at noon or water in the sea will find it, and so it necessarily follows that the evidence of God in nature is not of this kind. It tells us elsewhere: *Verily thou art a God that hidest thyself.*[29]

In essence, the critical difference between proper and improper efforts to prove God's existence, according to Pascal, hinges on the nature of faith itself. Pascal argues in this passage that those philosophers who use the resources of natural theology to try to bring others to faith misunderstand the place of the heart in the whole process of coming to faith. The real barrier to faith is not the apparent lack of external evidence for God's existence. What prevents people from encountering God is rather their natural unwillingness to seek God in humble need. Pascal presumes that the Christian God remains hidden to those who seek him for any reason other than that they feel a longing for God's presence. Pascal understands the gospel message of grace to mean that full access to God's presence is only through the person of Christ. Apart from Christ, we cannot even see our own need for God with enough clarity to overcome our inherent pride and acknowledge our need for grace. Until we seek God with our hearts properly humbled, God remains, according to his own incalculable wisdom, hidden from our sight. This fundamental relationship between faith and humility can be further clarified if we recall that for Pascal faith is rooted in love. To believe in God one must love God

29. Ibid., frg. 781.

not just as any ordinary person or being, but as the supreme person and the essential good for human life. To love God as God, one must esteem God as supreme and feel a deep longing to know God intimately as this personal reality. Both elements require humility. Hence, unless one humbly submits to God and renounces the proud tendency of humans to control their own lives and be their own masters, one cannot love God. But without this love, faith is impossible and all efforts to know God, who remains hidden from those who do not approach him in love, will falter.

We could well say, then, that Pascal attacks the practice of natural theology not because he opposes the very idea of using reason to discern signs of God's presence, but because some of the most important modern intellectuals who engage in natural theology think that reason apart from faith and love can lead us to knowledge of God. As Pascal remarks, those seekers who already love God and possess faith may well profit from the traditional proofs for God's existence. Such individuals, for instance, may be helped to perceive more clearly and fully the mark of God's wisdom in the contrivances of nature. There is thus nothing wrong with the proofs themselves, unless one holds, as Descartes does, that their premises must be indubitable, rational starting points, available from a standpoint of pure reason, from which knowledge of God may be attained. Pascal insists that knowing God in faith must be prior to any real profit, in terms even of spiritual enlightenment, to be garnered from the traditional proofs for God's existence. For Pascal, it is through the heart that we come to know God, which is to say that reason alone, apart from love and humility, profits us nothing.

By clarifying the real substance of Pascal's case against natural theology, we can see more fully how Pascal's paradox argument uniquely attempts to synthesize reason and the heart. Unlike the standard metaphysical proofs for God's existence, Pascal's paradox argument tries to awaken or transform the hearts of its readers in order to affect in them the necessary sense of humility that they may come to faith. Quite ingeniously, each level of the paradox argument calls forth a slightly different form of humility. On the initial level, coming to see how the Cartesian and Pyrrhonian sides negate each other forces on us the self-awareness that neither our natural reason alone nor our power to doubt can rule our lives. Having overcome the temptation to make either of these the autonomous ruling counsel in our lives, we then proceed to the next stage, that of natural faith, to see that we cannot even govern our commonsense beliefs by our own wills. Thus in a way that further humbles our cognitive aspirations, we find that our natures compel us to believe in certain realities that we cannot really prove to exist. Finally, for Pascal these basically secular forms of humility must give rise to a decisive kind of humility that acknowledges our need for God's assistance.

To prepare us for this Christian humility, Pascal tries to bring us to acknowledge two basic truths about ourselves: first, that we naturally seek to have firm knowledge of ourselves and to possess a fully satisfying good in our lives, even though we are unable through our own efforts, individually or socially, to find either such knowledge or such a good; and second, that the good we ultimately desire is the communion with a perfect God of love, who fills our souls and gives us consolation. If we acknowledge these inner realities of our human selves, then the Christian gospel can truly appeal to us as a rational solution to our existence. Having cultivated the proper virtues of humility and self-knowledge, which Pascal hopes to bring about in his paradox argument, we are able to become the kind of persons for whom the gospel message makes sense and is thus worthy of our reverence and respect. Believing in God appears rational to us, in other words, only when we come to see and feel its power for making sense of our paradoxical natures and providing a power we lack as natural persons to attain self-fulfillment.

Yet Pascal never suggests that we simply and voluntarily choose to believe in God after the rationality of this belief becomes evident to us. Rather, he thinks that seeing the rationality of belief in God will open us to receiving the gift of true faith. For Pascal, as for Augustine, faith is ultimately the transformation of the human will through divine grace. To open ourselves to the possibility of receiving God's gift of faith, we must finally seek God with the proper state of our hearts. By means of the paradox argument, Pascal writes specifically to those modern intellectuals who have become hardened to faith in part because they do not see its rationality. By opening the hearts and minds of his readers to the rationality of faith, Pascal hopes to assist his readers, and in particular his modern skeptical readers, to become the sort of persons who can will themselves to receive the gift of faith.

Pascal's Wager: Unmasking Skeptical Neutrality

Understanding the role of the heart in Pascal's conception of rational faith enables us to appreciate the real significance of Pascal's famous—or infamous—wager argument. The standard textbook version of Pascal's wager presents his argument in precisely the way Pascal himself never intended it—as an apologetic strategy stripped of its place in the *Pensées*, considered as a whole, and left to stand on its own. Such a presentation of the wager argument does it a grave disservice. The wager argument simply cannot be adequately understood in isolation from Pascal's overall apologetics of the heart. Properly understood, the wager makes a compelling but limited point. As Peter Kreeft observes:

> This is the most famous of all Pascal's ideas, the one history associates with his name. Yet it is not his central concern, the thing closest to his heart. It is only one step on the way, one possible means to the end. The end, the point, the goal, is Christ.

> The Wager is not an attempt to prove that God exists. It is not a new argument for the existence of God. Rather, it tries to prove that it is eminently reasonable for anyone to "bet" on God, to *hope* that God is, to invest his life in God. It moves on the practical, existential, human level rather than the theoretical, metaphysical, theological level.[30]

Kreeft clarifies here that the wager is best understood as just an intermediate step in a larger and more complex apologetic strategy. As we have seen, Pascal's fundamental concern in his *Pensées* is to show the reasonableness and attractiveness of faith in Christ. Pascal defends personal faith in Christ because only Christ makes sufficient sense of our human duality and provides us with an effective path for attaining the communion with the God of love our rational nature desires. At the heart of this faith is the denial of the autonomous self and the affirmation of love. Faith denigrates the self alone but exalts the self in relationship to God, neighbor, and all of creation. But the wager argument, as many of its critics have noted, operates merely on the level of self-interest. The wager urges the skeptic to take sober account of what he or she has to win or lose; curiously, the wager seems to say nothing about either self-denial or love. What can Pascal really have had in mind in presenting the wager as a means to faith?

Let us first consider how Pascal introduces the wager. He begins by noting the immense disproportion, the infinite distance, between God and humanity. As God's perfect being shares no actual, finite likeness to our contingent nature, we cannot through our natural faculties gain any direct or adequate knowledge of God. Yet, Pascal adds, this great disproportion between human and divine also means that we are incapable of disproving God's existence as we might disprove empirical claims about the order of nature. As finite creatures possessing a noble but limited reason, we are left suspended between certainty of God's existence and certainty of God's nonexistence. Left in such uncertainty, Pascal proposes simply to entertain the question of believing or not believing in God's existence as if we were playing the lottery or a game of poker. Pascal proposes that we entertain the rationality of betting for or against God by means of our "natural lights." In the context of the wager argument, following our natural lights means three things: (1) that we play by the rules of our rational limits, not knowing for certain whether God exists; (2) that we play by the rules of the rationality of betting, calculating not only the probability of winning and losing but also the prospects of what we stand to gain or to lose; and (3) that we limit our calculation to nothing higher than the self-interest of a betting person. Confined within these narrow but not inhuman limits of self-interested calculation, the wager argument seeks to lead the skeptic beyond a feigned neutrality to the recognition of the claim God has even on the most self-centered of human agents.

30. Kreeft, *Christianity for Modern Pagans*, 291.

Kreeft clearly portrays the rational efficacy of the wager for the self-regarding betting person as follows:

> We are all playing the same game (life) for the same two prizes. We all have two things we absolutely demand to win and not to lose: truth and happiness. No one wants to be deceived and no one wants to be miserable.
>
> Imagine the two prizes we are playing for as blue chips (truth) and red chips (happiness). Now we cannot calculate our chances of winning the blue chips. Reason cannot prove the truth of either theism or atheism. Therefore we must calculate our chances of winning the red chips, happiness.
>
> These are the two things everyone wants absolutely. No one wants to be a fool, stupid, ignorant, in error. "All men by nature desire to know"—this is Aristotle's premise and first line in the *Metaphysics*. And no one wants to be wretched and miserable. St. Thomas observes, in the *Summa*, that since no one can live without joy, one deprived of true joys necessarily seeks false joys in the form of worldly and carnal pleasures. We seek truth with our reason and joy with our will, and these are the two things that raise us above the animal. That is why they are absolute and nonnegotiable to us: they are the fulfillment of our essence. If we attain them, we are a success, no matter how else we fail. If we fail at them, no other success can compensate for this loss. For "what does it profit a man if he gain the whole world and lose his own soul?" (Mark 8:36 KJV).
>
> The red-chip calculation is as certain as the blue-chip calculation is uncertain. The only chance of winning the happiness we crave—adequate, total, eternal, unending, unlimited, infinite happiness—is the first of the four possibilities . . . namely, the combination "God exists and I believe." . . .
>
> Suppose you are offered a lottery ticket for free. Suppose you knew there was a 50 percent chance it was worth a million dollars, and a 50 percent chance it was worth nothing. Would it be reasonable to take the trouble to accept the gift, to *hope* at least in it, to trust the giver enough to accept the gift?
>
> It would be obvious insanity not to.
>
> To the objection that such "belief" is not yet true faith, the reply is: Of course not, but it is a step on the road to it. Even if it is sheer fear of God's justice in Hell, "the fear of the Lord is the beginning of [wisdom]" (Prov. 1:7). It is certainly not the end. Love is that. But "love stoops to conquer" and can use even fear as a beginning—like a loving parent shouting to a toddler to get out of the street.
>
> True faith is not a wager but a relationship. But it can begin with a wager, just as a marriage can begin with a blind date.[31]

As Kreeft helps us comprehend, Pascal's aim in confronting us with the wager is not to provide a direct bridge to faith, but to break down a key barrier preventing the skeptic from being willing to approach such a bridge. As Pascal knows, the root cause of our estrangement from God is not the insufficiency

---

31. Ibid., 300–301.

of evidence but the obduracy of our pride. Inordinate love of self, and our jealous determination, whether we are believers or unbelievers, to safeguard our cherished sovereignty over our own lives is the root cause of our separation from God at all levels. Pascal, in understanding the role of our will and our affections in forming our fundamental convictions, brilliantly sets out to meet the skeptic on his own terms. In an act of ingenious charity, in other words, Pascal deconstructs the barrier to God's love precisely by turning it on itself. If misguided self-interest prevents us from honestly and openly seeking the God of love, then what better means of reaching the proud human heart than by using its very self-love to bring about a nascent humility. The crucial point of the wager, then, is not to effect conversion, at least not directly to do so, but to reach out to the skeptic and appeal to him or her within his or her own frame of reference. The point of the wager is thus to unmask the real barrier to seeking God. Indeed, it is exactly this insight that Pascal's man of natural lights comes to experience:

> "I confess, I admit it, but is there really no way of seeing where the cards are?"—"Yes. Scripture and the rest, etc."—"Yes, but my hands are tied and my lips are sealed; I am being forced to wager and I am not free; I am being held fast and I am so made that I cannot believe. What do you want me to do then?"—That is true, but at least get it into your head that, if you are unable to believe, it is because of your passions, since reason impels you to believe and yet you cannot do so. Concentrate then not on convincing yourself by multiplying proofs of God's existence but by diminishing your passions. You want to find faith and you do not know the road. You want to be cured of unbelief and you ask for the remedy: learn from those who were once bound like you and who now wager all they have. These are people who know the road you wish to follow, who have been cured of the affliction of which you wish to be cured: follow the way by which they began.[32]

In a distinctively Augustinian way, Pascal's strategy in his wager argument modifies the pattern of the Socratic *elenchus* by transforming it in light of the centrality of charity. Just as Socrates sought first and foremost to bring about self-knowledge and to engender humility, so Pascal seeks to lead the natural man imprisoned in his own state of excessive self-regard to recognize the gross inadequacy inherent in his own self-regarding perspective. Put simply, the wager serves to break down a crucial barrier to our recognition of our own wretchedness. Until we acknowledge our wretchedness, we cannot see the need for a savior, and we will not be able to see within ourselves the "evidence" of sickness Christ appeals to in calling us to be his patients. In itself, the wager has no power to bring us home or to heal us; its purpose, as Pascal makes clear, is not to convert but to open our eyes to the fact that in

32. Pascal, *Pensées*, 418.

our natural self-regarding state we cannot reasonably maintain an indifference or aversion to God's call to us for eternal, loving fellowship. The wager
serves to expose the self-delusion within our natural condition of presuming that the existence of a loving God is a matter of indifference. Certainly
Pascal understands that true faith requires self-surrender and love of God—
what Pascal deems the annihilation of the "self-alone." But what good is
proclaiming such doctrine to a person convinced through intellectual pride
that he or she simply does not need God? What Pascal's wager so brilliantly
comprehends is the need to appeal to the natural, self-centered person on
his or her own terms. The wager thus functions not to "produce faith," but
to awaken desire and engender self-understanding. By bringing the natural
human to see the folly and dishonesty of proud, skeptical indifference to the
God of love, Pascal's wager is a profound act of love whereby Pascal seeks
to meet the modern skeptic on his or her own ground and awaken in such
a person an embryonic desire to resist our natural addiction to individual
autonomy.

Let me now return to the central issue of how Pascal conceives of faith in
God as rational. First of all, as we have seen especially from Pascal's critique of
natural theology, the real question of the rationality of faith, for Pascal, must
be posed from within a practical, existential context. To treat the justification
of faith as a purely theoretical matter, and to concentrate, in particular, on
the issue of whether such faith rests firmly on a basis of objective facts, is to
do violence to the real character of faith. Faith makes sense only when it is
left in its proper context, as a loving response of the human heart toward a
personal God who offers a cure for the human paradox. Faith functions in
the life of believers as a fundamental interpretative principle, the rationality
of which manifests itself only from the perspective of a humbled, suffering
self-awareness. As the ultimate, moral first principle for the community of the
faithful, its rationality must be shown dialectically in terms of its power to heal
human brokenness. This is to say both that belief in God is not self-evidently
true and that this belief cannot be justified—at least not in the primary sense
that relates to its essential character as salvific—by any mere appeal to facts
outside the human condition. What leads us to faith is not that the world outside of us needs an ultimate cause, for example, but that our own lives need a
healing we cannot, through our own power, achieve. The logic of faith hinges
on the issue of evidence, but only if one carefully specifies that the relevant
evidence is internal to human aspiration and feeling. If we concur with Pascal
that our lives do indeed suffer from the kind of incoherence he portrays as the
human paradox, then the evidence we need to see the rationality of faith is
available to us. Yet to call such aspects of human existence "evidence" might
misleadingly suggest that these are objectively verifiable facts evident to any
human observer, regardless of his or her moral intuitions and character. As
we have noted, the "facts" of human life are neither. To grasp these existential

facts, as Pascal perceives them, we must have humility about our power to cure ourselves, and we must feel the desire to know ourselves and to possess a good that transcends our limits. Hence we might well say that Pascal's case for the rationality of faith presupposes a particular, and inevitably uncertain, diagnosis of the human heart.

Pascal versus Fideism: Faith Is Not Contrary to Reason

I turn now to my earlier point that it is misleading to portray Pascal as an antirational, antiphilosophical fideist. In contradistinction to both Popkin and Penelhum, I think it is more illuminating to place Pascal in the Augustinian tradition that holds that one must first believe in order to understand. The key advantage to placing Pascal in this tradition is that we can more truly appreciate how, like Augustine, Pascal can attack the efforts of philosophers to know God apart from faith and nevertheless seek to show, as Augustine does, the rational integrity and superiority of faith over skepticism. Put simply, Pascal rejects the modern evidentialist stance that assumes that one must first understand, on the basis of objective evidential reasoning, in order to believe, but he accepts the Augustinian call of faith seeking understanding. Pascal is not a fideist, then, because he in no way recommends a life of faith essentially opposed to sustained rational inquiry and argumentation.[33]

If the fideist reading of Pascal were correct and Pascal had really meant to set aside the demands of reason entirely to prepare the way for faith, we might still find in the *Pensées* many instances of rational persuasion or the use of philosophical argument. Yet we would expect these rhetorical appeals to serve only to convince the reader that faith needs no support or approval from reason. As Popkin rightly notes, if Pascal meant to attack reason per se, he might well still use rational argument to confront the critics of faith on their own ground and fend off those opponents who mistakenly attempt to evaluate faith in terms of the standards of rational argument. Certainly if he really were a fideist, the one thing it would make no sense at all for Pascal to do would be to use reasoning in a positive manner to show how faith makes rational sense and is even rationally attractive. Yet it is precisely this latter strategy of arguing in defense of faith that Pascal adopts in his *Pensées*. Pascal does not contend that faith itself is "beyond reason" entirely, though the truths of faith may be, nor does Pascal ever say that faith is finally contrary to reason. Rather, he seeks to persuade us that the commitment of faith to our Redeemer is rationally preferable to that of unbelief.

33. Although Pascal embraces using reasoning as a legitimate avenue to faith, he does not fall prey to the gnostic tendency to disparage the simple faith of those who respond to God naturally, without any sophisticated exercise of rational reflection. See esp. frg. 110, where Pascal makes it clear that a life of simple faith is praiseworthy.

In further support of my characterization of Pascal as more of a Christian Socrates than a Christian fideist, consider the following two passages where Pascal steps back from his overall project to inform us of his underlying methodology:

> I do not mean you to believe me submissively and without reason; I do not claim to subdue you by tyranny. Nor do I claim to account to you for everything. To reconcile these contradictions I mean to show you clearly, by convincing proofs, marks of divinity within me which will convince you of what I am, and establish my authority by miracles and proofs that you cannot reject, so that you will then believe the things I teach, finding no reason to reject them but your own inability to tell whether they are true or not.

> The true religion would have to teach greatness and wretchedness, inspire self-esteem and self-contempt, love and hate.[34]

In the first of these passages, Pascal assumes the voice of God and addresses the reader as the "wisdom of God." Seeking to clarify how faith is neither tyrannical nor irrational, God's wisdom declares that people are not to be coerced to believe. God neither demands irrational assent nor renders himself so fully accessible and so transparently intelligible that we are compelled to believe in him. Rather, God reveals himself historically through proofs that will be convincing to those who see clearly enough why our human nature cries out to God for help. If taken out of context, our first passage might lead us to think that Pascal means here to endorse the kind of view he so passionately opposes elsewhere—namely, that reason apart from the heart can provide us with compelling proof of the existence of God. But there is no reason to suppose Pascal is making such an uncharacteristic move. Rather, Pascal is here addressing the person who possesses the right kind of humility and openness to God: for such a person, the signs of God's divinity in miracles and in God's providence provide compelling evidence for God's reality. Essentially, God reveals himself in such signs as a God who can solve the paradox of our contradictory dual state of greatness and wretchedness. It is rational for people to turn to God not because of any undeniable proofs in the form of external evidence, but because of the pairing of God's own revelations with the inner evidence of our own paradoxical existence.

In the second passage Pascal characterizes in summary form his own conception of the rational standard for judging true versus false religion. Note that the criteria for true religion do not rely on the evidence of external facts but rely instead on the paradoxical nature of our internal psychological and spiritual condition. We judge a religion to be true or false in terms of both its explanatory power in making sense of our own broken nature and its ability

---

34. Pascal, *Pensées*, frgs. 149 and 450.

to empower us to achieve our most desired goals. For Pascal, true religion must render us intelligible to ourselves and offer us a way to attain the self-completion that our hearts naturally and most deeply desire. In Pascal's view, the Christian faith is rational because it accounts for our inner suffering as paradoxical beings and offers a way of salvation. Pascal is by no means trying to say that Christian faith is rational insofar as we can prove its veracity by appealing to a set of undeniable, self-evident premises. On the contrary, this faith is rational only as a cure for those who have the self-understanding of themselves as sufferers in deep need of a healing they cannot provide through their own efforts. In other words, it is because we are finite creatures with a paradoxical character, a character that we recognize to be both great and wretched, that the God who reveals to us his divine grace makes rational sense to us. That embracing this grace is rational for humans is indeed the central thesis of Pascal's paradox argument.

Hence Pascal is not a fideist: he is committed to a project of rationally justifying faith, a project that, for the fideist, is the very thing to be resisted. A fideist such as Tertullian believes in effect that one cannot serve both God and reason because they are incompatible authorities. While sympathetic to the fideist's concerns to avoid the idolatry of relying on reason alone, Pascal rejects the fideist stance by holding that reason, like mammon, is a gift of God that, when used properly, aids us in serving God as our ultimate authority.

Pascal and Hume, Pascal and Aristotle: Conclusions

Throughout our investigation of the philosophies of Hume and Pascal we have been confronted with the question of what it means to believe rationally. On this subject, Hume and Pascal agree on at least two claims: first, that reflective humans ought to care whether their deepest beliefs about human nature are rationally justified; second, that human life cannot in practice be governed by the standards internal to the Lockean, modern foundationalist account of rational belief. It is one of Hume's notable contributions to modern thought to have shown, through his attacks on natural theology and the evidential basis for belief in miracles, how the Lockean model comes into conflict with Christian belief. Yet, as I have argued, Hume's most damaging case against theism and, in particular, Christian theism hinges on his diagnosis of the "popular" religious psyche as unhealthy and destructive. In developing this naturalistic psychopathology, Hume posits an alternative, very restricted "theism" that he characterizes, in a way that breaks free of the limits of the Lockean model, as philosophical and rational. Yet Hume fails insofar as his diagnosis of Christian spirituality is reductionistic and thus rationally unwarranted.

Not surprisingly, Pascal's diagnosis of human existence is the mirror image of Hume's. In Pascal's view, human life apart from God's grace suffers from a paradoxical disunity that undermines our happiness. For Pascal, we are by nature creatures seeking to possess knowledge of ourselves and to attain whatever it is that is our true good. Yet neither this knowledge nor our true good can come into our possession through our own natural endowments. Like Augustine, Pascal believes that we need God's help if we are to understand ourselves and if we are to fulfill our natures in contact with our highest good. To believe in this God is rational, according to Pascal, both because God's message to us about sin and grace makes coherent sense of our suffering nature and because God's grace provides our only access to the good for which we naturally yearn. The essential task of the *Pensées*, in Pascal's own words, is to show disbelievers, who are prone to proud indifference, that the message of Christ's gospel is "worthy of reverence and respect":

> Order: Men despise religion. They hate it and are afraid it may be true. The cure for this is first to show that religion is not contrary to reason, but worthy of reverence and respect.
>   Next, make it attractive, make good men wish it were true, and then show that it is.
>   Worthy of reverence because it really understands human nature.
>   Attractive because it promises true good.[35]

What makes the gospel message rational for Pascal has nothing to do with standard Enlightenment notions of being self-evident or being based on what is self-evident. Rather, as we have seen, Pascal envisions a more dialectical rationality of one's fundamental beliefs about being human. Belief in God is rational because it alone satisfies our natural longing as rational beings for self-knowledge and for our true good. Pascal presupposes here that there is an objective human nature, that this nature fuels in us longings for self-understanding and for a final good that will truly satisfy us. We are naturally constituted to seek a good beyond ourselves and to find this good in union with God if only we subdue our pride and open ourselves to embrace it. Insofar as Pascal projects this ideal of human flourishing, he operates within a clear, teleological framework. Like Aristotle, Pascal does not suppose that his account of the human *telos* has the status of a Euclidean proof or an indubitable first principle. To argue his case for this Christian *telos* as opposed to some other, Pascal proposes to show that the Christian narrative of sin, forgiveness, and salvation makes sense of our dual state of greatness and wretchedness and offers to us the good we naturally desire. But we will not be persuaded by such a line of reasoning, as we find it displayed in Pascal's paradox argument, unless we apprehend the same basic facts in human existence—namely, our suffering plight and the natural attractiveness of the Christian *telos*. As Pascal recognizes, for one thing, not everyone thinks that

35. Ibid., frg. 12.

human existence requires some radical, teleological corrective. Others, such as the Pyrrhonists, hold that our unhappiness stems from our misguided passion for attaining knowledge of what lies beyond appearances. Hume rejects the general Pyrrhonian strategy as unnatural but in the area of religion envisions an abstract, impersonal religion as alone affording a degree of stable, rational pleasure. And these three non-Christian alternatives represent only a fraction of the possible interpretations of the character of human life. The fact that there are so many competing perspectives on this subject presents an obvious challenge for a Pascalian diagnosis. How can Pascal defend his own account of human duality, one might ask, as anything other than one possible perspective, the truth of which is apparent only for those who share its perception of the human condition? The Pascalian answer to this question is to acknowledge that only those who possess certain moral intuitions in the first place can be persuaded by the kind of argument he develops.

On my interpretation, Pascal is an Augustinian in at least two significant respects. First, following Augustine, he opposes philosophical efforts to reach God apart from a faith rooted in love. Pascal expresses his Augustinian position by emphatically insisting on the role of the heart in knowing God. As does Augustine, so Pascal holds that one must first believe in order to understand. Second, while both Augustine and Pascal reject the demand for a proof that precedes faith, they adopt a dialectical stance on the rationality of faith. Although belief in God serves in their thinking as a fundamental first principle, one that is not self-evident, it can still be defended as rational. It is rational because it embraces the grace that people naturally long for and that alone reveals to us our nature as noble but fallen creatures. For Augustine, the path of wisdom must actually lead to communion with the good, and not just to an abstract knowledge describing what the true good is. By nature, according to both thinkers, people seek their own self-completion yet inevitably fall short of this state apart from grace. To accept divine grace becomes rational for us given the *telos* that we naturally seek. Both thinkers hold that it is only the loving and humble acceptance of grace that can lead us to true wisdom. Granted this exclusive power of God's grace to complete our rational nature, the life of faith, which they recommend, turns out to be preeminently rational. To be Augustinian, as Pascal is, thus involves a subtle ambivalence toward philosophical reasoning, one that neither exalts reason as supreme nor condemns it as inherently unreliable or impious.

One very important insight that emerges out of this Pascalian worldview and account of human nature is that what it means for a belief to be rational depends in part on the function or role that belief has, or on how that belief functions in a particular human practice. In the sense in which I am using the term here, we can say that our beliefs are rational when they result from the proper functioning of our cognitive faculties. Similarly, we can say that a person is being rational when his or her beliefs and actions are based on the proper functioning of his or her cognitive faculties.

Nevertheless, in Pascal's view, we can still assess with some rigor the rationality of our beliefs about ultimate meaning. The appropriateness or propriety of such ultimate beliefs turns out to be quite subtle for the Pascalian. As I have argued, Pascal conceives of the rationality of our ultimate beliefs in terms of two key functional criteria: (1) whether the belief functions properly in making coherent sense of our experience of ourselves; and (2) whether the belief functions properly in guiding us toward the genuine completion of our human nature. In this way, Pascal's account of the rationality of faith might well be called teleological, insofar as it judges this rationality in terms of the completeness and unity for which we naturally yearn as humans. Pascal's case for the rationality of faith turns on an account of who we are as persons seeking a good we cannot attain on our own. It is in the context of the supreme goodness of love, in particular, and of our failure as lovers of one another that faith makes rational sense for us. We can no more assess the rationality of faith apart from this existential context than we can assess that of a scientific hypothesis apart from the goals, values, and canons of rigorous scientific research. What all rational beliefs have in common is some dependence on the human heart, on our basic intuitions. But just as human life is complex, so is the human heart, and so are the specific and precise standards for judging the rationality of our various beliefs.

Pascal's subtle Augustinian vision of the synthesis of reason, knowledge, and the heart may be summarized as follows:

1. All types of human knowledge, whether mathematical, scientific, ethical, or religious, rest on some foundation of intuitive basic beliefs that (1) are held by the heart rather than by empirical or logical reasoning; (2) are not absolutely indubitable in the Cartesian sense; and (3) nevertheless have a strength and firmness about them that renders them either very difficult or impossible to doubt. Such beliefs are not derived from more fundamental beliefs; they are held as basic intuitions, logically uncertain yet psychologically compelling. Our fundamental beliefs are held through the heart and not through reason. Reason thus depends on the heart.

2. Humans naturally seek to fulfill their deepest aspirations and thus attain self-completion and wholeness. By nature humans desire to possess and have knowledge of an ultimate good that will satisfy their natural desire for self-unity.

3. An honest assessment of the human condition reveals to us a basic paradox and predicament of our human nature—namely, that we are incapable either individually or communally of attaining this self-unity, which is to say that we are both great and wretched.

4. The historic witness of the life and death of Jesus Christ provides a viable solution to the paradox of human life: it not only makes rational

sense of the human paradox, but also provides a viable way through grace for people to become unified and complete. That is, the story of Jesus Christ offers us the wholeness we yearn for, as the person of Jesus Christ promises satisfaction of the two most fundamental longings in the human heart—to understand who we are and to live our lives truthfully with fullness and integrity.

Put more specifically, Christ reveals to us that the meaning of our lives is bound up with our need to love and to be loved. Christ teaches us not only of our need for God's unconditional love but also of our own selfish refusal to put aside inordinate love of self so that we can love God with our full allegiance. Christ's sacrifice on the cross and his resurrection show us who we really are: creatures who need God's unconditional love but who are also too afraid and stubborn to let go of our self-centeredness. Faith in Christ is rational, then, as it provides us a way to become the sort of persons who can love well and who can understand who we really are. We can become whole and complete as humans only by responding to God's perfect love by allowing him to transform us into beings capable of loving him as our highest good and of loving our neighbor as our self. More importantly, we recognize that we are powerless to do this on our own. In other words, we are creatures who need grace.

5. Our recognition of our own incompleteness, of our desperate need but inherent inability to love adequately, naturally awakens in us a yearning for God's grace, even though this intuitive response can effectively be blocked by a proud refusal to acknowledge our own brokenness. Unlike specific "natural" intuitions that we hold involuntarily, this intuitive act of wishing for and being open to God's healing requires an act of human willing and thus is partially under our own control. Faith, however, is not simply a matter of human willing, for faith is ultimately a divine gift available to us only through the work of the Holy Spirit. Still, while faith is a gift, the acceptance of this gift necessitates our being willing to humble ourselves and to acknowledge our need to be healed by God's power. Ultimately, faith in the God of love and in Jesus Christ is a gift divinely bestowed, but faith still requires on the part of those who receive it a humble acknowledgment that we are the kind of creatures who can be healed only by a divine physician.

6. Faith, love, and rationality are thus inextricably interconnected. To see how faith in a loving God is rational, one must first acknowledge one's desire for self-unity, believe that God's love alone has the power to heal and lead one to this self-unity, and thus feel a yearning for grace. All three responses involve both intellectual judgment and human will. These responses to the human condition are intuitive and fallible. Those who hold them can see how an uncertain belief in God is rational as a fundamental

first principle that renders our lives coherent. Belief in God is rational not as the conclusion of a deductive argument but as an intuitive first principle that makes coherent sense of our beliefs and experiences about ourselves. Thus in order to understand the rationality of belief in God, one must first believe certain truths about human existence. Similarly, as one lives out the life of faith, one develops the capacity to appreciate more fully the goodness of love and grasp more clearly the imperfection in how one loves. Here again, one's basic intuitions play a major role in what appears rational to believe about the meaning of human life. In place of certainty, one is left with fallible intuitions and the attempt to make rational sense of them. What one understands about human life and the ultimate significance of all things depends on what one intuitively believes. Following Augustine, we can rightly say *"credo ut intellegam"*—that is, I must trust in certain basic intuitions about myself and God in order to be transformed by God's love so that I may finally come to understand God, my neighbor, and myself.

If we accept Pascal's diagnosis of human wretchedness and greatness, the question of the rationality of faith becomes a matter of whether faith succeeds for us, as Pascal contends it does, in unifying our lives. And insofar as faith serves in this fashion as an overarching, fundamental belief, it will appear rational only to those who experience their own lives as paradoxical in Pascal's sense. Clearly, then, not everyone should be expected to find Pascal's case rationally compelling. Like Aristotle, Pascal recognizes that philosophical accounts of the human *telos* must appeal to the basic intuitions and character of his audience. As we saw in chapter 1, however, the fact that teleological outlooks such as Pascal's are never absolutely certain and can be justified only from within a perspective of human beliefs and desires does not mean that any one such account is just as rational as any other.[36] As a teleological account of human nature,

36. In arguing for a nonrelativistic but dialectical conception of rationality, I should note my indebtedness to Alasdair MacIntyre's analysis of traditions of moral thinking found in *Whose Justice? Which Rationality?* (Notre Dame, IN: University of Notre Dame Press, 1988). In this work, MacIntyre argues that the Enlightenment conception of universal, necessary, and neutral standards of rationality and justice fails to appreciate how the standards of rationality and justice emerge from and are dependent on particular historical traditions. Yet, MacIntyre claims, while we cannot step outside all traditions to attain a privileged, autonomous perspective, we can nevertheless evaluate competing traditions by examining their success or failure in responding to challenges originating both internally from their own adherents and externally from rival traditions. According to MacIntyre, the fundamental test for judging rival traditions is whether they can coherently resolve their internal crises and respond to questions and refutations posed by their rivals in a way that coheres with their fundamental commitments and beliefs. Traditions fail when they are unable to formulate a coherent response to one or more serious objections, problems, or crises. One distinctive strength of MacIntyre's analysis is that he provides an account of the rationality of traditions that acknowledges the demise of modern foundationalism but still avoids succumbing to relativism. MacIntyre avoids relativism by insisting that in order

Pascal's analysis must be able to respond successfully to critical objections and challenges. Success in this process does not require that everyone agree with Pascal's position. Rather, it requires the defender of Pascal's outlook to clarify and defend it as a coherent account of human well-being. In the last chapter, I will defend Pascal against one line of contemporary criticism, namely that of the radical, secular postmodernist who rejects all metaphysical schemes as epistemologically naive and ethically oppressive, a current mode of criticism that I think warrants serious attention.

---

to be rational, traditions must satisfy the Socratic requirement to articulate a coherent defense of their positions in the face of dialectical challenges. Insofar as it is possible that more than one rival tradition will, at least for some period of time, be able to give a satisfactory *logos* for its outlook, MacIntyre admits that his account of rationality does not provide a neutral standard that will be sufficient for settling all the major disputes among competing stances.

4

A DIALECTICAL DEFENSE OF PASCAL'S PARADOX ARGUMENT

PASCAL VERSUS RADICAL POSTMODERNISM

I would like my country to be seen and known with an attentiveness that is schooled and skilled. I would like it to be loved with a minutely particular affection and loyalty. I would like the work in it to be practical and loving and respectful and forbearing. In order for these things to happen, the sciences and the humanities are going to have to come together again in the presence of the practical problems of individual places, and of local knowledge and local love in individual people—people able to see, know, think, feel, and act coherently and well without the modern instinct of deference to the "outside expert."

Wendell Berry, "An Argument for Diversity"[1]

The question before us, then, is an extremely difficult one: How do we begin to remake, or to make, a local culture that will preserve our part of the world while we use it? We are talking here not just about a kind of knowledge that involves affection but also about a kind of knowledge that comes from or with affection—knowledge that is unavailable to the unaffectionate and that is unavailable to anyone in the form of *information*.

Wendell Berry, *Sex, Economy, Freedom & Community*[2]

1. Wendell Berry, "An Argument for Diversity," in *What Are People For?* (New York: North Point, 1990), 115–17.
2. Wendell Berry, *Sex, Economy, Freedom & Community* (New York: Pantheon Books, 1993), 24.

Much of modern philosophy was long held captive by a humanistic vision of rational autonomy in which the essential spirit and authority of objective reason was set over against the tutelage of the human affections. In an Augustinian model of embedded rationality, however, reason and affection ought to function symbiotically, with the result that the highest level of assurance and clarity for which we can hope in defending our most deeply held convictions about human meaning is one that exhibits the deep and complex coherence of our beliefs, desires, and practices within our lived experience as limited, passionate, and incarnate individuals. Since this teleological coherence involves not only the formal consistency of one's beliefs but also a holistic consistency of one's philosophical theories within a complex matrix of intuitive moral beliefs, basic desires, affections, and cognitive limits, such a defense cannot help but be ad hominem. This is to say that in articulating any philosophy of what it means to be human, the Augustinian philosopher can aspire no further than to show the philosophy's rich and compelling coherence within a set of human beliefs, feelings, desires, and experiences. Hence, the persuasiveness of one's worldview will be felt only by those persons whose intuitions, feelings, and desires provide the lived context in which they will be able to recognize both the intelligibility and the power of such a worldview as an account of human meaning.

To assess the rationality of Pascal's account of human existence, in particular, I propose in a Socratic fashion to subject Pascal's paradox argument to a particularly powerful and timely line of dialectical criticism—what I will term "the postmodern objection" to Pascal's worldview. If we presume to judge the rationality of a philosophical outlook in a Socratic manner, we must concede that our conclusions will never be immune from later revision and further scrutiny. At best, we can hope to show how the outlook we find compelling can be defended as coherent in the face of the gauntlet of criticisms so far entertained, and as coherent in our lives as we have so far lived them. As we have noted, it is the very nature of Socratic critical inquiry to acknowledge that all human ethical perspectives must be open to future revision, for the standard of Socratic rationality is not proof but a robust dialectical coherence. From a Socratic vantage point, the more fully a philosophical outlook manifests its complex, lived coherence in our lives, the more assured its adherents can be of its rationality. Yet all religious and philosophical outlooks invariably put their adherents at risk; there is no standpoint, religious or secular, that affords immunity from the risk of misperception and misjudgment. Human fallibility is not so much an immature state to be outgrown as a fundamental limitation of human theorizing and inquiry; these limitations should be acknowledged with honesty and humility. In this spirit of Socratic humility, let us turn now to examine the postmodern criticism, a line of criticism that maintains, in effect, that the Pascalian perspective on the human condition utterly fails to present a rational and responsible vision of human existence.

The Radical Postmodern Challenge to Pascal's Paradox Argument

> Without the aid of trained emotions the intellect is powerless against the animal organism. I had sooner play cards against a man who was quite skeptical about ethics, but bred to believe that "a gentleman does not cheat," than against an irreproachable moral philosopher who had been brought up among sharpers. . . . The head rules the belly through the chest—the seat, as Alanus tells us, of Magnanimity, of emotions organized by trained habit into stable sentiments. . . . In a sort of ghastly simplicity we remove the organ and demand the function. We make men without chests and expect of them virtue and enterprise. We laugh at honor and are shocked to find traitors in our midst. We castrate and bid the geldings be fruitful.
>
> C. S. Lewis, *The Abolition of Man*[3]

In presenting his diagnosis of the human paradox, Pascal engages in a form of metaphysical theorizing that has come under repeated and relentless attack by mainstream, radical postmodern thinkers such as Gilles Deleuze, Jacques Derrida, Michel Foucault, François Lyotard, Richard Rorty, and Paul de Man, all of whom reject not only the Enlightenment quest for certainty, as does Pascal, but also the entire metaphysical enterprise of traditional philosophy that, in its various forms, attempts to articulate a rational perspective on the "real itself," on the nature of the world in itself. In his defense of an embedded reason, Pascal, like traditional metaphysicians before him, seeks to discover the fundamental unity, the *arche* or *logos*, of all beings. Radical postmodernism, in contrast, seeks to unmask just this sort of metaphysical project of traditional Western philosophy as self-negating, incoherent, and oppressive. Underlying the diverse and even radically dissimilar traditions of Western metaphysics is a basic yearning of the human spirit to make contact with the realm of being itself—with the world not merely as it appears to a given, particular, historical community or culture, but "as it really is." In radical opposition to both the spirit and project of Western metaphysics, radical postmodernists reject the metaphysical quest for objective truth as both intellectually and politically defective. Clearly, if the basic endeavor of philosophical and religious metaphysical traditions to gain enlightenment about the true nature of the self and world is profoundly deluded, if not debased, then Pascal's entire defense of the rationality of faith falls apart.

Before we examine the postmodernist objection to Pascal's *apologia* for Christian faith, we might do well to recall how, for both Augustine and Pascal, the driving impulse of the philosophical quest for the truth is a form of love. In certain respects, what we see in Augustine and Pascal is a deeply Platonic vision of the philosophical life. According to Plato, the philosopher's quest for wisdom is fueled not by acquisitive appetites or by self-assertive *thumos*

---

3. C. S. Lewis, *The Abolition of Man* (San Francisco: HarperCollins, 1944), 24–26.

or pride, but by a nonegoistic eros, by a love of what is beautiful, whose character and worth as beautiful is ours to receive as a gift, ours to apprehend and to imitate rather than to create or to own for ourselves. As I have argued, Augustine and Pascal affirm the Platonic aspiration to make contact with, and abide in, the fundamental unity and goodness of the cosmos; they disagree with Plato on the question of the adequacy of the Platonic eros, as a merely human impulse, for achieving this communion with ultimate reality. While Augustine and Pascal can affirm the basic spirit of Platonic eros, they must call into question the ultimate efficacy of a merely human eros to overcome the divide between the human and the divine. Platonism will inevitably leave us unfulfilled, according to Augustine and Pascal, because Platonic eros, however noble, is still merely a natural human power, which, apart from the grace of God, cannot heal the errant human will and lead us home. For Augustine and Pascal the true philosophical quest is Platonism completed by grace, and the true philosophical life is the life of faith seeking understanding. Such a grace-filled life is still deeply erotic: it carries out the search for wisdom fueled by the heart's yearning for eternal communion and relationship with absolute beauty and brought to fruition by divine assistance. Let us note further that the beauty sought for on this Augustinian and Pascalian view of philosophy is coequal with Being itself; for Augustine and Pascal, beauty is neither merely a subjective form of harmony, as Kant argues, nor is it our own creation, as Nietzsche envisions in his portrayal of the self-creating *übermensch*. Rather, for Augustine and Pascal beauty is coterminous with reality in two respects: first, with respect to God, to be in the fullest sense (to be the perfect Being) is to be beauty itself; and second, with respect to contingent being, to be as a created being is to be an icon of beauty itself. Insofar as Augustine and Pascal uphold this conception of the unity of beauty and being, they find themselves outcasts both in the modern and the postmodern worlds. For the modernist, beauty cannot be inherent in the world because the world is merely a neutral assemblage of facts. For the postmodernist, the Augustinian and Pascalian metaphysics of the beautiful and the real is no more than a dissembling, falsifying, and imprisoning artifice.

Certainly mainstream, radical postmodernism has a varied and by no means monolithic character. One must be duly cautious in characterizing in universal or comprehensive terms what it means to be postmodern or what all postmodernists really believe.[4] Nevertheless, as David Bentley Hart contends, one can

---

4. My analysis of postmodernism is especially indebted to the following fine works: Lawrence Cahoone, ed., *From Modernism to Postmodernism: An Anthology* (Oxford: Blackwell, 1996); David S. Dockery, ed., *The Challenge of Postmodernism: An Evangelical Engagement*, 2nd ed. (Grand Rapids: Baker Academic, 2001); John M. Ellis, *Against Deconstruction* (Princeton, NJ: Princeton University Press, 1989); Stanley J. Grenz, *A Primer on Postmodernism* (Grand Rapids: Eerdmans, 1996); David Bentley Hart, *The Beauty of the Infinite: The Aesthetics of Christian Truth* (Grand Rapids: Eerdmans, 2003); Hauerwas, *A Better Hope*; Charles Jencks,

justly characterize radical postmodernism in terms of certain basic contours or features that delineate some of the most significant layers of postmodernism's historical and hermeneutical identity. Hart notes, first of all, how postmodernism, like authentic Christian theology, seeks to expose the pretensions of the modern doctrine of autonomous and objective human rationality:

> If one conveniently over-simple definition (or aspect) of the postmodern is the triumph of (in classical terms) rhetoric over dialectic, or at least the recognition that the dialectical is always essentially rhetorical, theology should welcome this as a word of comfort. The great project of "modernity" (the search for comprehensive meta-narratives and epistemological foundations by way of a neutral and unaided rationality, available to all reflective intellects and independent of cultural and linguistic conditions) has surely foundered; "reason" cannot inhabit language (and it certainly has no other home) without falling subject to an indefinite deferral of meaning, a dissemination of signification, a play of nonsense and absence, such that it subsists always in its own *aporias*, suppression of sense, contradictions, and slippages; and "reason" cannot embody itself in history without at once becoming irrevocably lost in the labyrinth of time's interminable contingencies (certainly philosophy has no means of defeating such doubts).[5]

Hart further expounds on this distinction between postmodern rhetoric and Enlightenment dialectic—in the sense of unaided metaphysical reason—in the following terms:

> "Postmodern," to begin with, is a term that will serve rather loosely to indicate a variety of styles, perspectives, prejudices, and premises for which no single word is truly adequate. "Postmodernity," for the purposes of this text, marks out a certain territory in current intellectual culture, a general convergence of various ideologies and methods, each of whose proponents might justifiably object to so tidy and comprehensive an abstraction, because all other terms that could be used—"poststructuralism," "late modernity," "deconstruction," etc.—suffer from too confined a range of associations. In the exceedingly elementary, and perhaps misleading, sense given the word above—the ascendancy of rhetoric over dialect—the postmodern indicates an auroral astonishment following upon a nocturnal oblivion: the West at long last awakes from the

---

What Is Post-Modernism? 3rd ed. (New York: St. Martin's Press, 1989); Peter Augustine Lawler, *Postmodernism Rightly Understood: The Return to Realism in American Thought* (Lanham, MD: Rowman & Littlefield, 1999); MacIntyre, *Three Rival Versions of Moral Enquiry*; idem, *Whose Justice? Which Rationality?;* John McGowan, *Postmodernism and Its Critics* (Ithaca, NY: Cornell University Press, 1991); Harold Netland, *Encountering Religious Pluralism: The Challenge to Christian Faith and Mission* (Downers Grove, IL: InterVarsity, 2001); Christopher Norris, *Deconstruction: Theory and Practice* (London and New York: Methuen, 1982); Plantinga, *Warranted Christian Belief*; and James K. A. Smith, *Who's Afraid of Postmodernism? Taking Derrida, Lyotard, and Foucault to Church* (Grand Rapids: Baker Academic, 2006).

5. Hart, *Beauty of the Infinite*, 3.

nightmare of philosophy, even the last ghosts of Enlightenment reason having been chased away, to discover and rejoice in the irreducibly aesthetic character and ultimate foundationlessness of "truth." In a world of ungovernable plurality, composed of an endless multiplicity of narratives, there can be no grand meta-narrative that extracts itself from, and then comes to comprise, all the finite and culturally determined narratives that throng the horizons of meaning; no discourse can triumph over the particularities of all the stories that pass one another by in the general congress of cultures; there is no overarching dialectic by which a single and rationally ascertainable truth might be set above all merely contingent truths.[6]

Postmodernism, according to Hart, declares that rhetoric—discourse that celebrates particularity, subjectivity, and dissonance—trumps philosophical dialectic—discourse that aspires to universality, objectivity, and unity. As Hart explains, however varied and variegated its genealogy and permutations, radical postmodernism is a historical phenomenon the complex identity of which, though admittedly elusive, emerges through the recurring self-presentation of its most notable expositors.

Following Hart, I will argue that despite their differences, mainstream radical postmodernists promote a more or less stable self-image: they envision themselves as revolutionary strategists, if not frontline guerilla fighters, in an intellectual and political struggle against the false authorities and institutions of traditional Western culture. As a historical movement, postmodernism is predicated on a neo-Nietzschean conviction that the defining normative principles and institutions of modern Western culture and philosophy have lost their efficacy and legitimacy for the present-day world. Mainstream postmodernists seem especially to agree that among those aspects of modernity best consigned to the trash bin should be the traditional Judeo-Christian belief in God. Postmodernists thus tend to regard the declaration of Nietzsche's Zarathustra, "God is dead," as an incontestable starting point for mature, politically liberated, critical inquiry.[7]

Though there certainly are fundamental differences and disagreements on any number of significant points of doctrine among such contemporary postmodernists as Derrida, Deleuze, Foucault, Rorty, de Man, and Lyotard, one can discern in their writings four recurring—one might even say "identity conferring"—motifs or fundamental elements. While each of these features or motifs will, of course, permit a variety of intonations and nuances, they all

6. Ibid., 5.

7. A curious irony of mainstream postmodernism emerges here: postmodernism's sweeping declarations concerning the death of God are hard to reconcile with postmodernism's avowed antipathy toward totalizing metanarratives. In so confidently proclaiming that "God is dead," one suspects that postmodernists are not so much describing how things really stand in the general opinion, but how things look and feel to an elite subclass of Western intellectuals who feel free, and indeed duty-bound, to speak for the rest of us.

figure into the basic project of postmodernism as both an intellectual, critical program for debunking false metaphysical idols and a political platform for the liberation of the self-defining individual or community from the oppressive confines of metaphysical authorities. In examining these four key principles or fundamental tenets of postmodernism, I will characterize these postmodern teachings as embodying a form of a "hermeneutics of unmasking." In so doing, I will emphasize both the critical temperament of postmodernism—thus the term "unmasking"—and an elevation of hermeneutical concerns and linguistic context to a central role in critical thought. The postmodern emphasis on the place of words, signs, and interpretative constructs in all human cognition situates our being in the world within some humanly constructed horizon of meaning; all human experience is thus contextualized by the signs and symbols of human discourse. Radical postmodernism is a neo-Kantian and neo-Nietzschean discipline of "hermeneutics," which places special emphasis on the nature and role of interpretive linguistic process, form, and context in all of human experience.

Radical Postmodernism's Fourfold Hermeneutics of Unmasking

Political Hermeneutics of Unmasking

First of all, postmodernism espouses a "political" hermeneutics of unmasking toward Western metaphysics; that is, postmodernism rejects on ethical and political grounds the various metanarratives of Western metaphysics as subversive and oppressive. The key problem, according to the postmodernist, is that totalizing metaphysical metanarratives serve as legitimating myths that suppress opposing voices in the name of metaphysical authorities such as God, essential human nature, or the future state. Consider, for example, how Terry Eagleton characterizes postmodernism in terms of its aversion to the tyrannical and oppressive "fetishism" of modernity's belief in metaphysical absolutes:

> Post-modernism signals the death of such "meta-narratives" whose secretly terroristic function is to ground and legitimate the illusion of a "universal" human history. We are now in the process of awakening from the nightmare of modernity, with its manipulative reason and fetish of the totality, into the laid-back pluralism of the post-modern, that heterogeneous range of life-styles and language games which has renounced the nostalgic urge to totalize and legitimate itself. . . . Science and philosophy must jettison their grandiose metaphysical claims and view themselves more modestly as just another set of narratives.[8]

8. Terry Eagleton, "Awakening from Modernity," *Times Literary Supplement* 20 (February 1987): 194 (quoted in Grenz, *A Primer on Postmodernism*, 48).

Eagleton's impassioned description of the postmodern temperament emphasizes the political dimension crucial to most, if not all, postmodern thought. Driving the postmodernist aversion toward totalizing metanarratives is the ethical and political determination to liberate humanity from the supposedly despotic, exploitative consciousness inherent in the various Western traditions, especially as these espouse in some form or other a sovereign metaphysical authority—such as God, the future state, objective science, universal rational progress, and so forth. This postmodern suspicion toward metaphysics often takes the form of a protest against traditional metaphysical claims—that certain beings in the world have essential natures, that humans, in particular, have a universal, stable nature and individual self-identity. Such metaphysical, essentialist doctrines only sublimate and mask difference, plurality, and diversity, and in so doing lead invariably, in principle and in practice, to oppression and exclusion. The mainstream postmodern rejection of Western metaphysics thus is motivated in part by a political determination to be inclusive rather than exclusive, a determination to preserve difference from the "fetish of the totality." Eagleton's moral earnestness in his exposition of postmodernism's aversion to metaphysical terror is especially revealing: whether Eagleton himself acknowledges it, his characterization of the spirit of postmodern thinking reveals postmodernism's characteristically dualistic outlook. In spite of all its supposed plurality, ambiguity, and dissonance, the world inhabited by the postmodernist divides sharply into two opposing valences. First, there are the institutions, practices, theories, and beliefs of the benighted Western world with its specifically modern metaphysical order. These phenomena must not be left intact, but should be severely criticized, for they are repressive, subversive, exploitative, ethnocentric, logocentric, or in some other way politically and socially defective. Second, in carrying out the task of critical unmasking, the postmodernist aspires to more than merely opposing such illusions and degradations of human culture. The aim of the postmodernist is not merely to debunk, but also to provide an antidote to the diseases of traditional metaphysical illusions; in rejecting metaphysical claims to objective truth, the postmodernist seeks to enlighten humanity and liberate it from its bondage to oppressive modes of consciousness.

Antilogocentric Hermeneutics of Unmasking

Postmodernism also exhibits an "antilogocentric" hermeneutics of unmasking—that is, postmodernism rejects a particularly important underlying epistemological and metaphysical presupposition of traditional Western metaphysics: namely, the presupposition, going back at least to Parmenides, that "the real is the rational" and that the fundamental aim of human thought is to bring us into contact with the underlying rational unity and order of the cosmos. Indeed, while a number of traditional metaphysical thinkers such as Plato, Aristotle, and Aquinas seem to acknowledge the inability of mere human cognition to grasp the full character of the *Logos* that orders and sustains all beings, their traditional metaphysical systems nevertheless uphold the ultimate coherence of what is real; they affirm the ideals of unity and coherence as regulative principles for human thinking about what is real. For the traditional metaphysician, reality may be *mysterious*, but it is not ultimately *irrational* or *absurd*. Similarly, while human thought may inevitably fall far short of comprehending the real, this metaphysical outlook requires that such thought aspire to unity and coherence. In other words, a fundamental affinity holds between the conditions of human rationality and the nature of reality. Thus it is the basic character of human rationality to aspire to bring us into contact with the fundamental unity of the all that is. Any worldview, then, that provides us with no more than disordered and inconsistent utterances, leaving us mired in dissonance and multiplicity, would be rationally defective. Even if dissonance and disorder are inherent in the universe, it is the task of rational thought to give us a coherent and unified account of the nature of this dissonance and its ramifications for human life.

The postmodernist condemns such "philosophical faith" in the unity and coherence of the real; likewise, it disavows the fundamental affinity between the rational intellect and the totality of being—the affinity between the representational, analytical, conceptualizing mind on the one hand, and the world order, the horizon of human experience, or the fullness of all that is, on the other. For Derrida, this break with the metaphysics of rational unity takes the form of an insistence on the role of the inchoate, the unrepresentable, the self-negating *différance* or "trace" in all human thought and experience; incoherence and disorder are fundamental features of all human utterance and experience of the real. There is no realm of metaphysical presence, no world "out there" free from the inherent dissonances and contradictions of human discourse. For Lyotard, similarly, the "unpresentable" or "postmodern sublime" demarcates the limits of representational truth and rational unity, unmasks the illusion of the ultimate rational coherence of what is, frees us from the dogma of the coherent unity of being and thought, and liberates us from the metaphysical responsibility to grasp reality in its ultimate unity and intelligibility.

Contextualist Hermeneutics of Unmasking

Postmodernism displays as well a "contextualist" hermeneutics of unmasking—a rejection, that is, of any and all philosophical and religious worldviews that presume that human reason can attain a purely objective point of view, free from the influences of historical and cultural context. There is, in other words, no unfiltered, direct, translinguistic access to reality. Postmodernists thus reject all worldviews, such as that of the Enlightenment, that presume some "direct" access to "the real" beyond and outside the artifices of human language and interpretation. Postmodernism insists, in other words, that all presentation is representation, that no encounter with the self or the other is ever unmediated or free from contextualization. All human thought and experience is imbued with signs, metaphors, and other signifiers. No simple and direct act of listening to or encountering the world around us is possible; even such apparently mundane and other-directed acts as perceiving, listening, and reading are forms of self-assertion and linguistic imposition. All acts of rational cognition are thus expressions of power.

Perspectival Hermeneutics of Unmasking

Finally, postmodernism espouses a "perspectival" hermeneutics of unmasking toward truth—a rejection not only of the possibility of an unmediated or hyperlinguistic access to "reality in itself" but also of the very notion of a "real world" outside human language and humanly constructed, interpretive frameworks. In the famous—or infamous—words of Derrida, "*Il n'y a pas de hors-texte*" ("There is nothing outside the text"). As Richard Rorty remarks in his characteristically—perhaps also deceptively—lucid manner:

"There is no truth." What could that mean? Why should anybody say it?

Actually, almost nobody (except Wallace Stevens) does say it. But philosophers like me are often said to say it. One can see why. For we have learned (from Nietzsche and James, among others) to be suspicious of the appearance-reality distinction. We think that there are many ways to talk about what is going on, and that none of them gets closer to the way things are in themselves than any other. We have no idea what "in itself" is supposed to mean in the phrase "reality as it is in itself." So we suggest that the appearance-reality distinction be dropped in favor of a distinction between less useful and more useful ways of talking. But since most people think that truth is correspondence to the way reality "really is," they think of us as denying the existence of truth.

Our critics—the philosophers who agree that that is indeed what truth is—do not think that the useful-useless distinction can take the place of the old appearance-reality distinction. They believe that less useful ways of talking are descriptions of what only appears to be going on, whereas more useful ones are descriptions of what is really going on. For example: primitive scientists, or conformist members of a slaveholding society, describe what misleadingly appears to be going on. Our critics need the reality-appearance distinction to prevent the notion of "corresponding to reality" from being trivialized. For every belief, no matter how primitive or vicious, corresponds to some "world"—the "world" that contains the objects mentioned by the belief (Ptolemy's crystalline spheres or the subhuman nature of the slaves). So those who want to hang on to the notion of "correspondence" have to take the idea of how things *really* are seriously. . . .

I argue that philosophy will get along better without the notions of "the intrinsic nature of reality" and "correspondence to reality" than with them. For those who find these notions indispensable, but only for them, this will look like an argument that there is no truth. . . .

If pragmatists cannot offer a theory of truth, what can they do? They can point out . . . that truth is not a goal of inquiry. If "truth" is the name of such a goal then, indeed, there is no truth. For the absoluteness of truth makes it unserviceable as such a goal. A goal is something you can know that you are getting closer to, or farther away from. But there is no way to know our distance from truth, nor even whether we are closer to it than our ancestors were. For, once again, the only criterion we have for applying the word "true" is justification, and justification is always relative to an audience. So it is also relative to that audience's lights—the purposes that such an audience wants served and the situation in which it finds itself. This means that the question "Do our practices of justification lead to truth?" is as unanswerable as it is unpragmatic. It is unanswerable because there is no way to privilege our current purposes and interests. It is unpragmatic because the answer to it would make no difference whatever to our practice.[9]

Clearly in this passage Rorty is not merely asserting that human thought is fallible and incapable of achieving any incorrigible, direct apprehension of the world as it really is. And he is not simply asserting that we cannot know for sure the way the world really is; he is not simply declaring that we cannot attain a "God's eye point of view." Rather, Rorty is purporting to find the very notion of "how the world really is apart from our descriptions and interpretations of it" to be unintelligible and unfruitful. The notion of "reality in itself" is unintelligible because we cannot even think of reality except in some context of descriptive interpretation: our apprehensions of and reflections on "what is real" are always embedded within a pragmatic and linguistic matrix of human signs, symbols, and interests. Furthermore, since we have no access to this so-called reality in itself, we have no intelligible way of determining how or when our linguistically situated beliefs and practices might bring us closer to this realm of "how things really are." Traditional metaphysics thus fails on two fundamental counts: it both lacks an intelligible *telos* and cannot in principle provide any nonarbitrary method or criterion for determining when progress toward this unthinkable *telos* has occurred.

Consider, then, how Rorty defends himself in this passage against critics who charge him with rejecting the very existence of "truth." How, Rorty asks, can he be guilty of rejecting the existence of what is in fact an absurd and unthinkable chimera? As Rorty sees it, the traditional correspondence theory of truth depends on a distinction between appearance and reality that is muddled, unintelligible, and epistemically sterile. What truth means to us is not

9. Richard Rorty, *Truth and Progress*, vol. 3 of *Philosophical Papers* (Cambridge: Cambridge University Press, 1998), 1–4.

correspondence with "the real world out there," but agreement regarding what is useful within a human community pursuing its own interests and purposes. Truth is merely instrumental; to be true is to be useful for some communally agreed on linguistic practice within the perspective of some particular, historically situated community. Truth, then, is not some lofty, metaphysical ideal as much as it is a tool serving our own interests and ambitions. We might well say that the Rortyean postmodernist is the quintessentially American intellectual pragmatist whose role model for the philosophical life is not the Platonic erotic seeker but the eminently practical automobile manufacturer Henry Ford, who declared that "history is bunk." "Philosophy pragmatized" exchanges the Platonic account of the human—one who seeks communion with an order of beauty outside of oneself—with a Protagorean account of the human—one who seeks to satisfy one's interests by measuring the world according to one's own conventions. Thus Rorty embraces a postmodern marriage of Deweyian pragmatism and Nietzschean atheism: traditional metaphysical and religious perspectives have laden us with false and restrictive notions of authority and human flourishing. As a gesture of solidarity with the modern, Protagorean community of democratic liberalism, the Rortyean postmodern philosopher, qua critic, seeks to unmask the oppressive character of metaphysical authorities and declare that a new era of human creativity and liberation has dawned. Having rid ourselves of the bonds of metaphysical higher authority, we are now free to pursue our own projects of self-creation while at the same time promoting and enforcing our own political interests. Let those interests be decent, bourgeois, and sensitive, to be sure.

A distinctive virtue of Rortyean postmodernism—as opposed, say, to Derridean or Foucaultean—is the admirable clarity of both its antimetaphysical vision and its internal logic and justification. Rorty debunks traditional philosophy and religion for their unintelligibility and utter emptiness and impracticality. Yet while Rorty is a perceptive critic, he is profoundly mistaken on both counts. Ironically and incoherently, postmodernism is still committed to the basic metaphysical vision of autonomy bequeathed to us by modernity. Insofar as radical postmodernism endorses rather than challenges this modern doctrine of autonomy, we might be tempted to rename so-called radical postmodernism "*petit bourgeois* hypermodernism." Ultimately, postmodernism fails to grasp the inseparability of two forms of humility: acknowledgment of our limits as epistemological interpreters and our dependence as metaphysical seekers.

In contrast to these "really not-so-radical" postmodernists, I will defend what might be called "modest and yet genuinely radical postmodernism." My argument for this variety of modest postmodernism has its roots in the three historical figures I have presented thus far: Augustine, Pascal, and Hume. And it is especially indebted to two contemporary thinkers, Alasdair MacIntyre and Stanley Hauerwas. Ironically, insofar as it affirms both our epistemic limits and our metaphysical dependence, modest postmodernism turns out to be much more radical and much more "postmodern" than the really-not-so-radical hypermodern and academically fashionable models of postmodernism most visible in the academy today.

Following MacIntyre and Hauerwas, to understand the discourse of post-modernism, it is necessary to comprehend the complex phenomenon of post-modernism, no matter what its specific contours, in its historical context.[10] As we have noted, whereas the postmodern program certainly defies any simple formulaic definition, it is a characteristic feature of postmodern writers such as Derrida, Foucault, Lyotard, and Rorty that they exhibit a thoroughgoing antipathy toward modernity's primary articles of faith: postmodernists call into question modernity's belief in objective knowledge, in the unity of self and world, in the authority of objective reason, and in the very intelligibility of the notion of "a world out there" that is independent of human interpretative constructions. Summarizing the postmodernism of Derrida, Foucault, and Rorty in particular, Grenz provides a helpful overview of postmodernism's antipathy to such "idols" of modernity:

Postmodern philosophers applied the theories of the literary deconstructionists to the world as a whole. Just as a text will be read differently by each reader, they said, so reality will be "read" differently by each knowing self that encounters it. This means that there is no one meaning of the world, no transcendent center to reality as a whole.

On the basis of ideas such as these, the French philosopher Jacques Derrida calls for an abandonment of both "onto-theology" (the attempt to set forth ontological descriptions of reality) and the "metaphysics of presence" (the idea that something transcendent is present in reality). Because nothing transcendent inheres in reality, he argues, all that emerges in the knowing process is the perspective of the self who interprets reality.

Michael Foucault adds a moral twist to Derrida's call. Foucault asserts that every interpretation of reality is an assertion of power. Because "knowledge" is always the result of the use of power, to name something is to exercise power and hence to do violence to what is named. Social institutions inevitably engage in violence when they impose their own understanding on the centerless flux of experience, he says. Thus in contrast to Bacon, who sought knowledge in order to gain power over nature, Foucault claims that every assertion of knowledge is an act of power.

Richard Rorty, in turn, jettisons the classic conception of truth as either the mind or language mirroring nature. Truth is established neither by the correspondence of an assertion with objective reality nor by the internal coherence of the assertions themselves, says Rorty. He argues that we should simply give up the search for truth and be content with interpretation. He proposes

---

10. See esp. MacIntyre, *Whose Justice? Which Rationality?* idem, *Three Rival Versions of Moral Enquiry*; Hauerwas, *A Community of Character*; and idem, *After Christendom?*

replacing classic "systematic philosophy" with "edifying philosophy," which "aims at continuing a conversation rather than at discovering truth."

The work of Derrida, Foucault, and Rorty reflects what seems to have become the central dictum of postmodern philosophy: "All is difference." This view sweeps away the "uni" of the "universe" sought by the Enlightenment project. It abandons the quest for a unified grasp of objective reality. It asserts that the world has no center, only differing viewpoints and perspectives. In fact, even the concept of "world" presupposes an objective unity or a coherent whole that does not exist "out there." In the end, the postmodern world is merely an arena of "dueling texts."[11]

As Grenz observes, postmodernists are particularly skeptical of modernity's faith in the rationally autonomous self, of both the philosophical ideal of individual autonomy and of the doctrine of critical reason as functioning independently of historical, cultural, and linguistic influences. But if by "postmodernism" we mean to include all those varieties of contemporary critical thought that reject the modern doctrine of autonomous reason, then we need to distinguish, within postmodernism itself, two fundamentally dissimilar perspectives. For those postmodernists who tend to label themselves as such, the end of modernity entails the end of all traditional forms of philosophy and religion, precisely because such outlooks share the common belief that the goal of life is a matter of finding our proper place in an objective, metaphysical order. For such radical postmodernists, a crucial lesson of the collapse of the modern conception of rational authority is to come to see the untenability of believing in objective realities at all, whether this reality be that of a transcendent God or of any ordinary, everyday physical being. Such radical postmodernists also reject the very notion that it makes sense to believe in an objective human nature that could serve as the ground for ethical and political aspirations.

A more modest postmodern skepticism, if one might call it that, differs from radical postmodernism in a crucially significant way: the modest postmodernist does not find the beliefs in a transcendent or immanent objective reality problematic in themselves, but sees as problematic modernity's optimism that we can justify our beliefs about reality on the basis of purely rational, objective foundations. My intention in this chapter might then be stated as an attempt to defend a Pascalian and Augustinian version of modest postmodernism. The kind of postmodernism I will be attacking succumbs, as did Descartes and his modernist heirs, to the "lure of autonomy." A critical error of radical postmodernism lies in how it is not sufficiently "postmodern." More specifically, mainstream radical postmodernism fails to be genuinely radical, for it fails to overcome the most dubious article of faith in the whole dogma of modernity, the faith in human autonomy.

11. Grenz, *A Primer on Postmodernism*, 6–7.

Postmodernism as "Hypermodernism"

While I think postmodernism has serious defects, I do not mean to give the impression that postmodernism did not make important contributions to the intellectual debates in the last half of the twentieth century. It is clear, in my mind, that a defense of a Pascalian and Augustinian rationality ought to acknowledge that, with respect at least to some of its critique of modernity, postmodernism may turn out to be more amenable to Christian theism than many of the more influential modern Western metaphysical systems have been. In particular, the postmodernists' suspicion toward modern Western metaphysicians who uphold the sufficiency of human reason to comprehend the very depths of human existence would be welcomed rather than shunned by the Augustinian or Pascalian. For example, the "contextualist" hermeneutics of unmasking traditional metaphysics seems in particular to provide a healthy reminder of a basic defect in many—*but certainly not all*—metaphysical voices in Western thought. This reminder serves to highlight the hubris inherent in those metaphysical thinkers whose overestimation of the power of human reason exhibits, on an intellectual level, the unfortunate human tendency to rely solely on the resources of our fallen human nature. Two ideas pose no threat at all to the Pascalian or Augustinian: that every encounter of self with other and of self with the natural world is mediated through humanly generated concepts and language, and that all arguments and judgments of human reasoners are fallible, historically situated, and bound up with disordered affections. On the contrary, one might well see in Derrida's insistence on "*la différance*" or Lyotard's proclamation of the "postmodern sublime" an awareness of disorder in human thought and in the world that is absolutely essential to the Augustinian and Pascalian conception of the fallen created order.

In some respects, ironically, Derrida's purportedly radical proclamation of the ever-lingering penumbra of irrationality and incoherence in human language, of "*la différance*" lingering in every proposition, would strike the Augustinian or Pascalian as "radical" not in the contemporary, consumer sense of being brand-new, innovative, and shocking, but in the more original Latin sense of *radix*, of being firmly rooted and grounded in what is genuine and lasting. In urging us to recognize the imperfections and incoherences of human existence, postmodernism may serve to promote a "radical" recovery of a Judeo-Christian humility, reminding us that we are flawed creatures, merely distorted and distorting icons of divinity. In this respect, Derrida's insistence on the presence of shadows and dark recesses inhering in all human claims to the light of reason might well assist us in the radical endeavor to recover our Socratic and Pauline roots and deepen our understanding of human limitation.

The postmodernists' awareness of disorder in every human order, of a trace of the flawed in every seemingly ideal human work of art, of the elusive and unrepresented defect in every linguistic and performative act, reiterates the kind of

Christian understanding of truth passionately articulated by Augustine and Pascal. For Augustine and Pascal, all human truth is approximate, a flawed participation in the only Truth in which there is infinite depth and difference without disunity or self-violence. To some extent, in other words, the postmodern agenda serves to unmask the pretensions of modern Western metaphysicians; these thinkers exalt human reason far beyond its proper limitations—to the extent of upholding the power of that reason to transcend the limitations of human language and obtain direct and infallible supralinguistic access to reality. Against such intellectual pretensions, postmodernism offers a healthy antidote to modernity's idols of progress through technological reason, mastery through a supposedly disinterested reason, and the capacity of human reason to comprehend reality to its very depths. The Christian theist should thus treat charitably the self-congratulatory, self-adulatory rhetoric that seems to characterize so much of postmodernist discourse: postmodernists seem never to tire of portraying their program as a born-again phoenix of enlightened and liberated human consciousness arising out of the ashes of modernity's metaphysical tower of Babel.

Postmodernism's Liaison with Metaphysics

> I sit in one of the dives
> On Fifty-second Street
> Uncertain and afraid
> As the clever hopes expire
> Of a low dishonest decade:
> Waves of anger and fear
> Circulate over the bright
> And darkened lands of the earth,
> Obsessing our private lives;
> The unmentionable odor of death
> Offends the September night.
>
> Accurate scholarship can
> Unearth the whole offense
> From Luther until now
> That has driven a culture mad,
> Find what occurred at Linz,
> What huge imago made
> A psychopathic god:
> I and the public know
> What all schoolchildren learn,
> Those to whom evil is done
> Do evil in return.[12]

12. W. H. Auden, "September 1, 1939," stanzas 1 and 2, in *Anthology of Twentieth-Century British and Irish Poetry*, ed. Keith Tuma (New York: Oxford University Press, 2001), 316.

In what follows, I will argue that postmodernism subverts itself by surreptitiously promoting the very metaphysical and totalizing character it condemns in the philosophical traditions of supposedly oppressive Western culture. In seeking to articulate its fourfold hermeneutical suspicion, postmodernism ironically fails to sustain its own fundamental aversion to metaphysical realism: the postmodernist can unmask his or her opponents, the traditional metaphysical pretenders of systematic and comprehensive rational adequacy, only by both affirming and denying postmodernism's own identity as metaphysical pretender. Postmodernism thus ends up being one of the "coercive metanarratives" that it opposes in its program of liberation from metaphysics. As Hart explains:

> Where the discourse of fashionable postmodernism should become distasteful to theological reflection, in fact, is not in its alleged "relativism" or "skepticism," but in its failure sufficiently to free itself from the myths of modernity. Jean-Francois Lyotard has described the postmodern condition succinctly as "incredulity towards meta-narratives": an attitude commendable in itself, no doubt, but also one that can easily be translated into a dogmatic meta-narrative of its own. In the terms presumed by this salutary dubiety, all the magisterial projects of modernity—political, philosophical, scientific, economic, social— are recognizably *modern* insofar as they attempt to ground their discourse in some stable, transhistorical process, method, set of principles, or canon of rationality; the "totalizing" tendency of modernity is as much in evidence in Descartes as in Kant, as much in Rousseau as in Marx, etc. (supremely of course, in Hegel). The "modern" indicates not a single comprehensive narrative, but a single meta-narrative ambition: a desire to transcend the conditioned finitude and contingency of stories by discovering the meaning, limits, and motives of *all* stories, by way of a representation of the absolute, the universal, or the rational. The "postmodern" condition, however, is an awareness that all meta-narrative structures stand upon a shifting surface of dead and living metaphors, while all "truths" are endlessly fluid. So Nietzsche: "What, then, is truth? A mobile army of metaphors, metonyms and anthropomorphisms—in short, a sum of human relations, which have been enhanced, transposed, and embellished poetically and rhetorically, and which after long use seem firm, canonical, and obligatory to a people: truths are illusions about which one had forgotten that this is what they are; metaphors which are worn out and without sensuous power; coins which have lost their pictures and now matter only as metal, no longer as coins." Not that this is an extraordinary observation; one might learn as much from thinkers as diverse as Herder, Vico, various American pragmatists, even Anatole France; from no one more memorably than Wittgenstein. Indeed, nothing would be more misleading than a catastrophist model of the "postmodern," which depicts it as simply a spontaneous reaction to modernity; it is, rather, the culmination of the critical tradition of modernity, and has evolved quite naturally from the same (meta-narrative) ambition that led Kant to rewrite the project of philosophy as epistemology and ethics, consequent upon the collapse of metaphysics. And predictably (given its pedigrees), this rigorous

soupçon or critical incredulity becomes yet another attempt to extract thought from the quagmires of narrative; it becomes a meta-meta-narrative, the story of no more stories, so told as to determine definitely how much may or may not be said intelligibly by others who have stories to tell; it completes not only the critical but the meta-narrative projects of modernity (which prove to be indistinguishable). This is where the temper of the postmodern proves wanting in courage and consistency. The truth of no truths becomes, inevitably, truth: a way of naming being, language, and culture that guards the boundaries of thought against claims it has not validated.[13]

Following Hart, I will argue that postmodernism succumbs to self-negation by espousing its own metanarrative, or, if you will, its own metaphysics of identity.

One pervasive feature of postmodern writing is its suspicion of universality and its affirmation of particularity: in rejecting the modern philosophical doctrine of universal reason, postmodernists cultivate a suspicion about any metaphysics of self that would posit a universal human nature or final *telos*. To be postmodern in this sense is to reject not only modern, epistemological foundationalism—that there are luminously self-evident, "pure" foundations for human knowledge—but also with it any "foundationalist" story that grounds the meaning of human life in some ultimate objective reality.

Lyotard, in his articulate and in certain respects even humble work, *The Postmodern Condition*, articulates what it means to be postmodern by contrasting that outlook with modernity's misguided fondness for foundational metanarratives. Characterizing what it means to be postmodern specifically in terms of postmodernism's aversion to metanarratives, Lyotard writes:

Science has always been in conflict with narratives. Judged by the yardstick of science, the majority of them prove to be fables. But to the extent that science does not restrict itself to stating useful regularities and seeks the truth, it is obliged to legitimate the rules of its own game. It then produces a discourse of legitimation with respect to its own status, a discourse called philosophy. I will use the term *modern* to designate any science that legitimates itself with reference to a metadiscourse of this kind making an explicit appeal to some grand narrative, such as the dialectics of Spirit, the hermeneutics of meaning, the emancipation of the rational or working subject, or the creation of wealth. For example, the rule of consensus between the sender and the addressee of a statement with truth-value is deemed acceptable if it is cast in terms of a possible unanimity between rational minds: this is the Enlightenment narrative, in which the hero of knowledge works toward a good ethico-political end—universal peace. As can be seen from this example, if a meta-narrative implying a philosophy of history is used to legitimate knowledge, questions are raised concerning the validity of the institutions governing the social

13. Hart, *Beauty of the Infinite*, 6–7.

bond: these must be legitimated as well. Thus justice is consigned to the grand narrative in the same way as truth.

Simplifying to the extreme, I define *postmodern* as incredulity toward meta-narratives. This incredulity is undoubtedly a product of progress in the sciences: but that progress in turn presupposes it. To the obsolescence of the meta-narrative apparatus of legitimation corresponds, most notably, the crisis of metaphysical philosophy and of the university institution which in the past relied on it. The narrative function is losing its functors, its great hero, its great dangers, its great voyages, its great goal. It is being dispersed in clouds of narrative language elements—narrative, but also denotative, prescriptive, descriptive, and so on. Conveyed within each cloud are pragmatic valencies specific to its kind. Each of us lives at the intersection of many of these. However, we do not necessarily establish stable language combinations, and the properties of the ones we do establish are not necessarily communicable.

Thus the society of the future falls less within the province of a Newtonian anthropology (such as structuralism or systems theory) than a pragmatics of language particles. There are many different language games—a heterogeneity of elements. They only give rise to institutions in patches—local determinism.[14]

Lyotard proclaims that a new day has dawned for those who have witnessed the horrors of the wars of modernity. As one of the vanguard, Lyotard calls on intellectuals who are reasonable, sensitive, and politically concerned to see through the Western illusions of metaphysical authority so that they can effectively address social problems and read canonical texts in an authentically postmodern way, in a way that embraces difference, plurality, and newness rather than in a way that yearns for finality. We are no longer to be duped by the stifling completeness and exclusiveness of grand, totalizing metanarratives. With the unmasking of the classical metaphysical vision of "the True, the Beautiful, and the Good," Lyotard leads us to the inevitable conclusion that the traditional creeds of the church, and indeed the traditional Western belief in objective realities and objective authorities, have been thoroughly discredited. Whatever commitments we are able to find credible in our postmodern world cannot be of the sort that claim to have metaphysical authority transcending human conventions; thus we can no longer put our faith in authorities such as "God" or "reason" or even a "canonical text," which have been so influential for the Western traditions of church and metaphysics. As Nietzsche summoned his readers to acknowledge, long before postmodernism would become fashionable, life-affirming individuals must forge ahead and create their own authorities, their own forms of meaning, now that God, as both religious authority ("thou shalt") and grammatical article of faith ("God exists"), is dead.

14. Jean-François Lyotard, *The Postmodern Condition: A Report on Knowledge*, trans. Geoff Bennington and Brian Massumi (Minneapolis: University of Minnesota Press, 1989), xxiii–xxiv.

To solve the problems of the postmodern world, the Lyotardian postmod-ernist follows the way of Nietzsche, contending that we must not look to metaphysical authorities of our past. In thinking of the nature of authority, we must embark on a "revaluation of values" with a postmodern sincerity that looks with honesty and suspicion on the idols of the past. For the radical postmodernist, the question of whether it is wise to believe in such realities as God, freedom, and the immortality of the soul is no longer even a live op-tion. To be postmodern requires that we accept the finitude and uncertainty of all human believing and that we reject as unwise the quest to establish reason as an autonomous authority. But it also insists that we reject as inco-herent and naive the very notion of a transcendent God, or of any objective order of reality existing outside of and beyond our human interpretations. Unlike "modest postmodernists" or "antimodernists," such as Hauerwas or MacIntyre, the radical, secular postmodernist contends that the name of the game is not the discovery of what is but the creation of a diversity of images of self-expression and the promotion of a diverse community of self-creators. Whereas MacIntyre and Hauerwas pursue in a narrative and historical context a rationally sustainable but inevitably situated and uncertain perspective on our true self, the Lyotardian postmodernist invites us to reconcile ourselves to living within the worlds of our own creation, and indeed to affirm our potential to exercise our freedom as "self-creators." Thus to conclude his postmodern manifesto by returning to the central question, "What is postmodernism?" Lyotard writes:

> The postmodern would be that which, in the modern, puts forward the unpre-sentable in presentation itself; that which denies itself the solace of good forms, the consensus of a taste which would make it possible to share collectively the nostalgia for the unattainable; that which searches for new presentations, not in order to enjoy them but in order to impart a stronger sense of the unpresent-able. A postmodern artist or writer is in the position of a philosopher: the text he writes, the work he produces are not in principle governed by preestablished rules, and they cannot be judged according to a determining judgment, by ap-plying familiar categories to the text or to the work. Those rules and categories are what the work of art itself is looking for. The artist and the writer, then, are working without rules in order to formulate the rules of what *will have been done*. Hence the fact that work and text have the characters of an *event*; hence also, they always come too late for their author, or, what amounts to the same thing, their being put into work, their realization (*mise en oeuvre*) always begin too soon. *Post modern* would have to be understood according to the paradox of the future (*post*) anterior (*modo*).
>
> Finally, it must be clear that it is our business not to supply reality but to invent allusions to the conceivable which cannot be presented. And it is not to be expected that this task will affect the last reconciliation between language games (which, under the name of faculties, Kant knew to be separated by a chasm), and that only the transcendental illusion (that of Hegel) can hope to

totalize them into a real unity. But Kant also knew that the price to pay for such an illusion is terror. The nineteenth and twentieth centuries have given us as much terror as we can take. We have paid a high enough price for the nostalgia of the whole and the one, for the reconciliation of the concept and the sensible, of the transparent and the communicable experience. Under the general demand for slackening and for appeasement, we can hear the mutterings of a desire for the return of terror, for the realization of the fantasy to seize reality. The answer is: Let us wage a war on totality; let us be witnesses to the unpresentable; let us activate the differences and save the honor of the name.[15]

Two features of Lyotard's postmodern vision are especially noteworthy in this passage: first, unmasking metaphysics means to oppose the metaphysical yearning to apprehend the objective fabric of the real world, "to supply reality" in our theories, and to unify our beliefs and practices into a final, totalizing system; and second, celebrating the distinctively postmodern frees us from worrying about "metaphysical truth." Having achieved our liberation from the very nostalgia of totalizing metanarratives, Lyotard invites us to celebrate our radical freedom through artistic, interpretive acts of self-expression. Through these acts of "presenting the unpresentable," we create rather than discover ourselves, and we constitute rather than humble ourselves before those authorities that govern our lives. The postmodernist claims neither final knowledge nor partial apprehension of the real world outside our own interpretative constructs. Instead, the postmodernist wages war on the very notion of a higher authority, higher truth, or higher reality, seeing in these ideals only the potential for tyranny and intolerance. Behind this aversion to metaphysical ideals is a deeply held suspicion that upholding such ideals only invites villainy from those who claim privileged and unmediated access to them. As activists on behalf of "difference," postmodernists condemn as dangerous illusions the pretensions of universal metaphysical truth, of the enduring authority of what is, as opposed to the shifting impressions of what merely seems to be from a given, humanly created perspective. All higher truth is unknowable, unthinkable, and unpresentable; the only truth we can speak of and thus present to ourselves is the truth we constitute. To celebrate "difference" means to reject the traditional dichotomy in metaphysics of reality versus appearance, for the very notion of the real collapses into just another artifice of human inventing. Lyotard invites us to revel not as the bride before the Lamb but as the sheep lost without their Good Shepherd.

By linking postmodernism to this aversion toward metaphysical objectivity and authority, Lyotard exemplifies the post-metaphysical postmodern outlook that MacIntyre brilliantly critiques in *Three Rival Versions of Moral Enquiry*. MacIntyre's exposition and assessment of radical postmodernism is particularly useful to our inquiry, since MacIntyre helps us to see both the

15. Ibid., 81–82.

strengths and the weaknesses of the kind of strategy Lyotard employs. First of all, MacIntyre acknowledges that rooted in the writings of Nietzsche is the "genealogical tradition" of postmodernism that succeeds in exposing the incoherence and pretentiousness of the Cartesian and Enlightenment vision of attaining final and certain knowledge through our rational, autonomous deliberation. Yet MacIntyre argues that this Nietzschean tradition suffers its own particular form of incoherence, insofar as it must ironically presuppose in some way or another the very metaphysics of self it condemns.[16] A crucial defect of radical postmodernism lies in how, in order to articulate what it means to be postmodern, the postmodernist, such as Lyotard, must implicitly posit an enduring self who maintains his or her liberated, antimetaphysical character precisely by repeatedly committing itself, as an enduring self, to the rejection of all forms of metaphysical authority. In the case of Lyotard's exposition above, what then does it mean to characterize the postmodern self as Lyotard does, but to posit a newly liberated, enduring self whose defining and enduring features are (1) its skepticism about all claims to objective truth, and (2) its moral earnestness in warning against the incivility and inhumanity inherent in metaphysical aspirations to achieve a "totalizing" worldview? It is at least very difficult to make sense of either of these defining characteristics of the liberated postmodern psyche unless we take them seriously as enduring and "real" aspects of a self, trying in a persistent fashion to stay true to itself as a liberated, "non-metaphysical" self.

16. An important question to be raised here is whether the genealogical tradition that MacIntyre refutes is authentically Nietzschean. At times, as in his famous essay "On Truth and Lies," Nietzsche certainly looks as if he may be rejecting not only our ability to grasp objective truth by transcending the limits of our language and desires, but also the very idea of objective truth as rooted in the way the world really is outside all human perspectives. At other times, especially in his vehement diatribes against Christianity, Nietzsche seems to regard his own naturalistic philosophy of self-affirmation and the will-to-power as not only true for his own perspective, but true overall for any possible reasonable human perspective. To read *The Anti-Christ* or *Twilight of the Idols* merely as expressions of Nietzsche's own perspectivism reduces Nietzsche's challenging arguments to emotional discharge. There is no question that these texts suffer from and are marred by such animosity toward Christianity that Nietzsche—even more so than Hume—appears totally incapable of perceiving the role of love in the life of Christian belief. As with Hume's *Natural History*, Nietzsche's texts in opposition to the "blight" of Christianity are powerful not as an attack on genuine faith but as a sober and scathing indictment of the abuses and corruptions of Christian faith that have been both pervasive and tragic. I think the most plausible reading of Nietzsche, overall, is that Nietzsche is not a perspectivist after the fashion of Lyotard and Derrida. Rather, Nietzsche is a subtle and enigmatic practitioner of a kind of fiercely individualistic, naturalistic realism. Whatever the case, MacIntyre's refutation of Nietzschean genealogy does provide a compelling argument against radical postmodernism and against the standard reading of Nietzsche on the part of such postmodernists as Derrida, Lyotard, Rorty, and Deleuze. One should note, finally, the irony of postmodernists who defend Nietzsche against critics such as MacIntyre by arguing that MacIntyre has misrepresented what Nietzsche is really saying. Seeing their own prophet in harm's way, neo-Nietzschean postmodernists do not hesitate to "get metaphysical."

Put another way, is it not evident in the passage above that Lyotard succeeds in demonstrating both the seriousness and the validity of where he stands in contradistinction to those who still espouse "totalizing" worldviews? Does not this very act of self-description through opposition entail a commitment on Lyotard's part to a kind of real self, the postmodern self that he wishes us to comprehend? Perhaps the postmodernist would reply that I am misinterpreting the nature of postmodern self-description, that what Lyotard, for example, engages in is not the positing of an enduring "postmodern" self but merely the creation of a self as a form of expression, the creation of which self can be repeated continually without any commitment to some real postmodern self. But such a move only compounds the problem facing the postmodern apologist. In making this integrity-preserving move, the postmodernist now simply gets caught in the same incoherence on a new level. Note that the postmodernist would now be avoiding self-refutation by insisting that a critic such as MacIntyre has misrepresented the character of the postmodern self. In making this countermove, the postmodernist is simply once again relying on his or her own distinction of appearance and reality. What does it mean to defend oneself against misrepresentation when one insists that there is no self as such to be misrepresented? The postmodernist either has to say that MacIntyre's account of the postmodern self is just as real as Lyotard's own self-description, since both are equally real as fabricated conventions, or that MacIntyre has misrepresented the postmodern self. While Lyotard tells us that the task of the postmodern is not to "supply reality" but "to invent allusions," the earnestness with which he distinguishes the postmodern from its metaphysical counterpart involves a traditional assertion about what one really believes and where one really stands. Can we not imagine Lyotard's response to the naive reader who asks, "Are you not just another Platonist or Christian metaphysician? Is there really any difference between you and them?" The whole tone and content of Lyotard's presentation of what it means to be "postmodern" requires us to see that he would have to insist that anyone who characterizes him as a standard Platonist or traditional Christian theist is just *misrepresenting* what he is saying. Play as much as they wish to, when it comes to telling us why they are playing and what it means to play, postmodernists show the sincerity of the most impassioned realist: "Do not accuse me of espousing metaphysical metanarratives because that is exactly what I am not doing!" roars the postmodernist to the naive critic. But any such move of self-defense on the part of the postmodernist is a form of hypocrisy. While it may be the case that a postmodernist such as Lyotard has only the thinnest of metanarratives to offer us, in his own self-description, he cannot help but become engaged in the practice of metaphysical thinking.

By setting himself over against all those totalizing and oppressive forms of metaphysical identity, Lyotard does not simply mean that his preference for merely local language games is nothing more than an emotive expression of his own perspective representing the moral earnestness of his arbitrary authorial voice. The dilemma for Lyotard is this: either postmodernism's aversion to totalizing metanarratives and totalitarian coercion amounts to nothing more than a mere social construction, an arbitrary preference or perspective, with no more authority or urgency than that of the subjective tastes of a given Western intellectual community, or this aversion is rationally justified, and is indeed of urgent importance, because such a preference for freedom and peace over oppression and violence is rooted in an objective moral order of real selfhood that is not itself simply reducible to human preference.

One might counter here that this postmodern dilemma of metaphysical aversion is really no genuine conflict at all. Lyotard could, for example, simply accept the first horn of the apparent dilemma, admitting that the postmodernist's aversion to metanarratives is nothing more than a matter of taste, the authority of which is entirely dependent on the human perspective of those who share Lyotard's postmodern tastes. But such a move could not work for a postmodernist such as Lyotard, who clearly invests his vision of the liberated postmodern self with sincere moral earnestness. If this moral earnestness reflects no objective feature of the self, because the very notion of an objective self "out there" to be discovered by errant and wandering human selves is an illusion, then this sincere earnestness appears to command no more and no less seriousness than does an advertisement urging us to prefer one kind of commodity over another: all ethical appeals are merely social constructions and expressions of rhetorical self-creation. Apart from some notion of moral objectivity, such evils for the postmodernist as the metaphysically deluded self and the politically coercive political order are to be condemned simply on the grounds of intellectually elite fashion or style. There is nothing more real to back up the preference for freedom over despotism than an arbitrary human perspective.

This dual indictment of Lyotard's postmodern project is not irresponsible or misguided. With respect both to its political earnestness and its intellectual integrity, postmodernism takes very seriously the enemies to which it is opposed. My critique of postmodernism turns on the fact, first of all, that its self-stated character as antimetaphysical presumes the very kind of metaphysics of truth from which the postmodernist self seeks to liberate itself. The force and seriousness of postmodernism hinges on the fact that the metaphysical convictions and cultural forms it opposes are not merely the imaginative myths of postmodern critics, but are real errors against which the postmodernist forges his or her own identity as liberator. If we agree with Lyotard that "we have paid a high enough price for the nostalgia of the whole," then we should by all means oppose such nostalgia. Yet if we do so, do we not need also to ask: "Is your contention that traditional philosophy has fallen prey to an unhealthy nostalgia just a fiction of your own making, some postmodern linguistic creation on your part, some playful gesture or move in a mere game, or is it a real defect of these traditional systems to be guilty of oppressive, philosophical thinking?" If merely the former, then the whole legitimacy and urgency for a postmodern liberation is nothing more than a fancy, a chimera, of certain hermeneutically minded persons who like to think of themselves as "radical." If it is the latter, then the postmodernist is as much a metaphysical thinker as those he or she seeks to unmask.

The fundamental dilemma here, the dilemma of the "postmodernist poetics of aversion," is that postmodernism either is merely a fashion in the shopping mall of intellectual commodities or it is self-negating, because it must posit as real both the structures of oppression it opposes and its own liberating persona. This dilemma haunts any form of postmodernism in which the following two basic features are in place:

1. an earnest, sustained, and self-defining aversion toward and impassioned reaction against metaphysical institutions and doctrines of Western thought perceived to be oppressive and illusory;
2. an earnest, sustained, and self-defining reaction against the very concept of any objective, real order of things, of a reality that transcends mere human artifice and under whose authority all communities of human thinkers must find their proper place as seekers of what is true.

Whether one considers Lyotard's aversion to metanarratives, Derrida's distaste for the metaphysics of presence, or Foucault's and Deleuze's sustained antipathy to any transcendent ground of human experience, what it means to be postmodern hinges on not being duped and oppressed by certain "not so very enlightened" traditional theories and practices. That there are these negative forms of being and that they are definitely negative must, then, for the postmodernist be a matter of the real record of human history. That is, either these traditional metaphysical beliefs and practices are what they are—namely, false masks to be stripped away—and are not merely what the postmodernists say they are, because postmodernists have made all this up as part of their own free play of linguistic creativity, or postmodernism is itself a pathetic gesture of protest, for it refuses to take responsibility for its own identity defined in significant part in terms of the oppression it opposes. Yet every time the postmodernist declares what it means to be postmodern or defends postmodernism against some allegedly misguided criticism, the postmodernist makes a metaphysical move.

This rendition of "the dilemma of the postmodernist poetics of aversion" is a variation of Aristotle's critique of Protagorean subjectivism, itself a restatement of Plato's refutation of Protagoras in the *Theaetetus*. If the postmodernist means to be taken seriously when he or she proposes to have unmasked metaphysical thesis M, then there must be a real difference between what it means to be deluded by believing M and what it means to be liberated by not believing M. If not, there is nothing of cognitive seriousness in what the postmodernist utters, and his or her utterance is no more intelligible than a noncognitive bodily discharge. To be worth taking seriously, in other words, the *difference* between the state of believing delusory M and the state of aversion toward believing M, or, if you will, of anti-M enlightenment, cannot itself merely be a fabrication or preference of those who espouse anti-M. Note here that the postmodern legitimation of aversion toward M and the very reason for becoming and persisting in being anti-M is that one has come to see through the delusion of believing M and thus one believes, even if one's own epistemology publicly denies it, that M and anti-M are *really different*.

Now, I am of course not arguing that qua realist, the postmodernist must be able to step outside all language or have a translinguistic, direct insight into reality itself in order to articulate the oppositional character of postmodernism as antitraditional or antimetaphysical. All our speaking and thinking is immersed in the ether of human discourse. I am arguing instead that in terms of both its moral earnestness and its various formal self-descriptions as espousing an "antioppressed form of consciousness," postmodernism vaunts itself in the public arena of discourse as more than merely an arbitrary perspective of subjective game-playing. If the postmodernist protests that this critique is merely another trick of oppressive, metaphysical logocentricism or the misrepresentation foisted on postmodernism by a metanarrative fundamentalist, then we only return to postmodernism's same fundamental self-negation on a higher metalevel. What can it mean to be misrepresented or the victim of calumny except that one has really meant something that one's critic has distorted or even willfully misrepresented? If it makes sense to say that a critic has "failed to understand what the postmodernist means," then postmodernism must have an identity, even if it is in some respects a fluid and not fully representable stable identity. While this self-identity may be nuanced, protean, or even finally beyond full description, it is nevertheless an "identity of aversion" that is not simply whatever a given hermeneutical community says that it is.

Two important points bear mentioning. First, postmodernists are right in seeing two potential dangers to any metaphysics in which beings in the world are regarded, in some sense, as possessing essential identities and relating to one another in ways that reflect their inner natures. One potential danger is the characteristically modern one of treating these self-identical natures as atomistic, self-contained, and autonomous. A genuinely postmodern understanding of human relationships, and of ecology in general, should inform our theories of the human self and of nonhuman creatures in such a way that we acknowledge the communal dimension central to the nature of any individual. Postmodernists are right to insist on the communal and historical situatedness of all individual natures. To be human is to be a self whose very essence reflects his or her place in a variety of communities. Individuality can emerge only within a matrix of social relatedness. Every individual is an embedded individual.

Furthermore, just as belief in essences can lead to an excessive atomism, so too on a religious or political level, a vision of "essential types" of humans can perversely serve to legitimate the degrading and oppressive treatment of the "other." The history of both religious and political oppression testifies to the real dangers inherent in forms of essentialism that subordinate one race, gender, or tradition of humans to some supposedly superior type. But, of course, we must be careful in how we argue from such acknowledged examples of ill use and exploitation. Here we must acknowledge a crucial second point. From the fact that human history is replete with examples of atrociously bad metaphysical thinking, it of course does not follow that all metaphysical thinking is atrociously bad. *Abusus non tollit usum*, "the abuse of something does not destroy its proper use." Indeed, we should avoid the postmodernist's condemnation of all metaphysics if it turns out that the most compelling, and indeed the only coherent way of opposing bad versions of a metaphysical essentialism, is to rely on some alternative essentialism that insists on the dignity and inherent beauty of each and every person.

The best, if not the only, effective antidote to metaphysical schemes that promote intolerance and oppression are metaphysical schemes that do not. The unfortunate error—indeed a tragic error—of postmodernism is to think that we safeguard ourselves against human cruelty and hatred by relinquishing any vision of higher truth and moral authority by which human communities and institutions are to be measured. To declare, for example, as Rorty does, that truth is no more than "what our peers will . . . let us get away with saying,"[17] is to declare a muddle in which the author really is metaphysical despite himself. Clearly in making such a declaration, Rorty implies that he thinks truth *really is different* from what the metaphysical realist thinks it is! If the postmodernist replies that this objection to Rorty shows a misreading of what Rorty really means, then once again we confront the tiresome irony of the postmodern defender who both denies that there is a reality beyond our perspectives, that the distinction between "appears to be" and "really is" is a muddle, and then presupposes this very distinction when he or she insists that the critics of postmodernism play fair and listen more carefully to what the postmodernist really says. Ironically, we cannot avoid the ironic fact that a trace of metaphysical realism taints every draught of postmodernist apologetic rhetoric.

17. Richard Rorty, *Philosophy and the Mirror of Nature* (Princeton, NJ: Princeton University Press, 1979), 175–76.

Postmodernism and the Lure of Autonomy

> Exiled Thucydides knew
> All that a speech can say
> About Democracy,
> And what dictators do,
> The elderly rubbish they talk
> To an apathetic grave;
> Analyzed all in his book,
> The enlightenment driven away,
> The habit-forming pain,
> Mismanagement and grief:
> We must suffer them all again.
>
> Into this neutral air
> Where blind skyscrapers use
> Their full height to proclaim
> The strength of Collective Man,
> Each language pours its vain
> Competitive excuse:
> But who can live for long
> In an euphoric dream;
> Out of the mirror they stare,
> Imperialism's face
> And the international wrong.[18]

I shall argue in what follows that mainstream radical postmodernism fails to be sufficiently radical in its critique of modernity: while the postmodernist rightly objects to Enlightenment pride and its excessive confidence in the powers of unaided and autonomous human reason, postmodernism suffers from its own distinctive form of excessive pride derived from the modernist's self-image of the autonomous intellectual critic. Postmodernism fails to unmask the modern presumption of the human self as an autonomous critic of all claims to authority outside the legislative decrees of the autonomous self or community of selves. While the postmodernist critique of the totalizing human schemes of metaphysical theorizing has merit, postmodernism fails to own up to and confess its own illicit love affair with the modern harlot of human autonomy.

I turn now to develop my second line of criticism against postmodernism—namely that postmodernism fails as a corrective against modernity insofar as it simply is not sufficiently critical of one of the most problematic features of mainstream modern culture. Consider the following irony. Is it not a curious fact that Lyotard's postmodern discourse on the liberation from metaphysics

18. Auden, "September 1, 1939," stanzas 3 and 4, 316–17.

was sponsored by a United Nations project for world peace? Lyotard defends his postmodern philosophy of liberation from metaphysical thinking as a necessary stance for opposing the modern perversions of totalitarian grand narratives. Lyotard's case turns on a diagnosis of the modern perversity of totalitarian violence and prejudice in which the oppressive acts of modern totalitarianism are symptoms of a form of false consciousness that presumes that the totality of human experience can be subsumed under some overarching, grand, metaphysical narrative. Lyotard is certainly justified in thinking that modern totalitarian oppression has, in some horrendous instances and especially in the last century, derived its legitimization from a faith in some type of grand metaphysical narrative (the master race, the new rational society, and so forth); at the same time, he overlooks a dehumanizing facet of contemporary postmodern practice that turns his indictment on its head. Lyotard fails to take into account how comfortably his own perspective of a creative postmodern consciousness fits into the grand narrative of amoral global consumerism, a narrative quite willing to embrace any form of "radical thinking" that removes the possibility of subjecting amoral global capitalism itself to moral critique, one that is based on an objective—rather than a merely fabricated—standard of human dignity.

In declaring the postmodern conception of the self to be the one true friend of postmodern decency and peace, Lyotard commits the astounding oversight of failing to see how the postmodern self makes the perfect partner for intercourse with that demeaning and oppressive worldwide form of living and thinking called global capitalism. What do I mean here by this term? I do not at all mean that set of market-based practices by which the local producers and merchants exercise their economic independence. In contrast to the practices of local, free-market exchange, which is arguably the most defensible, though certainly corruptible, system of economic enterprise, the grand narrative of global capitalism goes beyond mere economic theory by embodying, promoting, and advertising an inhumane but alluring metanarrative or worldview of consumer autonomy. According to this global perspective, the only viable standards of value in human affairs are net profit and net loss; to have value is thus merely a function of the wants and preferences of consumers. In other words, according to this grand narrative, "to be is to be the function of price curves and individual preferences" and "to be just" is simply "to be the preferred standard of value of the majority of voting consumers for adjudicating the conflicts of individual freedom and social order."[19]

Intimately linked to this global capitalist "praxis" that is dominant in our postmodern world is the overarching, legitimating narrative of the promise of the ever-increasing good life made possible through capitalism's economic

---

19. For a lucid analysis of the worldview of global capitalism, see Max Oelschlaeger, *Caring for Creation* (New Haven: Yale University Press, 1994), 8–117.

efficiency. Sensitive postmodernists like Lyotard are deeply aware of the exploitative dark side of this amoral, global, capitalist worldview. Lyotard envisions postmodernism as a resistance movement to the degrading, monolithic institutions of finance capitalism. But just how effective a resistance movement can Lyotard's postmodernism be in the face of global capitalism's own postmodern character? The answer is: not very effective at all.

What is curiously absent in Lyotard's assessment of totalitarian oppression is any recognition on his part that his own playful postmodern philosophy of creative autonomy is elegantly fitted to be the suitor or valet of global consumerism, since it offers such a marvelously legitimating rationality for postmodern consumerism. Just how dangerous for the powerful elites of global capitalism is the proclamation of postmodernism that the only authorities governing our individual and social practices are themselves products of our own manufacturing? The answer to this significant question is that, far from being a dangerous threat, the postmodern doctrine of the autonomous, free self or self-defining community fits so harmoniously with the amoralism of global capitalism that the postmodern concern for human dignity has little hope of being anything but a powerless and obsequious voice in the presence of the powerful institutions of global capitalism. Ironically, it is hard to say which came first, the *praxis* of global consumerism, which appears more and more to be the dominant popular expression of postmodernity, or the *theory* of the postmodern, liberated, autonomous human creator. However one understands this complex interrelationship of postmodern *praxis* to postmodern *theory*, it is very hard to see how theoretical postmodernism can liberate us from the practical, popular postmodernism inherent in global capitalism. The crucial affinity of global capitalism and theoretical postmodernism is that both share a determination to oppose any traditional metaphysical account of value that could provide an objectively authoritative "sacred canopy" under which human claims and practices could be held up to scrutiny and exposed as defective.

One immensely important difference between Augustine's philosophy and Lyotard's postmodernism is that only the former can effectively call the global capitalist, consumerist psyche to an authoritative, higher standard and vision. Postmodernism can appeal only to standards of human dignity and nurture that, as mere human projections, are themselves no more authoritative than the consumerist ideals of global capitalism. Of course, a postmodernist might well deplore the brutality of totalitarian regimes animated by totalizing metaphysical narratives and the oppression of a postmodern global consumerism, a global worldview, that, dismissing all metaphysical narratives as unnecessary and unentertaining, simply takes as a given that all beings and the world in which they live are merely commodities. But the postmodernist has no adequate authority from which to critique the ethos of consumerism, for both perspectives essentially speak the same language of consumer/hermeneutical freedom, in which all claims of authority are merely human contrivances, themselves commodities, the value of which, like that of mass-marketed goods at the superstore, derives solely from consumer preferences. In this respect, the postmodernism of the intellectual academy is not so radical after all. It is the intellectual counterpart to consumer culture, in which debates about truth make no sense at all unless they are tied to considerations of subjective preference and thus ultimately to power. An Augustinian outlook, on the contrary, insists that considerations of power must be subsumed under those of objective human dignity. What is prior for the Augustinian is not the genealogy of power, as in Foucault, but the divine narrative of creation that reveals to us who we really are and what is truly good in our lives. Fundamentally, the postmodernist and the Augustinian articulate radically different conceptions of rationality, power, and freedom. In the world of global consumer society, where consumer preference is the ultimate arbiter of value and the exercise of personal preference the core meaning of freedom, postmodernism plays the part of the harlot with respect to the mainstream popular culture and the utilitarian, exploitative consciousness of amoral finance capitalism; Lyotard's thesis that postmodernism, armed with the power of antimetaphysical freedom, possesses a revolutionary power to oppose the tyranny of capitalist Western culture is a claim that is woefully and tragically overexaggerated and self-deceived.

At the core of the moderate antimodern position I intend to defend is an Augustinian skepticism about the modern conception of human autonomy. As I have already noted, radical postmodernists share with their modernist predecessors a deep attraction to the power of intellectual autonomy. A central part of my critique of radical postmodernism contends that it is not radical enough: having witnessed the sudden collapse of the modern Enlightenment citadel of autonomous reason, contemporary postmodernists ought to be as circumspect about the "lure of autonomy" as they are about the objectivity of reason. By "the lure of autonomy" I refer to the human temptation to rebel against all higher authority so that we can regard ourselves, either individually or collectively, as the final judges and highest authorities on matters of ethical and religious concern. The spiritual embodiment of the lure of autonomy is gnosticism: the gnostic presumes that we can liberate ourselves by breaking free from dependence on tradition and embodiment and thereby through elite enlightenment assert our own rightful independence over against the restrictive claims of tradition and the limits imposed on us by our embeddedness in the social and material world order. For the rationalistic proponents of the Enlightenment project, the lure of autonomy was articulated in the language of pure reason in which reason alone would liberate the rational individual, bring all claims of authority before the bar of pure reason, and, as a result, overcome the intellectual and social disorder that has plagued human history. For Descartes in particular, this meant that we would wipe clean the slate of all prejudices and customs and build a new system of *scientia* on foundations of our own reason.

Admittedly, if reason could indeed establish a set of foundations independently of the influences of tradition, passion, and culture, then the modern conception of objective reason would seem to offer something of immense usefulness for human life—the power to live well in a rational human community free from the instability and suffering caused by human ignorance. Let us acknowledge that the vision of Descartes and the later Enlightenment was as much a matter of what reason could enable us to do in the world as of what reason would finally allow us to know about the world. This is to say that the ends of this quest for autonomous reason were both practical and intellectual. In both cases, it was thought to be the unique province of purified reason to provide the power to achieve those ends. Because this power derives from reason relying only on itself, its exercise depends on radical freedom, the freedom, that is, of being final arbiter and judge. In this way, the lure of autonomy reflects a very human desire to free oneself from the need to depend on and submit to the power of some authority outside of oneself.

The lure of autonomy thus promises the individual an immense freedom to determine one's own identity. One of the great legacies of the Cartesian method was the belief that the rational individual can establish his or her identity and solve substantial problems facing people by means of a radical doubting of past beliefs and external authorities. The human intellect, freed of tradition and custom, offers us the power to determine who we are and how we shall live. It is important to appreciate how the radical postmodernists secure this same basic independence from the past, in particular from such traditions as church and metaphysics, without taking the modernist path of finding this freedom in pure reason. The distinctively postmodern path to autonomy lies not in the affirmation of the authority of pure reason but in the proclamation of the sovereign authority of our own historically conditioned and linguistically constituted interpretative constructions. The postmodern logic securing this new kind of authority proceeds as follows. Having come to realize how all human thinking is shaped by one's interpretative perspective, the postmodernist ingeniously finds a new "foundation" for radical autonomy, an autonomy now rooted in the power of critical interpretation. That our postmodern condition offers no standard for authority other than our acts of interpretative creativity turns on what might be termed the postmodern thesis of the priority of interpretation. Since no reality can assert its authority in our lives independently of the interpretive power that renders authoritative claims intelligible, the person or community itself becomes the ultimate authority. It is the human interpreter who provides the horizon or context of meaning that constitutes the necessary background for all claims to authority. It is thus the human qua interpreter who must be acknowledged as the ultimate authority in all human affairs. For the radical postmodernist, the highest freedom is not the freedom of the Enlightenment autonomous reasoner but the more elusive freedom of the autonomous, human architect of interpretive constructs. Like the Cartesian reasoner, the radical postmodernist endeavors to attain autonomy over any form of metaphysical authority that presumes to make normative claims about the nature of self.

For our radical postmodernist, then, the only realities that can impinge on our freedom are those we constitute through our own acts of interpretation. Ultimate authority thus resides in us, for we can be called to serve authority only by voices who submit to the terms of our own interpretative constructs. Author James Edwards characterizes a communal version of this hypermodern postmodern outlook quite effectively—and in a manner much more lucid than Lyotard's:

> If language, which one might call the ultimate and essential human social practice, is not—whether through rules, intentions, interpretations, or feelings—authorized by the individual self who speaks it, then no social practice is finally so authorized. If *linguistic* authority doesn't reside originally in the individual, if I cannot in the first instance make my words mean what I want them to mean (and I *cannot*), then *no* real authority resides there. And this is so because any claim to epistemic or ethical authority in a particular instance must itself be a claim made *in language*, and must therefore trade upon some prior linguistic authorization. All authority is finally linguistic authority: that is why a perspicuous presentation of language is the key to the question of philosophical nihilism.[20]

In this passage, Edwards elegantly sets forth the logic of postmodern, hermeneutical autonomy. As I have argued, insofar as postmodernists embrace such a radically modern vision of human autonomy, postmodernism is more appropriately to be understood as hypermodern rather than postmodern. In a way ironically reminiscent of Descartes, postmodernism reenacts the drama of assuming a posture of radical doubt in order to secure autonomous authority. Granted, for the postmodernist it is not the atomistic, rational ego but the linguistically constituted arena of human interpretation that reigns as the highest authority. In defense of this sovereign authority, postmodernists insist that all metaphysical claims to authority must submit to the bar of postmodern hermeneutics. Contrary to the Cartesian project, what grounds our freedom here is not the clear and distinct foundations of reason, the autonomy of reason purified of all "prejudice," but the linguistic creativity of our own interpretive practices. In an ingenious fashion, postmodernism thus satisfies modernity's demand for human autonomy without being encumbered with the responsibility imposed on us by the order of universal reason. With postmodernism, the reign of metaphysical idols—including, ironically, the modern idol of rational authority—ceases. As a consequence, we are faced with a human autonomy of a far more radical character than the rational au-

20. James C. Edwards, *The Authority of Language* (Tampa: University Presses of Florida, 1990), 217–18.

tonomy envisioned by such thinkers as Descartes or Kant. Modern philosophy, and in particular the Enlightenment, sought to liberate the universal rational self from the bondage of the "nonrational"; radical postmodernism seeks to expose modernity's universal reason as but another form of oppression limiting our radical freedom of linguistic self-creation. In so doing, radical postmodernism poses a serious and ingenious challenge to all metaphysical forms of authority, religious or secular.

The inseparability of postmodernism's zeal for autonomy and postmodernism's aversion toward metaphysics is spelled out with particular clarity in Rorty's analysis of Derrida's deconstructionist rhetoric in "Envois," the first half of Derrida's text titled *The Post Card*. For Rorty, it is in the text "Envois" that Derrida most authentically reveals himself as the antimetaphysical ironist who eschews the aim of discovering a final vocabulary of intellectual discourse and disavows the aim of traditional philosophy to seek "The Truth." To the question of what good end Derrida's playful, antimetaphysical rhetoric might serve, Rorty remarks:

> What is the good of writing that way? If one wants arguments which reach conclusions, it is no good at all. As I have said already, there is nothing propositional to be taken away from the experience of reading it—any more than from the writings of the later Heidegger. So it is to be judged by "literary" rather than "philosophical" criteria? No, because, as in the cases of the *Phenomenology of Spirit*, *Remembrance of Things Past*, and *Finnegan's Wake*, there are no antecedently available criteria of *either* sort. The more original a book or a kind of writing is, the more unprecedented, the less likely we are to have criteria in hand, and the less point there is in trying to assign it to a genre. We have to see whether we can find a use for it. If we can, then there will be time enough to stretch the borders of some genre or other far enough to slip it in, and to draw up criteria according to which it is a good kind of writing to have invented. Only metaphysicians think that our present genres and criteria exhaust the realm of possibility. Ironists continue to expand that realm.[21]

According to Rorty, one should not turn to Derrida to be confronted with philosophical arguments or to see the truth about anything. Rather, Derrida's text breaks free of the confinement of rational criteria, ignores the limitations of past genres, and prefers the open landscape of free expression over the confinements of metaphysical structures. In a word, for Rorty the value of Derrida's text lies precisely in its affirmation and instantiation of a daring form of radical autonomy. Rorty concludes his study of "Envois":

> To sum up: I am claiming that Derrida, in "Envois," has written a kind of book which nobody has ever thought of before. He has done for the history of

21. Richard Rorty, *Contingency, Irony, and Solidarity* (Cambridge: Cambridge University Press, 1989), 135.

philosophy what Proust did for his own life story: He has played all the authority figures, and all the descriptions of himself which these figures might be imagined as giving, off against each other, with the result that the very notion of "authority" loses application in reference to his work. He has achieved autonomy in the same way that Proust achieved autonomy: neither *Remembrance of Things Past* nor "Envois" fits within any conceptual scheme previously used to evaluate novels or philosophical treatises. He has avoided Heideggerian nostalgia in the same way that Proust avoided sentimental nostalgia—by incessantly recontextualizing whatever memory brings back. Both he and Proust have extended the bounds of possibility.[22]

On Rorty's reading, the value of "Envois" is its power to raise us up to the most liberating heights of interpretative autonomy. To write like Derrida is to achieve liberation from any and all preestablished rational criteria. Derrida has so extended the bounds of possibility that the only challenge impossible for his authorial voice is to allow itself to be held accountable for anything he has said. Here again we see the postmodern psyche not so much as antimodern but as hypermodern: whereas modernity freed us from the constraints of history, tradition, and affection to liberate our autonomous rational selves, postmodernity frees us from being selves accountable to any authority, rational or irrational, individualistic or communal.[23]

Derrida's desire to escape the confines of norms and standards and to emerge unencumbered by the burdens of the responsible self seems evident enough in Derrida's account of the poetics of playfulness. In this mode of playfulness, Derrida plays hide-and-seek with words, recognizing the inherent ambiguity in every description, the difference in every relation of sameness, and the absence in every manifestation of presence. So Derrida writes in "Structure, Sign, and Play":

> Besides the tension between play and history, there is also the tension between play and presence. Play is the disruption of presence. The presence of an element is always a signifying and substitutive reference inscribed in a system of differences and the movement of a chain. Play is always play of absence and presence, but if it is to be thought radically, play must be conceived of before the alternative of presence and absence. Being must be conceived of as presence or absence on the basis of the possibility of play and not the other way around. If Levi-Strauss, better than any other, has brought to light the play of repetition and the repetition of play, one no less perceives in his work a sort of ethic of presence, an ethic of nostalgia for origins, an ethic of archaic and natural innocence, of a purity of presence and self-presence in speech—an ethic, nostalgia, and even remorse, which he often presents as the motivation of the ethnological project

22. Ibid., 137.
23. For a sustained critique of Derrida's philosophy along these lines, see Ellis, *Against Deconstruction*.

when he moves toward the archaic societies which are exemplary societies in his eyes. These texts are well known.

Turned towards the loss or impossible presence of the absent origin, this structuralist thematic of broken immediacy is therefore the saddened, *negative*, nostalgic, guilty, Rousseauistic side of the thinking of play whose other side would be the Nietzschean *affirmation*, that is the joyous affirmation of the play of the world and of the innocence of becoming, the affirmation of a world of signs without fault, without truth, and without origin which is offered to an active interpretation. *This affirmation then determines the noncenter otherwise than as loss of the center.* And it plays without security. For there is a sure *play*: that which is limited to the *substitution* of *given* and *existing*, *present*, pieces. In absolute chance, affirmation also surrenders itself to *genetic* indetermination, to the *seminal* adventure of the trace.[24]

For Derrida the celebration of playfulness is a heralding of Nietzschean autonomy—an affirmation of creative innocence, the innocence of a playground, one might say, without any authority figures to monitor us and hold us responsible for our games of make-believe. The innocence of play here requires the absence of authority, for it is play without rules, without preexisting codes of success or failure, and without the nostalgia for truth or enduring significance. Derridean freedom would seem to be freedom from any sort of authoritative voice that would inhibit the literary free play of the momentary, transient self.[25]

24. Jacques Derrida, "Structure, Sign, and Play in the Discourse of the Human Sciences," in *Writing and Difference*, trans. Alan Bass (Chicago: University of Chicago Press, 1978), 292 (italic in the original).

25. At least for an outsider, it is hard not to suspect that in Derrida's dense discourses on liberation lies an adolescent, teenage fantasy: "If I could just get rid of Mom and Dad, let alone God, I could do whatever I want." At times, to be sure, Derrida's diatribes against God seem more a product of the infantile than of the adolescent imagination. Consider Derrida's "poetics of the toilet" in his essay "La parole soufflée":

> God is thus the proper name of that which deprives us of our own nature of our own birth; consequently he will always have spoken before us, on the sly. He is the difference which insinuates itself between myself and myself as my death. This is why—such is the concept of true suicide according to Artaud—I must die away from my death in order to be reborn "immortal" at the eve of my birth. God does not take hold of any one of our innate attributes, but of our innateness itself, of the innateness proper to our being itself: "There are some fools who think of themselves as beings, as innately being. / I am he who, in order to be, must whip his innateness. / One who must be a being innately, that is, always whipping this sort of nonexistent kennel, O! bitches of impossibility" (*CW* [Antonin Artaud, *Collected Works*, trans. Victor Corti (London: Calder & Boyars, 1971)], I:19).

Why is this original alienation conceived of as pollution, obscenity, "filthiness," etc.? Why does Artaud, bemoaning the loss of his body, lament a loss of purity as much as he laments dispossession, lament the loss of propriety as much as the loss of property? "I have been tortured too much . . . / . . . / I have worked too hard at being pure and strong / . . . / I have sought to have a proper body too much" (*84*, p. 135).

By definition, I have been robbed of my possessions, my worth, my value. My truth, what I am worth, has been purloined from me by some One who in my stead became

Yet surely this hypermodern—also known as postmodern—declaration of interpretative autonomy, whether Nietzschean or neo-Nietzschean, does not stand up to careful, responsible scrutiny. Like their Enlightenment forefathers, radical postmodernists succumb to the lure of a false autonomy. Essentially, what we must embrace if we are to be truthful about ourselves is a greater humility about the prospects for human autonomy than shown either by classic proponents of the Enlightenment or by radical postmodernists. In what follows, I will contend against "the lure of autonomy" that what we really need today is not more autonomy in the banal postmodern form of liberation from authority, but Socratic self-knowledge; we need the self-knowledge that embraces both our dependence on the divine and our need to engage in honest, critical, reflective thought. To solve our problems of injustice, greed, and loneliness, we need to accept and even embrace the authority of realities that stand outside our human consciousness. The position I uphold is that the drama of the "end of modernity" should lead us at least to suspect that, for all we know, the most viable solutions to our present problems may lie in the most unexpected places, perhaps even in those places deemed no longer fashionable by Western secular intellectuals. Put simply, before condemning all Western traditions of transcendent authority in a sweeping and wholesale fashion, we in the so-called postmodern academy would do well to look more closely at our own disorders, to concentrate our suspicious gaze not merely on the sins of our forebearers, but also on the blindnesses and obstructions in our own postmodern eye, even though the real problem may well reside more in our hearts. It is time for postmodernists, the vast majority of whom are members of the economically privileged classes of comfortable Western institutions, to be more sober and more suspicious about the modern myth of autonomy. Only then can postmodern critics of modernity act responsibly in the face of the degrading realities of industrialist and postindustrialist societies.

God at exit from the Orifice, at birth. God is false value as the initial worth of that which is born. And this false value becomes Value, because it has always already *doubled* true value which has never existed, or, amounting to the same thing, existed only prior to its own birth. Henceforth, original value, the ur-value that I should have retained within myself, as my value and my very being, that which was stolen from me as soon as I fell far from the Orifice, and which is stolen from me again each time that a part of me falls far from myself—this is the work, excrement, dross, the value that is annulled because it has not been retained, and which can become, as is well known, a persecuting arm, an arm eventually directed against myself. Defecation, the "daily separation with the feces, precious parts of the body" (Freud), is, as birth, as my birth, the initial theft which simultaneously depreciates me and soils me. This is why the history of God as a genealogy of stolen value is recounted as the history of defecation. "Do you know anything more outrageously fecal / than the history of God" ("Le théâtre de la cruauté," in *84*, p. 121). (Jacques Derrida, "La parole soufflée," in Bass, *Writing and Difference*, 181–82)

Atheism, relentless and formidable in Nietzsche's writings, succumbs in such passages from Derrida to a naughty, infantile preoccupation with fecal rhetoric.

One very good reason for taking the history of philosophy—even modern philosophy—seriously is that the failure of many ingenious and profound systems of thought should awaken in us a sense of intellectual humility about our ability to step back from our own situation, separate ourselves from our corruptions, and recognize our deepest assumptions and presuppositions. Achieving such a Socratic self-knowledge is never easy, and there is no sure sign at any point in our inquiries that we have actually succeeded. What I have hoped to do in this study is to show how the thought of two modern philosophers, both of whom were deeply skeptical about the modern faith in reason, can help us to achieve some self-knowledge in our postmodern world. The two figures I have focused on, Pascal and Hume, were in certain respects more postmodern than modern. Such at least has been the substance of my argument. Pascal and Hume, despite their own deep differences, agree for strikingly similar reasons that human life cannot be governed by autonomous reason. Their attacks against the excesses of the modern confidence in reason are instructive. Though clearly reformers in their own right, Pascal and Hume show a surprisingly prophetic, modest "postmodern" skepticism about modernity's intellectual reformation, the "reformation of reason." As critics of modern philosophical reformers, Pascal and Hume offer us two provocative and yet competing frameworks for living humbly and reasonably in our own postmodern world. In comparison with their outlooks, that of the radical, self-constituting, postmodernist shows less sensitivity to, and maturity about, our limits as humans.

In his essay "Writer and Region," Wendell Berry, with characteristic elegance, further clarifies the contrast between modest postmodern and hypermodern outlooks that I am trying to illuminate. Berry writes:

> Similar to the Territory of abstraction is the Territory of artistic primacy or autonomy, in which it is assumed that no value is inherent in subjects but that value is conferred upon subjects by the art and the attention of the artist. The subjects of the world are only *raw material*. As William Matthews writes in a recent article, *A poet beginning to make something needs raw material, something to transform*. For Marianne Moore, he says, "subject matter is not in itself important, except that it gives her the opportunity to speak about something that engages her passions. What is important instead is what she can discover to say." And he concludes: "It is not, of course, the subject that is or isn't dull, but the quality of attention we do or do not pay to it, and the strength of our will to transform. Dull subjects are those we have failed" ("Dull Subjects," *New England Review and Bread Loaf Quarterly* [Winter 1985]: 142–52). This assumes that for the animals and humans who are not fine artists, who have discovered nothing to say, the world is dull, which is not true. It assumes also that attention is of interest in itself, which is not true either. In fact, attention is of value only insofar as it is paid in the proper discharge of an obligation. To pay attention is to come into the presence of a subject. In one of its root senses, it is to *stretch*

toward a subject, in a kind of aspiration. We speak of *paying attention* because of a correct perception that attention is owed and that without our attention and our attending, our subjects, including ourselves, are endangered.[26]

As Berry observes, in the postmodern "territory of autonomy" artists regard their creativity as a radical expression of freedom—the freedom as artist to create one's own world and legislate one's own rules. For Berry, such a world, like the world of global consumerism, lacks a sense of place in which the artist as craftsman creates out of a sense of obligation and responsibility to a social order and land whose worth precedes, and provides the necessary context for, individual self-expression. For Berry, the tragedy of our economically privileged but displaced consumer society is that we as humans cannot live healthy lives apart from having a proper sense of our place, which, by providing us with the ethical and physical limitations of a real world, bestows on us an identity necessary for leading fulfilling lives in the pursuit of "good work." To do good work is to serve others and respect creation not as a reality dependent on our own cleverness and interpretative novelty, but as a part of a good world to whose Creator we owe service. But this means that to have a place is to be limited both historically by one's time and spatially by one's landscape. We could say here that living rationally as beings with a place is a matter of using one's reason well in coming to appreciate and to serve God and neighbor as an expression of gratitude for one's place in the created order. Neither the bare, autonomous Cartesian self nor the radically liberated hypermodern postmodern self can have a sense of place. It would be fair to say that my argument throughout this book in defense of Augustinian "postmodernism" is rooted in my own fallible intuition that human life without a deeply religious sense of place is a descent into self-absorption and insanity.

Postmodernism and the Illogic of Antirealism

> Faces along the bar
> Cling to their average day:
> The lights must never go out,
> The music must always play,
> All the conventions conspire
> To make this fort assume
> The furniture of home;
> Lest we should see where we are,
> Lost in a haunted wood,
> Children afraid of the night
> Who have never been happy or good.

---

26. Wendell Berry, "Writer and Region," in *What Are People For?* 83.

The windiest militant trash
Important Persons shout
Is not so crude as our wish:
What mad Nijinsky wrote
About Diaghilev
Is true of the normal heart;
For the error bred in the bone
Of each woman and each man
Craves what it cannot have,
Not universal love
But to be loved alone.

From the conservative dark
Into the ethical life
The dense commuters come,
Repeating their morning vow;
"I will be true to the wife,
I'll concentrate more on my work,"
And helpless governors wake
To resume their compulsory game:
Who can release them now,
Who can reach the dead,
Who can speak for the dumb?[27]

My case that radical postmodernism is guilty of an illegitimate liaison with an untenable and extreme form of autonomy calls us back to consider the profound character of the most striking *différance* confronting human life—the deep and ugly divide that lies between the authority of Truth itself and the fallibility of all our merely human worldviews and interpretative frameworks. Postmodernists rightly condemn those metaphysical systems that forget the persistent reality of this most sublime *différance* and assume for themselves the final authority of Truth Itself. All responsible human theorizing has an obligation to remember our inherent cognitive and affective imperfections; no human individual or institution may assume the authority of the ideal of Truth Itself. But this ethical responsibility of honest theorizing goes astray if it is not balanced in turn with the responsibility of upholding the ethical realism and seriousness inherent in this profound *différance*: our own socially constructed authorities pale before the final authority of Truth Itself, in the light of which all our conventions and all our authoritative communities are but crude traces and diminished shadows of reality. Tragically, as a result of its intoxication with the lure of autonomy, antimetaphysical postmodernism offers only a thin, "Hollywoodesque" sound bite of the profound drama of this deep and ugly *différance* in human history.

27. Auden, "September 1, 1939," stanzas 5–7, 317.

In what follows I will argue that mainstream, secular postmodernism fails to distinguish between two different types of contextualization: the first concerns how we encounter and apprehend beings in the world; the second concerns the nature of the being and the authority of truth itself, the authority not of our limited understanding of what the truth is, but of what the truth really is concerning the nature of the self and cosmos. Postmodernism typically exhibits an unfortunate conflation of these two very distinct realms. Indeed, postmodernism's hermeneutics of unmasking metaphysical claims about objective truth reflects a serious and tragic confusion of our fallible human understanding of truth, on the one hand, and the truth itself, independent of our paltry efforts to comprehend it, on the other.

Granted, the postmodernist poetics of *différance*, sublimity, and incomprehensibility may serve as useful reminders of our finitude and of the inadequacies of all of our narratives of human experience. And yet this poetics, insofar as it shares the antirealism of Derrida's "*Il n'y a pas de hors-texte,*" oversimplifies and diminishes the reality of dissonance, sublimity, and difference, and turns out to be too mild, too conventional, and too cosmetic. To appreciate the depth and breadth of disharmony and irrationality in human experience, we must recognize that beyond the traces of unintelligibility and conflict recurring within the collective consciousness of human history is an even more radical dissonance and distance—the immense gulf that lies between the totality of all human endeavors and ultimate reality itself. When we acknowledge that the Real is the incomprehensibly beautiful, that the Real is unconditional love, and that in and through this love the Real became incarnate in the realm of human unintelligibility and irrationality, then and only then can we begin to see the full extent of the appalling and horrendous nature of the discontinuous and disruptive *différance*. Only in light of God's perfect love and the blessedness of the eternal beauty of the Trinity can we begin to see the reality of that *différance* that negates and opposes our efforts to live and think harmoniously.

To uncover in more depth the problematic nature of the radical postmodernist's rejection of the ideal of objective truth inherent in the traditions of metaphysics, I want to first consider Richard Rorty's case against metaphysics—where metaphysics is understood as an inquiry into the true nature of the world—in *Contingency, Irony, and Solidarity*. Rorty's case is argued with impressive clarity, which is why it merits our consideration here, but it falls short in its lack of compelling reasoning. Interestingly enough, in his essay "The Contingency of Language," Rorty affirms the commonsense belief that there is an objective world independent of our interpretative perspectives, yet he seems to hold that since we can think only through language, truth is *merely* a property of language and has no relationship to the world outside of language. Defending the rejection of metaphysics on the grounds that all our descriptions of things reside within language, Rorty writes:

> The world does not speak. Only we do. The world can, once we have programmed ourselves with a language, cause us to hold beliefs. But it cannot propose a language for us to speak. Only other human beings can do that. The realization that the world does not tell us what language games to play should not, however, lead us to say that a decision about which to play is arbitrary, nor to say that it is the expression of something deep within us. The moral is not that objective criteria for choice of vocabulary are to be replaced with subjective criteria, reason with will or feeling. It is rather that the notions of criteria and choice (including that of "arbitrary" choice) are no longer in point when it comes to changes from one language game to another. Europe did not *decide* to accept the idiom of Romantic poetry, or of socialist politics, or of Galilean mechanics. That sort of shift was no more an act of will than it was a result of argument. Rather, Europe gradually lost the habit of using certain words and gradually acquired the habit of using others.
>
> As Kuhn argues in *The Copernican Revolution*, we did not decide on the basis of some telescopic observations, or on the basis of anything else, that the earth was not the center of the universe, that macroscopic behavior could be explained on the basis of microstructural motion, and that prediction and control should be the principal aim of scientific theorizing. Rather, after a hundred years of inconclusive muddle, the Europeans found themselves speaking in a way which took these interlocked theses for granted. Cultural change of this magnitude does not result from applying criteria (or from "arbitrary decision") any more than individuals become theists or atheists, or shift from one spouse or circle of friends to another, as a result either of applying criteria or of *actes gratuits*. We should not look within ourselves for criteria of decision in such matters any more than we should look to the world.
>
> The temptation to look for criteria is a species of the more general temptation to think of the world, or the human self, as possessing an intrinsic nature, an essence. That is, it is the result of the temptation to privilege some one among the many languages in which we habitually describe the world or ourselves. As long as we think that there is some relation called "fitting the world" or "expressing the real nature of the self" which can be possessed or lacked by vocabularies-as-wholes, we shall continue the traditional philosophical search for a criterion to tell us which vocabularies have this desirable feature. But if we could ever become reconciled to the idea that most of reality is indifferent to our descriptions of it, and that the human self is created by the use of a vocabulary rather than being adequately or inadequately expressed in a vocabulary, then we should at least have assimilated what was true in the Romantic idea that truth is made rather than found. What is true about this claim is just that *languages* are made rather than found, and that truth is a property of linguistic entities, of sentences. . . .
>
> The difficulty faced by a philosopher who, like myself, is sympathetic to this suggestion—one who thinks of himself as auxiliary to the poet rather than to the physicist—is to avoid hinting that this suggestion gets something right, that

my sort of philosophy corresponds to the way things really are. For this talk of correspondence brings back just the idea my sort of philosopher wants to get rid of, the idea that the world or the self has an intrinsic nature. From our point of view, explaining the success of science, or the desirability of political liberalism, by talk of "fitting the world" or "expressing human nature" is like explaining why opium makes you sleepy by talking about its dormitive power. To say that Freud's vocabulary gets at the truth about human nature, or Newton's at the truth about the heavens, is not an explanation of anything. It is just an empty compliment—one traditionally paid to writers whose novel jargon we have found useful. To say that there is no such thing as intrinsic nature is not to say that the intrinsic nature of reality has turned out, surprisingly enough, to be extrinsic. It is to say that the term "intrinsic nature" is one which it would pay us not to use, an expression which has caused more trouble than it has been worth. To say that we should drop the idea of truth as out there waiting to be discovered is not to say that we have discovered that, out there, there is no truth. It is to say that our purposes would be served best by ceasing to see truth as a deep matter, as a topic of philosophical interest, or "true" as a term which repays "analysis." "The nature of truth" is an unprofitable topic, resembling in this respect "the nature of man" and "the nature of God," and differing from "the nature of the positron," and "the nature of Oedipal fixation." But this claim about relative profitability, in turn, is just the recommendation that we in fact *say* little about these topics, and see how we get on.

On the view of philosophy which I am offering, philosophers should not be asked for arguments against, for example, the correspondence theory of truth or the idea of the "intrinsic nature of reality." The trouble with arguments against the use of a familiar and time-honored vocabulary is that they are expected to be phrased in that very vocabulary. They are expected to show that central elements in that vocabulary are "inconsistent in their own terms" or that they "deconstruct themselves." But that can *never* be shown. Any argument to the effect that our familiar use of a familiar term is incoherent, or empty, or confused, or vague, or "merely metaphorical" is bound to be inconclusive and question-begging. For such use is, after all, the paradigm of coherent, meaningful, literal speech. Such arguments are always parasitic upon, and abbreviations for, claims that a better vocabulary is available. Interesting philosophy is rarely an examination of the pros and cons of a thesis. Usually it is, implicitly or explicitly, a contest between an entrenched vocabulary which has become a nuisance and a half-formed new vocabulary which vaguely promises great things.[28]

Unfortunately, Rorty's reasoning here is flawed on several levels. First, he commits the fallacy of antirealism (see my subsequent critique of Putnam) by presuming that because language is an artifice, and because we cannot think except through language, then what we are thinking about when we describe the world must itself reside only within language. The fact that the truth of statements involves language does not mean that either truth or language is

---

28. Richard Rorty, *Contingency, Irony, and Solidarity* (Cambridge: Cambridge University Press, 1989), 6–9.

merely made up rather than discovered. The fact that we make up our sentences does not mean that we make up the truth.

Second, Rorty seems to know enough about the world out there to know that it cannot speak to us. But how does Rorty know that? Rorty's position would appear to make a huge metaphysical presupposition that whatever concerns us and whatever makes sense to us has no relation to the "indifferent" world beyond our language. Here, as I think Rorty at least comes close to admitting himself, Rorty the "ironist" is not so much arguing as declaring how post-Nietzschean secularists like Rorty himself *prefer* to look at things. Yet at times Rorty allows us to think that he is in fact arguing rather than merely "preaching to the choir"; indeed, Rorty is presenting arguments that are remarkably lucid but disappointing in their rigor.

Finally, Rorty appears both here and in his *Philosophy and the Mirror of Nature* to argue that we should junk the traditional metaphysical conception of truth as correspondence between human language and reality in itself because we cannot get outside of language to confirm when our assertions are true, and thus we have no means by which to know for sure when we are speaking the truth. But the lack of such certainty means only that we should be humble about our grasp of truth and acknowledge that all our believing has its roots in faith and trust. And Rorty may well be right in thinking that we cannot merely assume that even our best human explanations have any correspondence with the real world. It is true that we cannot know for certain that human reason is reliable in generating true beliefs about the world. But for the Christian who believes that we are made in God's image, it is reasonable *to believe* that human reason properly used is designed to put us in touch with reality. Of course, if Rorty means to say that we are better off giving up all beliefs and concepts that are uncertain and subject to disagreement among different communities of solidarity, then, unfortunately, not only would we have to divest ourselves of all metaphysical and commonsense beliefs and concepts, but we would have to reject Rorty's own case for doing so, on the grounds that nothing he says—attractive as it may be to some intellectuals—is certain to anyone!

I turn now to examine, in contrast to Rorty, a particularly lucid argument in favor of antirealism offered by the contemporary philosopher Hilary Putnam. I turn to Putnam, who is not a "postmodernist," because he brilliantly and clearly articulates the kind of argument against metaphysical realism that tends either to be presupposed by postmodernists—who often speak as if the case against metaphysics has already been made by Heidegger or some other pioneering thinker—or to be presented in their writings in a manner so dense and obscure as to be more oracular than dialectical.[29] Putnam has characterized his own

---

29. Lyotard's exaltation of the poetics of the sublime in the final pages of *The Postmodern Condition* and Derrida's rejection of *episteme* in Western philosophy in "Structure, Sign, and Play" are two vivid (and impressive) examples of postmodernism's triumphal rhetoric that as-

antirealist position as embodying an internalist's perspective in contradistinction to an externalist's stance that presumes to attain a "God's eye point of view." In defense of his internalism, Putnam offers the following version of a line of reasoning that I will subsequently deem the "logic of antirealism":

> The perspective I shall defend has no ambiguous name. It is a late arrival in the history of philosophy, and even today it keeps being confused with other points of view of a quite different sort. I shall refer to it as the *internalist* perspective, because it is characteristic of this view to hold that *what objects does the world consist of?* is a question that it only makes sense to ask *within* a theory or description. Many "internalist" philosophers, though not all, hold further that there is more than one "true" theory or description of the world. "Truth," in an internalist view, is some sort of (idealized) rational acceptability—some sort of ideal coherence of our beliefs with each other and with our experiences *as those experiences are themselves represented in our belief system*—and not correspondence with mind-independent or discourse-independent "states of affairs." There is no God's eye point of view that we can know or usefully imagine; there are only the various interests and purposes that their descriptions and theories subserve. ("Coherence theory of truth"; "Non-realism"; "Verificationism"; "Pluralism"; "Pragmatism"; are all terms that have to be applied to the internalist perspective; but every one of these terms has connotations that are unacceptable because of their other historic applications.)[30]

The crucial premise of Putnam's argument—that it makes coherent sense to talk of beings only within the context of some human perspective—leads Putnam to reject the traditional account of the nature of truth as a correspondence between human assertions and the way the world really is. For Putnam, the ways in which the world can be spoken of are always situated and relative to a given human perspective. There can be no "God's eye" point of view, Putnam adds, if all points of view intelligible to us are just those projected by some actual or possible human interpreter. In lieu of the correspondence theory of truth, Putnam speaks of truth in terms of idealized warrantability: asserting that the statement "A is F" is true means something along the lines of "This statement is and will remain rationally justified from a certain human perspective and no future set of rationally justified beliefs within this perspective will ever be found which require the rejection of this belief as rationally unwarranted." What Putnam proposes, in effect, is a metaphysically neutered theory of truth. Such a theory of truth is needed, of course, if indeed it is true that the traditional, fundamental metaphysical distinction between what appears to us and what really is, is incoherent.

---

sume rather than argue for the end of metaphysics and the traditional conception of truth as grounded in the nature of objective reality.

30. Hilary Putnam, *Reason, Truth and History* (Cambridge: Cambridge University Press, 1981), 49–50.

As I have interpreted Putnam, his decisive antirealist move is not first and foremost to reject the traditional metaphysical theory of truth but rather to attack as incoherent that theory's metaphysical presupposition regarding the meaning of being. In contradistinction to the traditional, metaphysical notion of being "in and of itself," Putnam maintains that to be is to be an object or a reality within some conceptual scheme. Once this antirealist account of the nature of being is granted, clearly the traditional correspondence theory of truth must be abandoned. For if we understand truth, in a simple and untechnical sense, to be a relation between what we say and what is, then, given Putnam's theory of what it means to be an object, and thus of "what is," truth cannot be defined as the proper accord between our statements and what lies outside of all human interpretations. In other words, if it makes no sense to speak of an object's having being outside of all human interpretive frameworks, then it surely cannot make sense to conceive of propositional truth as the relation of correspondence between an assertion and a "real" object that exists outside all human thought.

In another passage of the same essay, "Two Philosophical Perspectives," Putnam articulates his theory of the context-dependent nature of objects in the following terms:

> For an internalist like myself, the situation is quite different. In an internalist view also, signs do not intrinsically correspond to objects, independently of how those signs are employed and by whom. But a sign that is actually employed in a particular way by a particular community of users can correspond to particular objects *within the conceptual scheme of those users.* "Objects" do not exist independently of the conceptual schemes. We cut up the world into objects when we introduce one or another scheme of description. Since the objects *and* the signs are alike *internal* to the scheme of description, it is possible to say what matches what.[31]

Clearly Putnam does not presume to reject the everyday, commonsense conception of a statement's truth being a matter of its accurate reference to the state or condition of some object or objects. What Putnam criticizes is the "externalist's" interpretation of propositional truth as a relation of a statement to objects in themselves, to objects that have their being independently of our conceptual frameworks. In Putnam's view, the objects to which our utterances refer are always objects within some human perspective. To grasp Putnam's meaning, consider the ornithological thesis, still causing some degree of social and political unrest today, that "northern spotted owls are declining in the old-growth forests of the Pacific northwest and ought to be protected." The error of the externalist rendering of this thesis, a Putnamian would say, would be that it posits the existence of "owls

31. Ibid., 52.

in themselves." The externalist would say that it is the owls in themselves, which do not depend on any human conceptualization for their being, that are the proper objects of the ornithological thesis. Now, according to Putnam, the key problem with the externalist's account here is that, to speak of any individuals or events, we cannot help but view them through our conceptual structures, making use of those concepts that allow us to think of owls, declining populations, being northern, being spotted rather than great-horned, and so on. Unless we make these sorts of interpretative moves and rely on concepts that allow us to distinguish, identify, attribute, and so on, we cannot even think of owls, let alone of a certain subspecies of owls whose numbers are diminishing. The fact that we cannot bypass our conceptual schemes and directly grasp the metaphysical essence of "northern spotted owl" has, of course, nothing to do in particular with ornithological as distinct from other kinds of discourse. All human discourse about objects of any kind is situated in our complex worlds constructed through our conceptualizations. To be an object of any kind is thus to be an object in a world of human interpretation. Indeed, even to describe something as an object is to apply certain concepts to it, concepts that render it accessible to our apprehension. An object apart from all concepts is unintelligible to us since, as Putnam puts it, "objects do not exist independently of our conceptual schemes," so we must reject the externalist's idea of objects as they are in and of themselves as absurd. Since the very notion of a world of such objects is incoherent, the traditional, metaphysical conception of truth as correspondence with this world must also be abandoned as incoherent. Putnam's fundamental quarrel with the traditional metaphysicians as evidenced in these passages leads to the conclusion not, strictly speaking, that the world in itself does not exist, but that the idea of the world in itself is conceptually incoherent.[32]

32. In more recent essays, Putnam has sought to distance himself from relativistic implications of the rejection of metaphysical realism and to reconcile his position with our commonsense notions of a world existing independently of our conceptual manufacturing of it. In his essay "Craving for Objectivity," Putnam accuses Kuhn of falling into the incoherence of Protagorean perspectivism (see *Realism with a Human Face* [Cambridge, MA: Harvard University Press, 1990], 120–31). Putnam makes similar moves in opposition to Rortyean relativism in his essay "Realism with a Human Face" (ibid., 3–29). In the latter essay, it is unclear to me whether Putnam would object to the sort of dialectical metaphysics found—with major differences, no doubt—in both Pascal and Aristotle. What Putnam attacks is something he calls realism with a "Big R"—namely, a realism that insists on some narrow and fixed picture of truth and reality. Realism with a "Big R" insists on taking up the "view from nowhere" in which one envisions a finite set of true descriptions of an independent set of facts. It is unclear, however, just which philosophers in the history of metaphysics really espouse such a dubious view. For two insightful critiques of Putnam's original and revised versions of antirealism, see Robert Tad Lehe, "Realism and Reality," *The Journal of Philosophical Research* 23 (1998): 219–37, and Nicholas Wolterstorff, "Are Concept-Users World-Makers?" in *Metaphysics*, ed. J. E. Tomberlin, Philosophical Perspectives 1 (Atascadero, CA: Ridgeview, 1987), 233–67.

Any thorough analysis of the kind of antirealism espoused by Putnam in "Two Philosophical Perspectives" would certainly need to trace its historical roots to the transcendental idealism of Kant through the antimetaphysical arguments of Martin Heidegger and Ludwig Wittgenstein. Like Kant, Putnam stresses the role of the human subject in constructing an organizational framework within which the objects we experience can be known by us. Yet, quite obviously, Putnam departs from the Kantian position in his more radical critique of traditional metaphysics. Whereas Kant still insists on our need to think about realities independently of the structures of human experience, Putnam goes further and rejects as unintelligible the very idea of realities outside human interpretive frameworks. Interestingly enough, at one point Putnam concedes to Kant our apparent need to posit the world "out there." But, as Putnam remarks, the existence of a natural need to posit such a realm, if indeed there is such a need, would not obviate the fact that all our efforts to satisfy it lead us to absurdity. So, Putnam observes, "perhaps Kant is right: perhaps we can't help thinking that there is somehow a mind-independent 'ground' for our experience even if attempts to talk about it lead at once to nonsense."[33] What Putnam proposes, then, might well be termed "Kantianism reduced to appearances," as a way of indicating both its indebtedness to Kant and its more extreme disagreement with pre-Kantian metaphysics. No doubt much more ought to be said about the Kantian influence on Putnam's antirealism. At the same time, it is not really my concern to work out a plausible, detailed account of the historical roots out of which this antirealist view emerges. My interest is rather with the implications of such an antimetaphysical outlook, currently quite influential, for our study of Pascal's diagnosis of the human condition. More specifically, my aim is to call into question the merits of Putnam's lucidly argued case for the kind of antirealism fundamental to mainstream postmodernism. I shall argue that Putnamian antirealism suffers from a serious fallacy, and that exposing this fallacy in the context of a critical examination of Pascal's thought can help us to appreciate both the defective nature of mainstream postmodernism and the force of Pascal's metaphysical diagnosis of the human paradox.

The "fallacy of antirealism" is inherent in the following antirealist argument:

1. Humans can neither perceive nor think of a being or object without apprehending this being or object within a conceptual world or conceptual matrix of meaning.

33. Putnam, *Reason, Truth and History*, 62.

2. Because our thinking and perceiving of a given being entails our apprehending it as a being within such a complex network or matrix of meaning, we never simply think of or perceive any being as a pure object or as some being in and of itself apart from a world of meaning that provides the context of intelligibility for our apprehending it as "this sort of object."

3. Since we cannot think of or perceive any being except as a being in a world of meaning, as an object within a given, humanly constituted conceptual scheme, it makes no sense to speak of a being existing apart from our conceptual schemes or to talk of a world of objects "as it is in itself" apart from our conceptual schemes. It is absurd to think or talk about the world "as it really is," as if such a world existed independently of human interpretation. Thus for any object or thing, "to be" is "to be an object within a human interpretative world of meaning."

4. Since the traditional metaphysical theory of truth holds truth to be a correspondence between the world as it really is, in and of itself, and what we say about this world, the traditional metaphysical theory of truth must also be rejected as nonsense.

The crux of this logic of antirealism, as I have noted above, lies with the theory of the meaning of being—of what it means to be an object or entity—articulated in the third premise. According to the antirealist's logic, we must reject the traditional metaphysical theory of truth as correspondence because the conception of reality on which it is based is simply incoherent. In order of logical priority, the theory of being in this argument lays the initial groundwork, and the rejection of the correspondence theory then follows by logical necessity.

Putnam is not the first antimetaphysical thinker to espouse this line of reasoning. Basically the very same fallacy of antirealism can be found in the early, highly influential work of Thomas Kuhn, *The Structure of Scientific Revolutions*. In his 1969 "Postscript" to this work Kuhn offers the following reflection on the meaning of progress in scientific inquiry:

> Compared to the notion of progress most prevalent among both philosophers of science and laymen, however, this position lacks an essential element. A scientific theory is usually felt to be better than its predecessors not only in the sense that it is a better instrument for discovering and solving puzzles but also because it is somehow a better representation of what nature is really like. One often hears that successive theories grow ever closer to, or approximate more and more closely to, the truth. Apparently generalizations like that refer not to the puzzle-solutions and the concrete predictions derived from a theory but rather to its ontology, to the match, that is, between the entities with which the theory populates nature and what is "really there."

Perhaps there is some other way of salvaging the notion of "truth" for application to the whole theories, but this one will not do. There is, I think, no theory-independent way to reconstruct phrases like "really there"; the notion of a match between the ontology of a theory and its "real" counterpart in nature now seems to me illusive in principle. Besides, as a historian, I am impressed with the implausibility of the view. I do not doubt, for example, that Newton's mechanics improves on Aristotle's and Einstein's improves on Newton's as instruments for puzzle-solving. But I can see in their succession no coherent direction of ontological development. On the contrary, in some important respects, though by no means in all, Einstein's general theory of relativity is closer to Aristotle's than either of them is to Newton's. Though the temptation to describe that position as relativistic is understandable, the description seems to me wrong. Conversely, if the position be relativism, I cannot see that the relativist loses anything needed to account for the nature and development of the sciences.[34]

According to Kuhn, we should no longer seek to characterize the nature of scientific progress in traditional terms of apprehending the world as it really is. In his concise way, Kuhn presents what are essentially steps 3 and 4 of the logic of antirealism outlined above. As with Putnam, Kuhn clearly infers step 4 ("the notion of a match between the ontology of a theory and its 'real' counterpart in nature now seems to me illusive in principle") from step 3 ("there is . . . no theory-independent way to reconstruct phrases like 'really there'"). Now Kuhn no more wishes to throw out the idea of scientific progress than Putnam wishes to get rid of the everyday notion of speaking truthfully about things we experience. Kuhn instead proposes to replace the now outmoded or outré metaphysical conception of truth with a more pragmatic standard of success in discovering and solving puzzles.

Putnam and Kuhn concur in rejecting what they understand to be the paradigmatic, metaphysical account of truth. Further, both do so for the same basic reason that the very idea of the world as it really is—of the world existing apart from our theories and our conceptual modes of apprehension—is, as they see it, without intelligible meaning. In this way, Kuhn and Putnam espouse what is for all intents and purposes the same "logic of antirealism." If their argument succeeds, then certainly Pascal's own diagnosis of the human heart suffers a serious blow. If there is no meaningful way to make sense of the idea of a world really out there, how can it be reasonable for humans to turn to a God who really is "out there"? How can this *metanoia* be reasonable if, as Pascal recommends, it springs from our self-awareness as beings unable to attain knowledge of the way things really are and unable to achieve union with a good that alone will fulfill our real nature?

34. Thomas S. Kuhn, *The Structure of Scientific Revolutions* (Chicago: University of Chicago Press, 1962), 206–7.

It might be noticed at this point that I have not dealt specifically and in detail with any contemporary theologians who have embraced the antimetaphysical stance of antirealism and have called for a radical rethinking of traditional theistic beliefs concerning the nature and existence of God. I have not done so because such theological positions tend to appropriate the arguments against realism found originally among philosophers. As I am primarily interested here in the core reasoning behind the antirealist agenda, I have chosen to focus on the clearest articulation of that reasoning I have found.

Two recent theological efforts to purify theistic discourse of "outdated" realist presuppositions are Gordon D. Kaufman's *An Essay on Theological Method* and Joseph Runzo's *Reason, Relativism, and God*.[35] Both theologians echo the "fallacy of antirealism" of the contemporary antirealism rigorously articulated by Putnam (and less rigorously, but more dramatically, formulated by Nietzsche). So, Runzo writes, "conceptual relativism is not just the view that truth is conceptual-schema-relative. Rather, the conceptual relativist more fundamentally argues that since reality is itself conceptual-schema-relative and true statements are about reality, the irreducible plurality of adequate and consistent, but mutually incompatible conceptual schemes, leads to a plurality of truths."[36] A similar suspicion regarding the traditional realist's conception of a reality "out there" to which our assertions correspond is voiced by Kaufman as follows:

> The question of whether theological claims are *true*, and if so in what respects, has not been straight-forwardly addressed in this essay. This is because this question, as usually understood, presupposes what I have called the "perceptual model of reality," where the correspondence of our ideas with the reality "out there" is a proper issue. It is appropriate to raise the question of truth in this form with regard to every object or quality in the world, for here we are concerned with the way in which one item in our conceptual scheme relates to and represents one item in what we call (also in our conceptual scheme) experience or the world. But where it is the *world-itself* we are trying to conceive, the whole within which everything falls—including not only all facts but also our symbols—there is nothing outside our conception against which we can see whether it corresponds: just as every thing is within the world, so also everything must be conceived as included within the conception of the world. With this conception, then, criteria of correspondence cannot be applied: only criteria of coherence and pragmatic usefulness to human life are relevant and applicable. If these considerations hold for the concept of the world, how much more must they apply to the concept of God, built up as it is through even more elaborate imaginative constructive moves.[37]

35. Gordon D. Kaufman, *An Essay on Theological Method*, rev. ed. (Decatur, GA: Scholars Press, 1979); and Joseph Runzo, *Reason, Relativism, and God* (New York: St. Martin's Press, 1986).

36. Runzo, *Reason, Relativism, and God*, 62.

37. Kaufman, *Essay on Theological Method*, 71.

At the heart of Kaufman's analysis here is the move central to the "logic of antirealism," that in referring to reality, we are referring only to objects that exist within some constructed, human, conceptual world. If true, the consequences of such a thesis for theistic discourse are obvious: it no longer makes sense to think of God as "out there," living independently of human experience and interpretation.

The antirealist logic has also emerged in recent works of literary criticism. In his essay "Change," Stanley Fish echoes the same basic antirealist suspicion regarding traditional ideas of reality and truth.[38] Fish strikes at the traditional realist outlook as follows: "The problem [of accounting for the meaning of change] arises only when one thinks that by 'what really happened' is meant 'what really happened after all the competing descriptions have been discounted or set aside?' But it's hard even to give that question a sense, since the fact of what happened, like any other fact, can only be said to exist relative to some conceptualization or description."[39] One ought to wonder here if Fish is not speaking about how the world really is when he confidently declares that *all* facts are relative to some conceptual scheme. As I shall argue, such varieties of the basic reasoning of the "logic of antirealism" confuse the conditions of our thinking with those of the nature of being; the logic of antirealism confuses the limits of our human apprehension with the character of things existing outside us in the "real world." Texts certainly do not have a single meaning "eternally embedded" within them, but one can still misinterpret what a text really means. In this respect, texts bear a close resemblance to human nature and to God.

It will be instructive at this point to return to the debate over metaphysical realism and to clarify how Putnam's antirealist point of view and Edwards's postmodernist stance differ in important respects not only from Pascal's view but from the Humean's and Pyrrhonian's as well. Pyrrhonists recommend the way of doubt as a remedy for the distress of ceaseless metaphysical speculation. Since the philosophical quest for knowledge of reality leads only to aporia and uncertainty, the skeptic proposes as a cure the suspension of judgment on all nonevident matters. Unlike contemporary antirealists, Pyrrhonists do not hold that the basic conception of a reality beyond what appears to us is absurd. On the contrary, the traditional road to Pyrrhonian *ataraxia*, to that peace of mind consequent on the abandonment of the metaphysical project, is that of metaphysical inquiry. The self-discovery of the Pyrrhonist happens after one has engaged sincerely and rigorously in the practice of seeking the nature of reality. Pyrrhonian conversion, so to speak, presupposes that one has strained and suffered as a metaphysical pilgrim.

38. Stanley Fish, "Change," in *Doing What Comes Naturally* (Durham, NC: Duke University Press, 1989), 141–60.

39. Ibid., 158.

Only after traveling such a tortuous path can the Pyrrhonist genuinely arrive at his or her destination and find tranquility. Superficially, the Pyrrhonist's abandonment of metaphysics might seem to be of a piece with the anti-metaphysical program of the antirealists. Yet, unlike these contemporary antimetaphysicians, the classic Pyrrhonist never abandons the notion of a nonevident reality. Indeed, for the Pyrrhonist the skeptical resolve to suspend judgment follows on the recognition of our inability to know, either through reason or the senses, the nature of what is nonevident, of what is really out there. Hence it is built into the very program of Pyrrhonian self-discovery that it is meaningful to refer to and inquire into the nature of what really is. The conversion to Pyrrhonian *ataraxia* comes not with the insight that the idea of such a reality is nonsense but with the hard-won insight that no human account of this reality succeeds any better than its rivals in giving us knowledge of what it is. The Pyrrhonist's road to enlightenment, in other words, presupposes as meaningful the crucial idea that proponents of antirealism condemn as nonsense.

Undoubtedly, both Hume and Pascal are in one important respect even further from the antirealist outlook: although they disagree deeply on the question of faith, both thinkers concur in rejecting as unnatural the Pyrrhonist's call to suspend belief on all matters pertaining to nonevident realities. Hume argues in the first *Enquiry* that we cannot help but make judgments about causal powers, the regularity of the universe, and the existence of external objects. In a similar way, Pascal contends that we hold a number of intuitions about space, motion, and our own real state of wakefulness that defy the Pyrrhonist's injunction to suspend judgment. Of the three, the Pyrrhonian position is probably the closest to that of the antirealists who endorse the fallacy of antirealism. Yet unlike Hume, Pascal, and the Pyrrhonists, only the antirealists contend that we cannot meaningfully think of what exists outside our conceptual frameworks.

It is quite evident, then, that the antirealist offers a unique and radical form of skepticism. The real merits of this radical outlook are far from evident, however. As I have indicated, one serious problem with the antirealist's position is that inherent in the logic of antirealism is the "antirealist fallacy." To see just where the fallacy lies, we need to look carefully at step 3 of the argument: "since we cannot think of any object except from within a given, humanly constituted conceptual scheme, it makes no sense to speak of an object existing apart from our conceptual schemes or of a world as it is in itself apart from our conceptual schemes." Basically, this premise has two parts. The first asserts that we cannot think of any object without situating it within some conceptual scheme. We cannot think of or perceive an object without applying some concepts to it since our conceptual schemes provide the context within which that object has intelligible meaning for us. As a claim about human cognition, this part of the premise seems entirely justified. How indeed, we might ask, can we perceive or think of an object as something without conceptualizing it?

Consider the following example. At this moment, I pause from writing and gaze outside my living room window, noting the striking, brilliant red autumnal foliage of a dogwood. In looking at the tree, I understand what I perceive as a tree of a particular species at a certain time of year. One way to describe this act of perception is to say that I bring to my perceptual experience a set of concepts. Another would be to say that the object appears to me not as an isolated, bare "this," but as something in a world of concepts, as a thing that appears as something of a particular sort. Clearly the tree appears differently depending on the world of meaning in which it resides. Thus, for example, an experienced forester would no doubt apprehend the dogwood within a more sophisticated silvicultural "world" than does the ordinary suburban commuter. A child might doubt the tree's sturdiness for climbing; for the child the being of the tree relates to its suitability for a climbing adventure. A natural artist would very likely see the same tree with a different set of concepts or, if you will, within a different overall world or context of meaning. A woodworker might categorize the tree in terms of the grain of its wood. A landowner I once knew collected dogwood berries, selling them to nurseries to help pay her property taxes; for her the being of a dogwood was linked to its fertility. While all these individuals apprehend the same kind of tree, how they encounter that tree varies as a function of the different ways in which they relate to it. What they and all properly functioning human perceivers and thinkers share in are the basic, natural, interpretative practices necessary for apprehending particular objects as intelligible within a complex and many-layered world of meaning. An object on its own apart from all concepts and isolated from any context is neither thinkable nor perceivable.

The antirealist is right, then, to emphasize the essential role our concepts play in our cognitive apprehension of objects. It is true that we cannot think or speak of objects without situating them in some conceptual framework or other. From this feature of human cognition, the antirealist introduces the second part of the antirealist premise by drawing the conclusion that the very notion of a reality outside all our conceptual schemes is nonsense. Now one line of objection to the antirealist's conclusion might proceed from the stance of everyday, common sense. As Hume observes, it is natural for people to regard the objects of perception as having existence independent of the mind. Although we must conceptualize our perceptual experiences, what we take to be the objects of such experience are real things existing apart from our perceiving them. A commonsense response to the antirealist's contention that it makes no sense to speak or think of objects apart from our conceptual schemes might be that it must make sense because we do it all the time. Can it really be impossible for people with doctorates in critical theory to do what children and normal adults do all the time? Why do these intellectuals deny as meaningless what persons in common life seem to have no trouble understanding?

Taken by itself, this commonsense retort to the antirealist might strike us as missing the point. Is it not unavoidable that some of our commonsense beliefs will have to be rejected when we subject human experience to the critical scrutiny of philosophical reflection? Is it not the case that part of leading the examined life will inevitably involve the loss of some of our traditional beliefs and commonsense notions? Is the commonsense belief in the existence of real objects whose being does not depend on our perceiving them or on our conceptual schemes not just one of these unreasonable elements of our unreflective consciousness? The answer to these questions is clearly "no." Whether we should reject a commonsense belief depends at least on two things: first, on how fundamental such a belief is to our human nature; and, second, of course, on the cogency of the philosophical argument for rejecting it. If we view the nature of philosophical criticism from a Socratic perspective, we realize that the purpose of self-examination is to make coherent sense of our lives, in part by formulating specific first principles that explain our basic intuitions and enable us to defend those beliefs we honestly hold as true. Philosophical theories that violate one or more of our core beliefs can reasonably be looked on as suspect. But ultimately, what we must look for is a reasonable refutation of such theories. Honesty in dialectical thinking requires that we acknowledge perplexity when it confronts us. The commitment to rationality in dialectical thinking requires us to seek a resolution.

In the case of the antirealist's opposition to common sense, the resolution lies in noting that the second part of the third premise above just does not logically follow from the first. It is one thing to claim that we cannot talk about, think of, or perceive objects apart from our conceptual frameworks; it is quite another to say that we cannot talk about, think of, or perceive objects as realities that do have their own existence and natures independently of our conceptual worlds. The key problem with the antirealist's argument lies, I think, with the sort of assertion typically made, to the effect that "we cannot speak of objects except from the perspective of some conceptual scheme." The problem with this claim is that it is ambiguous. If it is taken as a claim about how we can think of objects, it seems reasonable. If it is understood, instead, as a claim about what we can think about—namely, objects existing apart from us—then it is not at all reasonable. Once we clearly differentiate between these two very dissimilar renderings of the same statement, we can grasp both why the antirealist's third premise *seems* right but why *in fact* it clearly is not. Note that the following two assertions might appear to be identical in meaning, but are not:

1. Unless we rely on some humanly constructed, conceptual scheme, we are unable to think of or in any way apprehend any being.

    2. We are unable to think of or in any way apprehend any being except as
       a being within some humanly constructed, conceptual scheme.

Essentially, I believe that the antirealist's basic logic commits the fallacy of
assuming that if one grants the truth of 1 then one is logically compelled to
affirm the truth of 2. But in fact 1 neither means the same thing as nor even
logically entails the truth of 2. In fact, 1 and 2 are radically different claims,
though it is easy to confuse them and regard them as equivalent. At the heart
of this confusion is a crucial fallacy, "the fallacy of antirealism." This fallacy
may be uncovered in the following way: the antirealist presumes that if one
grants the truth of the following proposition,

    1. Unless we rely on some humanly constructed, conceptual scheme, we
       are unable to think of or in any way apprehend any being,

then one is logically compelled to grant that the following is true as well:

    2. We are unable to think of or in any way apprehend any being except as
       a being within some humanly constructed, conceptual scheme.

As we have seen, this fallacy lurks in the writings of many antirealist discourses. The logic of antirealism fails to recognize the fundamental difference
between these two assertions, even though they in fact make radically different claims about the relationship of self and world. Basically, the antirealist
logic fails to distinguish the fundamental difference between 1, which sets
forth a contextualist thesis about the conditions of human consciousness, a
thesis about *how* we are able to apprehend beings in the world, and 2, which
informs us about the nature of reality, insofar as it stipulates the nature of
the objects we are able to think about. The fundamental confusion inherent
in the fallacy of antirealism is between 1, an epistemological claim about the
situatedness of all human consciousness, and 2, a metaphysical claim about
the nature of the real. Put another way, one can acknowledge that all human
cognition is embedded within a complex matrix of human signs, symbols,
and constructs without succumbing to the much more far-reaching view that
all reality, the totality of being of which we can coherently think, is merely a
human, social construction.

    Consider the following example. Right now I cannot think of my oldest son,
Nathaniel, without relying on a multilayered world of images, associations,
signs, and concepts. If I try to imagine him at college, I conjure up certain
images of him, and of his campus as well, that are themselves embedded
within a rich soil of feelings, memories, and conceptual associations. But do
I believe that his existence depends on the cognitive and emotional world I
reside in as I am now thinking of him? Clearly I ought not to go that far. It is

only my remembering and valuing of him that requires the complex horizon of meaning in which I am able to direct my mind toward his being. I rely on and must reside within a world of meaning in order to think of him, but I would be most deluded to confuse his being as a person of independent and inherent worth with that limited and flawed world of meaning from which I contemplate him. What I am thinking of is a young man, a real one, who is out there often enjoying life without me. Here my mental concepts serve more as the lenses through which I view him than as constituting the being of the object to which I attend. So to clarify the example by introducing another, when I use my Leica binoculars to look at a rare Kirkland's warbler, I certainly do not confuse my experience by thinking that the bird is the same thing as the optics. Similarly, in everyday life we naturally understand that what we perceive, under normal circumstances, exists independently of our act of perceiving it. Just what a warbler is in and of itself I may never know, but it hardly needs my concepts or those of any other merely human observer to migrate south at the approach of winter.

This is not to say that by "reality" we must now mean some unknowable thing-in-itself that exists as a being whose nature can in no way correspond to those signs, symbols, and concepts we rely on to apprehend its being in the world. My point is not that my son, existing independently of my consciousness, must be some "a-conceptual," mystical thing-in-himself whose identity is not bound up with his own real embeddedness in a narrative, social existence set within a rich, multilayered world of significance. Here, indeed, lies a common confusion among antirealists like Rorty about what it means to posit a mind-independent reality. Metaphysical realism merely claims that the real world of living and nonliving beings exists independently of humanly constructed, interpretative perspectives. The metaphysical realism I defend holds, furthermore, that all finite beings have a proper place in an intelligible creation and possess an inherent goodness whether or not a given person, community, or age grasps their true reality and treats them with the reverence they deserve as created beings. In other words, metaphysical realism simply contends that the existence and character of beings in the world are not human social constructions. Both Creator and creation have their inherent natures, and while it may well be the case that mere human thought cannot adequately grasp the fullness and distinctness of any being in the world, it is nevertheless true that we are reasonable to trust that our human minds, created in the image of God, can attain at least a partial comprehension of the nature both of ourselves and of the Creator and creation on which we depend. Reality in itself is not a reality "beyond any conceptual description," but simply a reality whose existence and character is not our own creation. It may well be a common confusion among antirealists to think that a reality "independent of human interpretation" must be a reality "beyond all description and to which none of our words, descriptions, or concepts may apply."

The crux of the problem with the antirealist's third premise is thus one of ambiguity. The claim, properly dissected, that we cannot think of anything apart from some conceptual scheme is both true and false. It is true if we take it to mean that "apart from some conceptual scheme or other, we cannot think of any object." It is false, however, if we mean that "we cannot apprehend or think of any object except as an object within one of our own conceptual schemes." Interestingly enough, the contemporary antirealist is not the first to commit the fallacy of confusing these two very different propositions. Basically the same confusion is evident in one of Bishop Berkeley's classic arguments against Lockean realism. Berkeley seeks to demonstrate that the Lockean conception of mind-independent objects is absurd. He supports his thesis as follows:

> But, say you, surely there is nothing easier than for me to imagine trees, for in-stance, in a park, or books existing in a closet, and nobody by to perceive them. I answer, you may so, there is no difficulty in it; but what is all this, I beseech you, more than framing in your mind certain ideas which you call books and trees, and the same time omitting to frame the idea of anyone that may perceive them? But do not you yourself perceive or think of them all the while? This therefore is nothing to the purpose; it only shews you have the power of imagining or form-ing ideas in your mind: but it doth not shew that you can conceive it possible the objects of your thought may exist without the mind. To make out this, it is necessary that you conceive them existing unconceived or unthought of, what is a manifest repugnancy. When we do our utmost to conceive the existence of external bodies, we are all the while only contemplating our own ideas. But the mind taking no notice of itself, is deluded to think it can and doth conceive bodies existing unthought of or without the mind, though at the same time they are apprehended by or exist in itself. A little attention will discover to anyone the truth and evidence of what is here said, and make it unnecessary to insist on any other proofs against the existence of *material substance*.[40]

The argument here takes the form of what we might call the "Berkeleyan chal-lenge." If in the name of commonsense realism we think Berkeley's opinion—that all material objects are really in the mind—rather odd, Berkeley simply asks us to provide him with a single example of a material object that lies outside the mind. "Try to conceive of an object that does not exist in your mind," Berkeley says to us. "Well," an ornithologically inclined skeptic might reply, "how about some rare penguin sitting on an ice floe in Antarctica no-where near any human perceiver?" But Berkeley is not persuaded, and to help us see why, he asks us to consider if it is not true that this thing we believe to exist outside any mind is in fact being thought by us at this very moment.

---

40. George Berkeley, *Treatise Concerning the Principles of Human Knowledge* in *Berke-ley's Philosophical Writings*, ed. David M. Armstrong (New York: MacMillan, 1965), 69–70, para. 23.

"Your challenge," Berkeley insists, "is to think of a being existing outside of your mind without at the same time thinking of it." Now, of course, we can never do this because every object we try to think of as existing outside any mind is at that very moment being thought of by our minds and thus would appear to exist within our minds. So it seems that it is simply impossible for anyone to win the Berkeleyan challenge, since the only way to win is to think of something without thinking of it! Quite ingeniously, Berkeley subjects us to this exercise of mental frustration in order to dissuade us of our entrenched but confused commonsense opinion that we can and often do think of things existing outside our consciousness.

Berkeley's argument here is as clever as it is confused. It may well be true that the conception I have of some being—say of my youngest son, Sasha, a birder in training—watching a yellow warbler fly south lies in some sense "within" my consciousness. But when I think of Sasha, I am certainly not thinking of my idea of him. The crucial lapse in Berkeley's reasoning is that he fails to acknowledge this phenomenological distinction. In constructing his argument, Berkeley confuses two very different realities—namely, the mind-dependent idea I have of some being, on the one hand, with the real object I in some sense direct or intend my idea to represent, on the other. The various ideas I have or use right now to think about my son's enjoyment of a bird depend on my thinking them; neither my son nor the bird do. Just what exactly using an idea to think of someone or something involves phenomenologically is difficult to say. We do not in any tangible way use an idea the way we use a hammer or a nail. Nevertheless, any plausible phenomenological analysis of conceiving of or perceiving another person or object outside us surely must distinguish our concepts as mental forms from the reality of which we are conscious. Berkeley's argument seems formidable only if we fail to grasp this crucial distinction. As in the case of the antirealist, we should note that it makes all the difference in the world whether we are referring to our thinking of an object or to the object, of which we are thinking, itself. It is true that we cannot think of an object without relying on mental ideas; it is false that anything we think about must itself depend on our mental ideas. Basically, then, Berkeley confuses the conditions of thinking with the conditions of being. As I have argued, this is essentially the same error made in the fallacy of antirealism. In conclusion, we may say that insofar as the antirealist's negation of metaphysics rests on the fallacy of antirealism, it is guilty of committing the "Berkeleyan fallacy."

A defender of antirealism might argue in response that the antirealist's account of conceptual schemes differs substantially from Berkeleyan idealism. For Berkeley, we cannot conceive of objects existing independently of separate, individual minds. Berkeley's idealism is subjective in the sense that he reduces Locke's material universe to a sphere of ideas existing within particular minds. To distinguish private fancies from real objects, Berkeley proposes at one point that we distinguish between true and false ideas—or, perhaps, beliefs about our ideas—in terms of whether they correspond with the ideas in the mind of God.[41] In this way Berkeley falls back on a metaphysical doctrine of correspondence. The apparent world for humans is the sphere of mind-dependent ideas. Not all of these ideas represent reality, however, since we do at times misperceive real objects or simply imagine something to exist that really does not exist. Only those ideas that accord with or resemble the ideas existing in God's mind are veridical. For Berkeley, then, to be is either to be a mind—that is, a finite or infinite mental substance—or to be an idea or set of ideas within some mind. In contrast, the antirealist espouses quite a different notion of conceptual relativity. For Putnam and Kuhn, to be is to be an intelligible object within some communally based conceptual world. Thus it is not just our talk of material objects that is "mind dependent." Rather, all our existential utterances, whether they refer to physical objects, human minds, or even God, are intelligible only within some community of discourse. In contrast to Berkeley, the antirealist's account of conceptual relativity is communal rather than individual. Conceptual schemes for the antirealist are not features of real particular minds so much as individual minds are intelligible to us only within some historically developed, social form of discourse. Furthermore, whereas Berkeley's idealism simply reformulates Lockean realism into a new version of traditional metaphysics, the antirealist's proposal does away altogether with traditional metaphysics. It is hardly appropriate, therefore, to condemn contemporary antirealism by citing a fallacy within Berkeley's very different metaphysical brand of idealism.

The virtue of this counterargument is that it serves to clarify more fully the special character of contemporary antirealism. It is true that the positions of Kuhn and Putnam differ crucially from Berkeley's subjective idealism. But the intent of my original comparison of their antirealist perspective with Berkeley's thought experiment was not to suggest otherwise. What I mean to show is how the same confusion underlies both Berkeley's clever argument and the seemingly persuasive logic of antirealism. Consider, for instance, Putnam's thesis in *Reason, Truth and History*, that we cannot speak of objects except from within some conceptual scheme.[42] At first glance, it seems impossible to argue against this claim: since our speaking about anything involves a complex web of concepts and beliefs, how can we deny the conceptual relativity to which Putnam refers? What I have argued is that we need not deny it at all as long as we avoid confusing our subjects. Of course, we cannot speak or think of anything without relying on those mechanisms and conditions that make speech or thought possible. Admitting all of this in no way puts in jeopardy our basic metaphysical instinct that things exist independently of human thinking. To hold that the conceptual relativity of human thought and speech entails the end of metaphysics is to confuse, as

41. For Berkeley's proposal that correspondence with the mind of God should serve as one criterion for judging whether our ideas are real, see "The Third Dialogue" of the *Three Dialogues between Hylas and Philonus*, in Armstrong, *Berkeley's Philosophical Writings*, 189–225.

42. See Putnam, *Reason, Truth and History*, 49–50.

Berkeley so clearly does, the conditions of human conscious activity with the conditions of being. Even though contemporary antirealism differs markedly from Berkeleyan metaphysics, both overlook the critical difference between thinking and being. In this respect, in particular, it is useful and appropriate to compare their otherwise very dissimilar positions.

The antirealist's stance is especially relevant to our study of Pascal for two reasons. If its rejection of metaphysics is rationally justified, Pascal's account of the rationality of Christian faith faces an insuperable dialectical refutation. For Pascal, faith in Christ makes sense to us once we recognize our own inability to achieve the ultimate good we need to become complete persons. Yet if the very idea of a transcendent Good is incoherent, and if the only coherent goods available to us are those that depend on our conceptual worlds, then our fundamental human desire, as Pascal sees it, can never be satisfied. In fact, it is hard to say whether it even makes sense to speak of such a desire, given that what it posits for an object is absurd. Either Pascal has simply misdescribed the character of this desire, and there is no such yearning in the human heart, or the human heart is destined to seek the impossible and any promise of fulfillment, such as is found in the Christian gospel, is irrational. Yet if my analysis of the fallacy of antirealism is cogent, the antirealist's challenge fails, at least when it rests on the fallacy of antirealism, because its foundation is itself illogical.

Let us return here to the radical postmodernist, who, as antirealist, finds the very idea of a world out there, outside of or transcendent over lived human experience, to be absurd and unthinkable. For postmodernists such as Derrida, the "metaphysics of presence," the metaphysics of objective, mind-independent realities, is an illusion, for to talk or conceive of objects or realities is necessarily to refer to things that can be spoken of only within some conceptual scheme or other. We cannot coherently think of or converse about what is beyond the boundaries of our concepts, since to talk of or think about any being, per se, or anything having a nature, is to operate within a conceptual context of human making. Thus it follows, for the postmodernist, that all philosophical and religious traditions rooted in a metaphysical vision of human life are illegitimate. According to such "radical" or "antirealist" postmodernists, while the failure of the Cartesian project undermines the essential project of modern philosophy, the incoherence of the very idea of the world "out there" reveals the emptiness of the whole Western tradition of metaphysical inquiry. From such a postmodern stance, the failure of modern foundationalism is merely an offshoot of the doomed enterprise of traditional philosophy. To be postmodern in this radical sense is to declare the end of philosophy as the Western tradition has known it.

Yet, as I have argued, antirealist postmodernism confuses such matters as how we know what we know and how imperfection and ambiguity haunt all that we claim to know in the matters of the reality of self, other, and cosmos with which traditional philosophy and religion concerns itself. My ultimate aim in addressing the antirealist's challenge to Pascal's thought is to embark on something more positive than simply to disarm this challenge. Indeed, our consideration of antirealism helps us to appreciate more clearly four of the strengths of Pascal's understanding of the human condition. First, in recognizing our natural disposition to form beliefs about how things really are, Pascal's philosophy accords better with our everyday commonsense outlook than does that of the antirealist. Second, in comparison with the antirealist, Pascal provides us a much better justification for engaging in moral inquiry. In a similar vein, I want to argue, third, that Pascal's metaphysical conception of human nature gives us today a much better reason for heeding the Socratic call to lead the examined life. Finally, and most decisively, I will argue that Pascal's Christian, fallibilist realism provides us with a much more satisfactory account of human *eros*. By arguing all four points, I hope at least to sketch the outlines for a positive dialectical defense of Pascal's thought. Taken together, the force of my arguments in defense of Pascal lead us to the conclusion that Pascal's vision of the human self finally puts us in touch with our nature as erotic beings in a way that radical postmodernism utterly fails to do.

Postmodernism as a Failure of Eros

All I have is a voice
To undo the folded lie,
The romantic lie in the brain
Of the sensual man-in-the-street
And the lie of Authority
Whose buildings grope the sky:
There is no such thing as the State
And no one exists alone;
Hunger allows no choice
To the citizen or the police;
We must love one another or die.

Defenseless under the night
Our world in stupor lies;
Yet, dotted everywhere,
Ironic points of light
Flash out wherever the Just
Exchange their messages:
May I, composed like them
Of Eros and of dust,
Beleaguered by the same
Negation and despair,
Show an affirming flame.[43]

43. Auden, "September 1, 1939," stanzas 8 and 9, 317–18.

I will argue now that postmodernism manifests a profound failure of erotic sensitivity. Given its first three failures, postmodernism can at best offer only a desolate and infirm account of what it means to love beauty, whether in another person, in creation, or in God's very person. Put rather colorfully, as a political movement, mainstream, secular postmodernism responds to what is in fact the world's desperate plea for romance in the presence of what is enduringly beautiful and merciful with nothing more romantic and sustainable than a titillating and adolescent urge to go to bed alone. Tragically, in short-circuiting our erotic nature, postmodernism liberates us not into a life of community in the presence of the beauty for which we really yearn, but into a self-congratulatory life of adolescent loneliness and self-manipulation.

Yet the postmodernist stance poses a powerful challenge to the epistemology of rational love I have been defending in this inquiry. Like Pascal and Hume, these contemporary antirealists reject the Enlightenment ideal of establishing absolute foundations for metaphysical beliefs. In a manner sharply opposed to both of these "mitigated skeptics," the radical postmodernists reject the whole project and aspiration of metaphysical thinking; they do so by rejecting as nonsense the very idea of a nonevident reality—of a world, that is, that exists independently of human forms of experience. The postmodernist's radical skepticism merits our attention not only because it is currently in vogue among the intelligentsia, but, more importantly, because it offers a serious challenge to philosophy in general and to Pascal's Christian apologia for the human paradox in particular. The postmodern demystification of metaphysics itself requires critical unmasking. In what follows I wish to explore further the basic question of whether the postmodern rejection of metaphysical realism, of the view that reality exists in and of itself, independently of our human concepts and cognitive constructs is valid. It is with this rejection that radical postmodernism most seriously threatens the Pascalian understanding of human life; the postmodern suspicion of transcendent or objective authority and the reduction of argument to power or self-expression are attitudes and practices that derive much of their plausibility from the posture of antirealism characteristic of radical postmodernism.[44]

44. But, one might ask, "Is the doctrine of antirealism really an *essential* feature of any position deserving of the title 'radical postmodernism'?" The prudent reply to this question might seem to be negative, simply on the grounds that no one thesis or doctrine in any one specific form is probably essential to all variants of postmodernism. Rorty, for example, espouses a radical postmodern outlook on the nature of truth, and yet it is unclear that Rorty consistently holds that it makes no sense to talk about a reality outside human interpretive frameworks (see *Philosophy and the Mirror of Nature*). Rorty's thesis that truth is nothing more than "what our peers will . . . let us get away with saying," seems in Rorty's overall outlook sometimes to be rooted not so much in an explicit antirealist's stance as in a pragmatic skepticism and suspicion about being able to determine which metaphysical claims are ultimately true. At times, in other words, Rorty seems to give up on objective truth simply on the grounds that we have no way of knowing, so at least he thinks, when our interpretations of reality actually do correspond with

A crucial detail in Pascal's portrait of human existence—our inability to satisfy our natural longing for knowledge of ourselves and for a good that can truly fulfill us—presupposes the existence of objective, nonevident realities, especially of an objective, human nature, and of a true good that will render that nature whole. Both realities, for Pascal, have a nature independently of what any given person or community thinks about them and entail the existence of a transcendent reality on which we utterly depend. The Reality that grounds our being does not depend on our concepts or our thoughts about him. God's independence from the realm of finite human artifice is essential to Pascal's whole account of the human paradox. In Pascal's portrayal of the nature of our plight, to be self-unified we need to be in communion with a divine love that is essentially unconditional and thus not dependent on our paltry creations or tentative efforts of belief. But are Pascal's diagnosis and cure just another species of metaphysical nonsense? What can be said for Pascal's metaphysical outlook in the face of the radical postmodern assault on reality and truth?

For both Hume and Pascal, philosophical theories of human nature must acknowledge our natural tendency to form beliefs about what really exists independently of human consciousness. According to Hume, true philosophy must accept the status and authority of these beliefs as evidence of the limited power of reason in human life. In a similar way, Pascal accounts for our basic beliefs about space, time, and number as intuitions of the heart. Both thinkers also agree to a limited extent on why modern philosophers in particular need to recognize the nonrational source of these beliefs. Having its roots in the fertile soil of Cartesian and Lockean rationalism, modern philosophy tends to exaggerate the authority of reason in human life. Both Pascal and Hume concur that our natural practice of forming beliefs about real objects outside us should serve as an antidote to the intellectual pride of rationalist philosophers. Seeing how our human nature does not always bow to the demands of "reason alone" promotes philosophical humility.

---

the world outside human thought. And yet without the support of an explicit antirealist argument, Rorty's views seem especially vulnerable to the kind of objections raised by Plantinga in his *Warranted Christian Belief* (429–36). The fact that we cannot know for sure whether our interpretations accord with reality in no way entails that we have no criteria of any kind for defending some accounts of reality as better than others. Plantinga finally accuses antirealist postmodernists as lacking in courage: all attempts at grasping how the world really is are risky; yet the seriousness of human life and suffering compel us to do our best. My own view is that without the support of an antirealist conception of self and world, the typical radical claims associated with radical postmodernism, such as Rorty's denial that truth involves more than conventional agreement, are for most of us just hard to take seriously, because they do not take the problems confronting human existence seriously enough, and they appear to be self-refuting. On the contrary, if antirealism were in fact a compelling outlook, then the rejection of objective truth in radical postmodernists like Rorty would be much more formidable. My contention, then, is that without its "hermeneutics of suspicion toward truth," postmodernism turns out to be more of a fashion than a philosophy.

As I noted previously, not every philosophical outlook historically has agreed on this need to take our commonsense beliefs very seriously. Whether a philosophical perspective should take commonsense beliefs seriously depends, in part, on the conception of the nature of philosophy internal to it. Those philosophies cast in a Cartesian mold propose to build a philosophical system on a set of undeniable foundations. If these foundations are indeed the certain starting points their proponents claim they are, then there probably is no good reason to worry about how one's conclusions accord with everyday, untutored common sense. But as many thinkers have come to believe, there seems little hope of finding such secure foundations, especially when the object of our inquiry is our own existence. On a Socratic dialectical account, the purpose of philosophical self-examination is to do the best we can to understand our lives and render our beliefs, feelings, and actions as coherent as possible. Since our commonsense beliefs constitute a major part of the self of which we are trying to make sense, it is necessary to treat these beliefs as innocent until proven guilty.

One way to express my criticism of the antirealists is to say that their denial of the commonsense belief in the existence of real objects outside human consciousness turns out to be inconsistent with their overall project. As both Pascal and Hume recognize, inherent in the belief structure of healthy humans is a natural and basic belief in the independent existence of objects beyond our subjective perceptions. In ordinary life, we naturally take the things we perceive, such as trees and rivers and the species that depend on them, not to depend on our minds for their being. If the antirealists understood their own philosophical project to involve luminously clear, Cartesian foundations, they might have a good excuse for promoting a thesis that so radically violates our common sense. But, of course, one of the central claims of the antirealists is that such foundations simply do not exist. The antirealist strives to purify philosophy of its hopeless Cartesian pretensions, to bring philosophical theorizing down to a human level, and, more specifically, to clarify how culture and historical context shape our philosophical and scientific theories. Ironically, however, if humans naturally and unavoidably do think of objects existing outside human consciousness, the antirealist only produces a new form of abstract philosophical theorizing that alienates us from our human nature. Rather than bring philosophy down to a human level, and reconcile our theoretical aspirations with our human limits, the antirealists would force us to confront a tragic opposition between our human experience and the dictates of abstract self-reflection. What makes this tragic conflict so ironic is that the ambition of the antirealist is to humble the impulse of human theorizing by making it acknowledge its dependence on human traditions and practices. But if Pascal and Hume are correct, one enduring feature of our everyday human traditions and practices is that we believe in the very way that the antirealist condemns as nonsense. In proceeding in this way, the antirealists fail to carry out their basic project of situating theory in the context of human life. One serious defect with antirealism is that it turns out to be just another dislocated theoretical stance that fails to accord with human experience; thus whatever its merits, it ultimately subverts itself by promoting an outlook deeply at odds with some of our most basic human beliefs and practices.

To return to Rorty, then, let us note how his postmodern expression of antirealism is only a counterfeit form of pragmatism. If the aim of pragmatism is to return philosophy to the interests and concerns of everyday, practical life, then what we see in Rorty is nothing of the sort. Rortyean pragmatism delivers only a distorted theoretical fantasy of practical life. In this respect, Rortyean postmodernism is just another expression of modernity's desire to re-create a new humanity rather than acknowledge the limitations that nature places on our philosophizing. Ironically, in a way reminiscent of Descartes's quest for final certainty, postmodernism's poetics of aversion is an exercise in intellectual escapism: in a world of real starvation, real cruelty, real violence, and real human limitation, the postmodernist retires to the safety and security of intellectual narcissism and fantasy.

As does Hume, Pascal provides us with a philosophy of human limitation and believing that more genuinely accords with our human nature. Indeed, one way to defend the rationality of Pascal's account of human nature is to show how it avoids the extremes of antirealism on the one hand, and Cartesian claims to absolute knowledge on the other. As Pascal remarks, an essential aspect of our human finitude is that we possess a sense of ultimate truth and yet have no natural rational ability to know this truth with certainty. So, Pascal states:

> *Instinct, reason.* We have an incapacity for proving anything which no amount of dogmatism can overcome.
> We have an idea of truth which no amount of skepticism can overcome.[45]

No amount of skepticism can undermine our belief in ultimate truth for Pascal, because our belief in objective truth, our belief that the nature of things does not depend on our thinking, is one of the basic intuitions of the heart. Since this belief is basic to our human nature, its rationality does not depend on our supporting it with rational proof. To try to prove this belief would be foolish, since the project of deducing a conclusion already presupposes the distinction between reality and appearance and between truth and falsity. Yet unlike Descartes, Pascal holds out little hope for our grasping this truth with unwavering certainty. If we are then to engage in philosophy within our limits as humans, we must deny neither our idea of truth nor our rational inability to be certain of just what the truth is. If we grant that the idea of truth does

45. Pascal, *Pensées*, frg. 406.

indeed lie at the core of our being as human agents and thinkers, and that we cannot honestly put our belief in truth aside, we must conclude that, at least in this respect, Pascal's analysis of human thought is rationally superior to that of the antirealists. In contrast to Pascal, the antirealist's project is irrational insofar as it proposes an account of what we mean by "reality" that we as humans cannot honestly embrace.

Pascal's insistence on our possessing an idea of truth leads to my second point concerning the relative superiority of Pascal's thought. My second basic point is that the idea of truth that Pascal relies on makes a significant difference in moral reflection. If we suppose that there are objective moral principles concerning human existence, and, in particular, that there is an objective *telos* for human nature, then engaging in moral self-examination becomes a deeply valuable activity. If there is an objective human nature, we should examine our moral beliefs for at least one reason: we inevitably live with the uncertainty that our moral beliefs accord with who we really are. Since we cannot attain moral certainty, we can never be absolutely assured that our actions are beneficial rather than harmful to ourselves and others. Subjecting ourselves to the pain and discomfort of dialectical scrutiny is worth the effort if we have so much to lose if we are wrong. Indeed, if our most basic moral intuitions, such as those regarding the wrongness of genocide and murder, are objectively true, we should realize how often in human history cultures have been lured into committing the most egregiously immoral actions. The grim historical record of human meanness and callousness should lead us to feel a great concern for our own integrity as moral beings. If there are objective moral truths, in other words, we must examine our own beliefs as part of our overall responsibility to take seriously our obligation to do what is morally right. While it may be excessive to claim that we should do whatever is in our power in order to promote what is good, it is surely reasonable to require that we make some genuine effort to make sure that our actions are not immoral.

If the antirealist is correct about truth in general, then, certainly all moral truths must be understood as valid only within particular human conceptual schemes. If the basic idea of truth apart from the perspective of some human world of concepts and beliefs is nonsense, then the specifically moral notion of an objective good and evil must be abandoned as irrational. This line of reasoning makes it much harder to see why moral inquiry is vitally important. Why, we might ask, should Socrates trouble himself and actually jeopardize his life to call into question the values of wealth and honor so fundamental to the outlook of his Athenian contemporaries? Of course, an antirealist could say that we should examine our moral beliefs because we simply do care about such issues as violence, intolerance, and injustice. But why care deeply enough about such matters to risk one's happiness and even one's life if these values are true only relative to some human moral point of view? Clearly Socrates risks his own life because he believes he has a duty to help his fellow

Athenians achieve greater moral enlightenment. But if human moral health is itself just a matter of human preferences, then Socrates is not so much a benefactor as a violent disrupter of established social tradition. Unlike the antirealist, Pascal, in admitting our basic idea of objective truth, provides us with a much more forceful rationale for taking moral inquiry seriously. If objective moral truths by which our actions are measured really exist, then we should care enough about both ourselves and others to subject our moral beliefs to rational scrutiny. It is very hard to see why moral disputes deeply matter, on the contrary, if even the most heinous of crimes ultimately violate nothing more than human constructs.

One of Pascal's great insights is to connect our idea of truth with the basic moral conception of human dignity. One of our most fundamental moral intuitions shared by many different traditions is that we should care about how our actions affect others because all humans possess a special dignity or moral worth. According to Pascal, an essential aspect of our dignity as humans is precisely that as rational beings we have an idea of objective truth. As Pascal observes, though we are in many ways at the mercy of natural forces beyond our control, our greatness lies in our ability to transcend them through our self-consciousness. I am not just a mere reed pushed in whatever direction the wind prevails; I am a "Thinking Reed" capable to a limited extent of my own self-determination:

> Thinking Reed. It is not in space that I must seek my human dignity, but in the ordering of my thought. It will do me no good to own land. Through space the universe grasps me and swallows me up like a speck; through thought I grasp it.[46]

In a significant way, for Pascal, our idea of truth symbolizes or, perhaps better, embodies our true condition as both wretched and great. Our ability to reflect on what is true affords us greatness; our inability to know the truth profoundly humbles us and reveals our weakness. By emphasizing this duality of our cognitive human nature, Pascal affords us an account of our humanity that makes sense of another basic intuition, one that is held by many but certainly not all persons, that there is a special dignity or worth inherent in all humans. When we deny our idea of truth, we lose sight of an essential part of our unique dignity as humans. For those who possess this moral intuition of human dignity, one advantage of Pascal's account of human nature is that it serves to explain at least part of our sense of the intrinsic moral worth of every person.

A predictable antirealist response to my reasoning would be to challenge my thesis that our conception of moral dignity needs any metaphysical grounding

46. Ibid., frg. 113.

at all. The antirealist might well say that if a community of human agents adopts a point of view according to which all people possess inherent worth, and as a result upholds such values as tolerance and freedom of choice, then for all practical purposes we have all the basis we need to maintain a certain kind of moral community. Thus to ask for some further metaphysical grounding for this community and its moral practices is both unnecessary and misguided. It is unnecessary since the basic agreement among members of this community regarding moral dignity provides all the foundation needed for sustaining its existence as a moral community. The conventional agreements among those adhering to a shared moral vision suffices for sustaining that vision and the social world that upholds it. According to the antirealist, in addition, to look beyond the agreements of convention to a metaphysical foundation is misguided. So the antirealist might observe that in order to defend any so-called metaphysical foundation for ethics, we must, of course, still appeal to some shared intuitions about moral worth. If we could discover independent, Cartesian intuitions to establish our metaphysical account, then such an account might provide additional evidence and serve as a reputable metaphysical justification for our moral outlook. But, according to the Socratic conception of moral reasoning I have been working with throughout this inquiry, there are no such independent standards transcending our fallible intuitions on which we can securely rest our moral first principles. If our only recourse for justifying some theory of the objective good is these fallible intuitions, then why not simply operate from the basis of the intuitions by themselves? What is there to be gained, asks the antirealist, from additional metaphysical explanations, the validity of which we can judge only by reference to these original intuitions?

This line of counterargument falls short for two reasons. The first has to do with the essential character of moral intuitions themselves, and in particular of the intuition that humans ought to be respected because of their moral worth. Whether one accounts for this idea of human dignity along Kantian lines—in terms, that is, of our autonomous rational nature—or along Pascalian lines—as grounded in our being rational creatures created for fellowship with a perfect God—it is clear that we cannot separate the intuition from its metaphysical roots, and treat it merely as a human convention, without fundamentally changing the character of the intuition itself. Consider how for both Kant and Pascal people have a kind of moral status that demands the respect of social communities. Historically, we find that human societies often act and believe in ways that seriously violate the dignity of certain classes, cultures, or races. The intuition of human dignity shared by Kantians, Pascalians, and others leads those who possess it to condemn violations of our duty to respect one another, not because we constitute a moral community that as it so happens upholds certain ethical conventions, but because humans really possess a moral dignity regardless of whether our moral community acknowledges this to be the case. In this way, it is built into the very core of this moral intuition of human worth that our worth has a metaphysical basis and serves as a standard for judging our social conventions. To treat the intuition in question here simply as a product of human convention is to make it unrecognizable to those who take it seriously. Hence, one very important reason to seek a metaphysical theory to support one's moral idea of human dignity is to clarify one's implicit sense of metaphysical grounding already present within the intuition itself. At least some of our moral intuitions have this metaphysical reference internal to their nature. At least, some of us find ourselves compelled to think they do.

In a similar way, we hold intuitively that our sense perceptions, under normal conditions, refer to objects existing independently of our consciousness. The antirealist could propose as well that we regard these perceptual intuitions merely as agreed-upon contrivances of human society. But to do so is again to transform the intuitions in question from having an essential metaphysical reference to having only a conventional one. One cannot, without distorting their common life character, strip away all reference to a mind-independent world from our ordinary sense perceptions, for one cannot plausibly argue that reducing our everyday intuitions about external objects to mere conventions leaves those original intuitions intact. Now, in the case of what many persons have historically understood by the concept of human dignity, there is a profound reason why we should not affirm the antirealist's conventionalist reductionism. To deny that people really possess moral worth, independently of whether a given society affirms and respects it, is simply to deny the intuition. The intuitive sense many persons have, that humans must be respected, points to some objective basis. The Socratic call to determine as best we can what that basis could be serves to help us make sense of and defend this intuition. If our basic moral intuitions are especially of profound importance, seeking to account for them by formulating the best account we can of their objective foundations is the most rational way of taking them seriously. We seek such an account, in other words, because the matter at issue—how all humans can possess a moral dignity—is of such great importance to us.

Let me present a further reason for rejecting the antirealist response. One obvious feature of postmodern society is the great diversity of outlooks on human life and welfare. If the basic disagreements among moral perspectives are ultimately conventional, then what grounds are left for encouraging genuine, rational debate among rival outlooks? If these rival outlooks accept the rational standards of what I have called Socratic, teleological thinking, then despite their radical disagreements they can acknowledge a common commitment to dialectical examination. If there exists an objective human nature and our well-being depends on our living in accordance with it, then we all have a very good reason to engage in dialogue with one another. But if even our most basic moral beliefs are simply the products of human contrivance, then how can we insist on rational dialogue? If there is no truth out there to be reached, why not just use force, either institutional or physical, to safeguard the "integrity" of one's moral community? Apart from the commitment to an objective human good, a community might approve of tolerance but, then again, it might not. How would communities committed merely to convention-based notions of tolerance seek to persuade others? If their persuasive tactics are also mere conventions, then why is their own form of argumentation not just another subtle form of domination? Here the classic Socratic distinction between the philosophical pursuit of truth and the sophistical practice of persuasion breaks down—if there is in fact no truth about ourselves to be discovered. Without a real set of human virtues to aspire to, Socratic philosophy reduces itself to just another form of the assertion of power. Stripped of the objective ideals that underlie it, is not the call to the examined life and the commitment to challenge the core beliefs of others merely a way to enforce one's own agenda? Put simply, if there is no true self, and if justice is no more than a communal artifact, then all arguments attacking injustice are in principle coercive. My argument here leads us back to the basic idea of an objective human dignity. If we believe that people should be respected because of their inherent moral status, we possess a good reason to engage in rational dialogue and rational self-examination, a reason the antirealist seems to lack. Our reason is that such practices serve to help us live in accordance with our nature as beings with moral dignity. If we all really possess such dignity, then these practices really matter, because the subject of their inquiry really matters.

My third argument in favor of Pascalian realism builds on the preceding ones. But in this case my concern is not with the seriousness of moral reflection but with the value of philosophy in general. In the Socratic tradition, philosophy is essentially the love of wisdom. The wisdom we seek as finite thinkers requires us to possess a self-reflective account of human life by which we can live well. Suppose, though, we raise the question in this context of why this activity of philosophical thinking matters. Why, especially, does it make sense to engage in the search for wisdom if we cannot ultimately know, as mortal thinkers, the truth about ourselves? Why is the Pyrrhonist not right to recommend his or her skeptical program for overcoming this supposedly universal human desire to know? For Socrates and Pascal, the answer to these questions is basically that we must search because we deeply care about what our lives really mean. We understand enough to be able to doubt and ponder the objective meaning of our lives. Our basic moral intuitions lead us to distinguish between healthy and unhealthy ways of being and to understand the importance of getting in touch with our real nature. Since being true to ourselves—that is, living in accordance with our true objective nature—matters to us, it makes sense to confront the uncertainty of our condition and risk discomfort for the truth. Subjecting ourselves to the critical force of Socratic questioning may well cause us distress. To turn such questioning on one's neighbors, as Socrates does, may cause others discomfort, threaten social stability, and infect others with doubts and uncertainties. Why should we follow Socrates and risk such personal and social suffering unless the alternative of being unknown to ourselves is a form of woeful ignorance?

Now again, if the antirealist is right about truth and there is no objective human good to find or to lose, why should philosophical inquiry really matter and why should we suffer at times while we confront our own self-contradictions and inadequacies? Put another way, if truth is itself relative to some one or other conceptual scheme, how much is getting in touch with it really worth? Perhaps it is still worth something to those who find it pleasurable to think like an antirealist. Perhaps for those who desire to think philosophically while being self-consciously aware of the lack of any metaphysical ultimacy of their beliefs, there need be no more justification for philosophy than that one's conceptual scheme includes some value that supports it. Perhaps antirealists just like being decent intellectuals.

It is hard to see, however, how philosophical thinking for such an outlook can have the same seriousness and importance as it does for metaphysical realists searching for the objective truth about the human condition. Why pursue this truth when we have cashed it in for all the pleasure it has to offer us? Why entreat new generations of students to study Plato's *Republic* when reading the latest tabloids would likely provide them with more immediate pleasure and perhaps a much better idea of present communal beliefs and practices? To these questions, the antirealist has a kind of answer, of course: namely that the practice of philosophy has its own conventions, one of which is to apply certain standards of argumentation as a means to solve a range of so-called philosophical problems. Those who engage in philosophy from an antirealist orientation need look no further than these agreed-upon conventions in order to justify their project or to defend their choice of careers. Yet while the antirealists can appeal to various conventions in justifying their philosophical practices, is such an "apology" adequate to account for the seriousness with which some philosophers have approached their philosophical questions and perplexities? It is hard to see how mere institutional or communal agreements can lend the same force to philosophical questions as does the commitment to metaphysical realism.

The Western tradition of philosophical inquiry has, of course, been guided by certain more or less agreed-upon conventions about how philosophy ought to be done. Generally these agreements were themselves animated by a desire to understand who we really are and what our real place is in the cosmos. If there is a truth about human life to be discovered rather than simply fabricated, if we naturally find ourselves desiring to understand this truth, and if we believe that human life somehow is important because people possess an objective human dignity, then we can clearly justify taking philosophical thinking seriously. That all humans by nature desire to know themselves and their world would make perfect sense. We might even on this view argue that everyone capable of reflective thinking ought to spend some time pondering and examining what life is all about. Drawing on culinary imagery, we might say that the philosophical enterprise deprived of its realist moorings is not so much philosophy decanted as philosophy decaffeinated.

If we follow the spirit of the Platonic tradition and envision philosophy as the pursuit of wisdom driven by love, by an erotic desire for communion with an independently real, supreme good, then we could more fully articulate our misgivings about the antirealist project by concluding that it denudes reasoning of its *eros*. On the one hand, then, we find a conception of philosophy in which pursuing the truth is a passionate response to our fundamental need both to know ourselves and to find our true home in the cosmos. The postmodern, antirealist conception, on the other hand, follows the postmodern path of demythologizing such a traditional narrative—in this case, that of humans pursuing wisdom—in order to help those seeking enlightenment to stick to the postmodern facts and avoid fantasy. The view one takes of the nature of philosophical inquiry certainly makes a fundamental difference regarding what it means to do philosophy. Just how seriously the practice of philosophy should be taken depends largely on whether people desire wisdom by nature or simply by convention.

The worth of philosophy, we might well say, depends on the worth of its practitioners. One advantage of Pascal's fallibilist realist perspective is that it provides us with a better reason for taking seriously inquiry into human existence. Simply put, philosophy is a serious enterprise because human life really has a serious value. In the end, I suspect here that my argument cannot help but be of limited power. For those who already have a strong moral or philosophical intuition about objective human meaning, my argument may succeed in showing why Pascal's overall idea of truth makes a great difference in our lives. If I am right, our idea of truth is of far more importance than just as an intellectual presupposition. It is, more importantly, indispensable for making sense of the earnestness many persons feel in the face of our moral and philosophical uncertainty. We should heed the call to examine ourselves not solely because our social community places value on it, but because our lives really matter. Not surprisingly, my "prorealism" argument here turns on the presence of particular intuitions, the truth or falsity of which is ultimately in this mortal life fully transparent to none of us.

One might well query in response, why should we pursue the Socratic way of inquiry and subject ourselves to critical, dialectical examination if the truth we do in fact long for will never become luminously evident to us? For Pascal, in particular, we know our first principles, including our basic beliefs about our highest good, only through the heart. Some of our intuitions of the heart, such as our belief in external objects, we probably do hold involuntarily. Others, such as the belief in a loving God, involve a willing affirmation of our need for divine aid and thus seem in part dependent on individual choice, even though faith is finally a supernatural gift of grace. Yet why should we trust either those fundamental beliefs about which we have no choice or those that seem partially within our control to affirm or deny? What grounds do we have for thinking that the commitments of our hearts put us in contact with reality? Why is it reasonable to trust our hearts when it is possible that what our hearts naturally incline us to believe may not correspond to either our real selves or the real world around us?

Perhaps it seems misguided to raise this question of reasonableness in the case of those fundamental beliefs of the heart that are so ingrained in our cognitive nature that we have no power to withhold our assent to them. At least in the context of Socratic self-examination, it might not be misguided to accuse someone of being irrational in holding a belief that he or she was at some time honestly incapable of doubting, if such a person were unwilling to allow his or her holding such a belief to be challenged. On a Socratic view, reasonableness is not so much a property of particular beliefs as it is a virtue of the person who has succeeded in achieving a unified and coherent psyche, one in which the multiplicity of one's intuitions, inferred beliefs, emotions, passions, dispositions, and attitudes fit together into a coherent life. According to this Socratic account of dialectical rationality, a reasonable person is also committed to a never-ending, open-minded examination of what he or she believes and feels about human life. A reasonable person remains committed to the philosophical search out of a sense of humility. He or she recognizes the need for faith to seek for greater understanding.

From a Socratic dialectical perspective, it is only in the larger context of a person's life as a narrative quest for self-understanding that it is possible to determine the reasonableness of a person's particular beliefs, attitudes, or actions. The Socratic standard for judging the reasonableness of particular beliefs requires an assessment of how such beliefs relate both to one another and to one's whole psyche and thus to one's historical existence. Consider, for example, the person who finds himself or herself strongly convinced that murder is ethically wrong. Let us suppose that such a person holds this belief so firmly that he or she cannot entertain either giving up this belief or accepting any moral theory that fails to uphold the wrongness of murder. How, from a Socratic point of view, does one assess whether such a person is "reasonable" in holding this specific moral belief with such tenacity? First of all, the Socratic standard for testing this person's reasonableness requires judging the status of this basic conviction within this person's complex moral world of beliefs, feelings, and commitments. If, for example, this person refuses to entertain any prospect that this belief might need revision or that his or her own understanding of why murder is wrong is flawed, then such a person would be unreasonable to a significant degree. However, if this person were both open to dialectical challenges and capable of defending his or her belief in the wrongness of murder in the context of other beliefs about such matters as the dignity of life, this person would exhibit a much higher degree of reasonableness. Socratic assessing of a person's reasonableness scrutinizes a person's complex psyche and does not merely consider the status of someone's beliefs in and of themselves, abstracted from the historical existence of the person who holds them. Thus, on the Socratic view, rationality or reasonableness is primarily a characteristic of a narrative existence. The highest level of reasonableness one can hope to attain, on the Socratic view, is to be able to provide a *logos* of one's moral self.

Now the specter of skeptical doubt might seem once more to plague us. The best we can hope for, according to the Socratic account of human rationality, is to justify our beliefs within the context of our own narrative moral life. Even if one can show how one's faith or fundamental moral belief in human dignity is rational within one's life, what reason is there for trusting that this life itself reflects the real world or corresponds with one's real human nature? Put another way, if the standard of rationality is unavoidably person-relative, are there any good grounds for believing that in our endeavors to be rational we are making progress in the quest to understand the truth itself—the quest to come into contact with reality not as we construct it or interpret it, but as it is in and of itself?[47]

How one answers this disturbing question depends, inevitably, on one's understanding of the world. In Pascal's account of the paradox of human existence, to be human means that we both long for the true and the good and yet must acknowledge our inability through our own efforts to satisfy our basic human longing. Given the generosity of divine grace, it nevertheless makes sense for the Pascalian to have faith that when our hearts and minds are properly receptive to God's grace, they will ultimately, but only in and through God's help, lead us correctly to see the truth about ourselves and attain our proper good. It makes sense to hold such a faith despite our limited resources and as finite and sinful lovers of the good, not because we are autonomously self-sufficient, but because the object of our faith is a perfect God of grace who seeks our happiness and promises to lead us and transform us if only we die to self alone and engage fully to trust in him. The Pascalian, in other words, is in a very good position not to prove that our hearts supply us with true intuitions, but to believe coherently that we are justified in following our hearts if the Being to whom they lead us has promised us true fulfillment if we open our hearts to his healing grace.

As long as we must struggle in our efforts to live out our faith, and are not yet so transformed as to be able to encounter God face-to-face, our confidence in God's promise must serve as our own portion. Our quest for wisdom, we are promised, is neither absurd nor in vain, and so we must be content to

---

47. For a thorough discussion of this problem of trusting our cognitive faculties, see Plantinga, *Warrant and Proper Function*.

acknowledge that we must walk by faith rather than by our own autonomous reason. As our hearts lead us to depend on God, so God in turn, insofar as he is the God of perfect love, enables us to understand him more clearly and to trust in him more fully. Thus we cannot, without circularity, try to prove that our hearts are reliable by citing God's promise to us as if it were neutral evidence. Indeed, on a Pascalian view we ought to have no ambition to prove the reliability of our most fundamental intuition or belief in God.[48] Our trust in our hearts and our trust in God work together to make more reasonable our faith that we are advancing toward the truth. This argument, based on such a dual trust, is not meant to imply that no other form of theism or religious tradition can offer similar good grounds for searching for the truth about ourselves. In comparison with any secular, materialistic metaphysics, however, or in comparison with any variant of postmodernism, which rejects this faith in the ultimate moral goodness of what is real, Pascal's philosophy offers a clear line of justification for trusting that we are indeed so made that our natures will, through God's transforming power, be led to the final truth.

Just as Pascal's theism provides a good reason for trusting that our natural cognitive faculties are reliable, it also offers reason to hope that, after death, our enjoyment of the good will not be so severely curtailed by our natural limits and rebellious hearts. The fact that God promises to give us the grace to "see him face-to-face" and enjoy an eternal good of infinite depth and breadth further justifies our imperfect efforts to attain the good and seek the truth in this life. We know by faith that the hard work of seeking to love God and to love our neighbor as ourselves is not in vain despite how we fall so far short in this life of loving in a pure and uncorrupted manner. As so many of the saints in the church have testified, the path of spiritual growth is not simply a journey of an ever more vivid and sanctified awareness of one's nearness to Christ. On the contrary, what the saints of the church teach us is that as one grows closer to God, one sees ever more clearly and painfully how imperfect and self-centered one's efforts at loving God and neighbor really are. It is in the face of such an ambiguity, one that lies at the very core of the journey of the heart in love, that we must acknowledge an arresting paradox inherent in the life of faith. If the experience of nearness to God in this life is inextricably linked to its very opposite, to the awareness of one's own unworthiness to be loved and of one's own

48. Note that my argument concerning the mutual coherence between trusting in God and trusting that one's basic intuitions accord with reality differs crucially from Descartes's endeavor to prove the reliability of reason by proving the existence of God. Descartes's fundamental error is to suppose that the appropriate strategy for defeating the skeptic is to provide an indubitable proof for the veracity of reason. My strategy, following Aristotle, is to argue against the skeptic dialectically—that is, to show how the principle of noncontradiction serves as a basic first principle of reason essential to the practice of intelligible discourse; rather than attempt to prove the veracity of reason by means of deductive argument, Aristotle shows Socratically how the skeptic presupposes rationality in his or her very attempt to debunk it. Of course, the skeptic can still resist this refutation but only by violating his or her essential nature as a rational thinker.

failure to love well, then it might appear that the nihilist is right after all. To be human is to be doomed to either a life of senseless effort or one of resignation to despair. And yet the nihilist is right only if there is no real power of divine grace and no reliable promise of new life beyond the grave. Put another way, apart from the faith that we will finally be transformed into new creatures who are capable of loving rather than loathing the good for whom we most deeply hunger, the prospects for the life of faith are not very reassuring. Of course, in Pascal's view our paltry efforts to love unselfishly do not stand on their own merits. Our efforts to live out the life of faith in love possess grandeur and no-bility because they will, through God's love, be part of a story leading to full and blessed communion with God. The Pascalian has a compelling response to the nihilist only because he or she hopes in a God who will not abandon us to fend for ourselves.

The Pascalian outlook, as I have tried to articulate it, shares with Platonic and Aristotelian theories of human nature the belief that we seek naturally to realize our essential capacities and live a life of self-completeness. As a Christian philosopher, Pascal's vision of human fulfillment is fundamentally transformed by the concept of a loving God who is the creator of the material and immaterial world. Central to Pascal's defense of his faith is his claim that only by grace can people enjoy the fulfillment sought after but never attain-able in the classical philosophical search for wisdom. By fulfilling rather than destroying the philosophical tradition of seeking wisdom, Christian doctrine thus respects rather than negates human reason.[49] Pascal's skepticism is thus far from being antirational. What Pascal attacks is not reason per se, but a Cartesian model of reason that overlooks our human limits. In so doing, Pascal engages in the curious practice of using that human faculty uniquely capable of reflecting on its own limits. Rather than be coerced by the author-ity of faith, reason, aware of its own limits, submits rationally to grace. Thus Pascal himself reflects, "St. Augustine. Reason would never submit unless it judged that there are occasions when it ought to submit."[50]

I have argued in defense of Pascal's synthesis of faith and reason by sup-porting both its metaphysical realism and its theistic belief in divine grace. The substance of my case is that those who have reason to accept metaphysical realism—which I believe means all people—and who take ethical and philo-sophical inquiry seriously, have good reason to embrace Christian faith as "worthy of reverence and respect." It is only by trusting in God's unconditional love and perfect grace that we can acknowledge the full seriousness of human life and not fall into despair. Before closing, I would like to supplement this

---

49. That Christian faith respects human nature while at the same time seeking to redeem it is no contradiction. Of course, philosophers such as Nietzsche refuse to embrace such a distinction.

50. Pascal, *Pensées*, frg. 174. For Pascal's understanding of the submission of reason to faith and of the rationality of trusting in God's grace, see esp. frgs. 167–73.

line of argument with a final reflection related to the significance of human love. Clearly, it is the common experience of many persons to find one of the most meaningful and fulfilling experiences in their lives to be loving and being loved by other persons. What I wish to argue is that our experience of love is not metaphysically neutral, for being a lover of another person makes one, wittingly or unwittingly, a metaphysical realist.

How can it be that only metaphysical realists can be true lovers? In making this claim, I do not mean that a person must be familiar with some theory of metaphysical realism in order to love another person. Such a view would surely be ludicrous. What I mean to argue is that loving another person, whether as stranger, friend, intimate erotic companion, child, or parent, commits one to believing that the beloved person possesses an independent, inherent worth or goodness, and that this conception of the inherent worth of another person makes no sense apart from a background or context of metaphysical realism.

Loving another person requires more than simply finding that person plea-surable or desirable; this is to say that we have not experienced love for someone if we value him or her merely instrumentally. If I genuinely love my wife, for example, must I not, at least to some degree and however imperfectly, desire her well-being not simply in order for her to serve my needs, but for her own sake? And does not the same requirement hold if I love someone other than my wife and in a way different from my wife—say, a stranger, colleague, friend, child, or parent? Let us grant, then, that to love another human means to love that person as a being who is not merely worthwhile just as a means to one's own happiness, but who is a person whose dignity and worth is not contingent on his or her serving my own interests. To carry this logic further, would we not also say that insofar as loving another person means wishing his or her own good, in loving someone I wish for that person to live well and thus, among other essential aspects of human flourishing, to know what it means to love? Put another way, if I love someone, I regard him or her as a person whose presence should be a source of joy to at least some other person, if not just myself, and whose own love for another should in return be a source of encouragement and a reason for living to that person. Such is arguably the case, for I cannot love another person if I do not wish him or her to experience a relationship of mutual love, as such an experience is one of the essential components of a flourishing, good human life. Indeed, perhaps the enjoyment of such mutual love means more to most of us than that of any other earthly good, even of such wonderful goods as listening to Bach, reading a short story by Flannery O'Connor, or watching my daughter Nadia turn her perfect cartwheels or pirouettes or ride a bike for the first time without training wheels. At least I find it intuitively compelling to hold that no experience within the order of finite beings, setting aside for the moment that relationship between human creature and God, is of greater worth and is more essential to human happiness than that of a genuine love that acknowledges the independent worth of some person outside oneself.

Quite significantly, however, it is the very nature of this love to negate the thesis of the antirealist that all reality and value have being only within some human conceptual scheme. If I understand the basic nature of the experience of love, at least as I am analyzing it, I cannot allow that the beloved person's worth depends on any desire or act of my own, nor can I allow that his or her worth is contingent on any desires or acts of other humans. Put simply, to love another person means that one feels and assents to the worth of the person one loves, and that this worth cannot be accounted for on the basis of any human constructs, whether private or social, whether premodern, modern, postmodern, or hypermodern. What I as a lover rejoice to behold in my beloved is that person's worth that I humbly acknowledge rather than arrogantly presume to constitute. It would seem then that true love simply defies an antirealist universe, for within such a universe there is no way to make sense of the worth of the beloved.

Now a romantically inclined, or otherwise lovingly disposed, antirealist might object at this point that I am confusing two very different matters. Am I not, this antirealist might contend, failing to distinguish the valid claim that loving another person requires not reducing that person merely to a commodity serving one's own private interests from the invalid claim that loving another person requires at least an implicit acknowledgment that the beloved possesses a value whose ground is independent from any humanly constituted scheme of values? In response to this important objection, I would say that while these two claims are indeed distinct in meaning, they are not distinct in their truth-value. In defense of this latter claim, I wish to argue that the affirmation of the worth of the beloved inherent in the act of loving that person does require us to reject any account of the beloved's worth that makes that worth contingent on any act of human estimation, on any mere human assessment of what should be deemed estimable. Put more simply, when I behold the person I love and acknowledge his or her worth, I must necessarily oppose any community or individual who would deny the worth of my beloved on the basis of any humanly constituted standards of evaluation. My basis for doing so must not be simply that I, qua individual or qua member of some human interpretative community, grant supreme worth to the one I love. For if my only basis for opposing those who would unjustly harm or kill the person I love is that my humanly constituted scheme of value opposes it, then I have no basis for arguing that the person I love deserves to be treated with respect regardless of the personal or political agenda of the individual or community intending to do that person harm. If I love another person, in other words, I must uphold the view that not only I but also others *ought* to acknowledge the worth of my beloved, because such an act of acknowledgment is demanded of us whether or not I or someone else accepts this obligation.

At the heart of my argument is the thesis that part of what it means to love another human, in whatever specific form that love takes, whether romantic, filial, or neighborly, is to appreciate a worth in the beloved person that neither I nor any other person has merely constructed or created. My thesis here is not meant to deny the profound reality of forgiveness and unconditional love, as if the person loved had to earn his or her worth through his or her own actions, nor am I here presupposing some one religious or philosophical account of exactly what it is that grounds the worth of a person. I do not mean, first of all, to contradict the Christian teaching that we must not presume to be lovable on the basis that our own actions merit either the love of God or that of other people. While I believe that we as humans possess a dignity independent of how we are esteemed by our fellow humans, I also believe that each one of us must be forgiven for the ways in which we deny and abuse that dignity. I also believe that our inherent worth is a gift rather than something we have earned. Furthermore, I do not mean in presenting my basic case here to bias my argument by presupposing a specifically Christian account of what it is that bestows this dignity and honor on the person. The basic gist of my argument here would be amenable to a diversity of religious and philosophical outlooks. I mean to argue that when I genuinely love someone outside myself, I intuitively feel a sense of humility in that person's presence, for, whether or not I can articulate it, I feel myself ennobled in the presence of something beautiful, a beauty of which I am not the author. One might say that I love the beloved because he or she is worthy, but the beloved is not worthy because he or she is loved by me or any other human person. The worth of the beloved may well be a gift of God's love, but it is not contingent on my own imperfect love or on the love of any other human person. Through the act of loving another person, the human lover does not so much bestow worth on the beloved as he or she becomes, by being one who beholds the beauty of the beloved, a recipient of a special worth, a lover enriched in the presence of the beloved by receiving an ennobling worth. This is a worth that I as lover am given; it is a gift I receive as I experience being a lover, as I find myself a partaker in the worth of my beloved.

If this model of appreciative human love does indeed accurately reflect our experience as lovers, then it follows, I think, that human love makes metaphysical realists of all who experience it. For to deny that our beloved spouse, friend, child, parent, or neighbor has "metaphysical" worth, a worth that endures even if all our human conventions fail to acknowledge it, is to betray the reality of human love. And if such human love is indeed fundamental to a healthy human life, then is it not clear that, tragically, the antirealist does not so much liberate us by freeing us from the chains of metaphysics as lead us into the nihilism of residing in a world incapable of love? For how, indeed, could life be worth living if ultimately all our loves collapse into lust, into some form of esteeming in which it is we as lovers who constitute the worth of our beloved?

This human experience of love affords us a second lesson. If loving others, not for what they can do for us but in affirmation of their own true self-worth, is essential for human flourishing, then must we not admit that apart from the hope we have in God's grace, the prospects for human life are not very encouraging? Two factors in particular are inherent in human life and related to this form of love, both threatening to undermine our sense that human life is worth living. First, few, if any, people are very good at loving unselfishly. Our acts of love toward others, whether toward our friends, parents, spouses, or children, are all too often tainted with our own need for self-assurance and our own tendency to look primarily to ourselves, treating others as mere means. The truly selfless love offered to us on the cross is the very love we need, and yet we seldom if ever extend anything very much like it to those we claim to love. Second, what we ultimately desire in loving others is to enjoy communion with them and meld our lives into theirs. But the inevitable end of mortal existence poses an eternal negation of this desire. We can love today and perhaps tomorrow, but some day death will forever separate us from those we love. Surely such a final negation of love is both inevitable and lamentable, if there is no hope for life after death. Love seems then to have a curious status in human life: it both enriches us in a deeply profound way and seems ultimately tragic for imperfect mortal humans. The fact that humans find solace and joy in loving others seems indisputable. The fact that our imperfections and impending mortality threaten to destroy the meaning this love gives us seems indisputable as well. Ironically, if we are mere mortals and must live without hope in a future life in communion with one another and the God of love, then the meaning we find in loving is finally negated by death. Although we can still love in the present, finally our love and all human love is doomed to end without fulfillment. This tragic defect in our lives is a condition from which our love, by its very nature, must recoil and find abhorrent.

Even as the imperfect lovers we are, in other words, we cannot in all sincerity affirm or be indifferent toward the prospect of the eternal loss of the one whom we love. Lovers primarily care about their beloved and desire to rejoice in the beloved's success and well-being. As Augustine himself argues in *Contra Academicos*, our desire for happiness cannot be content merely with itself—the mere presence of our love of wisdom, the mere seeking of happiness for ourselves and others cannot by itself satisfy us. Our love of the good seeks to possess the good. Our love of a second self seeks that person's good and seeks to rejoice in it. A love that finds contentment merely in itself, a love that says, "All that matters is the quality of my loving and no death can rob me of that," is not love at all but self-absorption. Hence, to affirm love of neighbor or parent or child or husband or wife in the face of our mortality requires either that we accept that the best we can hope for is our own imperfect and temporary love, an option that violates the nature of love itself, or that we believe, based on God's promise of eternal life, that ultimately human life will know true love and thus true fulfillment.

Anyone who loves another must, if he or she is honest, deeply wish that neither the beloved nor his or her love of the beloved will end with the grave. If we, indeed, find that our lives have meaning only as we love beyond our individual, private selves, and that love cannot simply accept the loss of its object, then our experience as lovers should open us to, and make us aware of, our inner longing for the revelation of eternal life with Love Itself.

Clearly, what I am now arguing reflects my own Christian outlook. In effect, I am arguing that love of neighbor leads us inexorably to love of God. And our pathetic efforts at both lead in turn to embracing God's love for us. If, as Pascal believes, we naturally, through our heart's basic desire, seek complete fulfillment, then we will, if we allow our nature to lead us, be drawn to God's grace. Clearly in this case, far from destroying human nature, this faith in God's grace alone can give us grounds for reasonable hope in love's fulfillment. Our experience of ourselves as lovers serves then as a symbol of our peculiar status as humans. It is our imperfect capacity to love others that propels us to see ourselves in this mortal life as pilgrims on our way to, rather than having already found, our true home. It is my contention, then, that Pascal's Augustinian vision of human life—a vision affirming the goodness of reason and faith and the indispensability of hope and love—offers a powerfully compelling solution to the problem of human existence. Pascal presents an honest picture of human life, one that acknowledges both our strengths and our weaknesses and makes sense of our human longings.

I turn, in closing, to one further noteworthy strength, as well as unavoidable limitation, of Pascal's analysis of human life. As I have sought to show, Pascal is more a Christian Socrates, committed to making an "apology" for the life of faith, than he is a fideistic skeptic, eschewing reason for blind faith. Whatever specific form one's Socratic outlook takes, the Socratic thinker can do no better as a human philosopher than to engage in philosophical reflection from one's own particular point of view and test one's deepest commitments from within the world of one's own beliefs and passions. All Socratic thinking is thus, in one form or other, a matter of "faith seeking understanding." I have throughout this investigation stressed the responsibility of each of us to heed the call of Socrates. But much more could be said on this matter regarding the role of communities and traditions in shaping our characters and assisting us in becoming the sort of persons for whom the Word that changed Pascal's life can make sense. For Pascal, of course, what changes human lives toward the acceptance of grace is ultimately the power of God's love. Those who are moved by this love are incapable of remaining impartial spectators or neutral skeptics. Those who are moved by this love have a profound responsibility to declare to the world, both in their words and their deeds, that human loving is not in vain.

Furthermore, if Pascal is right, those who are moved by God's love are also incapable of knowing, in this life at least and with any philosophical certainty, that the source of their experience of this love is indeed the God of Abraham,

Isaac, Peter, and Paul. And yet, although we can have no such "rational" certainty, we can reasonably expect that such a gracious love, if real, would have the power to transform our lives and give us the certainty of faith. One of the highest responsibilities of the historical church and its individual members is to witness to this power. Thus although it certainly does not provide the kind of neutral evidence sought by Enlightenment philosophers, the power of God's love evident in the lives of those who experience it and proclaim it provides a kind of evidence, an evidence internal to the human heart, that we would only expect to find if God's message of the intersection of human depravity and divine forgiveness, proclaimed on the cross, is true. In this study, I have tried to show how the commitment to rational self-reflection, for a Pascalian, provides us with a way of life that accords with intuitions that many people share. In this respect, a Pascalian view of life appears to be rational insofar as it provides us with self-knowledge by making sense of our lives; thus in living by this faith we develop toward becoming fully rational persons as we learn how to make proper use of our cognitive faculties. Finally, however, as Pascal reminds us, Christian faith in God will appear rationally compelling only for those who feel the need for, if not the reality of, the power of God's amazing grace. In closing, we must confess with Augustine that with respect to this internal evidence of the reality of divine love and the trustworthiness of its author, one must believe in order to understand.

Undoubtedly in every age and in every culture, Christians have tragically compromised themselves and relinquished their responsibility to challenge, by the light of the gospel of grace, the prevailing forms of cultural hegemony. But we must never forget that the history of the church is not merely the all-too-apparent drama of human failure and brokenness, for as Gerard Manley Hopkins beautifully reminds us, despite all the folly and self-destructiveness of God's weak and spineless followers, "the Holy Ghost over the bent / World broods with warm breast and with ah! bright wings."[51] As Hopkins knew, the Holy Spirit continues to redeem and transform the mistakes and follies of those who claim to be Christians. Following Hopkins, those who proclaim the good news of God's grace in Jesus Christ today may affirm both in word and deed the vital message that both Augustine and Pascal offer our post-Christian world of globalized and intellectualized *cupiditas*: until we who call ourselves believers in Jesus Christ commit ourselves in word and deed to recovering the art of living as his creatures, saved by his grace—until we learn, in other words, how to honor both the God of love and the inherent goodness of his creation, how to love one another as dependent beings beloved of this God, and how to embrace, rather than flee from or rebel against, the limits of our created nature and our utter dependence on him—neither we nor our children will find real peace or rationality in this life.

---

51. Hopkins, "God's Grandeur," 27.

BIBLIOGRAPHY

Allen, Diogenes. *Three Outsiders*. Cambridge, MA: Cowley Publications, 1983.

Allen, R. E. *Socrates and Legal Obligation*. Minneapolis: University of Minnesota Press, 1980.

Alston, William. "Knowledge of God." In *Faith, Reason, and Skepticism*, edited by Marcus Hester, 6–49. Philadelphia: Temple University Press, 1992.

Aristotle. *Nicomachean Ethics*. Translated by Terence Irwin. Indianapolis: Hackett, 1985.

Audi, Robert. "Direct Justification and Theistic Belief." In *Rationality, Religious Belief and Moral Commitment*, edited by Robert Audi and William Wainwright, 139–66. Ithaca, NY: Cornell University Press, 1986.

Augustine. *The Advantage of Believing*. Translated by Luanne Meagher. Vol. 4 of *The Fathers of the Church*. New York: CIMA, 1947.

———. *Confessions*. Translated by F. J. Sheed. Indianapolis: Hackett, 1993.

———. *Eighty-Three Different Questions*. Translated by David Mosher. Vol. 70 of *The Fathers of the Church*. Washington, DC: Catholic University of America Press, 1982.

———. *The Essential Augustine*. Edited by Vernon Bourke. Indianapolis: Hackett, 1974.

———. *Homilies on the Gospel of John*. Translated by John Gibb. Vol. 7 of *A Select Library of Nicene and Post-Nicene Fathers of the Christian Church*, edited by Philip Schaff. Grand Rapids: Eerdmans, 1956.

———. *Letters*, vol. 2. Translated by Sister Wilfrid Parsons. Vol. 18 of *The Fathers of the Church*. New York: Fathers of the Church, 1953.

———. *Of True Religion*. Translated and edited by John Burleigh. Vol. 6 of *Augustine: Earlier Writings*. Library of Christian Classics. London: SCM, 1953.

———. *On Christian Doctrine*. Translated by D. W. Robertson. Indianapolis: Bobbs-Merrill, 1958.

———. *On Free Choice of the Will*. Translated by Anna S. Benjamin and L. H. Hackstaff. Indianapolis: Bobbs-Merrill, 1964.

———. *On the Trinity*. Translated by Arthur Hadden and William Shedd. Vol. 8 of *A Select Library of Nicene and Post-Nicene Fathers of the Christian Church*, edited by Philip Schaff. Grand Rapids: Eerdmans, 1956.

———. *Sermons*. Translated by Edmund Hill. Vol. 2 of *The Works of Saint Augustine*, edited by John E. Rotelle. Brooklyn, NY: New City, 1990.

———. *Soliloquies*. Translated by Thomas F. Gilligan. Vol. 1 of *The Fathers of the Church*. New York: CIMA, 1948.

Bacon, Francis. *Novum Organum*. Edited by Joseph Devey. New York: P. F. Collier and Son, 1902.

Berger, Peter. *The Sacred Canopy*. Garden City, NY: Doubleday, 1967.

Berger, Peter, Brigette Berger, and Hansfried Kellner. *The Homeless Mind: Modernization and Consciousness*. New York: Vintage, 1973.

Berkeley, George. *Three Dialogues between Hylas and Philonus*. In *Berkeley's Philosophical Writings*, ed. David M. Armstrong, 189–225. New York: Macmillan, 1965.

———. *Treatise Concerning the Principles of Human Knowledge*. In *Berkeley's Philosophical Writings*, ed. David M. Armstrong, 42–128. New York: Macmillan, 1965.

Berry, Wendell. *The Art of the Commonplace: The Agrarian Essays of Wendell Berry*. Edited by Norman Wirzba. Washington, DC: Shoemaker and Hoard, 2002.

———. *Home Economics*. New York: North Point, 1987.

———. *Sex, Economy, Freedom & Community*. New York: Pantheon Books, 1993.

———. *What Are People For?* New York: North Point, 1990.

Broome, J. H. *Pascal*. London: Edward Arnold, 1965.

Cahoone, Lawrence, ed. *From Modernism to Postmodernism: An Anthology*. Oxford: Blackwell, 1996.

Chesterton, G. K. *Orthodoxy*. Garden City, NY: Image Books, 1959.

Clifford, W. K. "The Ethics of Belief." In *God, Man and Religion*, edited by Keith Yandell, 505–9. New York: McGraw-Hill, 1973.

Cottingham, John, Robert Stoothoff, and Dugald Murdoch, eds. and trans. *The Philosophical Writings of Descartes*. Cambridge: Cambridge University Press, 1984.

Craig, William Lane. "The Problem of Miracles: A Historical and Philosophical Perspective." In *The Miracles of Jesus*, edited by Craig Blomberg and David Wenham, 9–48. Gospel Perspectives 6. Sheffield: JSOT Press, 1986.

Davis, Stephen T. "The Miracle at Cana: A Philosopher's Perspective." In *The Miracles of Jesus*, edited by Craig Blomberg and David Wenham, 419–42. Gospel Perspectives 6. Sheffield: JSOT Press, 1986.

Derrida, Jacques. "La parole soufflée." In *Writing and Difference*, translated by Alan Bass, 169–95. Chicago: University of Chicago Press, 1978.

———. "Structure, Sign, and Play in the Discourse of the Human Sciences." In *Writing and Difference*, translated by Alan Bass, 278–94. Chicago: University of Chicago Press, 1978.

Descartes, René. *Discourse on Method and Meditations on First Philosophy*. Translated by Donald A. Cress. 3rd ed. Indianapolis: Hackett, 1993.

———. *The Philosophical Writings of Descartes*. Translated by John Cottingham, Robert Stoothoff, and Dugald Murdoch. Cambridge: Cambridge University Press, 1984.

Dickens, Charles. *Hard Times*. Edited by George Ford and Sylvere Monod. 2nd ed. New York: Norton, 1996.

Dockery, David S., ed. *The Challenge of Postmodernism: An Evangelical Engagement*. 2nd ed. Grand Rapids: Baker Academic, 2001.

Edwards, James C. *The Authority of Language*. Tampa: University Presses of Florida, 1990.

Eiseley, Loren. *The Star Thrower*. San Diego: Harcourt Brace, 1978.

Ellis, John M. *Against Deconstruction*. Princeton, NJ: Princeton University Press, 1989.

Evans, C. Stephen. *Faith Beyond Reason: A Kierkegaardian Account*. Grand Rapids: Eerdmans, 1998.

———. *The Historical Christ and the Jesus of Faith*. Oxford: Clarendon, 1996.

———. *Kierkegaard's Fragments and Postscript: The Religious Philosophy of Johannes Climacus*. Atlantic Highlands, NJ: Humanities, 1983.

Fish, Stanley. "Change." In *Doing What Comes Naturally*, 141–60. Durham, NC: Duke University Press, 1989.

Flew, Anthony. *The Presumption of Atheism*. London: Pemberton, 1976.

Giddens, Anthony. *The Consequences of Modernity*. Stanford, CA: Stanford University Press, 1990.

———. *Modernity and Self-Identity: Self and Society in the Late Modern Age*. Stanford, CA: Stanford University Press, 1991.

Gilson, Etienne. *The Christian Philosophy of Saint Augustine*. London: Victor Gollancz, 1961.

Grenz, Stanley J. *A Primer on Postmodernism*. Grand Rapids: Eerdmans, 1996.

Hart, David Bentley. *The Beauty of the Infinite: The Aesthetics of Christian Truth*. Grand Rapids: Eerdmans, 2003.

Hartle, Ann. *Death and the Disinterested Spectator*. Albany: State University of New York Press, 1986.

Hauerwas, Stanley. *After Christendom? How the Church Is to Behave if Freedom, Justice, and a Christian Nation Are Bad Ideas*. Nashville: Abingdon, 1991.

———. *A Better Hope: Resources for a Church Confronting Capitalism, Democracy, and Postmodernity*. Grand Rapids: Brazos, 2000.

———. *A Community of Character: Toward a Constructive Christian Social Ethic*. Notre Dame, IN: University of Notre Dame Press, 1981.

———. *The Peaceable Kingdom: A Primer in Christian Ethics*. Notre Dame, IN: University of Notre Dame Press, 1983.

Hazelton, Roger. *Blaise Pascal*. Philadelphia: Westminster, 1974.

Hume, David. *Dialogues Concerning Natural Religion.* Edited by Richard H. Popkin. Indianapolis: Hackett, 1980.

———. *Enquiries Concerning Human Understanding and Concerning the Principles of Morals.* Edited by L. A. Selby-Bigge and P. H. Nidditch. 3rd ed. Oxford: Clarendon, 1975.

———. *Essays: Moral, Political, and Literary.* Edited by Eugene F. Miller. Rev. ed. Indianapolis: Liberty Classics, 1987.

———. *The History of England.* Edited by William Todd. Indianapolis: Liberty Classics, 1983.

———. *The Natural History of Religion.* Edited by H. E. Root. Stanford, CA: Stanford University Press, 1956.

Irwin, Terence. *Aristotle's First Principles.* Oxford: Clarendon, 1988.

Jencks, Charles. *What Is Post-Modernism?* 3rd ed. New York: St. Martin's Press, 1989.

Kaufman, Gordon D. *An Essay on Theological Method.* Rev. ed. Decatur, GA: Scholars Press, 1979.

Kierkegaard, Søren. *The Concept of Anxiety.* Translated by Howard V. and Edna H. Hong. Princeton, NJ: Princeton University Press, 1985.

———. *Concluding Unscientific Postscript.* Translated by Howard V. and Edna H. Hong. Princeton, NJ: Princeton University Press, 1992.

———. *Philosophical Fragments.* Translated by Howard V. and Edna H. Hong. Princeton, NJ: Princeton University Press, 1985.

Konyndyk, Kenneth. "Faith and Evidentialism." In *Rationality, Religious Belief, and Moral Commitment,* edited by Robert Audi and William J. Wainwright, 82–108. Ithaca, NY: Cornell University Press, 1986.

Kreeft, Peter. *Christianity for Modern Pagans: Pascal's Pensées—Edited, Outlined, and Explained.* San Francisco: Ignatius, 1993.

Kuhn, Thomas S. *The Structure of Scientific Revolutions.* Chicago: University of Chicago Press, 1962.

Lasch, Christopher. *The Culture of Narcissism.* New York: Norton, 1979.

Lawler, Peter Augustine. *Postmodernism Rightly Understood: The Return to Realism in American Thought.* Lanham, MD: Rowman & Littlefield, 1999.

Lehe, Robert Tad. "Realism and Reality." *The Journal of Philosophical Research* 23 (1998): 219–37.

Lewis, C. S. *The Abolition of Man.* San Francisco: HarperCollins, 1944.

———. *Miracles.* New York: Macmillan, 1960.

———. *Selected Literary Essays.* Edited by Walter Hooper. Cambridge: Cambridge University Press, 1969.

Livingston, Donald. *Hume's Philosophy of Common Life.* Chicago: University of Chicago Press, 1985.

Locke, John. *An Essay Concerning Human Understanding.* Edited by Alexander Campbell Fraser. New York: Dover, 1959.

Lyotard, Jean-François. *The Postmodern Condition: A Report on Knowledge.* Translated by Geoff Bennington and Brian Massumi. Minneapolis: University of Minnesota Press, 1989.

MacDonald, Scott. "Theory of Knowledge." In *The Cambridge Companion to Aquinas,* edited by Norman Kretzmann and Eleonore Stump, 160–95. Cambridge: Cambridge University Press, 1993.

MacIntyre, Alasdair. *After Virtue.* Notre Dame, IN: University of Notre Dame Press, 1984.

———. *Three Rival Versions of Moral Enquiry: Encyclopaedia, Genealogy, and Tradition.* Notre Dame, IN: University of Notre Dame Press, 1990.

———. *Whose Justice? Which Rationality?* Notre Dame, IN: University of Notre Dame Press, 1988.

McClay, Wilfred M. *The Masterless: Self and Society in Modern America.* Chapel Hill: University of North Carolina Press, 1994.

McGowan, John. *Postmodernism and Its Critics.* Ithaca, NY: Cornell University Press, 1991.

McInerny, Ralph. "Ethics." In *The Cambridge Companion to Aquinas,* edited by Norman Kretzmann and Eleonore Stump, 196–231. Cambridge: Cambridge University Press, 1993.

McMullin, Ernan. "Rationality and Paradigm Change in Science." In *Philosophy of Science,* edited by Martin Curd and J. A. Cover, 119–38. New York: Norton, 1998.

Montiero, Joao-Paulo. "Hume, Induction and Natural Selection." In *McGill Hume Studies,* edited by David Norton, Nicholas Capaldi, and Wade Robison, 291–308. San Diego: Austin Hill, 1979.

Morris, Thomas V. *Making Sense of It All: Pascal and the Meaning of Life.* Grand Rapids: Eerdmans, 1992.

———. *Our Idea of God.* Notre Dame, IN: University of Notre Dame Press, 1991.

Netland, Harold. *Encountering Religious Pluralism: The Challenge to Christian Faith and Mission.* Downers Grove, IL: InterVarsity, 2001.

Neuhaus, Richard John. *The Naked Public Square: Religion and Democracy in America.* Grand Rapids: Eerdmans, 1986.

Noll, Mark A. *The Scandal of the Evangelical Mind.* Grand Rapids: Eerdmans, 1994.

———. *Turning Points: Decisive Moments in the History of Christianity.* Grand Rapids: Baker Books, 1997.

Norris, Christopher. *Deconstruction: Theory and Practice.* London and New York: Methuen, 1982.

Norton, David Fate. *David Hume: Common-Sense Moralist and Sceptical Metaphysician.* Princeton, NJ: Princeton University Press, 1982.

———. "Hume, Atheism, and the Autonomy of Morals." In *Hume's Philosophy of Religion,* edited by Anthony Flew, 97–144. Winston-Salem, NC: Wake Forest University Press, 1985.

O'Connell, Marvin R. *Blaise Pascal: Reasons of the Heart*. Grand Rapids: Eerdmans, 1997.

O'Connor, Flannery. *The Habit of Being*. Edited by Sally Fitzgerald. New York: Farrar, Straus and Giroux, 1979.

Oelschlaeger, Max. *Caring for Creation*. New Haven: Yale University Press, 1994.

Pascal, Blaise. *Blaise Pascal: Selections*. Edited by Richard H. Popkin. New York: Macmillan, 1989.

———. *Pensées*. Translated by A. J. Krailsheimer. Harmondsworth: Penguin Books, 1966.

Penelhum, Terence. "The Analysis of Faith in St. Thomas Aquinas." In *Faith*, edited by Terence Penelhum, 113–33. New York: Macmillan, 1989.

———. *God and Skepticism*. Dordrecht: Reidel, 1983.

———. *Hume*. London: Macmillan, 1975.

———. "Hume's Skepticism and the Dialogues." In *McGill Hume Studies*, edited by David Norton, Nicholas Capaldi, and Wade Robison, 253–78. San Diego: Austin Hill, 1979.

Peterman, James F. *Philosophy as Therapy: An Interpretation and Defense of Wittgenstein's Later Philosophical Project*. Albany: State University of New York Press, 1992.

Peters, James. "Reason and Passion in Plato's *Republic*." *Ancient Philosophy* 9 (Fall 1989): 173–87.

Plantinga, Alvin. "Coherentism and the Evidentialist Objection to Belief in God." In *Rationality, Religious Belief and Moral Commitment*, edited by Robert Audi and William Wainwright, 109–38. Ithaca, NY: Cornell University Press, 1986.

———. "Is Belief in God Rational?" In *Rationality and Religious Belief*, edited by C. F. Delaney, 22–77. Notre Dame, IN: University of Notre Dame Press, 1979.

———. "Reason and Belief in God." In *Faith and Rationality*, edited by Alvin Plantinga and Nicholas Wolterstorff, 16–93. Notre Dame, IN: University of Notre Dame Press, 1983.

———. *Warrant and Proper Function*. Oxford: Oxford University Press, 1993.

———. *Warranted Christian Belief*. Oxford: Oxford University Press, 2000.

Plato. *The Dialogues of Plato*. Translated by R. E. Allen. 4 vols. New Haven: Yale University Press, 1984.

Putnam, Hilary. *Realism with a Human Face*. Cambridge, MA: Harvard University Press, 1990.

———. *Reason, Truth and History*. Cambridge: Cambridge University Press, 1981.

Rist, John. *Augustine: Ancient Thought Baptized*. Cambridge: Cambridge University Press, 1994.

Rorty, Richard. *Contingency, Irony, and Solidarity*. Cambridge: Cambridge University Press, 1989.

———. *Philosophy and the Mirror of Nature*. Princeton, NJ: Princeton University Press, 1979.

———. *Truth and Progress*. Vol. 3 of *Philosophical Papers*. Cambridge: Cambridge University Press, 1998.

Runzo, Joseph. *Reason, Relativism, and God*. New York: St. Martin's Press, 1986.

Russell, Bertrand. *A History of Western Philosophy*. New York: Simon & Schuster, 1945.

Seeskin, Kenneth. *Dialogue and Discovery*. Albany: State University of New York Press, 1988.

Smith, James K. A. *Who's Afraid of Postmodernism? Taking Derrida, Lyotard, and Foucault to Church*. Grand Rapids: Baker Academic, 2006.

Stump, Eleonore. "Atonement According to Aquinas." In *Philosophy and the Christian Faith*, edited by Thomas V. Morris, 61–91. Notre Dame, IN: University of Notre Dame Press, 1988.

Swinburne, Richard. "The Christian Scheme of Salvation." In *Philosophy and the Christian Faith*, edited by Thomas V. Morris, 15–30. Notre Dame, IN: University of Notre Dame Press, 1988.

———. *The Concept of Miracle*. London: St. Martin's Press, 1970.

Taylor, Charles. *Sources of the Self: The Making of the Modern Identity*. Cambridge, MA: Harvard University Press, 1989.

Teloh, Henry. *Socratic Education in the Early Dialogues*. Notre Dame, IN: University of Notre Dame Press, 1989.

Toulmin, Stephen. *Cosmopolis*. New York: Humanities, 1990.

Tweyman, Stanley. *Skepticism and Belief in Hume's Dialogues Concerning Natural Religion*. Dordrecht: Martinus Nijhoff, 1986.

Wainwright, William J. *Reason and the Heart: A Prolegomenon to a Critique of Passional Reason*. Ithaca, NY: Cornell University Press, 1995.

Weber, Max. *From Max Weber: Essays in Sociology*. Translated and edited by H. H. Gerth and C. Wright Mills. New York: Oxford University Press, 1946.

Weiner, E. S. C., and J. A. Simpson, eds. *The Compact Edition of the Oxford English Dictionary*. 2nd ed. Oxford: Oxford University Press, 1991.

Wirzba, Norman. "The Challenge of Berry's Agrarian Vision." In *The Art of the Commonplace: The Agrarian Essays of Wendell Berry*, by Wendell Berry, vii–xx. Washington, DC: Shoemaker and Hoard, 2002.

———. *The Paradise of God*. Oxford: Oxford University Press, 2003.

Wolterstorff, Nicholas. "Are Concept-Users World-Makers?" In *Metaphysics*, edited by J. E. Tomberlin, 233–67. Philosophical Perspectives 1. Atascadero, CA: Ridgeview, 1987.

———. "The Migration of the Theistic Arguments: From Natural Theology to Evidentialist Apologetics." In *Rationality, Religious Belief and Moral Commitment*, edited by Robert Audi and William Wainwright, 38–81. Ithaca, NY: Cornell University Press, 1986.

———. *Reason within the Bounds of Religion.* Grand Rapids: Eerdmans, 1976.

Wood, Ralph. *Flannery O'Connor and the Christ-Haunted South.* Grand Rapids: Eerdmans, 2005.

Yandell, Keith. *God, Man and Religion.* New York: McGraw-Hill, 1973.

———. *Hume's Inexplicable Mystery.* Philadelphia: Temple University Press, 1990.

Zagzebski, Linda. "Religious Knowledge and the Virtues of Mind." In *Rational Faith: Catholic Responses to Reformed Epistemology,* edited by Linda Zagzebski, 199–225. Notre Dame, IN: University of Notre Dame Press, 1993.

INDEX